DONS AND WORKERS

DONS AND WORKERS

Oxford and Adult Education since 1850

LAWRENCE GOLDMAN

CLARENDON PRESS · OXFORD

1995

Oxford University Press, Walton Street, Oxford OX2 6DP
Oxford New York
Athens Auckland Bangkok Bombay
Calcutta Cape Town Dar es Salaam Delhi
Florence Hong Kong Istanbul Karachi
Kuala Lumpur Madras Madrid Melbourne
Mexico City Nairobi Paris Singapore
Taipei Tokyo Toronto
and associated companies in
Berlin Ibadan

Oxford is a trade mark of Oxford University Press

Published in the United States
by Oxford University Press Inc., New York

British Library Cataloguing in Publication Data
Data available

Library of Congress Cataloging in Publication Data
Goldman, Lawrence, 1957–
Dons and workers : Oxford and adult education since 1850 /
Lawrence Goldman.
p. cm.
Includes bibliographical references (p.) and index.
1. University of Oxford—History—19th century. 2. University of
Oxford—History—20th century. 3. University extension—England—
Oxford—History—19th century. 4. University extension—England—
Oxford—History—20th century. 5. Adult education—England—
Oxford—History—19th century. 6. Adult education—England—
Oxford—History—20th century. 7. Working class—Education—
England—Oxford—History—19th century. 8. Working class—
Education—England—Oxford—History—20th century. I. Title.
LC5325.092G654 1995
374′.942′57—dc20 95–20283
ISBN 0–19–820575–9

1 3 5 7 9 10 8 6 4 2

Typeset by Graphicraft Typesetters Ltd., Hong Kong
Printed in Great Britain
on acid-free paper by
Bookcraft Ltd.,
Midsomer Norton, Nr Bath, Avon

TO MY PARENTS

ACKNOWLEDGEMENTS

FOR permission to consult and quote from manuscript materials in their possession I wish to thank the Director of the Department for Continuing Education, University of Oxford; the Master and Fellows of Balliol College, Oxford; the Warden and Fellows of Nuffield College, Oxford; Ruskin College, Oxford; the Archives Department, University of Keele; the Fawcett Library, Guildhall University, London; the Central Library, Swindon; the Workers' Educational Association, Temple House, London; the South-Eastern District of the Workers' Educational Association; the North Staffordshire District of the Workers' Educational Association (now part of the West Mercia District); and the late Sir Richard and Lady Anne Acland.

I wish to thank the Warden and Fellows of All Souls College, Oxford, for permission to reproduce the photograph of the Revd Arthur Johnson; the Master and Fellows of Balliol College, Oxford, for permission to reproduce the photograph of Arnold Toynbee; the Bodleian Library, Oxford, for permission to reproduce the photograph of J. A. R. Marriott; and Mr Michael Sadleir for permission to reproduce the photographs of Michael Sadler and 'Arthur Acland and "The Inner Ring"'. The Workers' Educational Association, Temple House, London, has kindly permitted reproduction of the photographs of the 'Joint Committee of Oxford University and Working-Class Representatives, 1909'; 'R. H. Tawney and the Rochdale Tutorial Class in Industrial History'; 'R. H. Tawney and the Chesterfield Tutorial Class [1910?]'; 'Dinner Party at Balliol, August 1909'; 'Lindsay, Cartwright and Mansbridge at the 1912 Oxford WEA Summer School'; and 'The WEA Summer School, Balliol College, Oxford, [1912?]'. I wish to thank the Director of the Department for Continuing Education, University of Oxford, for permission to reproduce the following items: 'The 1888 Summer Meeting', 'The 1891 Summer Meeting, Balliol College' (and close-up); 'Tutors at the 1909 Summer Meeting'; 'University Extension Centres on the Oxford List, 1893–4'; 'Handbill for the first Oxford Tutorial Class in Longton, 1908'; 'North Staffordshire Miners in Balliol College, 1954'.

In writing a book of this sort one incurs many personal obligations and debts. I would like to acknowledge the contribution of the late Marshall Rachleff, who introduced me to the practice of adult education on a memorable evening in Bridgeport, Connecticut, in September 1979. I must thank Dick Smethurst, Provost of Worcester College, Oxford, who, when Director of the Department for External Studies in 1986, suggested that I organize an exhibition on the history of Oxford and adult education from which this book has emerged. For their help in presenting that exhibition, I would like to thank Liza Denny, Melanie Steiner, Anna Sandham and Nina Shorter at Rewley House. Alan Trump and Anne Rees, librarians at Rewley House, dealt with my many queries and requests with unfailing good humour. I am also grateful for assistance from the staff of the Bodleian Library, Oxford. The former university archivists, Ruth Vyse and Maggie McDonald, introduced me to the Oxford University Archives, but Simon Bailey, the current university archivist, has borne the brunt of my demands, and has been assiduous in finding obscure items in a dense and complex collection of papers. Penelope Bulloch, Alan Tadiello and Richard Darwall Smith made work easy in the Balliol College library.

Linden West, formerly District Secretary of the Workers' Educational Association in Buckinghamshire, Berkshire and Oxfordshire; Vernon Hull, Secretary of the WEA South Eastern District, and the staff of the former North Staffordshire District of the WEA at Cartwright House, Hanley, provided me with help and facilities for research. Hilary Gura and Richard Ross assisted with the papers and photographs of the Workers' Educational Association at Temple House, London. Mr M. J. Phillips guided me through the Lindsay papers at the University of Keele. For hospitality on various research trips, I would like to thank Lionel and Eva Alexander, Gerald and Maria-Elena McDonald, and the late Sir Richard and Lady Anne Acland.

Don Porter of Charlbury and Trevor Cockbill of Swindon provided me with valuable information on, respectively, Joseph Owen and Reuben George. The late Mr Frank Singleton of the *Guardian* found articles by R. H. Tawney and Raymond Williams for me. Joanna Innes and Pauline Adams helped with details concerning Somerville College, Oxford. John Jones of Balliol College brought to my attention various manuscripts in his college's archive. Harold Marks, Bridget Hill, John Vickers and the late Charles Wenden provided me with recollections of their experiences teaching extramural classes for the University of Oxford. Harold Pollins and Anne McCartney allowed me to see an early version of their piece on the university extension and settlement movements which will appear in the forthcoming volumes on the nineteenth-century history of Oxford. Ed Gallagher of Oakland Community College, Auburn Hills,

Michigan; Hal Miller of the University of Minnesota; Dan Rodgers of Princeton University; and Milton Stern of the University of California, helped me to understand the history of adult education in the United States.

I am grateful to Gerald Aylmer and Eric Swyngedouw for their insights on R. H. Tawney and Raymond Williams respectively, and to my close colleagues, Henrietta Leyser and Henry Mayr-Harting, for constant support and interest in this project. I am also grateful to the Master and Fellows of St Peter's College, Oxford, who were good enough to grant me an early sabbatical from college teaching to write this book. My former academic colleagues at Rewley House, Oxford, including Kate Tiller, Michael Lockwood, Raymond Flood, Bob Elmore, and Ed Coker gave encouragement and ideas. Karen and Douglas Hewitt not only shared with me their experiences of teaching, and their personal knowledge of some of the people discussed towards the end of this book, but gallantly read through drafts of the typescript. Mark Curthoys and Dan Greenstein gave freely of the knowledge they accumulated while working on the nineteenth- and twentieth-century volumes of the *History of the University of Oxford*. Janet Howarth generously shared the fruits of her work on Edwardian Oxford with me. For reading all or part of the manuscript, I am extremely grateful to her, Alon Kadish, and especially to Mark Curthoys, David Grylls, Brian Harrison and Colin Matthew. They have saved me from many errors, and they have made many helpful suggestions, as well. Those mistakes that remain are my responsibility alone.

Many of the students I have taught in recent years in adult education classes organized by the Department for Continuing Education in Oxford, and by the Workers' Educational Association, have shown an interest in this book. I am grateful to them for their encouragement, and for demonstrating to me that the ideals of the movement described in the pages that follow are still held dear by many in our society. I am also grateful to my students at St Peter's College, Oxford, whose comments in tutorials has helped me to shape some of the material and ideas in this book. I am indebted to Geoffrey Thomas, Director of the Department for Continuing Education in Oxford, who encouraged me to write this book, for his good humour, support, practical advice, and tolerance as the project changed and stretched beyond the serviceable institutional history that we first planned. My greatest debts are to my wife Madeleine, who believed in the subject, watched it grow, and who, among many other things, made it possible for me to write a first draft in three months of relative peace and domestic quiet.

CONTENTS

LIST OF PLATES

Between pp. 180 and 181

INTRODUCTION

THIS book is a history of the relationship between the University of Oxford and adult education since the mid-nineteenth century. It thus explores one of the less well-known aspects of the University's past—one that may be of surprise to some who feel they know the institution and to many more who hold one of several popular images of Oxford. This is also a study of the relationship between intellectuals and the working class in Britain, or perhaps more accurately, between a specific section of intellectuals and a specific section of workers. The relationship is described historically as it has developed through the shared enterprise of adult education.

In the history of modern Oxford, adult education has a secure but essentially peripheral place. Seen from the reverse perspective, in the history of adult education, or to be more accurate, liberal adult education as shaped by British universities over the last century or so, Oxford has an important and perhaps pre-eminent position. This book explores this paradox—the paradox of a creative enterprise on the margins of university life, that may well be among Oxford's most significant modern achievements, not least because through adult education Oxford has been brought into contact with many of the great themes and trends in modern British social and political history. The paradox is illustrated in the use that researchers make of the University's archive: though this covers eight hundred years of Oxford's past, and though it might be thought that the internal history of the University would offer the richest prizes to historians, it is that section of the archive devoted to the history of Oxford and adult education which attracts the most interest. This book will try to explain why this is the case.

As a study in educational history, the pages that follow focus on the organization of adult education, on the tutors who taught in it, on the students who came to classes, on what was studied and learnt, and on what was contributed to the educational life of the nation. But this book pays rather more attention to intellectual and political history than is customary in the literature on the history of adult education. In so doing I believe I have been faithful to a movement that always cherished political as well as educational objectives—indeed, which saw the two as indistinguishable—and which in Oxford has been led since the 1870s by a succession of major figures in British intellectual life. The political project of adult education as seen from Oxford was to integrate the working class into the nation and educate it for the tasks of social and political leadership that would inevitably fall to it with the advent of democracy—'to ensure a peaceful transition from the old society to the new by educating working people for power' as Brian Harrison has recently put it.[1] The complex tensions within this project form one of the central themes in this book; they have been present throughout, but were most obvious at the time when Oxford helped form and sustain the Workers' Educational Association at the turn of the twentieth century. There were many who questioned then whether the working class had much to gain from contact with Oxford, and feared that the consequences of any alliance with the University would be political incorporation.

The history of Oxford's involvement in adult education is not without conflict, therefore, though these conflicts help define the development of the intellectual left in British politics over the past century. Through Oxford's engagement with adult education, a succession of students and dons, from T. H. Green and Arnold Toynbee to Hugh Gaitskell and Dick Crossman, have made contact with the labour movement in Britain and offered it leadership. In tracing their involvement in adult education, this book may help clarify aspects of the political evolution of the left in Britain from the progressive social Liberalism of the 1880s, held by the founders and concerned to assimilate the workers into the new democracy, through broad convergence with the labour movement and support for the new Labour Party in the first half of the twentieth century, and on to the more complex political situation of the 1950s and beyond, when doubts and disputes about Labour's mission were evident, and the alliance of dons and workers began to dissolve.

Oxford's involvement in adult education was conceived and led by a succession of dons with influence and prestige above the ordinary, and understanding why they were attracted to adult education and what they gained from it for their own intellectual and political development is another main component of this study. In each generation attention is paid to certain key figures, either because of their role in establishing and furthering Oxford's engagement with the working class, or because of the intrinsic interest of their work

---

[1] Brian Harrison, 'Politics', in id. (ed.), *The History of the University of Oxford*, viii, *The Twentieth Century* (Oxford, 1994), 397.

in adult education. This 'tradition' began with Benjamin Jowett, T. H. Green, and Arnold Toynbee in the formative period up to the 1880s. They made the initial commitment to working-class education in Oxford and established the aims of the movement, aims that were followed with limited success by Arthur Acland, Michael Sadler, and Halford Mackinder after them. In the early years of the twentieth century a fresh generation came into adult education and took up the challenge in a new political context; it included William Temple, A. D. Lindsay, R. H. Tawney, Alfred Zimmern and, slightly later, G. D. H. Cole. More recently, in the post-Second World War era, Oxford's project in adult education influenced and shaped the work of Raymond Williams. In constituting these figures as a tradition I do not pretend that they can easily be bracketed together: the academic statesmanship of Jowett is hardly a natural companion for the academic Marxism of Williams. They were all committed to widening educational opportunities and furthering the interests of the majority cut off from higher education, but these aims hardly make them distinct as a group: they were held throughout the adult education movement and beyond. Rather, I mean to denote a lineage and historical succession: each of these figures in turn engaged with adult education, learnt from it, and used the experience so gained to inform a mature political and social outlook. Each in turn was conscious of what was owed to those who had gone before; each saw his own involvement in adult education in terms of the history of the movement up to that time. And, with the exception of Williams, they were all educated in Oxford, taught in the university, and were loyal to it. This book is not an intellectual history of adult education pure and simple. But it pays considerable attention to the ideas that inspired the movement at different times, and to the intellectual biography of some of its key figures.

If I have deliberately related the history that follows to wider issues and trends in national life, then I can at least feel that I am in good company. The historical introduction to one of the most important documents in the development of British adult education, the so-called *1919 Report*, which was written by several important figures in the account that follows, including R. H. Tawney, Arthur Greenwood, Albert Mansbridge, and A. L. Smith, noted 'the intimate relationship between adult education and other departments of social life' such as 'religious growth, economic reconstruction, scientific discoveries and inventions, political agitation and social ferment'. Because adult education has attracted a disproportionate number of socially engaged people, because in the tradition this book describes, it has sought to link education and social change, and because it has been a voluntary movement whose students have come out of choice rather than compulsion, and have shaped their learning in ways they believed both useful and relevant, it has always been open to a wide range of influences and able to contribute, in turn, to a range of social and political endeavours. And because, as the *1919 Report* observed, 'it is concerned with minds which are already mature' it 'cannot be interpreted in isolation from the interests and pre-occupations which form the background to the intellectual activities of each generation'.[2] Like many before me, I have let this insight inform my own approach and shape the nature of this book.

What follows is in the form of a narrative: the relationship of dons and workers in modern Britain is described and analysed through the history of Oxford and adult education over more than a century. But buried in the narrative are recurrent issues and themes which were of relevance to each generation, and may still be significant today. At various stages the educational movement described here has attempted to define and redefine its audience: if workers, what sort of workers, and if not the working class, then who? This in turn has thrown up questions about the the type of education offered. Should adult tutors sent out by Oxford replicate the liberal education of the university's internal curriculum? Or should they offer a different service altogether, with a syllabus designed to assist students to take their place in society, be that in the form of an 'education for citizenship' or in the transfer of marketable skills and training for a vocation? A movement linked so closely to the political aspirations of tutors and students has experienced recurrent disputes over the fine divide between education and propaganda—disputes within the movement, with other organizations that have broken away from the tradition described here, with political opponents outside the movement, and with the state. Yet some of those most closely associated with Oxford and adult education have eschewed politics altogether and understood their involvement in essentially moral and spiritual terms: they have sought to spread knowledge and an appreciation of the higher life in order to satisfy the needs of individuals for meaning and purpose. The education of individuals, their liberation from ignorance, and their personal development, have been the motives for their participation. Conversely, for many tutors and students described here, adult education has been valued because it offered a means to the collective advance of the working class as a whole. At a certain level this book thus

---

[2] *Ministry of Reconstruction: Adult Education Committee, Final Report* PP 1919, Cmd. 321, xxviii. 9.

examines the conflict between 'collectivist' and 'individualist' conceptions of adult education. They have been present throughout, often in unacknowledged tension: at different times one or other has been uppermost in the movement.

This study is not a history of adult education *in* the University of Oxford because most of the educational activity it surveys has taken place far from Oxford: it was only comparatively recently that the University began to draw adult students to it on a regular basis as well as sending out tutors to teach them *in situ*. Thus it would be mistaken to regard what follows as a 'history of Rewley House', the home of the present Department for Continuing Education in Oxford. This has been an administrative centre for adult education in Oxford for less than half the period covered by this book, and figures only occasionally in the later pages of this account. Nor is this a conventional institutional history of the several bodies with different names that have been charged with the oversight of adult education by the University since the 1870s. I have judged that administrative history is the least interesting aspect of this subject and placed emphasis elsewhere—on students, on tutors, on what was learnt, and on the place of the movement in cultural and political history. While the University has always retained a number of staff under these bodies whose full-time occupation has been the teaching of adult students, a great deal of the teaching and educational administration has been undertaken by part-time enthusiasts more likely to have regarded themselves as members of a college in the University, or as tutors for the Workers' Educational Association, or as freelance lecturers without any institutional affiliations at all, than as agents of the Delegacies and Departments which have organized adult education in Oxford.

The subject of this book is best conceived, therefore, as an aspect of wider university and intellectual life in modern Britain, to which a wide range of people with varied affiliations have contributed, and I have deliberately avoided presenting it in terms of internal developments within specific institutions. The history of Oxford and adult education should be understood as the history of an educational and social project that has caught up many individuals, groups, and institutions both inside and outside the University. It has no easy and obvious delineations, no clear and unambiguous margins; it spills across educational and institutional boundaries. It should be regarded as a 'movement'; Oxford has helped to organize the movement, but many other organizations have played a role in it and the history that follows has tried to be faithful to the movement's pluralism and complexity. However, I have not attempted to provide a chronicle of all that has been done in the name of adult and workers' education by Oxford. This study ignores some side-shoots that flourished for a while but had no direct impact on the main development of the enterprise. It does not mention every fine tutor or efficient administrator who played his or her part to the full, and it deliberately pays more attention to some periods than others. I am conscious of the omissions and the imbalances, but with limited space I have chosen to concentrate on what I take to be the essence of the movement.

The account that follows is weighted towards the period up to 1945, an emphasis dictated by the particular history of Oxford's relationship to adult education. It is possible to contend that until the end of the Second World War Oxford had a special role in the sphere of university adult education. Though it was not the first in the field, it assumed a kind of ideological pre-eminence in the movement as a whole. From the 1880s, Oxford sought to speak for the movement and define its ends. In the early 1900s Oxford inspired a series of initiatives that reformulated the movement and brought the universities much closer to the working class. The University's central role in these events, at a time when the adult education movement had its greatest political impact in Britain, has led to a special concentration on the years before 1914, therefore. A succession of gifted academic leaders, many of them from Balliol College, ensured that even though more British universities in the early twentieth century began to provide for adult education, Oxford remained at the centre of the movement and represented it. But after the Second World War the whole context of adult education began to change and it was no longer either possible or fitting for any university to presume authority.

The treatment of Oxford and adult education since the Second World War is therefore more general than in earlier chapters. I have attempted to relate adult education in the University to the broad social changes of this period, rather than narrate a purely institutional history and risk parochialism. Proximity to the period makes it more difficult to assess what was historically significant, especially during an era which has seen the dissolution of the settled patterns of university adult education described in earlier chapters of this book, and its rapid diversification into different functions and services offered to new types of student. Because of the fluidity and complexity of adult and continuing education in recent years, any attempt at a conclusive discussion of developments in Oxford runs the risk of becoming irrelevant very quickly. The tradition this book describes has been in rapid transition since the 1970s and I have tried to explain why this should be without following the twists and turns within a single university. I have also followed the convention of refraining from the discussion of recent events and decisions involving people who are still alive and, in many cases, still active in the field.

Nevertheless, it must be emphasized that what is now known as continuing education is an important part of the academic life of the University of Oxford today. Benefactions from the W. K. Kellogg Foundation have enabled the University's Department for Continuing Education, the direct descendant of the first University committee to organize extramural lectures in Oxford in 1878, to rebuild and re-equip Rewley House, to matriculate students on part-time degree courses, and to form a society of fellows from among its staff which was incorporated into the collegiate university in 1990, and named Kellogg College in 1994. Currently, the Department provides part-time courses for over thirteen thousand students a year—which is approaching the number of full-time, matriculated students in the University—in the traditional subjects of liberal adult education, and in newer programmes of professional and vocational education, also. In the years since 1988, Manchester College, previously an independent foundation, which originated as a 'dissenting academy' for religious nonconformists in the eighteenth century, and moved to Oxford at the end of the nineteenth century, has become part of the University, and has turned itself into a college for mature students studying for Oxford degrees.[3] Meanwhile Ruskin College, whose troubled relationship with the University in the early years after its foundation in Oxford in 1899, forms an important aspect of the history related in this book, continues in its influential role as an independent college of higher education for trade unionists.

I am conscious that in the way I have written this account, concentrating on Oxford, emphasizing its leadership of the movement, and setting it into various national contexts wherever possible, I may have distorted the history and experience of adult education in other universities. Locality, history, and tradition have made each university extramural department different; the view from universities set in industrial centres like Manchester, Liverpool, Leeds, and Birmingham cannot have been the same. My instinct, however, has been to generalize, both because Oxford frequently affected to speak for the movement as a whole, and because without generalization we may be left with several discrete institutional histories of adult

---

[3] Barbara Smith (ed.), *'Truth, Liberty, Religion': Essays Celebrating Two Hundred Years of Manchester College* (Oxford, 1986).

education of limited relevance to wider national history and of limited assistance to other historians. I have written with the conviction that a history of Oxford and adult education is something more than an interesting institutional history of an aspect of the life and work of a major university—that it illustrates a number of significant themes in recent British intellectual and social history.

I hope that my debts to the work of historians who have written about aspects of the history of Oxford and adult education are clear from my footnotes. I would like particularly to draw attention to the work of Alon Kadish, Sheila Rowbotham, Stuart Marriott, Bernard Jennings, Brian Harrison, and Roger Fieldhouse from which I have learnt a great deal and which I have incorporated into my own account. I may disagree with Professor Fieldhouse's conclusions, but I respect the scholarship on which they are based and the critical tradition his work embodies. A good deal of my own account depends on documents and materials drawn from the University Archives in Oxford. The collection relating to the history of adult education is used frequently by scholars, but is extensive and has not yet been catalogued. In using it myself I have concentrated on certain key events and figures, notably from the period 1900–14. I have sampled other material and occasionally tried serendipity and invariably found something of relevance. I am conscious of having only partially exploited the wealth of evidence in the collection and I hope that the account I have written may be improved on by others who use it in the future.

I originally intended to entitle this book 'Intellectuals and the Working Class in Modern Britain'. The publication of John Carey's controversial study of *The Intellectuals and the Masses* led me to change my mind.[4] This was not because the titles might be thought too similar, nor because of any disagreement with Professor Carey's argument. He has sustained a brilliant and persuasive polemic against the literary movement we know as modernism. He convicts it of a self-conscious élitism and a contempt, if not worse, for the new mass culture of the late-nineteenth and early twentieth centuries. Indeed, Professor Carey demonstrates how the very desire for education and self-improvement that moved the working- and lower-middle-class students described in these pages, provoked the disrespect and sneers of the literary class of the age. But it was Professor Carey's book that led me to reflect on the term 'intellectual' and reject it in favour of the more accurate appellation of 'don'. British

[4] John Carey, *The Intellectuals and the Masses. Pride and Prejudice among the Literary Intelligentsia 1880–1939* (London, 1992).

historians are generally rather shy of the word 'intellectual' and conscious that it frequently blurs the distinctions they feel bound to make between very different groups and social types. That the term could be applied by Professor Carey to one group of imaginative writers who so manifestly hated the new mass democratic society after about 1880, and also to another group of university teachers who, through adult education, positively encouraged it, may make the point.

But the term 'don' is not without its problems, since the majority of lecturers and tutors in the history to follow did not hold established positions in the University of Oxford: adult education has always relied on the enthusiasm of part-time and occasional tutors. Nevertheless, those who led the movement were dons and they imprinted it with their particular approach and outlook. Indeed, it is an object in what follows to emphasize that the achievements of adult education in and through Oxford owe much to the natural sympathy and public spirit of the dons involved. Oxford and Cambridge were among the first universities in the world to take up systematic adult education, and, in England at least, they helped to give it a distinctive style, notable for the close personal relationships and rapport between students and tutors. This owed a good deal to the traditional role of the don as teacher and mentor. In calling this book *Dons and Workers*, therefore, I feel that I am being more accurate to my subject than if I had used the term 'intellectual'. I also hope that in so doing I may draw attention to the virtues of a vocation and an academic style which is frequently caricatured, and which is now under threat of extinction as universities are remodelled to fit a pattern dictated by government.

In the course of researching and writing this book I became aware that many of the ideals and methods of the adult education movement which were taken for granted only a generation ago are now the stuff of history. I have also been made aware of how much the University of Oxford has changed in recent years. *Dons and Workers* describes a period when the University had broad political influence in state and society: in particular, the history of adult education in Oxford opens up a number of themes in the history of the relationship between Oxford, the Labour Party, and the wider labour movement. This book describes an age when the alliance of some Oxford dons and students with that movement, and with progressive politics in general, was an aspect of national political culture. Adult education brought dons and workers together in the first years of the twentieth century, but recent changes in the nature of all the elements of the alliance—in universities, among dons, in the working class, and in the Labour Party—have made the association much harder to sustain. This book records what was achieved when it was an acknowledged feature of both educational and political life.

It would be impossible to write about Oxford and adult education without being conscious, at almost every turn, of Thomas Hardy's *Jude the Obscure* and Jude's vain struggle, over several years, to study at Oxford. The novel was published in 1895 by which time 'university extension', as university adult education was first known, was already well established. 'Poor Jude' remarked one adult student in 1910 in a letter to one of the most active of Oxford dons in the cause of workers' education: 'Let us hope his descendants have a bit better luck and that there will be no cause for them to chalk their contempt for the University upon the walls of Balliol.'[5] The man who wrote this was to enter Balliol himself only three years later and study there, before devoting the rest of his life to teaching in Oxford's programme of adult classes in his native region, the Potteries of North Staffordshire. But *Jude* reinforced a prevalent view of the University's exclusivity and sums what is still a common image. This book has not been written with the intention of defending Oxford from such charges or to try and change those common images, though it does present a different side to the University and may help establish a more balanced view of Oxford and university life in general. If it has any sort of message at all, it is rather to draw attention to the achievements of the 'great tradition' of adult education as it has developed in many British universities this century. It is a tradition that has bound together education and social activism, though as will be seen, it is not without purely academic and intellectual distinction. In what is now an exceptionally difficult period for British universities it is all too easy to focus exclusively on internal problems and lose contact with the social aims of this 'great tradition'. I hope this account, in emphasizing them, will be read as a manifesto against insularity.

[5] Albert Emery to Alfred Zimmern, 15 March 1910, Zimmern Mss., Bodleian Library, Oxford, 12, fo. 125. See ch. 4, p. 145.

I

UNIVERSITY REFORM AND NATIONAL CULTURE: THE ORIGINS OF OXFORD UNIVERSITY EXTENSION

I

It is ironic that Oxford and Cambridge, so often taken as bywords for social and educational exclusivity, should have been among the first universities in the world to have become involved in the systematic extramural education of adults. Cambridge in 1873, and Oxford five years later, signalled a recognition of their responsibility to the community in general, and not just to their own matriculated students, when they began to send lecturers out into the towns and cities of late-Victorian England in an attempt to spread university culture more widely among adult audiences. They thus entered a field that had seen a variety of halting initiatives over the preceding sixty or seventy years. In the early nineteenth century adult education was provided by adult schools, generally designed to assault illiteracy and develop godliness among the poor, and by mechanics' institutes that emerged in the 1820s to spread a knowledge of science and its applications among artisans. There were many dozens of mechanics' institutes, but their limited curriculum and the overbearing influence of their middle-class sponsors deterred the working men for whom they had been established. In the 1830s and 1840s both the range of opportunities and the curriculum broadened, as authentic popular movements began their own experiments in adult education. 'Knowledge Chartism' with its lectures and classes, was one of the forms of activism developed by the Chartist movement. The Owenites had their 'Halls of Science' for education in the principles of co-operation, and local co-operative societies undertook adult education work that continues to this day.

The long-standing tradition of lecturing within the working class, going back at least to the London Corresponding Society of the 1790s, developed out of a spontaneous enthusiasm for improving knowledge. It was in response to this enthusiasm that a characteristic form of political agitation and propagandism of the early-Victorian period was developed—the public address by an itinerant lecturer, sent out to spread the message of Chartism or Owenism or, indeed, free trade in corn under the auspices of the Anti-Corn Law League. This enthusiasm for knowledge and moral uplift, and the educational traditions it gave rise to, explain the success of many of the 'university extension' lecturers in working-class communities somewhat later. In addition, the mid-nineteenth century saw the establishment of several Working Men's Colleges in centres like Sheffield, Wolverhampton, Manchester, and Salford. The most famous of these, the London Working Men's College, was founded in 1854 by F. D. Maurice and other Christian Socialists. It offered a more challenging academic education with less emphasis on the practical and vocational than had been available hitherto. In parallel with these formal initiatives, meanwhile, were a host of ill-documented informal ones—here a series of 'improving lectures' organized by an enthusiast in a local hall, there a reading class meeting in a cramped Victorian parlour.[1]

By the 1860s there were a variety of uncoordinated efforts under way, therefore. Some were provided *by* the working class and some *for* them: the tension between these contrasting types of educational provision forms a theme in what is to follow, and will be manifest in many of the initiatives and movements to be examined in this book. Why should Cambridge, Oxford, and also the London Society for the Extension of University Teaching, a private, voluntary body which was incorporated into the reformed University of London in the early years of the twentieth century, have become involved in a movement for adult higher education at this stage?[2] Why should the universities have accepted the responsibility of educational provision for groups and whole social classes, not to mention genders, hitherto ignored by the system of higher education? The answer must knit together themes in the history of the universities and their reform in the mid-Victorian period, with wider educational and social history.

[1] For general surveys of the development of adult education in the nineteenth century see Thomas Kelly, *A History of Adult Education in Great Britain*, 3rd edn. (Liverpool, 1992; first pub. 1970) 112–215 and J. F. C Harrison, *Learning and Living 1790–1960: A Study in the History of the English Adult Education Movement* (London, 1961), pts. 1 and 2.

[2] John Burrows, *University Adult Education in London: A Century of Achievement* (London, 1976), 2; Edwin Welch, 'The London Society for the Extension of University Teaching 1875–1902', *Guildhall Studies in London History*, 3/1 (Oct. 1977), 56. As the University of London was then limited to the function of examining only, the Society, which began classes in the capital in 1876, could not be established within the university and its sponsors were obliged to set it up in this form. The Society was dissolved and its functions transferred to the reorganized University of London in 1902.

The general mid-Victorian reform of education provides one point of departure. Royal commissions in the 1850s and 1860s investigated the elementary, secondary, and public schools, and legislation followed in the form of the 1869 Endowed Schools Act and the 1870 (Elementary) Education Act. Investigation and reform were evidence of growing public and political concern over the accessibility and quality of education in England—issues that also affected the two ancient universities. Their religious and social restrictions, their relatively poor academic standards when compared with the scholarship and natural science of German universities, and their supposedly wasteful and inadequate use of large endowments, prompted growing criticism of their failure to fulfil a truly 'national' role. Within the walls, there was widespread apprehension that if the universities failed to reform themselves adequately the mid-Victorian state would reform them against their will. There was growing appreciation of the hostility of the provincial middle classes to the curriculum, culture, and cost of the universities. With the formal admission of religious dissenters to Oxford and Cambridge in the 1850s and the passage of the Second Reform Act of 1867, there was a new awareness that the development of political democracy, and of social and religious pluralism, posed a new set of questions about the function of universities in a broader and heterogeneous culture. And some dons feared that Oxford and Cambridge would lose their cultural centrality and academic pre-eminence unless they found ways of reaching and bringing in new audiences. It was as a response to these concerns and challenges that Oxford and Cambridge began to debate the merits of what became known as university extension.

But the origin of university extension, perhaps because of its complexity, has generally been presented in inadequate fashion in terms of the initiatives of one young Prize Fellow of Trinity College, Cambridge, James Stuart, in the late 1860s and early 1870s. It will be the purpose of this account to present Stuart not as a far-sighted pioneer but as a product of institutions and outlooks that had been seeking an enlarged role for the universities in a new social context for at least a generation before he took up the question.

Stuart discovered for himself the 'vast masses who desire education' by going out to teach them.[3] Aged twenty-four, in 1867 he was asked to give several series of lectures to groups of women in Leeds,

[3] James Stuart, 'On the Work of the Universities in Higher Education', *Transactions of the National Association for the Promotion of Social Science 1871* (London, 1872), 373.

Sheffield, Manchester, and Liverpool affiliated to the newly formed North of England Council for Promoting the Higher Education of Women. Stuart, a future Professor of Mechanical Engineering in Cambridge, and from 1885 a Liberal MP, chose as his subject the history of astronomy.[4] He was not the only young fellow of an Oxford or Cambridge college engaged by the Council; indeed, the Council itself, under the presidency of the redoubtable campaigner for women's rights, Josephine Butler, included such well-known dons as James Bryce, T. H. Green and Henry Sidgwick.[5] But in choosing Stuart they hit upon a teacher very much in sympathy with the needs of educated middle-class women with no prospect of taking their studies further. Travelling through the industrial heartlands, Stuart discovered a demand for higher education among working men as well. In the following two years he gave lectures at the Crewe Mechanics' Institute and for the famous Rochdale Equitable Pioneers' Co-operative Society. The experience here was crucial. Stuart drew an audience of 'upwards of 1000', including mothers 'with babies in their arms'; as he later commented, 'it all served greatly to impress me with the desire these people had to get education'.[6] He went on to lecture at other notable co-operative societies in Bury, Leeds, and Dewsbury. There is evidence that at this stage Stuart began to project an alliance of the North of England Council and the co-operative movement who would together 'engage a group of teachers of the highest class and "utilize them as peripatetic professors of a Co-operative University"'.[7] Funds for this would come from the 2 per cent of the net annual profits of co-operative societies that was set aside by them for educational purposes, though frequently left unused.[8] But the scheme was overambitious and the

[4] Edwin Welch, *The Peripatetic University: Cambridge Local Lectures 1873–1973* (Cambridge, 1973), 25–44; James Stuart, *Reminiscences* (London, 1911), 155–68.

[5] H. J. Mackinder and M. E. Sadler, *University Extension: Past, Present and Future*, 3rd edn. (London, 1891) 18–19. For the origins and work of the North of England Council for Promoting the Higher Education of Women see F. W. Myers, 'On Local Lectures for Women', *Transactions of the National Association for the Promotion of Social Science 1868* (London, 1869), 450. Myers was also a Fellow of Trinity College, Cambridge, and it was he who was approached first by the North of England Council to give a course of lectures, but suggested they contact Stuart instead.

[6] James Stuart, 'Inaugural Address', *Report of the Second Summer Meeting Held in Oxford, August 1889* (Oxford, 1889), 27–8.

[7] W. H. Draper, *University Extension: A Survey of Fifty Years, 1873–1923* (Cambridge, 1923), 14.

[8] Alon Kadish, *The Oxford Economists in the Late Nineteenth Century* (Oxford, 1982), 78.

co-operative movement was reluctant to commit itself.[9] It is important none the less, because the later pioneers of Oxford extension would attempt to establish something like it after 1878. Unable to set up an independent organization for the provision of higher education, therefore, in 1870 Stuart began a campaign to build support in Cambridge for a formal system of lectures for such audiences.

Stuart's *Letter on University Extension Addressed to the Resident Members of the University of Cambridge*, issued in late 1871, and subsequent memorials from the groups and institutions to which Stuart lectured, had their effect.[10] Stuart played upon the fear that the universities would lose influence unless they responded to new educational expectations. Extension would thus be 'a great step towards making the Universities truly national institutions and be no less beneficial to them than to the country'. He also pointed out that most working people who sought higher education could never leave their homes and jobs for residence in a university; for them, anything other than peripatetic lectures was simply inappropriate. The university investigated the proposal, reported in favour of an experimental scheme and in the autumn of 1873 Stuart was able to organize, under the auspices of the university's new Local Lectures Syndicate, a series of successful trial lectures. They were on three subjects—physical science, political economy, and English literature—and were given by other members of Trinity College in Nottingham, Leicester, and Derby, three cities which had shown an especial interest in his proposals. The university extension movement thus began under the auspices of Cambridge and was organized to meet the demands for higher education of two groups in particular whom Stuart picked out in his *Letter*, 'women and working men'. Two years later the Cambridge local lectures were being given in thirty different centres, while a London Society for the Extension of University Teaching had been established to engage in extension work in the capital. Crucially, Stuart had been forced to accept that the local lectures should be self-supporting—that the costs should fall on the centres and audiences attending rather than be met, in whole or part, by the university. He recognized that 'it would be impossible to bring the matter to a successful issue if the Scheme were to involve any proposal for a charge upon University or College Funds'.[11] As the Vice-Chancellor, Henry Cookson Master of Peterhouse, commented when transmitting documents about the local

[9] Draper, *University Extension*, 15.
[10] James Stuart, *Letter on University Extension Addressed to the Resident Members of the University of Cambridge* (Cambridge, 1871).
[11] Quoted in Welch, *Peripatetic University*, 43.

lectures to the secretary of the Cleveland Commission, then investigating the finances of Oxford and Cambridge, 'it is understood that the necessary funds for carrying on a scheme of education like that which is contemplated will be provided from local sources, and that such a scheme may be chiefly, if not entirely, self-supporting'.[12]

II

Stuart presented a highly personal account of this six-year period in his *Reminiscences*, written in old age, divorcing himself from the contexts of university reform and provincial initiatives that really explain the origins of university extension. He wrote that extension 'for the first half-dozen years depended so much on myself as to become almost a personal matter'.[13] He even claimed first use of the term 'university extension' itself when he employed it in the title of his 1871 *Letter*.[14] In truth, the phrase had been current for a generation, bound up with the processes of university reform in general, and certainly familiar in Oxford since the 1840s.

Mid-Victorian reform of the universities, carried out between the early 1850s and early 1880s, was largely imposed from outside by the state. It was intended to open Oxford and Cambridge to all religious denominations, modernize their curricula, quicken the educational life and utility of the institutions, and encourage academic research. Much of this was to be achieved by the establishment within the universities of an academic career structure open to merit. The focus was on secularization, specialization, and the so-called endowment of research. In Oxford, in the space of a generation, college fellowships were thrown open to competition; celibacy as a condition for holding a fellowship was ended; intercollegiate lectures began to break down the educational isolation of the colleges; the University's governing structures were made more representative as the Hebdomadal Board of heads of colleges was replaced by a broader Hebdomadal Council; the professoriate was expanded; academic research was recognized as a legitimate university function; natural science was added to the curriculum, and religious tests were abolished for matriculation, graduation, and election to fellowships.[15]

---

[12] *Report of the Commissioners Appointed to Inquire into the Property and Income of the Universities of Oxford and Cambridge*, PP 1873, C. 856, xxxvii, pt. 1, app. I.

[13] Stuart, *Reminiscences*, 155.   [14] Stuart, 'Inaugural Address', 31.

[15] Arthur Engel, *From Clergyman to Don: The Rise of the Academic Profession in Nineteenth Century Oxford* (Oxford, 1983).

The social composition of the universities—who the students were and where they came from—was a consideration in these changes, but was always less important than purely institutional reform. Nevertheless, the cumulative effects of external investigation, parliamentary legislation, and reform, were to create by the 1860s a new generation of young, Liberal dons 'who were characterised not only by high intelligence, but by public-spirited enthusiasm' and for whom the social basis of university education was an issue.[16] James Stuart was one of these young 'lights of liberalism'.[17]

In fact, 'the extension of university education' had been an issue in Oxford since November 1845 when an address was presented to the university's governing Hebdomadal Board asking it to make 'academical education accessible to the sons of parents whose incomes are too narrow for the scale of expenditure at present prevailing among junior members' by expanding existing, and founding new colleges in the university. It bore the signatures of, among others, several leading Conservatives and churchmen, including Lord Sandon, Gladstone, Ashley, Sidney Herbert, Samuel Wilberforce, and A. C. Tait.[18] It was designed, essentially, to provide more candidates for ordination in the Church, a form of university extension that was eventually realized in the foundation of Keble College and its incorporation in the University in 1871. The Hebdomadal Board responded to the address in 1846 with a series of negative arguments and took no action.[19] But the question was raised again by the first and most famous Royal Commission on Oxford between 1850–2. In evidence before the Commission, Mark Pattison, later Rector of Lincoln College and one of the most influential internal advocates of change, pictured a reformed Oxford as 'a national University . . . co-extensive with the nation'. He advocated 'opening the University to the Nation and the world'.[20] And the Commission certainly recognized the claims to admission of the sons of 'the

[16] Lewis Campbell, *On the Nationalisation of the Old English Universities* (London, 1901), 235.

[17] On the relationship between university reform and political Liberalism in the mid-Victorian period see Christopher Harvie, *The Lights of Liberalism: University Liberals and the Challenge of Democracy 1860–1886* (London, 1976).

[18] See 'Appendix E. Report of a Committee of the Hebdomadal Board, in Answer to an Address upon the Extension of University Education. Presented to the Board of Heads of Houses and Proctors, March 16 1846', in *Report of Her Majesty's Commissioners Appointed to Inquire into the State, Discipline, Studies and Revenues of the University and Colleges of Oxford*, PP 1852, 1482, xxii (hereafter *Oxford University Commission 1852*).

[19] W. R. Ward, *Victorian Oxford* (London, 1965), 138–40, 264–7.

[20] *Oxford University Commission 1852*, Evidence, 44.

manufacturing and mercantile class, which has arisen by the side of the landed aristocracy'.[21] Evidence was also provided by another liberal, Benjamin Jowett, then Fellow and Tutor of Balliol College, who saw in the expansion of the university and its extension into new social classes 'the possibility of supplying an increased number of clergy', for 'providing a better class of school-masters', and of 'opening to the lower and middle classes an honourable way of advancement in life'. Jowett favoured expansion through 'establishing new Halls in connexion with Colleges'.[22]

The Commissioners' report enumerated the possible means by which such 'university extension' could be achieved: the establishment of new, cheap halls, whether in connection with colleges or as independent foundations; allowing undergraduates to live inexpensively out of college in private houses; permitting students to be members of the university, but without the expense of a college attachment; and providing admission to lectures only for non-resident and unassociated scholars. But it discounted a fifth option of affiliating external institutions with Oxford, singling out for opposition the ideas of William Sewell, Fellow and Senior Tutor of Exeter College, that the university 'should apply funds for establishing Professors in Birmingham and Manchester' and other provincial cities.[23] In the past Sewell has been referred to as 'the father of Oxford extension' because his suggestions in a pamphlet of 1850 prefigured the debate on extension and the actual scheme adopted in the 1870s. In fact, Sewell had no positive wish to extend university learning and culture and was advocating a means by which he believed he could ensure 'the preservation of the old Oxford he loved'.[24] The university could be retained in an unreformed state if surplus funds and surplus dons could be applied to the education of new classes in new cities *in situ* rather than in Oxford itself.[25] He was, in truth, an 'impetuous nostalgic' and conservative, and the Commission gave his ideas short shrift.[26] They favoured bringing poor scholars to Oxford 'to make the university a great seat of learning', not 'to multiply places in which Teachers inferior in learning

---

[21] Ibid., Report, 19.   [22] Ibid., Evidence, 33–4.

[23] See 'University Extension', *Oxford University Commission 1852*, Report, 29–54.

[24] Ward, *Victorian Oxford*, 284. See also Campbell, *On The Nationalisation of the Old English Universities* (London, 1901), 80–1.

[25] See William Sewell, *Suggestions for the Extension of the University: Submitted to the Rev. The Vice-Chancellor* (Oxford, 1850).

[26] Stuart Marriott, *Extra-Mural Empires: Service and Self-Interest in English University Adult Education* (Nottingham, 1984), 17.

and capacity . . . would train inferior students'. Such schemes, involving university expenditure beyond its confines 'should not be entertained till it has been shown that there is no demand for men and money in the University itself'.[27]

Here, in brief, were all the arguments and suggestions which formed the basis of discussion of 'university extension' until the 1870s. It is notable that the term originally applied to the provision of increased opportunities within Oxford itself. Only later was it given a more literal interpretation and associated with University teaching outside the walls. Indeed, Stuart's appropriation of the term to describe the system of peripatetic lecturing he established may have actually limited opportunities for those who still sought a broadening of the universities' social base. From the 1870s 'university extension' out there, remote from Oxford and Cambridge, ceased to carry any implications of internal reform.

But neither internal nor external reforms of the student body, as opposed to the academic structure of the university, followed the first Oxford Commission and the subsequent Oxford University Act in 1854. On the other hand, a useful symbol of the university's new national role and renewed social purpose came in the shape of the Oxford 'middle class examinations' or local examinations which it first sponsored in 1858. These were designed for boys in secondary, 'middle class schools' that were otherwise unregulated. The examinations would allow comparability between schools, it was hoped, thereby raising standards; provide a good measure of the achievement of individual pupils; and provide a means by which the university could remodel the secondary curriculum. The success of the experiment, extended to girls' schools in 1870, and also taken up by Cambridge, made the 'middle class examinations' a fixture in later Victorian education. It provided an example of educational endeavour beyond the ancient universities that university extension would build on in the 1870s: indeed, it was as an aspect of the work of the Delegates for Local Examinations that Oxford university extension was first organized. A precedent that university extension could build on had also been established, in that local examinations combined university recognition of wider educational obligations with co-operation between the university and external bodies.[28] And the Oxford middle-class examinations were also linked to later Oxford university extension by familial lines and familial

---

[27] *Oxford University Commission 1852*, Report, 53–4.
[28] Ward, *Victorian Oxford*, 280–1; Mackinder and Sadler, *University Extension*, 15–17. On the local examinations, see J. P. C. Roach, *Public Examinations in England, 1850–1900* (Cambridge, 1971), 35–102.

traditions of public service through education. The examinations
had been projected and advocated by two men above all, Sir Thomas
Dyke Acland and Frederick Temple. Acland, from a notable West-
Country landowning family with large estates at Killerton in Devon,
had been educated at Christ Church and held a fellowship at All
Souls in the 1830s. He was a Conservative free trader, who, like his
contemporary at Oxford and close friend, Gladstone, became a
Liberal. His third son, Arthur Acland, was to serve as the secretary
of the committee charged with organizing Oxford extension lectures
in 1878. Frederick Temple was variously a Fellow of Balliol who
retained close connections with Oxford reformers and liberals around
Jowett after leaving Oxford; an inspector of training colleges for
teachers; headmaster of Rugby; Bishop of London and ultimately
Archbishop of Canterbury at the end of the century. His son was
William Temple, who, as a fellow of Queen's College, Oxford, was
instrumental in the development of new forms of working-class
education in the Edwardian period. William Temple served as president of the Workers' Educational Association, and became a yet
more famous Archbishop of Canterbury.[29]

In November 1865, meanwhile, a powerful group of dons sympathetic to ideas of extension and broadly composed of university
liberals like Goldwin Smith, J. E. Thorold Rogers, Pattison, and
Jowett, and high churchmen, were elected by the University's convocation to a set of complementary committees 'to consider the
question of the Extension of the University, with a view especially
to the education of persons needing assistance and desirous of admission into the Christian ministry'.[30] As this suggests, the enterprise, under the chairmanship of the Provost of Oriel, was as much
concerned with solving the problem of the shortage of clergy as
opening up Oxford to new classes. Potential solutions, very much
in keeping with those suggested by the 1852 Commission were
investigated and published. As Jowett wrote to his mother, 'This
place is all in a stir about University Extension and probably something will be done. At present it is certainly a great grievance that
a young man has to pay about £200 a year for 6 months in the
year.'[31] Pattison echoed his sentiments in his book published two
years later, *Suggestions on Academical Organisation with Especial*

[29] Roach, *Public Examinations*, 66–72. See also T. D. Acland, *Some Account of
the Origin and Objects of the New Oxford Examinations* (London, 1858).
[30] *Oxford University Extension* (London, 1866), 5.
[31] Benjamin Jowett to Mrs Jowett, 9 Dec. 1865, Jowett Papers, Balliol College,
Oxford, II A7/16.

Reference to Oxford, which reviewed the very limited progress in cheapening the cost of a university education.[32] Yet in the same year, 1868, an advance was made with the establishment of the 'non-collegiate system' by which students were admitted as members of the university, lived in licensed housing, but were not members of a college. For forty years or so it was a partial success, drawing poorer boys to Oxford, yet it was unable to provide the full experience of university life for non-collegiate students, and they were unable to escape the social stigma that comparative poverty carried in Oxford.

1868 is also important because it saw the first active involvement in university extension of the two great Balliol figures, Jowett and T. H. Green, who together projected and established Balliol Hall as a hostel for poorer students. For the next decade Jowett would oversee the practical development of university extension in Oxford, and Green would inspire the movement long beyond his untimely death in 1882. Their collaboration and involvement drew extension towards the centre of university affairs and helped establish it as a quintessential expression of the social engagement of late-Victorian Oxford.

It is difficult to do justice to Jowett's role and reputation in Oxford, and Victorian Britain more generally, as a religious controversialist, scholar of Greek, and Master, after 1870, of the most influential and prominent Oxford college.[33] University extension was but one component of Jowett's lifelong project to modernize, liberalize, and energize the university and create, thereby, a newly responsible and educated ruling élite. He was convinced that, as he wrote to Florence Nightingale, 'not a twentieth part of the ability in the country comes to the university', a waste of talent that had to be redressed if Oxford was to be reformed and produce a moral and meritocratic class of leaders and servants of the nation.[34] Thus, in the immediate aftermath of the 1852 Royal Commission, Jowett was projecting a means of bringing deserving scholars to the university. As he wrote to A. P. Stanley, who had served as secretary of the Oxford Commission, 'the scheme is shortly a Hall attached to Balliol College with intercommunion of Lectures. Tuition to be free—Room Rent also free—the total expenses to be reduced (by common

---

[32] Mark Pattison, *Suggestions on Academical Organization with Especial Reference to Oxford* (London, 1868), 56–60.

[33] On Jowett see Evelyn Abbott and Lewis Campbell, *The Life and Letters of Benjamin Jowett*, 2 vols. (London, 1897).

[34] Jowett to Florence Nightingale, Oct. 1866, in ibid., i. 377.

meals etc.) to the lowest point, say £50 a year'. Where others saw the social composition of the university as of secondary importance, to Jowett 'nothing else would give an equal impulse to University Reform'. Writing a month later to A. C. Tait he went further, justifying the scheme to a future Archbishop of Canterbury as a means of 'providing an increased number of well-educated clergymen' and of affording opportunities 'to men of ability of rising in life not merely through the means of trade and business but through the far better one of a liberal education'. Where university extension was concerned, liberals and high churchmen could make common cause, though their ends were different. Jowett explained that his object was 'not to raise poor men but to educate men of ability at a lower rate'.[35] Nothing came of these ideas at this stage, perhaps because the next years, following Jowett's publication of an edition of St Paul's epistles in 1855, and his contribution to the infamous volume *Essays and Reviews* in 1860, embroiled him in public theological controversy. But from the mid-1860s he was able to use his influence over his colleagues to prompt his college to provide means and accommodation for poorer scholars. As he explained to Miss Nightingale in October 1866,

I found that my scheme of University Extension was very favourably received. I want men (1) to live in Lodgings which we are to build and furnish and let at a rent of £10 a year: (2) to be allowed to attend College lectures free: (3) to have small Exhibitions of £25 a year given away by examination. I reckon that paying £10 a year on rent, and having nothing to pay for instruction, they could live for the academical year of twenty-four weeks on £50 a year, or deducting the Exhibition, for £25 a year.[36]

This compares with average student expenditure of over £200 each year, as estimated by the 1850 Royal Commission. In 1867 Balliol established a scheme of five annual exhibitions for deserving scholars (actually setting them at £40 rather than £25) and in the following year opened Balliol Hall, a rented house at 26 St Giles, as a residence for them, supervised by T. H. Green and his wife.[37]

---

[35] See Jowett to A. P. Stanley, 6 June 1852; Jowett to F. T. Palgrave, 8 June 1852; Jowett to A. C. Tait, 9 July 1852. Jowett Papers, III S 57; I F 10/48; IV B5/5.

[36] Jowett to Florence Nightingale, Oct. 1866, in Abbott and Campbell, *Benjamin Jowett*, i. 377.

[37] John Jones, *Balliol College: A History 1263–1939* (Oxford, 1988), 208–9. See also H. P. Smith, 'A Note on the Contribution of Balliol to the Making of the Tradition of Extra-Mural Education', uncatalogued MS, Balliol College, Oxford, 1–2.

III

Balliol Hall was only one part of Jowett's conception of university extension, however. For from this period also dated his interest in using Oxford's prestige and resources to promote institutions of higher learning in the provinces—to extend the university in a literal sense by constructing a network of provincial colleges linked in certain ways with Oxford. This was not a new idea; it had been considered and rejected by the 1850 Commission as we have seen. But it received renewed attention in the late 1860s, as an authentic provincial movement for the spread of higher education emerged that has been largely ignored by historians of university extension. The movement can be traced in the pages of the *Transactions* of the National Association for the Promotion of Social Science, or the Social Science Association as it was known, an important mid-Victorian forum for the discussion of social policy and an information exchange on social initiatives.

The Association served to bring together metropolitan and provincial élites, generally of a Liberal outlook, and was thus a natural place of meeting for reforming dons and provincial educationalists.[38] When James Stuart was engaged in his campaign to win support for local lectures he naturally gave a paper to the Social Science Association at its 1871 Congress in Leeds.[39] Five years earlier, at the Manchester Congress of 1866, one Oxford graduate of the 1840s who was to return to the university in the 1870s as a tutor at Hertford College, the Revd James Rumsey, addressed the Social Science Association on 'Oxford Extension'. In remarks that foreshadowed the establishment of Balliol Hall, he called for the 'adaptation' of Oxford 'to the purposes of national education' by founding 'places of reception'—hostels, houses, colleges—cheaply run and offering 'efficient and skilled tutorial provision' for those currently excluded from a university education.[40]

Rumsey and Stuart were sure of a sympathetic hearing: almost all participants in the annual discussions on university extension at the Social Science Association shared a commitment to changing the universities. As Mark Pattison commented when addressing the Association in Birmingham in 1868, 'I shall take it for granted that

[38] See Lawrence Goldman, 'The Social Science Association 1857–1886: A Context for Mid-Victorian Liberalism', *English Historical Review*, 100/1 (1986), 95–134.   [39] See n. 3 above.
[40] Revd James Rumsey, 'Oxford Extension', *Transactions of the National Association for the Promotion of Social Science 1866* (London, 1867), 379–85.

this Section has made up its mind that the Universities are national institutions, and that the education and the endowments ought to be accessible, as widely as possible, to all who wish to avail themselves of them'.[41] Provincial Liberals, with a cutting edge to their radicalism, were seeking at the Social Science Association to make the universities serviceable 'for the diffusion of higher education throughout the country'. They also gave evidence that initiatives in higher learning were under way in several locations without any connection with the universities, reporting on lectures given for the benefit of middle-class, artisan, and female audiences.[42] One such Liberal was Robert Spence Watson, an active Quaker, a follower of John Bright, a leader of north-eastern Liberalism, and later president of the National Liberal Federation in the 1890s. He had been instrumental in arranging lecture series in the late 1860s at the Newcastle Literary and Philosophical Society; a decade later he was instrumental in bringing the Cambridge local lectures to the north east.[43] In 1870 at the Social Science Association he called on the universities to assume national responsibility for the higher education of the people and to employ some of their otherwise idle fellows in peripatetic lecturing: 'if they could only be stationed in small bodies in different large towns, and required to teach, instead of being retained in large bodies in two small towns and permitted to do nothing'. Oxford, Spence Watson continued, might 'look down with regret, no doubt, upon the flippancy and thoughtlessness, upon the gigantic Philistinism, which everywhere prevail, but they have no right to regard it with scorn unless they are prepared to deliver us from it'.[44]

The reference to 'Philistinism' must have been deliberate. Spence Watson was responding to Matthew Arnold's famous lectures as Professor of Poetry in Oxford, delivered in the Sheldonian Theatre and published as *Culture and Anarchy* in the previous year, 1869.

[41] Mark Pattison, 'What Measures are Required for the Further Improvement of the Universities of Oxford and Cambridge?', *Transactions of the National Association for the Promotion of Social Science 1868* (London, 1869), 385.

[42] See J. N. Langley, 'The South Staffordshire Association for the Promotion of Adult Education'; Edwin Smith, 'The Educational Work of the Birmingham and Midland Institute'; Rev. Canon Gover, 'Report of the Edinburgh Ladies' Educational Association'; all in, *Transactions of the National Association for the Promotion of Social Science 1868* (London, 1869), 447–52.

[43] Percy Corder, *The Life of Robert Spence Watson* (London, 1914), 147. *The Times*, 3 Mar. 1911, p. 11.

[44] R. Spence Watson, 'On the Best Method of Providing Higher Education in Boroughs', *Transactions of the National Association for the Promotion of Social Science 1870* (London, 1871), 365–6.

The debate on university extension, indeed on university reform more generally, was quickened by Arnold's assault on 'the bad culture' of the middle classes. Money-making, protestant nonconformity, and provincial insularity—this was 'philistinism' and, in Arnold's opinion, it had pinched and debased the culture of the English middle classes. Spence Watson evidently believed that such criticism was illegitimate, since it emanated from an exclusive culture and institution which had together done nothing to raise the middle classes towards what Arnold famously termed 'sweetness and light'. Other participants at the Social Science Association were less combative, however, fearing the consequences of a prolonged division between the two cultures, the 'Hebraism' of the middle classes and the 'Hellenism' of the élite, and they saw in university extension a remedy for it: it might bridge the cultural abyss as well as meet a growing demand for higher learning. One of these was John Percival, then the first headmaster of Clifton College and later President of Trinity College, Oxford, headmaster of Rugby, Bishop of Hereford, and mentor to many who took up adult and workers' education. Percival was an important reforming influence in the universities and public schools. A Liberal, a broad churchman, and a follower of Dr Thomas Arnold, he was also a friend of Jowett's, sharing many of his views.[45] Percival spoke at Newcastle in 1870 as well, and he warned against the 'permanent separation between the practical and the speculative sides of English life, between the centres of culture and the centres of practical activity, such as no nation can risk with impunity'. In other words, in the late 1860s and early 1870s the debate on the meaning and attributes of national 'culture' promoted a new argument for extension. In Percival's view, only by 'radical reforms' in the universities could they retain their cultural hold on the nation and prevent 'our town life from becoming hopelessly commercial and unintellectual'.[46]

IV

It is against the background of a growing provincial demand for higher education from the old universities, and a pervasive fear of

[45] William Temple, *The Life of Bishop Percival* (London, 1921); Kadish, *Oxford Economists*, 8.

[46] Revd John Percival, 'By What Means can a Direct Connection be Established between the Elementary and Secondary Schools and Universities?', *Transactions of the National Association for the Promotion of Social Science 1870* (London, 1871), 315–6.

the cultural consequences of doing nothing to meet that demand, that we must understand the origin of university extension in the 1870s. In Oxford, Balliol Hall had provided a working model of one solution, but on a small scale. Now Jowett turned to a grander plan. In one of his notebooks for 1871 there appears a brief jotting: 'University revenues should be applied to found universities in the large towns say at Newcastle, Liverpool—Aberystwyth—Derby—Birmingham—Leeds—Sheffield—Plymouth—Bath—Brighton (10). The two universities to give [£]8000, [£]6000 a year each to these New Colleges. The towns to raise a similar sum by the rates. The Government to pay half the cost of Buildings.'[47] These ideas were eventually consolidated in his 'Suggestions for University Reform', a memorandum drafted in 1874, though not published until after Jowett's death, which reviewed the progress of university reform and projected further changes.[48] Jowett estimated total annual university income in Oxford at £50,000 and total annual college income at £350,000. Remarkably, he advocated an expenditure of £40,000 per annum of this on establishing and supporting ten new 'colleges in large towns'. They would be affiliated to Oxford and would pass on worthy students who had completed preliminary courses at them for their final education in Oxford. Their curriculum would be conformable with Oxford's, though only Oxford could grant degrees. As he explained, 'colleges planted in the great centres of population would continue school education; they would afford to the more active-minded of the working classes the opportunity of self-culture; they would solve the problem of a higher education for women'. They would also introduce 'a body of highly educated men into a commercial and manufacturing society' and so assist in the development of a national as opposed to sectional cultures.[49]

When Jowett wrote this he could have been fairly confident that this form of university extension was viable since Balliol had already been involved for some two years in the founding of what later became the University of Bristol. At the first college meeting of 1872, the Master had proposed a committee to assist provincial efforts at university education.[50] And when in 1873 a committee was established in Bristol to found a local 'technical school of science', Jowett offered the services of Balliol.[51] He was alerted to

---

[47] Quarto notebook, untitled. First written page begins 'Lectures on Natural Religion' [1871?], Jowett Papers, I A17, fo. 67.

[48] Benjamin Jowett, 'Suggestions for University Reform, 1874', in Campbell, *Nationalisation of the Old Universities*, 183–208.   [49] Ibid. 202–3.

[50] Abbott and Campbell, *Jowett*, ii. 57–8; Balliol College Minutes, English Register 1794–1875, fo. 253, 19 Jan. 1872.   [51] Ward, *Victorian Oxford*, 285.

the opportunity by Percival who, as headmaster of Clifton, was one of the members of the local committee. Indeed, Percival used the opportunity to publish a pamphlet on *The Connection of the Universities and the Great Towns* which called on Oxford to assist provincial culture and learning by planting members of faculty in cities and towns in England and expending university resources on them as they lectured, taught, and directed the growing interest in higher education.[52] Jowett won the support of his college and was able to enlist the services of New College also. Both put up £300 annually for five years to assist the projected college, stipulating that women and working adults should be able to benefit and that the curriculum should be literary as well as scientific.[53] Jowett, attended by the Warden of New College, J. E. Sewell, and the historian E. A. Freeman, spoke at the founding meeting in June 1874 in Clifton: as he summed it up, 'They could not bring this class to the universities, and therefore they must take the universities to them'.[54] Bristol University College opened in 1876, and in the following year appointed its first Principal, the economist Alfred Marshall. T. H. Green was a member of its Council.

But Jowett's vision of Oxford transformed into the centre of a great federal university which she would direct in the national interest was already being superseded by events, and was unable to win the support of opinion in Oxford itself, outside Balliol. First, the beginning of Cambridge local lectures and their swift success, offered a much simpler and cheaper means of doing something for higher education in the nation. Jowett's ideas would have revolutionized Oxford; Stuart's practical scheme had no discernible impact on the University of Cambridge. It is not clear what Jowett thought of Stuart's experiment; he was briefly gracious about it in his address in Bristol in June 1874. But in Percival's pamphlet on *The Connection of the Universities and the Great Towns* there was criticism of the 'signs of movement' in Cambridge in 1873 because they were so limited.

[52] Revd John Percival, *The Connection of the Universities and the Great Towns* (London, 1873); see Temple, *Percival*, 263.
[53] Balliol College Minutes, fo. 262, 11 Oct. 1873; Jones, *Balliol College*, 218; Basil Cottle and J. W. Sherbourne, *The Life of a University* (Bristol, 1951), 1–13.
[54] *Report of a Public Meeting held at Bristol to Promote the Establishment of a College of Science and Literature for the West of England and South Wales* (Bristol, 1874). See also 'Bristol University College—Speeches by the late Professor Jowett in 1874 and 1875' and 'College at Bristol 5/74', in Jowett's Commonplace Book, Jowett Papers, I D7, and I H25 fos. 65–7.

In all this I hope we are only looking upon the preliminary experiments which are to issue, not in a few courses of lectures to working men and others, or in some larger growth of local examinations of an elementary character, but in an extension of the real work of the universities, in their own proper sphere. As a citizen of a provincial city, I am most anxious that the universities should come down and expend upon us some portion of their resources.[55]

This captures, in brief, the differences between Cambridge and Oxford over university extension: those in Oxford around Jowett who gave the movement their support wanted to build institutions in the provinces, endow them, and affiliate them to the central university. In Cambridge, meanwhile, a start had been made by adopting a much more limited conception of 'university extension', and its very limitations made it the more acceptable and durable— though in its defence, it must be explained that the success of Cambridge 'local lectures' in several provincial cities in the 1870s and 1880s such as Sheffield, Nottingham, and Exeter, quickened interest in higher education, and assisted efforts in them to found local universities.

But Jowett's grand design also proved unpopular. As he summed up the problem in a letter to Percival in March 1874, 'There is a great jealousy about taking College Funds out of Oxford and many persons are greatly provoked with us for offering'.[56] He was opposed even by other university reformers, especially those favouring 'the endowment of research'. One compromise suggested at this time by a former fellow and tutor of University College, C. S. Parker MP, would have reduced the number of tutorial and prize fellowships in Oxford by half (from approximately 400 to approximately 200) and used the surplus income released on new professorships in Oxford and in the support of professors in university colleges in provincial cities. Extension and research would both gain, in other words.[57] But the plan was never considered seriously. Indeed, it shortly became clear that the payments to Bristol by Balliol and New College were *ultra vires* and were discontinued, though it is characteristic that Jowett and Green continued to offer financial assistance from their own pockets.[58] At the Social Science Association meeting in Glasgow in 1874 the arguments against the endow-

---

[55] Percival, *Connection of the Universities*, 23.

[56] Jowett to Percival, 15 Mar. 1874, quoted in Temple, *Percival*, 263–4.

[57] C. S. Parker, *Academical Endowments* (London, 1875).

[58] Melvin Richter, *The Politics of Conscience: T. H. Green and His Age* (London, 1983 repr.; first pub. 1964), 361. Among legacies to be paid after the death of his wife, Green left £3,500 to Balliol College 'for promoting education in large towns', *DNB*, vol. viii, 499.

ment of provincial higher education by Oxford were put forcefully by George Brodrick, later Warden of Merton College. 'What the University could really supply,' he argued, 'was not money, but brain power; and he wholly objected to frittering away resources which ought to be concentrated at Oxford upon the great cities of England and Scotland.' He went further, with critical remarks about the failure of provincial Britain to develop higher education for itself: 'The true policy was to endeavour to make the fire burn more brightly, and not to distribute the resources in order to benefit towns possessing wealth vastly out of proportion to that of the universities, and which, had they been in America, would have supplied themselves with local universities, and endowed them richly, long ago.'[59] As may be imagined, Brodrick reawakened cultural resentment on both sides, and the discussion grew angry and tense.

Yet Brodrick's opinions were both representative of Oxford and probably correct: indeed, he may well have spoken with foreknowledge of the conclusions of the Cleveland Commission, 'appointed to inquire into the property and income of the Universities of Oxford and Cambridge', which published its report in the same month that he made these remarks, October 1874. For this Royal Commission established that Oxford and her colleges were not fabulously wealthy as was commonly believed, nor profligate with such resources as they did possess. The accounts showed that 'there was no useful margin anywhere for endowing provincial colleges . . . the commissioners' figures supported the contention of Jowett's critics that Oxford could help the new foundations only by man-power and not by money'.[60] Jowett had wanted Oxford to fund and so direct the development of provincial higher education. Brodrick and others replied that the higher education of the great cities was their own responsibility. And following the Cleveland Commission, opinion in Oxford was clear that the funds were not available in any case. That opinion only hardened as the agricultural depression of the late nineteenth century set in, depressing land values, reducing college incomes, and hence 'making essential the choosing of priorities'.[61] Extension was never a priority, and was treated accordingly. In a sense, the field was now open for the Cambridge version of university extension.

Jowett hung onto his scheme of a federation of colleges focused on Oxford until his death: at an Oxford conference on the progress of university extension in 1887 he was still seeking to draw the

---

[59] *Transactions of the National Association for the Promotion of Social Science 1874* (London, 1875), pp. 393–4.
[60] Ward, *Victorian Oxford*, 295.   [61] Engel, *Clergyman to Don*, 257.

movement towards the establishment of provincial colleges as a primary aim rather than the occasional (though notable) by-product of university extension that it became.[62] When he appeared before the subsequent Selborne Commission in 1877 to provide evidence on 'the extension of the university in large towns', he continued to advocate a role for Oxford in directing the development of new colleges, the better to guide them towards the liberal education he prized so high. 'I dwell upon the fact that we ought not to allow a great movement to slip entirely out of our hands, and become instead a mechanics' institute movement, instead of a real extension of such an education as the university would wish to see given'. He still advocated that non-resident fellowships be awarded to 'persons lecturing or holding professorships in the large towns'. He still could not 'see how you are to connect yourself with this movement at all unless by giving some pecuniary assistance'.[63] But over the course of the next year he must have come to recognize that it would be half a loaf or nothing—something akin to 'local lectures' or no university extension in Oxford at all. For on 5 March 1878, Congregation in Oxford debated a statute that the 'Delegates of Local Examinations shall receive proposals for the establishment of lectures and teaching in large towns of England and Wales and shall be authorised to appoint Lecturers and Examiners for carrying out such proposals'. The motion was introduced by the mathematician Henry Smith, Savilian Professor of Geometry and among the most naturally gifted of all Oxford scholars of the nineteenth century.[64] He noted 'considerable opposition in Council' to the idea. Indeed, the Hebdomadal Council appears to have stipulated that the scheme could only proceed with 'the consent of Convocation to each case of co-operation' with an outside body—a condition that never seems to have been honoured. T. H. Green answered one don who saw the whole thing as a subsidy 'to assist the wealthy towns that could help themselves', explaining that the costs were to fall on the local lecture centres, and not the university. And Jowett, reconciled to the project, enumerated 'the general reasons for the step':

[62] *Report of a Conference in the Examination Schools, Oxford, of Representatives of the Local Committees Acting in Concert with the Committee of Delegates of Local Examinations Appointed to Establish Lectures and Teaching in Large Towns and of others Interested in the Extension of University Teaching on April 20 and 21 1887* (Oxford, 1887), 96.

[63] *University of Oxford Commission 1877: Part I: Minutes of Evidence taken by the Commissioners*, PP 1881, C. 2868, lvi, 'Evidence of The Rev. Benjamin Jowett, M.A. (Master of Balliol College)', 2646–52.

[64] See *Dictionary of National Biography*, xviii. 458–61.

First, there was the desire for a higher education on the part of that class who were the men who, when in after life successful, founded colleges like Nottingham and Sheffield. They wanted something to sweeten the toils of commerce, and that the University now proposed to give them. Secondly, it was desirable to furnish an outlet for the energies of her own young men, whose sympathies were directed towards the poor and neglected, but who from various reasons were unwilling, as was so often the case, to take orders. Thirdly, it combined female education.[65]

Jowett stressed the mutual benefits, in other words, accruing to students of extension and to their university tutors as well: it was to be a common formulation in the subsequent history of university extension. He was conscious, also, of the role that university extension might play for a generation of students and dons no longer able to express their social commitment through conventional Christian means. As Haig has shown, from the 1860s, the most academically distinguished graduates of Oxford rejected ordination and tended to seek careers in education. Extension thus met the demands of the uneducated for access to national culture with a supply of socially conscious graduates whose experience of the social and intellectual changes of the mid-Victorian period—Darwinism and the general advance of natural science, higher biblical criticism, and divisions within the Church itself—had left them lacking in faith.[66]

V

The new venture was administered by a Standing Committee of the Delegates of Local Examinations composed of six men: the chairman T. H. Green; Professor Henry Smith; J. E. Thorold Rogers, the noted Liberal politician and economic historian; Bartholomew Price, a mathematician, Sedleian Professor of Natural Philosophy, secretary of the university press, and eventually Master of Pembroke College; Revd J. F. Bright, Fellow and later Master of University College; and Revd Hereford George, Fellow and Tutor of New College. Arthur Acland, formerly a tutor at Keble College, acted as organizing secretary. The first Oxford extension lectures on 'The History of England in the Seventeenth Century' were subsequently delivered by the Revd Arthur Johnson, 'late fellow of All Souls and Lecturer in Modern History at Trinity, St John's, Wadham and Pembroke

---

[65] *The Times*, 6 Mar. 1878, p. 10; see also *The Times*, 21 Feb. 1878, p. 6.
[66] See A. G. L. Haig, 'The Church, the Universities and Learning in Later Victorian England', *The Historical Journal*, 29/1 (1986), 187–201.

Colleges' in the Board Room of King Edward VI School, New Street, Birmingham on 26 September 1878.[67] They were given under the auspices of the Birmingham Higher Education Association, established in 1875 to promote adult education in the city. The lectures cost the Association £60, of which £40 went to the lecturer as his fee.[68] Johnson was accompanied by T. H. Green, who must have been instrumental in organizing these first lectures on the basis of a long-standing connection with the King Edward VI School, dating back to his experience in 1865–6 as an assistant commissioner for the Taunton Commission, collecting information on secondary education in four Midland counties. Green assisted in remodelling the schools of the King Edward VI foundation under the terms of the Endowed Schools Act. He then served as the representative of the schoolteachers on the reformed governing body.[69] In introducing the first Oxford extension lecturer, Green explained the aims of this relatively new educational movement.

The considerations which had led the Universities to undertake these provincial lectures were something of this kind. They believed that there was a large body of people in provincial towns who were anxious to continue their education after they had left school. They believed in the first place that among the superior artisans there was a great eagerness for knowledge, especially on certain subjects ... as political economy, history and some branches of physical science. They also believed that there were many young men engaged in business who were eager to leave school at the age of 15 but who a few years later found that they had still a great deal to learn; and they had also to consider the claims of women. The latter were at present excluded from the Universities—perhaps necessarily excluded so long as residence was considered a necessary qualification. It seemed only fair that as there were insuperable difficulties in admitting women to the Universities, the Universities should try to bring their help to women at their own homes. Thus there was reason to think that there was a strong demand for adult education of a higher kind. They thought there was no lack of money, but that in many cases men were not forthcoming in provincial towns themselves fitted to give the lectures. Therefore it appeared that the Universities could advantageously co-operate with educational institutions in the large towns.[70]

[67] For Johnson's appointment, see 'Committee for University Extension, Minutes of Meetings, vol. 1', Oxford University Archives DES/M/1/1, fo. 1. For Johnson's syllabus for these lectures, see DES/EP/1/3, 'Early Papers 1877–97', fos. 3–6.

[68] See Oxford University Archives, DES/M/1/1, fo. 1.

[69] For Green's links with the King Edward VI School see R. L. Nettleship, 'Memoir', in id. (ed.), *Works of Thomas Hill Green*, 3 vols., (London, 1888), vol. iii, pp. lv–lvi.

[70] 'University Extension: Meeting in Birmingham', *Birmingham Daily Gazette*, 27 Sept. 1878.

The Revd Johnson was a remarkable figure, described accurately at his death as 'a country gentleman in holy orders' and 'one of the most prominent figures in Oxford life for upwards of sixty years'. He was a hunting, shooting, and fishing don, whose attachment to field sports was legendary and accomplishments at them prodigious. He was 'one of the very finest riders with any pack of hounds that could be reached from Oxford, an indefatigable shot, and an almost perfect fisherman'. An undergraduate at Exeter College in the 1860s, he began and ended his academic career as fellow and chaplain of All Souls. In between he was a tutor and lecturer 'at nearly half the colleges in Oxford' and his perambulations between them made him something of a legend in his own lifetime. Johnson, known as 'the Johnner', was an historian apparently 'at home in all periods of English and European history since the fall of the Roman Empire' who was famed for his teaching and played a part in building up the new School of Modern History in Oxford.[71] He published several books, ranging across the centuries from the Normans to the Victorians, expounding everything in a heartily unacademic style: 'he seldom took paradoxical views' we are told, 'and perhaps rather mistrusted "clever" ones'. To complement this he was a college chaplain who cared 'nothing for dogma' and knew 'nothing of theology'. He was the old Oxford incarnate, every inch of his large frame the muscular Christian with forthright views and uncomplicated opinions. Johnson was 'fond of telling his pupils that nature had destined him for a groom or a gamekeeper, for anything but a scholar'. He is not forgotten; his exploits on the left wing of the University soccer team in 1874 in a famous victory over the Royal Engineers in the third Football Association Cup Final have been recalled recently.[72] The pairing with T. H. Green on that first evening brought together two opposites, the old and new Oxford. Certainly the extension lecturers who followed were more likely to be young idealists and radicals in the mould of Green, than Oxford men of the unreconstructed variety. But Johnson probably did a good job: we are told that he was 'remarkably free from the common academic habits' including 'the professorial way of speech and manner' and that his lectures were 'clear, methodical and solid'.[73]

---

[71] Peter Slee, *Learning and a Liberal Education: The Study of Modern History in the Universities of Oxford, Cambridge and Manchester 1800–1914* (Manchester, 1986), 104, 128, 144.

[72] 'With God in your Goal', *Guardian*, 22 Oct. 1988, 18.

[73] See the obituaries of Johnson in *The Times*, 1 Feb. 1927, p. 17 and *Oxford Magazine*, 17 March 1927, pp. 409–10. See also Henry Sanderson Furniss, *Memories of Sixty Years* (London, 1931), 50–1.

Three more lecture courses, all historical, began shortly afterwards at Wolverhampton in association with the local Ladies' Educational Committee, and at Stourbridge and Kidderminster under
the auspices of the local Ladies' Useful Work Association. Not all
the lecturers had Johnson's gifts: an early report on progress at the
second and third of these locations noted that 'At both places several persons spoke to me of their appreciation of [Mr Doyle's]
lectures. All the same, while his hearers are impressed with his real
knowledge of the subject, they find his delivery a little heavy.'[74]
Both the ancient universities were now at work, but it is important to recognize that the form this took was a severely limited
conception of university extension. The term had initially implied
internal reform of the universities so as to make them national and
open to men of talent irrespective of means. It had been transformed by Jowett into a scheme to spread the influence of the
universities by federation with new provincial colleges. Now it meant
only the arrangement of lecture courses in provincial centres without any financial commitment to the spread of higher learning.
James Stuart is usually presented as the hero of this story, cutting
through mere talk and devising a workable model of extension.
According to one historian of Cambridge extension, 'Mr Stuart
was a great pioneer. He has the honour of being the first man to
take successful action in this field, and of inducing a great University to enter upon the path which he himself opened.'[75] In one sense
this is just. He recognized that a more ambitious scheme would
have been controversial, and proceeded accordingly. But what he
did as well, perhaps unwittingly, was to narrow options and hence
ensure that there would be no more fundamental reform of the
social composition of the universities. He pioneered what was, in
truth, the least disruptive of schemes, involving the least outlay of
funds, and thereby placed university extension on the margins of
university life. Perhaps this is unfair to Stuart, who was a realist to
Jowett's dreamer. Nevertheless, the history of the origins of university extension, which is much more complex than hitherto appreciated, is the history of a movement for reform being channelled into
the weakest of several alternatives.

Yet university extension in this minimal form was a successful
venture, as we shall see. And one element of its success was, ironically, to help change public perceptions of the universities. As early

---

[74] 'Report of the Secretary of the Standing Committee of the Delegates Nov. 27
1878' in 'Early Papers 1877–97', DES/EP/1/3, Oxford University Archives.
[75] Draper, *University Extension*, 15.

as 1875 a *Times* leader on Cambridge university extension noted the recent decline of 'an avowed antagonism' between the great manufacturing towns and the universities.[76] And there are grounds for believing that university extension, symbolizing the universities' recognition of wider social obligations, assisted considerably in raising them in public esteem in the late-Victorian period after the hostilities of the 1850s and 1860s—though this is also attributable to wider political and ideological changes as mid-Victorian liberal radicalism waned. When Jowett wrote to *The Times* in 1887 to call for state funding of the new university colleges of the 1870s and 1880s, he commented that 'Nothing has more tended to attach the mass of the people to our seats of learning than the proof which was given to them that there were many persons in both Universities who were interested in their welfare'.[77] In the same year the then Vice-Chancellor of Oxford, the President of St John's, Dr Bellamy, noted of the university's extension lecturers, that 'as far as Oxford is known in their persons, I may say the more that is seen of us the more we are respected'.[78] Addressing the same conference, the then Secretary of the London Society for the Extension of University Teaching, R. D. Roberts, was more definite still:

I am sure, until this University Extension movement was started, it was not at all realised what a wealth of affection, devotion and reverence there was in the country ready to be lavished upon the Universities if once they spread out their hands and showed they were ready to help the people, and I do not shrink from saying that I believe the University Extension movement has really saved the Universities.[79]

It had certainly saved them from further reform. When the first Secretary of the Oxford Extension Delegacy, Arthur Acland, wrote to his successor, Michael Sadler in 1892, he noted that 'owing to the popularity of Extension operations there is no demand in the country for reform. Unless some demand comes from inside it is doubtful if anything will be even suggested.'[80] James Stuart, indeed, was perfectly clear that extension had endeared 'an ancient institution to the great masses of the people' and in his *Reminiscences* he almost justified university extension in terms of raising respect for the universities: 'I felt equally strongly that the Universities would

---

[76] *The Times*, 23 Sept. 1875, p. 7.
[77] *The Times*, 3 March 1887; Marriott, *Extramural Empires*, 30–2.
[78] See *Report of a Conference in the Examination Schools, Oxford*, 28.
[79] Ibid. 86.
[80] Arthur Acland to M. E. Sadler, Oct. 1892, Papers of M. E. Sadler, Ms. Eng. misc. c. 550, Letters and Papers 1885–1903, Bodleian Library, Oxford, fo. 117.

have before long to face a fire of criticism, and their position would be greatly strengthened if they ministered to the needs of a wider area than they then did.'[81] But in ministering in the fashion devised by Stuart, they effected only cosmetic change, as some, at least, understood.

In 1877 T. H. Green gave a lecture to the Birmingham Teachers' Association in which he reflected on the course of university reform. He acknowledged that Oxford had been opened up in some ways, but the university still remained closed to all but a few:

The hope on which the Oxford reformers of my generation have fondly fed, of drawing from a stratum of society previously unconnected with the university, has been hitherto unfulfilled . . . On the whole, Oxford is still fed by the classes with whom it is traditional to look to it, the landed gentry, the people of private fortune, the clergy of the Establishment, and the wealthier members of the other professions.[82]

Six years later, when the last Victorian Royal Commission on the universities had reported, and the resulting legislation had been passed, the Liberal don, James Bryce, who was of Scottish descent, and who retained Scottish conceptions of a democratic university system after coming south, reflected in similar style on what had been achieved by a generation of changes to Oxford and Cambridge. In addition to precise criticism of the timidity of the Selborne Commission's recommendations in respect of internal reform, Bryce complained that the universities had not been made 'serviceable to the whole nation, instead of only to the upper classes': 'With all her unrivalled advantages, all her wealth, all the dignity and influence she enjoys in the country, all the eminent men who have adorned her, Oxford seems likely to continue to be little more than a training school of literary rhetoric for the upper classes.'[83] Bryce, writing about 'The Future of the English Universities' thus left open for another generation the task of widening access to Oxford. It would be taken up by the university extension movement in the context of new social and political configurations in the Edwardian era.

[81] Campbell, *Nationalisation of the Old Universities*, 236; Stuart, *Reminiscences*, 165.

[82] T. H. Green, 'Lecture on the Grading of Secondary Schools', in Nettleship (ed.), *Works of T. H. Green* (1888), iii. 391–2.

[83] James Bryce, 'The Future of the English Universities', *Fortnightly Review*, NS 33 (March 1883), 385, 399.

2

RELIGION, PHILOSOPHY, AND WORKERS' EDUCATION: ARTHUR ACLAND, ARNOLD TOYNBEE, AND T. H. GREEN

I

For the first seven years of its existence Oxford extension was a movement without formal machinery or organization. Indeed, the years up to 1885, when extension lecturing was effectively refounded on a different model, were years of failure: few successful lecture courses were given, audiences were often thin and no cadre of dedicated tutors was established. Yet the period is not without interest: what was attempted reveals a great deal about the motives of those involved in the movement and the spirit of late-Victorian Oxford. And the three central figures of Oxford extension in these years, Arthur Acland, Arnold Toynbee, and T. H. Green, each present a different though archetypal face to the movement. In Acland's case university extension was a substitute for faith; for Toynbee it reaffirmed a sense of Christian mission and duty; in the case of Green, extension was one of many social engagements that together helped transmute religious into secular dedication. In university extension each in turn was responding to the loss of faith that characterized many of their generation of university men.

Arthur Acland was appointed Secretary of the Standing Committee of the Delegates of the Local Examinations, with responsibility for university extension, in late May 1878. As he noted in his journal, 'It gives me a position here in Oxford and many of my friends are very kind about it. I foresee pleasant work.'[1] He began that work in the autumn, submitting an initial report on a series of visits made to inspect courses being given by both Oxford and Cambridge extension lecturers.[2] He also visited some of the newly established provincial colleges and met Stuart in Cambridge. 'I paid

---

[1] The Journal of A. H. D. Acland, in the possession of the Acland family, 'College', Broadclyst, Devon, 29 May 1878, fo. 131.

[2] See 'Report of the Secretary of the Standing Committee of the Delegates Nov. 27 1878', Oxford University Archives, DES/EP/1/3, Early Papers 1877–1897.

visits to Wolv[erhampton], Midd[lesborough], Birm[ingham], Stourbridge where we had lectures and also to Sheffield, Nottingham, Liverpool, Leeds, York, mostly in November to learn about my work.'[3] To understand why Acland was chosen and why he approached the work in the way he did, it is necessary to know something about his background.

Arthur Acland, as we have seen, was the son of an educational reformer, Sir Thomas Dyke Acland. His uncle, Henry Acland, was Regius Professor of Medicine in Oxford. Arthur was educated at Rugby, where Frederick Temple, who had collaborated with his father in establishing the Oxford local examinations, was his headmaster, and then Christ Church, taking his degree in 1869. He then accepted an assistant tutorship at Keble College in Oxford, only just established to fulfil one of the longstanding aims of university extension, the education of the sons of the clergy for ordination in the church. Acland himself was ordained deacon in 1872 and in the following year married Alice Cunningham, daughter of the vicar of Witney. But a crisis of religious doubt followed, precipitating an emotional breakdown in 1874. Though Acland allowed himself to be ordained a priest in 1875 he lacked conviction in his faith, and spent a long period in the mid-1870s grappling with his conscience. Finally in 1879, after taking up his position in university extension, he announced that he would seek to resign his orders, and despite great family opposition, he did so early in the following year.[4] Acland's family blamed a winter spent in the company of T. H. Green and his wife in Florence in 1875–6 for his loss of faith. Looking back, Acland discounted this: 'I remember talking with Green about orders etc. especially once on the [Venice?] Lido. He was always reluctant to advise.'[5]

Crucially, as Acland divorced himself from the church, he found a new vocation in workers' education. Late in 1875, Acland and his wife went on a tour of the north of England which took them to Rochdale. They visited the co-operative cotton mill and store there; they also spent an evening in the local working men's club, and Acland sensed in himself the potential to turn this casual acquaintance with the respectable Victorian working class into something

---

[3] Acland's Journal, 12 Jan. 1879, fo. 133.

[4] Anne Acland, *A Devon Family: The Story of the Aclands* (London, 1981), 110–33; M[ichael] E[rnest] S[adler], 'Sir Arthur Acland', *Oxford Magazine*, 21 Oct. 1926, 13–14; 'Acland, Sir A. H. D.', in *Dictionary of Labour Biography*, i. 6–7; *The Times*, 11 Oct. 1926. See also the draft synopsis of the 'Later Stages of A. H. D. Acland's Life', written by Lady Anne Acland.

[5] Acland's Journal, 1898, fo. 98.

greater.[6] He visited Rochdale again in the following year and lectured there. Indeed, he seems to have made several visits to northern cities in the late 1870s, and to have begun to discern a role for himself and for his generation. He was at home in provincial, urban England, and liberated from the introspection and intellectualism of Oxford. As he wrote to an Oxford friend from Leeds in 1880, 'Is it not the case that in Oxford we are many of us perpetually picking holes, and avoiding any enthusiasm or thorough belief in anything or anybody! I feel much affected by the spirit myself. Being in a town where one gets down to the heart of the nation as it is (not, perhaps, as it ought to be) is a great thing occasionally.'[7] When writing to his father in 1881 he explained that

The things I really care most about are the things that working men are doing for themselves or the work of Charity organisations and other matters of that kind and it is just on these matters more than at any time previously in my knowledge of Oxford there are many young men (chiefly at Balliol and New College) genuinely anxious to be interested—genuinely anxious to make themselves useful in work for the poor and others.[8]

Acland was drawn towards the idea of workers' education in particular. When visited by two co-operators in Oxford 'We had a striking conversation about the result of increased education in the lower classes. Will it not bring a great development quite unlike anything that increased educn. does for upper classes [?]—Witness classes and soc[ietie]s mentioned by Smith for reading H. Spencer, Mill etc.'[9] Acland was more confident and secure in social and educational work than in the gospel; as he explained, 'whereas say in Coop[erati]ve or any social matter I knew the body I was addressing would follow me, on religion I felt they would not'.[10] The education of the citizen became his aim and project. In his journal for 1881 he asked himself a characteristic question: 'What is the best use to make of one's knowledge not for conceit or glory but for real use—so as not to waste one's life—but to help on others a little bit [?].' Five years later he committed his answer to his diary: 'Educate, educate in citizen's duties. This is the best thing I can

---

[6] Ibid., fos. 95–6; Acland, *A Devon Family*, 114.

[7] William H. Draper, *Sir Nathan Bodington: First Vice-Chancellor of the University of Leeds. A Memoir* (London, 1912), 55.

[8] A. H. D. Acland to Sir T. D. Acland, 4 Nov. 1881, quoted in Peter Gordon and John White, *Philosophers as Educational Reformers: The Influence of Idealism on British Educational Thought and Practice* (London, 1979), 95.

[9] Acland's Journal, 4 June 1877, fo. 105.

[10] Ibid., 15 Feb. 1880, fo. 135.

do—Read and work for this.'[11] Many more Oxford extension lecturers were to take up the work for similar reasons in the future.

Acland's growing links with the co-operative movement became known to friends in Oxford and he seems to have been a natural choice for organizing secretary of the new venture. It must have been expected that he would try to base Oxford's extension lectures on those working-class organizations he knew, and this is clearly what he set out to do. It suggests that from the very beginning university extension was seen in Oxford not merely in terms of spreading university culture through the nation, planting lecture courses wherever demanded, but in terms of a particular mission to working-class groups and communities. This was to be a distinctive feature of Oxford's educational work for the next century; it was precisely this relationship between dons and workers that was to inspire its most effective and influential tutors, even if much of the routine work was with socially mixed groups.

Acland was seeking to establish a direct relationship with working-class communities in much the same way that James Stuart had been in the late 1860s when he initially projected the idea of a 'Co-operative University'. But Stuart, as we have seen, was forced to reconsider his plans, and adopted the scheme of local lectures instead. Consequently, when Oxford entered the field under Acland after 1878, the difference in approach as compared with Cambridge extension was immediately evident. The Cambridge movement sought to replicate the university curriculum as it was taught inside the university and was, in these early years, more academically rigorous. Cambridge worked with local committees of enthusiastic students, building up a network of 'centres' which could be relied on to sponsor and organize lectures. Acland was more concerned with the political and social ends of extension. He contended that the 'more general topics of social and economical interest which touch the lives of all who want to live useful and capable lives as any ordinary citizen' were of greater importance to university extension than scientific and technical subjects.[12] He thus saw in the co-operative movement a fit partner and basis for the university's civic rather

[11] Ibid., 17 Apr. 1881, fo. 156; 15 Aug. 1886, fo. 218.

[12] A. H. D. Acland, 'The Education of Co-operators and Citizens', in *The Co-operative Wholesale Society Ltd. Annual Diary 1885* (Manchester, 1885), 423, quoted in Alon Kadish, 'The Teaching of Political Economy in the Extension Movement: Cambridge, London and Oxford', in Alon Kadish and Keith Tribe (eds.), *The Market for Political Economy: The Advent of Economics in British University Culture 1850–1905* (London, 1993), 97. See also Alon Kadish, *The Oxford Economists in the Late Nineteenth Century* (Oxford, 1982), 77–84.

than purely academic mission. As he was to explain somewhat later, 'If we have struck out a new line, it has been especially in appealing to certain classes of Working Men's Societies, especially Co-operative Societies in the north, which have already made considerable grants for educational purposes'.[13] Indeed, Acland and Arnold Toynbee, at a meeting in James Stuart's rooms in Trinity, seem to have ceded to Cambridge the provision of formal academic courses in centres in the north of England; they would focus on informal 'citizen's education' instead.[14] The emphasis is clear in the titles of some of the lecture courses given to co-operative societies during this period: 'The Education of Citizens', for example, and 'The Systematic Education of Co-operators in their work as Co-operators and Citizens'.

But all depended on the links that could be established with the co-operative movement and on convincing it that it could benefit from the kind of social education Oxford wished to provide. Acland himself joined the Oxford Co-operative Society in the year he was appointed, and in 1880 organized for it a series of lectures given by university men.[15] He was also instrumental in bringing the 1882 Co-operative Congress to Oxford. It was a singular moment in the history of late-Victorian Oxford and Acland took great satisfaction in 'the general enthusiasm between the Delegates and the undergraduates and others who entertained them'.[16] Senior members involved included Percival, W. R. Anson, the Warden of All Souls, Green's Balliol colleague, R. L. Nettleship, and two dons who were to play an important role in adult education in the future, T. H. Warren, later President of Magdalen College, and A. L. Smith, later Master of Balliol.[17] In his welcoming address to the delegates Acland described the union of the two institutions that he contemplated as 'a platform, a basis, a foundation upon which any number of hopeful movements and any amount of hopeful progress may be raised'.[18] And Arnold Toynbee, in his famous address to the conference on 'The Education of Cooperators', filled out the programme, describing the type of social and political education that Oxford could

---

[13] *Report of a Conference in the Examination Schools, Oxford, of Representatives of the Local Committees Acting in Concert with the Committee of Delegates of Local Examinations appointed to Establish Lectures and Teaching in Large Towns and of others Interested in the Extension of University Teaching on April 20 and 21 1887* (Oxford, 1887), 45.

[14] Alon Kadish, *Apostle Arnold: The Life and Death of Arnold Toynbee 1852–1883* (Durham, NC, 1986), 186.

[15] Ibid. 174.   [16] Acland's Journal, 27 Aug. 1882, fo. 168.

[17] Kadish, *Oxford Economists*, 78–9.

[18] *The Fourteenth Annual Co-operative Congress of 1882* (Manchester, 1882), 23–4.

provide to help break down 'the division of men into capitalists and labourers'. According to Toynbee, 'the education of the citizen' implied 'the education of each member of the community, as regards the relation in which he stands to other individual citizens, and to the community as a whole'.[19] Acland undertook several lecture tours to co-operative societies in the north to realize this project, taking in Manchester, Hebden Bridge, Rochdale, Accrington, and Heckmondwike in December and January 1882–3, for example.[20] As Charles Rowley, a founder of the Ancoats Settlement in Manchester, and keen adult educationalist, put it of Acland, 'One of his methods was to come among us, staying in our cottages, and meet us all on equal terms. His view evidently was that you must go for yourself to the people, and help them, by knowing them.'[21]

Meanwhile, in Oxford, Acland sought to quicken enthusiasm for the project inside the University. As his protégé and successor, Michael Sadler, later recalled, 'Acland was the centre of a group of young dons and undergraduates who, through him, got to know many of the leaders of working men's organizations in the North of England, especially those of the Co-operative movement'.[22] Sadler, indeed, accompanied Acland on lecture tours in 1883 and 1884. They called themselves the 'Inner Ring'—'a little society in which we can try to thrash some matters out social, political etc.' as Acland described it in June 1883.[23] Besides Acland and Sadler, members included J. A. Spender, Charles Mallet, L. T. Hobhouse, and the future archbishop, Cosmo Lang.[24] It was here, rather than in any formal university committee, that Oxford extension work was planned and executed in these years.[25]

But the enterprise was not a success. The co-operative movement

---

[19] Arnold Toynbee, 'The Education of Co-operators', in Arnold Toynbee, *Lectures on the Industrial Revolution in England* (London, 1884), 226. As Albert Mansbridge, another co-operator and adult educationalist, later wrote, 'The name of Toynbee is classical in the movement, and those who heard him read his paper . . . and were inspired by his ringing challenge to them to meet the passion for the dividend by the passion for education, recount it as their most splendid co-operative experience' (Albert Mansbridge, *Arnold Toynbee* [n.d.], 10).

[20] Acland's Journal, 25 Dec. 1882 and 4 Mar. 1883, fos. 174, 177–8.

[21] Charles Rowley, *Fifty Years Work Without Wages* (London, 1912), 214.

[22] S[adler], 'Sir Arthur Acland', 13.

[23] Acland's Journal, 10 June 1883, 4 Jan. 1884, 16 June 1884; fos. 181, 189, 193.

[24] Michael Sadleir, *Sir Michael Sadler: A Memoir by his Son* (London, 1949), 68.

[25] The minute book of the Standing Committee of the Delegates of Local Examinations which was formally charged with the organization of lectures, records four meetings only before 1885, all in the second half of 1878 and early 1879. Committee for University Extension. Minutes of Meetings I, Oxford University Archives, DES/M/1/1.

was never wooed and won. Many of its leaders remained suspicious
of the university's intentions and more concerned to educate co-
operators in the principles of the movement than in the wider idealism of the late-Victorian university.[26] And local co-operative
societies were less enthusiastic than had been expected. In addition,
Oxford's approach to the working class was launched at a moment
of economic downturn when communities had little to spare for
education. Acland blamed 'bad times', and his successors, Sadler
and Halford Mackinder described 'an uphill fight to keep the courses
going. In many the work fluctuated, and then for a time went out.'[27]
Quite how hard Acland fought is open to debate. For during these
years, 1878–85, he had personal ambitions of his own to fulfil, first
in Oxford and then in national politics. From 1879, Acland was
successively Treasurer of the newly projected Somerville Hall; then
Steward of Christ Church and from 1884, Bursar of Balliol. He also
tutored and lectured at Somerville and Christ Church and looked
after all this in addition to his work organizing extension lectures.[28]
Then, from 1884, he seems to have become interested in a political
career. This was a natural development of his work in working-
class communities as a lecturer and cultural ambassador. He failed
narrowly to win the Liberal nomination for Barnsley, but was then
invited to stand at Rotherham where he was elected with a handsome majority in 1885.[29]

His links with the working class had won him his job in Oxford
in 1878; they now provided him with a distinctive and respected
political identity as a Liberal who could sustain the often difficult
relationship between his party and late-Victorian working-class institutions. Acland acted with a group of younger, talented Liberals in
parliament including Asquith, Edward Grey, Tom Ellis, and R. B.
Haldane.[30] As Haldane wrote of him to the Liberal chief whip at the
time that Gladstone was forming his fourth administration in 1892,
'He has, as none of us younger men has, the personal respect of not
only prominent leaders like Tom Mann and Burns, but of the great
body of artisans of the northern and midland counties'.[31] As Acland's

---

[26] Kadish, *Apostle Arnold*, 186–8; id., *Oxford Economists*, 82–3.
[27] Acland's Journal, 15 Feb. 1880, fo. 138. H. J. Mackinder and M. E. Sadler,
University Extension: Past, Present and Future, 3rd edn. (London, 1891), 30.
[28] See Acland's inventory of tasks in his Journal for 9 Oct. 1881 (fo. 162) which
makes no mention at all of extension.
[29] Acland's Journal, 13 June 1885, fo. 206; 31 Jan. 1886, fo. 213.
[30] Peter Clarke, *Liberals and Social Democrats* (Cambridge, 1978), 24.
[31] R. B. Haldane to Sir Algernon West, quoted in Dudley Sommer, *Haldane of
Cloan* (London, 1960), 88.

mentor, John Morley, recollected, 'to Acland belongs special credit
for keeping in touch with the labour people and their mind'.[32] He
seemed set for a great political career, especially after his creative
direction of the nation's education policy as the first vice-president
of the Committee of Council on Education (effectively minister for
education) to have a seat in Cabinet in the two Liberal administrations between 1892 and 1895. His interest in social reform and the
working class suggests that Acland was a forerunner of what became known, in the early twentieth century, as 'new liberalism'. But
the physical weakness and hypochondria that had been with him
since his crisis of faith in the 1870s overcame him and he resigned
his seat in 1899. He lived on until 1926, by which time he had
switched his political allegiance to the Labour Party.

Acland's biography thus tells us about the earliest years of Oxford extension, which have often seemed obscure. It also presents
him as archetypal in two ways: first, he found a substitute for faith
in specifically workers' education; second, he used his experience of
working-class life, derived from extension lecturing, as a platform
on which to launch a political career. Acland brings to mind Jowett's
prescient observation to Congregation in Oxford in 1878 that extension would provide a vocation for Oxford graduates no longer
able to go into the church but 'whose sympathies were directed
towards the poor and neglected'.[33] Education would take the place
of religion in harmonizing and moralizing society. The religious
impulse did not wither but found new forms and modes of expression. As one who knew him commented of Acland, 'there was still
a clergyman inside him when you cut him open, and he carried into
politics much of the zeal and serious-mindedness that he had brought
to the cure of souls'.[34] And Acland used his knowledge of working-
class life and institutions as a way into politics, as his special claim
to a voice and preferment within the Liberal Party. Acland and
those who followed him into 'Lib-Lab' and later Labour politics,
were certainly not the first university graduates and intellectuals to
have made contact with the working class. In the 1850s Christian
Socialists like J. M. Ludlow and F. D. Maurice had made contact
with the co-operative movement. In the 1860s and 1870s, the Positivists, including E. S. Beesly, Frederic Harrison and J. H. Bridges,
had assisted the mid-Victorian trade union movement in its struggle
for social acceptance and legal recognition in a notably successful

---

[32] John Morley, *Recollections*, 2 vols. (London, 1917), i. 324.
[33] *The Times*, 6 March 1878.
[34] J. A. Spender, *Sir Robert Hudson: A Memoir* (London, 1930), 20.

alliance of university men and workers. But extension in the next generation was to forge new sorts of links with specific working-class communities and provide, thereby, the experience of working-class life that aspiring politicians required if they were to speak for the new democracy.

II

At about the same time that Acland was sensing a future role for himself in Rochdale in 1875, a similar discovery was being made by Arnold Toynbee. In the long vacation of that year Toynbee went to live in the East End of London at the invitation of Samuel Barnett, the vicar of St Jude's, Whitechapel. It was during this period, spent experiencing the life of the metropolitan poor, that Toynbee first addressed a working-class audience (on 'religion and politics') at the Tower Hamlets Radical Club, and, exhilarated by his success, also found a vocation in guiding the working-classes towards spiritual regeneration.[35] Toynbee was a delicate youth from a professional middle-class background. His father, Joseph, had been a noted aural surgeon, an active philanthropist, and a sanitarian who had helped found the Health of Towns Association in the 1840s.[36] Arnold had come up to Pembroke College, Oxford in 1873, but then migrated to Balliol, having come to the notice of Jowett and being attracted by its more earnest atmosphere. From 1878 until his famous death in 1883, he was a lecturer and tutor in the college. He began his extension lecturing in 1880 and in three successive years addressed audiences of working men and employers in such cities as Bradford, Bolton, Leicester, Sheffield, and Newcastle during the university vacations.[37] He seems to have organized these lectures with the help of friends and associates rather than through the Delegates for Local Examinations in Oxford, technically the body responsible for extension. As Alon Kadish has written, they were 'part of a wider educational goal aimed at the improvement of the workers' understanding of the moral implications of their newly acquired political power and their anticipated higher wealth . . . Toynbee's work in political economy, his popular lectures, and his work on behalf of church reform were all part of an effort to help the nation gain a

[35] Kadish, *Apostle Arnold*, 45.
[36] Gertrude Toynbee, *Reminiscences and Letters of Joseph and Arnold Toynbee* (London, n.d.).
[37] C. M. Toynbee, 'Prefatory Note', in A. Toynbee, *Lectures on the Industrial Revolution in England* (London, 1884), p. xxxi.

moral sense of direction.'[38] Toynbee found an eager audience in the industrial north for lectures that one of his friends and contemporaries at Balliol, Alfred Milner, who himself gave extension lectures in London, accurately described as 'strange mixtures . . . of dry economic discussion with fervent appeals to the higher instincts of his audience'.[39]

Toynbee came before his audiences with the ostensible aim of deriding conventional economic thought as both technically wrong and morally offensive. 'Political economy' was the common enemy for both dons and workers. Working men knew only too well how much conventional economic wisdom and the resulting organization of economic life oppressed them. And Toynbee's lectures assured them that their experience and their instincts were right—that political economy was an abstraction, bearing no relation to actual economic life, its methodological and doctrinal rigidities 'an insult to the simple natural piety of human affections'.[40] The critique itself was the point of contact between lecturer and audience; as Toynbee was to put it on the first page of his *Lectures on the Industrial Revolution in England*, 'the obstinate, blind repulsion of the labourer is approved by the professor'.[41] The instinctive dissent of workers from the economic nostrums of the age now had the scientific backing of a new generation of academic critics of economic orthodoxy. In what he termed 'the bitter argument between economists and human beings'[42] Toynbee stood on the side of humanity, not least because he prized social cohesion and unity above all, whereas orthodox *laissez-faire* doctrine was 'a sower of discord . . . an instrument of social division'.[43]

As was the case with many economists of the late nineteenth century—in Germany and the United States as well as in Britain—who had come to doubt conventional economic wisdom, Toynbee's approach to these questions was historical. Many of his lectures took the form of historical narratives, and in these narratives he tried to assess what the great industrial transformation over the preceding century had achieved for the working class. As Kadish has argued, Toynbee believed that this transformation gave grounds for optimism: social advance was achievable in the long term, and was already underway in some aspects of social life.[44] Nevertheless,

[38] Kadish, *Apostle Arnold*, p. 80.

[39] Lord Milner, 'Reminiscence', in A. Toynbee, *Lectures on the Industrial Revolution of the Eighteenth Century in England*, 3rd edn. (London, 1908), p. xxvi.

[40] A. Toynbee, 'Ricardo and the Old Political Economy', in id., *Lectures on the Industrial Revolution* (1884), 1.

[41] Ibid.   [42] Ibid.   [43] Ibid. 10.

[44] Alon Kadish, 'Oxford Economics in the Later Nineteenth Century', in Kadish and Tribe, *Market for Political Economy*, 71–2.

his assessment of the gains made by the working class as a consequence of industrialization thus far, was bleak:

The fact is, that the more we examine the actual course of affairs, the more
we are amazed at the unnecessary suffering that has been inflicted upon
the people. No generalities about natural law or inevitable development can
blind us to the fact, that the progress in which we believe has been won
at the expense of much injustice and wrong, which was not inevitable.[45]

The realization 'that free competition may produce wealth without
producing wellbeing' evoked in him a sense of guilt, both personal
and collective.[46] His very last lecture ended, famously, with an
apology to his audience for the historical neglect of the working
classes on the part of the middle classes: 'instead of justice we have
offered you charity, and instead of sympathy, we have offered you
hard and unreal advice'.[47] The guilt is reminiscent of Beatrice Webb's
famous description of 'a new consciousness of sin among men of intellect and men of property' that developed from the mid-Victorian
decades. She did not mean personal sin: 'the consciousness of sin
was a collective or class consciousness amounting to a conviction,
that the industrial organisation, which had yielded rent, interest and
profit on a stupendous scale, had failed to provide a livelihood
and tolerable conditions for a majority of the inhabitants of Great
Britain.'[48]

Toynbee's inspiration was always essentially religious: his extension lecturing was not merely designed to express solidarity with
working men and teach them how to understand their economic
and social position; it was also a means of spreading religious values and moral uplift more widely. His lectures always ended with
a challenge to his audiences to raise themselves in spirit. Higher
wages would 'enable the working man to enter on a purer and more
worthy life'.[49] 'Increased material welfare' should not be wasted on
'a few more coarse enjoyments' but open up 'a purer and higher
life'.[50] In addition, Toynbee did not come before his working-class
audiences as their advocate, seeking their advancement pure and
simple, but always expressed his sympathy in terms of a wider
commitment to class harmony and social cohesion. He preferred to
lecture to audiences that included both workers and employers.

---

[45] A. Toynbee, 'The Industrial Revolution', in id., *Lectures on the Industrial
Revolution*, 58.   [46] Ibid. 93.

[47] Arnold Toynbee, *Progress and Poverty: A Criticism of Mr Henry George*
(London, 1883), 53.

[48] Beatrice Webb, *My Apprenticeship* (London, 1926), 179–80.

[49] A. Toynbee, 'Wages and Natural Law', in id., *Lectures on the Industrial
Revolution*, 176.   [50] A. Toynbee, 'Are Radicals Socialists?', in ibid. 220.

According to Milner, he sought a position 'as an impartial, public-spirited mediator between conflicting interests and prejudices of class and class'.[51] Or as Toynbee himself put it in a letter following a triumphant lecture in Bradford in early 1881, 'The enthusiasm was quite moving, and I believe both employers and workmen were convinced of the justice of my claim to speak with impartiality'.[52]

It was not just that Toynbee wanted to preserve a position above the battle; he positively desired a society characterized by harmony and reciprocity, and feared the consequences of growing working-class interest in the ideas of socialism. His mission was to win back his audiences for radical Liberalism under middle-class guidance. As he stated at the end of his lecture on 'Industry and Democracy',

There never has been a time when such a union between classes has been so possible as it is today or soon will become. For not only has the law given to workman and employer equality of rights, but education bids fair to give them equality of culture. We are all now, workmen as well as employers, inhabitants of a larger world; no longer members of a single class, but fellow-citizens of one great people.[53]

Toynbee was not alone in possession of these hopes or in his belief that university extension, by going out and showing the solidarity of the privileged with the underprivileged, would assist in unifying British society. Indeed, it was a standard assumption of all who took up the work in the later Victorian period. James Stuart had projected extension in just this way a decade before Toynbee's lectures. As Stuart had explained in 1871, 'nothing could more tend to work against that class distinction than any efforts which we may make towards a system in which our rich and poor, our men and women, should be taught by the same individuals'.[54] And when Acland came to introduce Michael Sadler's lectures on 'Social Economy' at Bolton in January 1885, he justified university extension in the Oxford style as 'intended to be not merely an official teaching work, but to develop relations of personal friendship between cooperators and university men' the better to 'break down the barriers and remove the class feeling and the class prejudice which were such dangerous elements in the present state of society'.[55]

[51] Milner, 'Reminiscence', p. xxiv; see also C. M. Toynbee, 'Prefatory Note', p. xxxi.

[52] A. Toynbee to Albert, 4th earl Grey, c. Feb. 1881, quoted in Kadish, *Apostle Arnold*, 110.

[53] A. Toynbee, 'Industry and Democracy', in id., *Lectures on the Industrial Revolution*, 201.   [54] James Stuart, *University Extension* (Leeds, 1871), 12.

[55] 'University Extension Work Among Co-operative Societies', *Co-operative News*, 24 Jan. 1885, p. 69.

Two months later Sadler himself apparently told co-operators in Wombwell that extension 'would be the best safeguard of the country from revolutionary and all wild socialism and would enable the people to pass from one stage of happiness to another'.[56] When he succeeded Acland as the organizing secretary of Oxford extension— he was evidently satisfied that extension 'brings together students of very different ranks' and he could applaud the fact that in examinations held at one lecture-centre 'among those to whom were awarded certificates of distinction were a national school-mistress, a young lawyer, a plumber and a railway signalman'.[57] The next generation of extensionists, in the first years of the twentieth century, would redefine workers' education in terms of the promotion of working-class, rather than general social interests. But for the first lecturers, and Toynbee pre-eminently, the work was attractive just because it could be made conformable with a social philosophy emphasizing unity and harmony.

It was with a certain tragic irony that Toynbee's last and mortal lecture was delivered to a London audience that was hostile to this message of social solidarity. Toynbee's second of two lectures on 'Progress and Poverty', designed to refute the economic ideas of Henry George that were then in vogue, and delivered in February 1883, was a disaster. He came before a radical audience who were loud for socialism and land nationalization. They did not take to the Oxford man before them who said he was a radical but, as they heard it, preached moral arguments to them in churchy tones. After the lecture, punctuated by heckling, and questions, Toynbee suffered a mental and physical collapse from which he never recovered and he died in the following month, honoured as both a prophet and a martyr.[58] As Michael Sadler, one of his admirers and followers, was to put it somewhat later, 'Toynbee's sudden illness and early death drew to his work and personality the thoughts of students of history and social reformers throughout the country . . . he, by his very death, consummated and revealed the greatness of the achievement of a short life.'[59]

---

[56] *Barnsley Chronicle*, 21 Mar. 1885, quoted in Sheila Rowbotham, ' "Travellers in a Strange Country": Responses of Working Class Students to the University Extension Movement 1873–1910', *History Workshop Journal*, 12 (autumn 1981), 64.

[57] Mackinder and Sadler, *University Extension*, 70; *Annual Report of the Committee of the Delegates of Local Examinations Appointed to Carry into Operation the University Statute for the Establishment of Lectures and Teaching in the Large Towns of England and Wales 1889–90* (Oxford, 1890).

[58] Kadish, *Apostle Arnold*, ch. 8.   [59] Sadleir, *Sir Michael Sadler*, 31–2.

It was easy to extract the stuff of legend out of Toynbee's life and demise, and his memory was appropriated by several different Oxford causes including university extension. Of these, Toynbee Hall in Whitechapel, the university settlement established in 1884, is the most famous. But the circumstances of his death, stripped of the mythology, are revealing. For in his demise can be seen the ideological parameters of university extension: its association with élite culture, élite institutions, and some essentially religious impulses evoked considerable hostility among radicals and socialists in the 1880s and 1890s who rejected the learning being offered to them from on high. But not all were of this mind. A very different kind of extension lecturer and economist, J. A. Hobson, commented that in the late 1880s and early 1890s 'in (his) lectures upon Political Economy about the country', he had

found in almost every centre a certain little knot of men of the lower-middle or upper-working class, men of grit and character, largely self-educated, keen citizens, mostly non-conformists in religion, to whom Land Nationalisation, taxation of unearned increment, or other radical reforms of land tenure, are doctrines resting upon a plain moral sanction.[60]

III

Toynbee died only a few months after the third figure who helps explain the motivation and ideology of university extension in Oxford, Thomas Hill Green. But Green illuminates much more than the urge to go out and make contact with the working class through education. For Green was the dominant intellectual and social influence on Oxford in the last years of his life up to 1882, and for many years thereafter. He embodied and shaped late-Victorian Oxford. Through him it is possible to understand more clearly the intentions and aims of the extensionists and to set them in the context of the ideas then animating the University more generally.

Green was the first layman to be elected a fellow of Balliol and the college's first philosophy tutor. He eventually became White's Professor of Moral Philosophy in the University. Teaching a creed of social and political engagement by example, he was a member of the Oxford School Board from 1874, and in the following year became the first don elected to the Oxford Town Council in his own right. He was a Liberal and a committed university reformer, possessed a deep interest in, and knowledge of, education at all

---

[60] J. A. Hobson, 'The Influence of Henry George in England', *Fortnightly Review*, NS 372 (Dec. 1897), 841.

levels, and followed all issues of social reform. He was also a philosophical idealist and in this capacity made his greatest impact on the age.[61]

Idealism may be defined most easily in terms of what it opposed: individualism, utilitarianism, and social atomism. It was characterized by attachment to 'corporate identity, individual altruism, ethical imperatives and active-citizen participation'.[62] It was thus, in its English guise, a conscious departure from the hitherto dominant social philosophy of the nineteenth century, and it drew most notably on the German philosophical tradition embodied in Kant and Hegel. To Green and other idealists, individuals could only be understood and could only realize their potential in a collective context. Men and women were intrinsically part of social and political communities from which they could not be divorced either for analytical or practical purposes. And they were linked together by culture, values, and institutions rather than a web of economic relationships; the commonwealth of shared ideas and beliefs was a more powerful agent of solidarity than materialism. Indeed, materialism was understood as the cause of atomization. It followed from this that the state, as the embodiment of the social community who made it and who controlled it in the collective interest, was a beneficent guardian of citizens rather than a coercive and intrusive opponent of the individual. The state protected, nurtured, and reformed for the collective good. It also followed that idealism was especially attractive to those who valued social and cultural cohesion; this, as we have seen, was a powerful impetus to the pioneers of university extension and it was at the heart of the idealists' social vision. Finally, for Green and other idealists, education had a special role as the means by which the shared values and ideas of the community—its essence—could be disseminated and passed down the generations. Acland and Toynbee's commitment to 'the education of the the citizen' takes on a new significance in this context; it was through such education that people would learn of their obligations to others and so would be made true citizens of the community. Education would sustain and bind together the members of a society.[63]

---

[61] Melvin Richter, *The Politics of Conscience: T. H. Green and His Age* (London, 1983 repr.; first pub. 1964).

[62] Jose Harris, 'Political Thought and the Welfare State 1870–1940: An Intellectual Framework for British Social Policy', *Past and Present*, 135 (1992), 137.

[63] For helpful discussions of Green's idealism see Richter, *Politics of Conscience*; Gordon and White, *Philosophers as Educational Reformers*; W. S. Fowler, 'The Influence of Idealism upon State Provision of Education', *Victorian Studies*, 4/4

These ideas are intrinsically attractive. They were especially compelling for a generation that was losing its faith in conventional Christianity. Religion had previously supplied a sense of individual purpose and had guaranteed social solidarity: in the context of the 1870s and 1880s 'the doctrine of citizenship and reform developed by Green can best be understood as a surrogate faith appealing to a transitional generation'.[64] Crudely, Green offered the spirituality of idealism, complete with the promise of community and commonality, in place of a Christianity that was increasingly unpersuasive to young minds in the generation after Darwin. According to Richter, 'He would direct the zeal of Christianity into a religion of citizenship . . . Accurately aimed and powerfully argued, Green's theology enlisted emotions essentially religious in the cause of social reform.'[65] This perceptive judgement on Green brings to mind another of Beatrice Webb's insights: that 'during the middle decades of the nineteenth century . . . the impulse of self-subordinating service was transferred, consciously and overtly, from God to man'.[66] Idealism spoke to a generation which acknowledged as its primary task the construction of a plural, harmonious, and democratic society. Idealism offered a set of ethical and communitarian prescriptions for holding society together at a time of rapid economic and political transformation that otherwise threatened disintegration.[67] Since the protagonists of university extension in Oxford also saw their function as smoothing the transition to democracy, it is hardly surprising that they were attracted to Green's teaching.

And Green did more than offer a substitute for conventional social and economic philosophy and conventional Christianity; he enjoined his students and readers to give practical form to these ideas, and personally led by example.

It is no time to enjoy the pleasures of eye and ear, of search for knowledge, of friendly intercourse, of applauded speech or writing, while the mass of men whom we call our brethren, and whom we declare to be meant with us for eternal destinies are left without chance, which only the help of others can gain for them, of making themselves in act what in possibility we believe them to be.[68]

University extension was one means of giving 'the mass of men' a chance, though one means among many. Green welcomed the

(June 1961), 337–44; Jonathan Rée, 'Idealism and Education', *History of Education*, 9/3 (1980), 259–63.

[64] Richter, *Politics of Conscience*, 19.   [65] Ibid. 132–4.
[66] Webb, *My Apprenticeship*, 143.   [67] Harris, 'Political Thought', 140.
[68] T. H. Green, *Prolegomena to Ethics* (London, 1883), para. 270.

willingness of some Oxford graduates to take up teaching positions in ordinary day schools rather than the public schools and thereby enter 'into the educational life of the cities'.[69] It was the shortest of steps to recommend that they also consider lecturing to working-class and mixed audiences as extensionists. Moreover, Green's own family background linked him to the new movement. His uncle, Revd David Vaughan, was a Christian Socialist and vicar of St Martin's, Leicester (now Leicester Cathedral) from 1860 to 1893. He not only addressed audiences of working men on social and industrial topics; he also founded a flourishing working men's college in the city (now part of Leicester University). As a former fellow of Trinity College, Cambridge, Vaughan was an obvious link in the chain that James Stuart was creating in the early 1870s and Leicester was a perfect place to begin the Cambridge 'local lectures' in 1873. We know that Green made frequent visits to his uncle, and, through them, learned something of the nature of working-class life. We know also that the example of his uncle almost led him to take holy orders and influenced him considerably thereafter.[70] It is surely not idle to speculate that Green involved himself in the new movement as a result of these associations as much as for other reasons.

After Green died, his widow received a letter from her brother, John Addington Symonds. He wrote that

Green's practical grasp on political conditions and his sympathy with the vast masses of a nation, the producers and breadmakers, the taxpayers and inadequately represented, strike all alive. Personally I may say that he has inducted me into the philosophy of democracy and socialism . . . [He had] the faculty of feeling by a kind of penetrative instinct that modern society had ripened to a point at which the principles of democracy and socialism had to be accepted as actualities.[71]

This was Green's legacy to his age. He was a man of the middle class who had spanned the social divide. He was a don who not only came to know the workers but who understood the new social forces they represented. He was a philosopher who had thought about social questions and bequeathed a system that promised to contain the expected violence and disruption in the interests of all

[69] T. H. Green, 'Lecture on the Grading of Secondary Schools', in R. L. Nettleship (ed.), *Works of Thomas Hill Green*, 3 vols (1888), iii. 409–10.

[70] Richter, *Politics of Conscience*, 42, 81, 360–1; A. J. Allaway, 'David James Vaughan', *Transactions of the Leicestershire Archaeological and Historical Society*, 33 (1957), 45–58.

[71] J. A. Symonds to Mrs Green, [7 Oct.] 1883, T. H. Green Papers, Pt. I, Biography: B, Recollections of Green, Balliol College, Oxford.

groups. And Green was a teacher whose personal commitment to the education of all classes of the nation offered a vocation to those who followed.

IV

The question of Green's influence has long interested historians. Collingwood believed that 'the philosophy of Green's school might be found, from about 1880 to about 1910, penetrating and fertilizing every part of the national life'.[72] Indeed, the influence and persistence of idealism in British social thought into the 1930s and 1940s has recently been emphasized.[73] And in an admirable study of the influence of philosophical idealism on the development of British educational thought and policy in the decades after Green's death, Peter Gordon and John White have argued for the primacy of idealism as the inspiration of the reform and modernization of the English educational system down to the 1930s.[74] They have constructed an idealist lineage of educationalists who came under the influence of Green himself or his ideas, and apparently acted accordingly. Since the majority of figures in this educational tradition— Arthur Acland, Robert Morant, Michael Sadler, R. H. Tawney, and A. D. Lindsay—figure prominently in the history of Oxford extension and in the wider history of the relationship between intellectuals and the working-class in Britain, the argument cannot be ignored. The intellectual and spiritual home of philosophic idealism until the mid-twentieth century was Balliol College, and Balliol had a uniquely close association with adult education, and was an important national educational influence in its own right. It could be argued with plausibility that the history of adult and workers' education in Britain takes its cue from Green and Balliol idealism above all else—though for all Green's influence, it will not be the argument of this book, which will take a more pluralistic position. Moreover any attempt to write educational and social history by reference to ideas rather than in conventional administrative terms is to be welcomed and applauded.

Yet it is doubtful if the argument can be sustained without exaggerating the influence of Green and Oxford idealism in the development of state policy and in the motivation of many who took up extension lecturing at this time. And the argument cannot be

---

[72] R. G. Collingwood, *An Autobiography* (Oxford, 1939), 17.
[73] See Harris, 'Political Thought', *passim*.
[74] Gordon and White, *Philosophers, passim*.

advanced with confidence unless it can be shown that other competing educational ideologies were uninfluential. Moreover, that individuals educated in Oxford in an often only vaguely idealist tradition came to influence educational policy does not necessarily imply that idealism itself had an impact on what was said and done. There is also a danger in the argument that Green's influence is made to stand for the more general impact of university liberals and reformers from the 1860s: Green was not the first or only don to unite scholarship with activism, nor was an interest in educational questions unique to him and his followers. And Green's idealism could be used, and was used, to underpin very different social philosophies—both the new Liberal interventionism of the Edwardian era and the old poor law mentality of the Charity Organization Society claimed Green as their own.[75] This may reinforce arguments for Green's impact on the succeeeding generation, but it makes it rather more difficult to be sure what that influence amounted to.

Green's message was unclear. While Idealism seemed to point towards collective and state action, and while Green frequently seemed to favour this, he also remained loyal, as Melvin Richter shows, to independent and voluntary action as the basis for social improvement, and he was careful to lay down prescribed limits for state action. Green may have visualized the state as a moral agency, but he seems to have hung back from endowing it with complete moral authority over citizens. In this sense, he never broke totally with conventional liberal ethics. What he offered was a transitional social philosophy for a transitional generation. Elements of the new and the old jostled together. This left Green's philosophical legacy open to interpretation and makes it difficult to be precise about the application of his ideas.[76]

Above all, in considering Green's influence and the influence of his ideas it needs to be remembered that, in many circumstances, it was not idealism that made a certain type of outlook and personality: it was a certain type of personality that was attracted to idealism. To an extent this can be seen in the relationship of Toynbee and Green. They knew each other well and Toynbee edited Green's two famous *Lay Sermons*. They could agree on such matters as the desirability of state intervention in certain circumstances and they both held up 'devotion to the community', in Toynbee's phrase, as the end of social life.[77] But this does not prove the influence of

[75] Harris, 'Political Thought', 126.
[76] Rée, 'Idealism and Education'; Richter, *Politics of Conscience*, 339–40.
[77] The phrase can be found in A. Toynbee, *Progress and Poverty*, 25.

Green over Toynbee, for we know that Toynbee had been interested in all these matters long before he met Green. Jowett related that at eighteen, before coming up to Oxford, Toynbee spent a year 'revolving in his mind ... the social and religious problems of the age'.[78] And writing of the relationship of Toynbee and Green, Milner commented perceptively that 'they had arrived, by very different roads, at an almost identical position in religion, philosophy and social questions'.[79] Toynbee could easily assimilate the teachings of idealism because they corresponded with his own imperatives to serve, to educate and to heal. But he came to these conclusions by a personal route, and one that did not involve a break with Christianity. This is not to diminish Green's importance; no one summed the philosophical and social currents of the age as he did. But it does imply that in a period notable for the decay of fixed and sanctioned beliefs, it was possible to feel a social calling for a number of reasons—and it was possible that different motives might nevertheless be conformable and end in common action.

By implication, the philosophical and social inspiration of university extension was similarly pluralistic and complex. As these three portraits of the leading figures in Oxford extension in its earliest phase suggest, the movement grew out of internal university reforms, the consequences of religious doubt, a sense of social obligation to new and underprivileged classes, a fear of social disharmony, the development of a new 'social liberalism', and philosophical idealism. We can be no more precise than that: the social outlook of late-Victorian Oxford was peculiarly complex, and rich with motives and possibilities for action. Whatever its sources, the late-Victorian university was palpably different in atmosphere and tone when compared to the preceding generation. According to the *Oxford Magazine*, founded in early 1883 and the organ of high-minded, socially conscious Oxford,

The question has been asked, 'Is the new Oxford Movement to be a Socialistic one?' and if this is interpreted to mean, 'Is the most living interest of Oxford now that in social questions?' the answer must be distinctly, Yes! Oxford has turned from playing at the Middle Ages in churches, or at a Re-Renaissance in cupboards; and a new faith, with Professor Green as its founder, Arnold Toynbee as its martyr and various societies for its propaganda is alive among us.[80]

[78] Benjamin Jowett, 'Memoir', in A. Toynbee, *Lectures on the Industrial Revolution*, p. vii.

[79] Milner, 'Reminiscence', in ibid. (1908 edn.), p. xviii.

[80] *Oxford Magazine*, 1 (21 Nov. 1883), 384. The quotation is taken from a comment on William Morris's speech on 'Democracy and Art' in the hall of

Or as Acland put it after reading Mark Pattison's *Memoirs* two years later, 'I think Oxford is more influenced by the idea "whatever our future is we must try and do some good" than it ever was before'.[81] University extension emerged out of the complex institutional history of university reform, but it took its inspiration from this 'new faith', this new idea.

An authentic portrait of the new Oxford can be found in fictional form in the novels of Mrs Humphry Ward. *Robert Elsmere*, published in 1888 and one of the most successful serious novels of the late-Victorian period, is justly celebrated. The story of a young clergyman with a strictly evangelical wife who undergoes a crisis of faith, leaves his parish, and goes to live and work in a settlement house in the East End of London, captured many of the essential religious and cultural themes of the age. As is well known, the authoress, who was a granddaughter of Thomas Arnold, had lived in Oxford during the 1860s and 1870s, married a don, and had mixed with the university's leading figures.[82] She was thus able to provide her readers with thinly disguised characterizations of Jowett (the Provost of St Anselm's College, 'the Liberal headquarters'), Pattison (Squire Wendover), and Green (Professor Grey, 'this great son of modern Oxford'), to whom the book was dedicated. In the character of Robert Elsmere furthermore, Mrs Ward captured both the turmoil of religious uncertainty and the powerful calling to social activism that dominate this period, and in so doing she captivated her readers. But her success with her central characters should not surprise us, since they, too, may have been modelled on real people: it was said that Elsmere and his wife were loosely based on Arthur and Mrs Acland and the turmoil of their lives in the 1870s as Arthur lost his faith and found his real vocation. The Aclands and Humphry Wards had been good friends up to the novel's publication; thereafter Acland and his wife would have no contact with Mrs Ward, who had so publicly abused them as they saw it.[83] Whether or not Elsmere was based on Acland (and there are grounds for doubt, certainly, and other candidates for Acland's place), the

University College in which he declared his conversion to socialism and called for student support. Hence the oblique references to Pre-Raphaelitism which Morris and now Oxford had thrown over.

[81] Acland's Journal, 22 Mar. 1885, fos. 203–4.

[82] John Sutherland, *Mrs Humphry Ward: Eminent Victorian, Pre-Eminent Edwardian* (Oxford, 1990).

[83] Stuart Marriott, 'Dr Welch on "Oxford and University Extension": A Critical Note', *Studies in Adult Education*, 11/1 (Apr. 1979), 13; Anne Acland, *A Devon Family*, 156, questions the identification of Acland and Elsmere.

novel evokes the reformed and moralized university remarkably well.[84]

In the same author's *Marcella* meanwhile, published six years later, a key figure is one, Edward Hallin, a student at Trinity College, Cambridge and 'a leader among the best and keenest of his fellows'—an embodiment, indeed, of the new spirit in the universities. Hallin studies history and sociology 'with a view to joining the staff of lecturers for the manufacturing and country towns which the two great Universities, touched by new and popular sympathies, were then beginning to organize'. And on leaving Cambridge he does indeed lecture 'on industrial and economical questions' in the north. Hallin was, in fact, a composite character resembling both Michael Sadler and Arnold Toynbee. Like Toynbee, Hallin also has a weak constitution, could only manage 'a couple of hours' serious brainwork in the day' and took a pass degree. Yet he also possessed, like Toynbee, 'a magnetic and personal charm which soon made him a remarkable power, not only in his own college, but among the finer spirits of the University generally'. Meanwhile, Hallin's father 'had been a factory inspector, well known for his share in the inauguration and revision of certain important factory reforms' and this is a thinly disguised portrait of Michael Sadler, Acland's successor as Secretary of Oxford extension, whose great-great uncle, M. T. Sadler, had been a famous pioneer factory reformer in the 1830s.[85] For a novelist seeking to capture the intellectual and social life of late-Victorian Britain, the extension movement provided fictional opportunities and representative figures in abundance. It was an authentic outgrowth and an embodiment of the institutional reforms, intellectual revisions, and awakening social consciousness of the universities from the 1850s.

But a final note of caution may be necessary. The relationship between dons and workers may have been based on a complex of factors specific to the ancient universities at this particular moment. But it was not a unique relationship. All over the developed world in the late-nineteenth and early twentieth centuries, from Chicago to St Petersburg, intellectuals of different sorts were making contact with working-class groups and seeking to educate them, usually in the principles of socialism. It is natural to differentiate the tradition

[84] According to William S. Peterson, 'Elsmere himself is a composite figure, with bits and pieces taken from a number of clergymen whom Mrs Ward knew or about whom she had read'. See William S. Peterson, *Victorian Heretic: Mrs. Humphry Ward's* Robert Elsmere (Leicester, 1976), 134–6.

[85] Mrs Humphry Ward, *Marcella*, Virago edn. (1984; first pub. 1894), 44–6. I am grateful to Karen Hewitt for these references.

of university extension in Britain from the 'political education' that lecturers from the Fabian Society or Social Democratic Federation or, indeed, from the Conservative and Unionist Party also offered at this time. And this is a reasonable distinction since, as we shall see, university extension and the tutorial classes movement that developed out of it in the Edwardian period, presented an academic curriculum for general educational purposes. But as this exploration of its origins in Oxford suggests, university extension embodied a series of complex ideological assumptions and aims. Some were only dimly understood by the founders themselves; others provided the very reason why they took up the work. Unsurprisingly, the politics of university adult education was always a difficult and contentious subject and the history that is to follow is marked by frequent disputes over the motives and aims of tutors, co-operating organizations, students, and the state. Frequently, we shall find un-acknowledged tensions between the educational and political pro-grammes of individuals who took a leading part in the movement.

If it may be accepted that university extension was irreducibly 'political' in a general, and not necessarily party-political sense from the outset, then it not only assists appreciation of the history of this tradition, but makes possible some meaningful comparisons with other societies. Rather than taking a parochial view of the subject, it should be acknowledged that extension was one form of the relationship between intellectuals and the new working classes that became generally apparent from the 1880s.[86] In Britain, an intellectual class at the very heart of the national culture made advances to-wards an already well-organized and increasingly powerful working-class movement in the name of a new and humanized liberalism. In Berlin, the leaders of the most prominent and successful socialist party in the world debated whether they would gain more by offer-ing a general education to workers in the party school, or a specifi-cally 'workers' education' based on Marxist principles.[87] A similar debate would dominate discussion of workers' education in Britain after 1900. In St Petersburg, isolated socialists from an intelligentsia utterly alienated from state and society, made contact with workers' circles and offered their services, only to discover that their students were more interested in education for its own sake than for purposes of revolution. And in these circles, worker-students read Darwin

[86] See Carl Levy (ed.), *Socialism and the Intelligentsia 1880–1914* (London, 1987).
[87] Nicholas Jacobs, 'The German Social Democratic Party School in Berlin, 1906–14', *History Workshop Journal*, 5 (spring 1978); see also *Ministry of Reconstruction: Adult Education Committee, Final Report*, PP 1919, Cmd. 321, xxviii. 368.

and Spencer and responded to the scientific utopianism of Edward Bellamy's *Looking Backwards* just as British and American students did.[88] Though the differences between these cases are clear, in each we see at work a characteristic intellectual urge of the age—to win the workers for the ideology of the future.

[88] Richard Pipes, *Social Democracy and the St. Petersburg Labor Movement 1885–1897* (Cambridge, Mass., 1963), 9–10.

3

EXTENDING OXFORD: UNIVERSITY
EXTENSION IN THE LATE-VICTORIAN
AND EDWARDIAN AGE

I

Acland was elected to Parliament in 1885 and his translation to politics provided the opportunity to refound university extension in Oxford. John Percival, then at Trinity College, was instrumental in this, assisted by Jowett, who was then Vice-Chancellor, and two other heads of house, the Provost of Queen's, Dr Magrath, and the Master of University, Dr Bright. The Delegates for Local Examinations were persuaded 'to resuscitate their committee for local lectures', Michael Sadler was appointed secretary at the end of April 1885, and new regulations for extension lectures were drafted and approved.[1] Under Sadler a more formal administration of the programme developed, and Oxford came to follow the pattern laid down by Cambridge. Oxford extension was similarly dependent on the voluntary efforts of local enthusiasts who organized, planned, and publicized courses. Like Cambridge, the curriculum became more formal and conventionally academic. Whereas Cambridge had tended to develop its centres in the north and east of England, Oxford moved into the south and west. But the demarcation was never that rigid and Oxford had several centres of its own in Yorkshire, for example. By the end of the century, Oxford was organizing lectures 'from Cornwall to Cumberland, from Dover to Carlisle'.[2] Progress was rapid: in 1885–6 Sadler estimated total student attendance at lectures at six thousand; three years later it was over thirteen thousand, and by 1890–91 Oxford extension was

[1] 'Minutes of Meetings etc. of the Committee of Delegates for Local Examinations appointed to carry into operation the Statutes for the Establishment of lectures and Teaching in Large Towns of England and Wales', in Committee for University Extension. Minutes of Meetings I, DES/M/1/1, fos. 1–4. See also William Temple, *The Life of Bishop Percival* (London, 1921), 265–6. H. P. Smith, *Labour and Learning: Albert Mansbridge, Oxford and the WEA* (Oxford, 1956), 32.
[2] J. A. R. Marriott, *Memories of Four Score Years* (London, 1946), 102.

reaching over twenty thousand students.[3] As Sadler wrote to Jowett in early 1891, 'Since last October our whole work has entered upon a very critical stage. Its growth has been very rapid, 180 courses having been already arranged for this session.'[4] The final total for the year actually reached 192. Ninety of these were in history, five in political economy, thirty-three were in literature and the arts, and the remaining sixty-four were in aspects of natural science.[5] That was an outstanding year, but somewhat later, during the Edwardian period, Oxford extension reached the height of its early influence, the programme attracting over twenty thousand students on a regular annual basis to a network of around 140 local centres.[6] In other words, it was reaching and providing some sort of education for approximately eight times the number of students then in residence in the University. Sadler's success was marked in 1892 with the transformation of the Standing Committee into a formal Delegacy for the Extension of Teaching Beyond the Limits of the University which was housed in offices in the Examination Schools.

By the 1890s the elements of an extension education had been established. As Sadler put it, Extension 'means everywhere the use of the same educational method—of the lecture, the class, the use of the printed syllabus, the paper or essay written after each lecture by the student at home and the test of the final examination'.[7] Lectures were given at weekly or fortnightly intervals and were followed by a more intimate class for committed students where issues were discussed and questions answered. Lecturers provided a detailed syllabus and reading list in advance, set and marked weekly essays for the keener students, and entered them for optional examinations administered from Oxford. In the 1890s approximately one in ten students sat the examinations, and the successful candidates were awarded one of three different types of certificate which apparently had some sway with employers. Schoolteachers in particular found the extension examinations a useful way of improving their formal qualifications: the Vice-Chancellor's Certificate was recognized by

---

[3] 'Third Meeting of the Committee, 12 Dec. 1885', DES/M/1/1, fo. 9. See the *Annual Report(s) of the Committee of the Delegates for Local Examinations Appointed to Carry into Operation the University Statute for the Establishment of Lectures and Teaching in the Large Towns of England and Wales (Oxford)*. (Hereafter referred to as *Annual Reports*).

[4] Sadler to Jowett, 3 Jan. 1891, Jowett Papers, Balliol College, Oxford, I E5/10.

[5] *Annual Report 1890–91*, 1.

[6] Between 1901 and 1910 there was only a single year, 1904–5, when total enrolment fell below 20,000. The peak year was 1907–8 when 23,428 students attended Oxford extension lectures.   [7] *Annual Report 1887–8*, 10.

the Education Department 'as excusing the holder from the Queen's Scholarship Examination'.[8] The problem of providing access to books for the students was solved by the invention of the 'travelling library', a box of books packed at the Extension Office in Oxford and transported by train to the local centre.

The lecturers sent out from Oxford travelled the country, moving from one extension centre to another on a weekly or fortnightly circuit, a train timetable in every pocket, staying overnight in the homes of members of the local extension committee: university extension was another by-product of the railway age. The qualities needed in an early extension lecturer were many and varied. According to Sadler, and his most important collaborator, Halford Mackinder, 'any lecturer who is to take an active part in the work must be strong enough to bear the considerable fatigue' of 'long and frequent journeys'. He must be a 'man of sound knowledge and many interests' rather than a learned specialist, capable of putting himself in the place of his students and 'taking an outside view of the subject.' He had to be 'a good platform-speaker' and yet be capable of 'intellectual sympathy' with his audience. He had to be adaptable, able 'to lecture to ladies in the afternoon and working-men at night'. He needed 'moral earnestness'. He would also need entrepreneurial flair for organization and promotion. 'University Extension, in a word, needs men who belong exclusively neither to the academic nor the business worlds, but who can sympathise with the aims and interests of both.'[9]

This serves admirably as a portrait of Sadler himself. He was born in Barnsley in 1861, the son of a physician. Educated at Rugby, he enjoyed a celebrated career as an undergraduate at Trinity College, Oxford between 1880 and 1884, taking a first in Greats and presiding over the Union. He was apparently influenced deeply by Ruskin, whom he heard lecture in the University Museum during his second year in Oxford, and also by Toynbee as befitted a member of Acland's 'Inner Ring'.[10] Sadler had charisma: his confidence, ease, and eloquence led many to believe 'that going into politics he would rise to be eventually Prime Minister'.[11] But personal gifts were allied to social conscience. He was described by his close

---

[8] *Annual Report 1892–3*, 3.

[9] H. J. Mackinder and M. E. Sadler, *University Extension; Past, Present and Future*, 3rd edn. (London, 1891), 103–6.

[10] Michael Sadleir, *Sir Michael Sadler: A Memoir by his Son* (London, 1949), 30–3.

[11] L. L. Price quoted in Alon Kadish, *The Oxford Economists in the Late Nineteenth Century* (Oxford, 1982), 14.

friend, D. S. MacColl, in the year prior to his appointment as Secretary as 'the most missionary spirit I know'.[12] The description is particularly apt; not only was it customary for contemporaries to draw attention to Sadler's evident sense of mission, but the term suited an enterprise that grew from essentially religious roots. When someone described university extension as 'the Salvation Army of education' Sadler was initially 'put out', but he came to recognize 'the grain of truth in it after all', and drew attention to 'the missionary spirit—the spirit of sympathy' as the mainspring of the movement.[13] As he wrote to one of his closest collaborators, G. W. Hudson Shaw, in 1886,

The work is stimulating and useful. It brings a man into contact with many bracing influences. It leaves him free to say his mind while giving him the distinction of a University appointment. It enables him to do good and to help men who need guidance and sympathy. In fact it is missionary work on a broad basis welcomed by all sects and classes.[14]

According to R. H. Tawney, Sadler was 'more of a thinker than an administrator, and more of a missionary than either'.[15]

Sadler was attracted to extension lecturing as a student and Acland groomed him as his successor. Writing to his father in 1884 Sadler described the opportunity, on graduating, of 'a lecturship to co-operative and extension classes in Social and Political economy with the view of eventually in a year or two becoming secretary to the Oxford University Extension. This is grand work with a great and useful future and I confess that I incline to it.'[16] Sadler's achievements depended on charm, hard work, and the possession of a thick skin. He administered the growing enterprise with the aid of a single secretary and one clerk, and he combined extension with his position as Steward of Christ Church from 1886. He was innovative, unscrupulous, and did not abide by the rules. He tried to ensnare in the Oxford circuit local centres previously loyal to

---

[12] D. S. MacColl to M. E. Sadler, 24 Jan. 1885, M. E. Sadler Papers, 'Letters and Papers 1885–1903', Ms. Eng. Misc. c. 550, fo. 109, Bodleian Library, Oxford.
[13] Linda Grier, *Achievement in Education: The Work of Michael Ernest Sadler 1885–1935* (London, 1952), 21.
[14] M. E. Sadler to G. W. Hudson Shaw, 1 Feb. 1886, A. Maude Royden MSS, Fawcett Library, Guildhall University, London, Box 222, 'Documents, Correspondence and Papers Relating to W. Hudson Shaw 1883–1952'.
[15] Quoted by Asa Briggs in the foreword to M. E. Sadler, *Selections from Michael Sadler: Studies in World Citizenship*, ed. J. H. Higginson (1979).
[16] Sadleir, *Sir Michael Sadler*, 57.

Cambridge or London.[17] He laid attractive bait for successful lecturers from competing universities. He introduced short, six-lecture courses which many deprecated as intellectually shallow. Sadler argued that if working-class students could not afford to attend the standard twelve-lecture extension courses, then something had to be done to make them affordable: 'the only chance for such a town is to have a cheap course ... the shortness of the course is not necessarily a bar to the thoroughness of the study.'[18] It was a plausible defence, though Sadler was determined to expand Oxford's influence and short, cheap courses were an attractive means of winning the loyalty of students and local extension committees.[19]

During Sadler's ten years as Secretary he not only established extension in Oxford but also had influence over the development of educational thinking more generally. He wrote widely in the journals of the day and with Mackinder published in 1890 *University Extension: Past, Present and Future*, the most authoritative statement of the movement's aims and methods. He gradually came to see that much of the value of extension work was lost because of the early age at which students had been forced to leave school and he used his position to draw attention to the inadequacies of secondary education for which the state then made no provision.[20] He worked closely with Acland in this project, especially once his former mentor had reached office in 1892: Acland immediately wrote to him to ask for advice on 'what we need nationally and can do, even with a small majority behind us'.[21] It was Sadler who promoted the famous conference in Oxford in October 1893 to assess the future of secondary education, which stimulated the appointment of the Royal Commission on Secondary Education, chaired by Bryce. Sadler was a member of the commission, and its recommendations laid down the principles for the 1902 Education Act. Though there were offers of employment in journalism and politics, Sadler remained committed to work in education. When he did leave the Delegacy

[17] For examples of competition between Oxford and, respectively, Cambridge and London in university extension work, see 'Correspondence with the Secretary to the Cambridge Syndicate on the subject of a Proposed Course at Halifax by Mr. MacColl' and 'Correspondence about the Establishment of Lectures at Ealing, March 1889', DES/EP/1/3 fos. 61–6, 134–41, Oxford University Archive.

[18] *Annual Report 1887–8*, 8–9.

[19] Stuart Marriott, *Extramural Empires: Service and Self-Interest in English University Adult Education 1873–1983* (Nottingham, 1984), 62; id., 'Dr. Welch on "Oxford and University Extension": A Critical Note', *Studies in Adult Education*, 11/1 (Apr. 1979), 20.   [20] Grier, *Achievement in Education*, 25–6.

[21] Acland to Sadler, 1 Sept. 1892, M. E. Sadler Papers, fos. 114–15.

in 1895, he accepted Acland's invitation to become Director of Special Inquiries and Reports in the Board of Education, 'a sub-department of educational research and publication' as Sadler later described it, which Acland, Sadler, and Tom Ellis had apparently planned and discussed while on holiday together in Switzerland.[22] For eight years he administered a comprehensive programme of pioneering research into education both in Britain and abroad, which made him the pre-eminent British educationalist of the period.[23] As Acland wrote to Sadler when making him the offer, 'It is a great opportunity for us to combine in laying the foundations quietly for a great modification of the State to National Education'.[24] This was only the first of several occasions in its history when the extension movement in Oxford played a part in the reform of schooling in Britain.

II

Oxford extension offered Sadler, like Acland before him, the opportunity of building a career in public service and using experience and knowledge gained through lecturing in the wider cause of social reform. His most important legacy to Oxford, meanwhile, was the cadre of dedicated tutors he established and nurtured. Many of the lecturers were recent graduates as yet unsure of their career, who offered extension two or three experimental years. As Sadler explained in 1887, 'The greater part of the lecturing staff will always be composed of young Graduates who are glad to have a University engagement for a year or two after taking their degrees, partly because it gives them in each year twenty eight weeks of unbroken vacation in which they can continue their studies more uninterruptedly than would be possible in almost any other remunerated occupation.'[25] Others were more serious scholars awaiting a fellowship or the opportunity of a position in one of the new provincial universities. And others still, took up lecturing as a career in itself. All,

[22] M. E. Sadler, 'Note A. The Department of Special Inquiries and Reports on Education. Robert Morant' (n.d.), M. E. Sadler Papers, Letters and Papers 1885–1903, fo. 8.
[23] Peter Gordon and John White, *Philosophers as Educational Reformers: The Influence of Idealism on British Educational Thought and Practice* (London, 1979), 139–43.
[24] Acland to Sadler, 17 Oct. 1894, M. E. Sadler Papers, Letters and Papers 1885–1903, fos. 118–20.   [25] *Annual Report 1886–7*, 12.

without exception, complained about the hard work, low fees, and low esteem accorded to this new class of 'democratic don'. Acland had recruited like-minded men from the 'Inner Ring': Sadler's significant break with what went before was his employment of all-comers, irrespective of politics and belief. Christian social activism, Conservative benevolence, Liberal progressivism and socialist radicalism—all these positions were represented after 1885, even if a style of advanced Liberalism was probably the predominant strain. John Marriott, Sadler's successor as Secretary of the Delegacy, wrote of 'a small group of like-minded men, strongly opposed to each other in political opinion and social outlook.'[26] The description is not a contradiction because they shared a commitment to the spread of higher education, and through it, of civic culture, even while coming at the task from different positions in formal politics. As Sadler put it in 1894, 'Our most immediate, pressing and urgent duty is to make a strenuous attempt to educate the English democracy . . . In University Extension work we are dealing with politics but not as party men'—though it is difficult to believe that tutors were not also trying to capture elements of the new democracy for the particular creed they espoused.[27]

Many of the graduates of late-Victorian Oxford went out east in the colonial service; others went instead to the East End. And some tried to make these two destinations conformable in an ideology of imperialism and social reform. This was true of Mackinder, Marriott, and also W. A. S. Hewins, who moved from Oxford Extension to become the first Director of the London School of Economics and was briefly Under-Secretary for the Colonies at the end of the First World War.[28] Oxford Extension also provided opportunities for more mainstream conservatives. It accommodated F. E. Smith, later Lord Birkenhead, who in 1898 was giving lectures in Chesterfield, Colwyn Bay, and Llandudno. It offered work to Cosmo Lang, later Archbishop of Canterbury, who took up lecturing during the three years between graduating with a first in Modern History and his election to a fellowship at All Souls in 1888. Lang nursed 'political ambitions' and in his own words 'wanted to get alongside working men in their real thoughts and interests, as my Tory Democratic ideas convinced me that no party could be either useful or successful which did not understand and sympathise with them'. Perhaps

[26] J. Marriott, *Memories*, 93.
[27] Quoted in S. Marriott, 'Dr. Welch on "Oxford and University Extension"', 19.
[28] See Richard Symonds, *Oxford and Empire: The Last Lost Cause?* (London, 1986).

this is why Sadler described him as 'a Tory of the kind who in the end becomes good Liberal'.[29] Lang left a fascinating vignette of his experiences lecturing at Bolton, Rochdale, Wallsend and Hebden Bridge.[30]

Oxford extension also found room for the unconventional. J. A. Hobson was temporarily prevented from lecturing on political economy in London because of the 'heretical' argument he advanced in 1889 in *The Physiology of Industry* that 'over-saving' could result in the underemployment of capital and labour and hence in depression.[31] But he was 'allowed by the greater liberality of the Oxford University Extension Movement to address audiences in the provinces, confining myself to practical issues relating to working class life'.[32] Extension lecturing suited an economist with a suspicion of the strictly academic, cloistered lifestyle.[33] And Hobson valued contact with extension students who taught him about actual economic conditions and practices. In Michaelmas 1892 and 1893 he taught courses on 'Problems of Poverty', and paid tribute in his class reports to the information his students provided on 'common questions too often left to the discussion of imperfectly informed theorists'.[34] Many lecturers, like Hobson, learnt as they taught.

Among others, C. R. Ashbee, the influential exponent of the arts and crafts movement, lectured for Oxford through the 1890s, seeking to mix personally with manual workers and artisans, and develop among them new ideas on design and the organization of work. He eventually gave up in frustration: his audiences were mainly composed of the middle classes, and university extension could not be made amenable to the more practical as opposed to the conventional academic curriculum he favoured.[35] Hilaire Belloc gave nearly

---

[29] Sadleir, *Sir Michael Sadler*, 43.

[30] C. G. Lockhart, *Cosmo Gordon Lang* (London, 1949), 47–8.

[31] A. F. Mummery and J. A. Hobson, *The Physiology of Industry: Being an Exposure of Certain Fallacies in Existing Theories of Economics* (London, 1889).

[32] J. A. Hobson, *Confessions of an Economic Heretic* (London, 1938), 30–1. Hobson probably exaggerated his ostracism by fellow-economists. See Alon Kadish, 'Rewriting the *Confessions*: Hobson and the Extension Movement', in Michael Freeden (ed.), *Reappraising J. A. Hobson: Humanism and Welfare* (London, 1990), 145–7 and J. H. Burrows, 'The Teaching of Economics in the Early Days of the University Extension Movement in London 1876–1902', *History of Economic Thought Newsletter*, 20 (spring 1978), 8–14.

[33] Kadish, 'Rewriting the *Confessions*', 151–2.

[34] Oxford University Extension. Lecturers' and Examiners' Reports, Oxford University Archive, DES/R/3/13 fo. 256 (autumn 1892) and DES/R/3/16 fo. 233 (autumn 1893).

[35] Alan Crawford, *C. R. Ashbee: Architect, Designer and Romantic Socialist* (New Haven, 1985), 51–3.

fifty Oxford extension courses between 1895 and 1905.[36] John Cowper Powys brought to extension lecturing in the 1890s and 1900s a theatricality and sexuality that made him especially successful.[37] Tall, handsome, and wonderfully expressive, Powys was the matinée idol of the movement, adored and admired in many English provincial towns for the hundred or so courses he taught for Oxford between 1899 and 1908.[38] He was so successful that in 1910 he transferred to the American lecture circuit, where he built up an equivalent reputation and following, before turning to the novels for which he is remembered. And even the famous emigré anarchist, Prince Kropotkin, applied to become an Oxford lecturer in 1893, and waited eleven months for the refusal.[39]

Among this heterogeneous group three figures stand out who deserve greater attention: Mackinder, Hudson Shaw, and Marriott. Mackinder is important not only because of the political project he brought to university extension, but for his institutional and curricular innovations. Like Sadler, Mackinder was also the son of a physician and also enjoyed a distinguished undergraduate career at Christ Church during which he too, was President of the Union. He took a first in Physical Sciences in 1883 and then read for the Final Honour School in Modern History in a year. This was no accident; the two subjects were related in Mackinder's ambitious project to develop a 'new geography' that would synthesize the humanities with natural science and focus on the relationship between social life, economic activity, politics, and the physical environment. With no means of developing this new discipline in an academic position within the university—for such a position did not exist—Mackinder was rescued from a career in the law by Sadler's invitation to become an extension lecturer, and he began to develop his ideas before enthusiastic audiences, many of them predominantly working class, on the extension circuit.[40] He gave his first lecture to an

[36] For Belloc's reports as a lecturer, see Oxford University Archives, DES/R/3/22–7 and 30–4.

[37] John Cowper Powys, *Autobiography* (London, 1934), 284–8; Richard Perceval Graves, *The Brothers Powys* (Oxford, 1984), 43–4; H. P. Collins, *John Cowper Powys: Old Earth-Man* (London, 1965), 32.

[38] On Powys as an extension lecturer, see Oxford University Archives DES/R/3/28–34 and 37–8.

[39] Oxford University Extension Minutes, 1 Dec. 1893 and 2 Nov. 1894, Oxford University Archives.

[40] W. H. Parker, *Mackinder: Geography as an Aid to Statecraft* (Oxford, 1982); E. W. Gilbert, *Sir Halford Mackinder 1861–1947: An Appreciation of his Life and Work* (London, 1961); Brian Blouet, 'Sir Halford Mackinder 1861–1947: Some New Perspectives', Research Paper No. 13, University of Oxford School of Geography, 1975.

audience of four hundred members of the Artisans' Co-operative Society in Rotherham in November 1885 and he was appointed to the formal position of University Extension Lecturer in Natural Science and Economic History in 1886.[41] He went on to give almost five hundred lectures in over fifty centres up to 1892.[42] Within a year he was ready to present his ideas more formally and his famous paper to the Royal Geographical Society in January 1887 on 'The Scope and Method of Geography', often taken as the point of origin of modern geographical studies in Britain, led to his appointment as Reader in Geography in Oxford—though students in the university were few and far between for this new subject, and the stipend was poor, so he was not deflected from extension work.[43] In 1899 he became Director of the Oxford School of Geography, the first university department for the subject in Britain. He went on to further distinction as second Director of the London School of Economics (1903–8) after Hewins, and, after breaking with the Liberal Imperialism of his youth when he came out for tariff reform, as a Conservative MP (1910–22). From extension and an academic interest in geopolitics, came a notable career in education and public service, dedicated to the maintenance of the Empire.

'The establishment of geography in Britain as a respectable academic discipline, and the promotion of imperial unity' were related missions for Mackinder.[43] The former would encourage reflection on the best means of achieving the latter, and would generally increase consciousness of empire. Mackinder believed 'that geography was essential for the elementary education of an imperial people', and thus devoted his life to evangelizing educational projects in the service of the discipline he helped create.[44] That these efforts should have begun in university extension is not surprising, for the new movement offered opportunities to develop and experiment with the traditional university curriculum. Extension attracted academic mavericks who refused to be bound by conventions and who enjoyed the relative freedom from public examinations and the scrutiny of colleagues inside the university. Mackinder's 'new geography' was just the most notable example of several creative developments in extension at the margins of academic life. As Alon Kadish has shown, university extension provided an arena for the study and teaching of political economy at a time when opportunities in the discipline were limited within the university. It was

[41] Gilbert, *Sir Halford Mackinder*, 8; Parker, *Mackinder*, 6.
[42] L. M. Cantor, 'Halford John Mackinder', in J. E. Thomas and Barry Elsey (eds.), *International Biography of Adult Education* (Nottingham, 1985), 376.
[43] Parker, *Mackinder*, 8–9.   [44] Ibid., p. v.

particularly attractive to young men involved in the Oxford Economic Society, founded in 1886, who, like Toynbee before them, took an inductive, historical, and institutional approach to the study of economic life.[45] In bringing lecturers into contact with working-class audiences and communities, extension encouraged research into the actual conditions of life and labour. To a very large degree, the modern discipline of economic history developed out of university extension and the tutorial classes movement which followed it, in the years between 1880 and 1914.[46] The difficulty, meanwhile, of teaching classics, the staple diet of an Oxford education, to audiences in which few, if any, possessed familiarity with Greek and Latin, led the movement to concentrate on the study of English texts, and to play a role in the institutionalization of English itself in the universities. John Churton Collins, who was eventually elected to the chair of English at Birmingham University in 1905, was one of the pioneers of the university study of modern English literature. He had been tutored by Green while an undergraduate at Balliol between 1868 and 1872, began teaching for the London extension society in 1880 and gave his first Oxford extension course in 1887. For a generation, using university extension as his base, Collins led the campaign to put English at the centre of the modern curriculum, and demonstrated its validity as a university discipline by his success in teaching literature in the extension movement.[47]

The other innovation that marked Mackinder's involvement with Oxford extension was his participation in the establishment of Reading University Extension College of which he was Principal between its foundation in 1892 and 1903. Reading was one of Oxford's most successful extension centres, and in the early 1890s Sadler and Mackinder chose it as the location for an 'extension college'—a properly organized local centre for the Oxford extension programme which would help develop both liberal and technical education in the area. The college was funded by subventions from

[45] Alon Kadish, 'The Teaching of Political Economy in the Extension Movement: Cambridge, London and Oxford', in Alon Kadish and Keith Tribe (eds.), *The Market for Political Economy: The Advent of Economics in British University Culture 1850–1905* (London, 1993), 100–1.

[46] Kadish, *Oxford Economists, passim*; T. C. Barker, 'The Beginnings of the Economic History Society', *Economic History Review*, 2nd ser., 30/1 (1977), 4; Norman Chester, *Economics, Politics and Social Studies in Oxford 1900–85* (London, 1986), ch. 1.

[47] Anthony Kearney, *John Churton Collins: The Louse on the Locks of Literature* (Edinburgh, 1986); Stuart Marriott, 'John Churton Collins' in J. E. Thomas and B. Elsey (eds.), *International Biography of Adult Education* (Nottingham, 1985), 104–10.

central government, surrounding county councils, Reading Town Council, and Christ Church in Oxford, which Sadler had roused and persuaded to support the scheme. At Sadler's prompting, Mackinder was elected to a Studentship at Christ Church which allowed him to devote his time to the new project. The extension college was formally opened by the Dean of Christ Church on 29 September 1892. Ten years later, shortly before Mackinder moved to the London School of Economics, and by which time the college had over two hundred full-time students in addition to its extension classes, Reading received its charter as a university college. In this way Sadler and Mackinder helped to realize a small part of Jowett's earlier conception of the ends of university extension.[48]

Mackinder was an administrator, a public servant, and a politician who left many monuments to his ideals and career. A rather different kind of extension lecturer, who left none at all and is now forgotten, but who was considered to be the most effective and accomplished lecturer of them all, was George William Hudson Shaw, for twenty-six years Senior Lecturer in History for the Oxford Delegacy. Hudson Shaw was born in Leeds in 1859, the son of a civil engineer. His father died when he was twelve and the rest of his family emigrated to Australia. But Hudson Shaw stayed in Britain, secured an education with the assistance of an aunt, and from Bradford Grammar School he went up to Oxford in 1879 as a non-collegiate student to read Modern History. Balliol then elected him to an exhibition. At Oxford he was influenced, in common with his friend Sadler, by Ruskin. Like Sadler, and also like Mackinder and Lang, he became President of the Union.[49] Graduating with a disappointing second and without money, Hudson Shaw contemplated emigration also, but remained in England when an anonymous benefactor, in fact a member of his college, offered him an allowance so that he might fulfil his ambition to work 'among the poor, and especially among the poor of the great cities'.[50]

---

[48] 'Opening of the University Extension College, Reading', *Oxford University Extension Gazette*, 3/25 (Oct. 1892), 1. See also William M. Childs, *Making a University: An Account of the University Movement at Reading* (London, 1933), ch. 1; Gilbert, *Sir Halford Mackinder*, 12–13; Parker, *Mackinder*, 12–14; *Annual Report 1892–3*.

[49] Stuart Marriott, 'George William Hudson Shaw', in Thomas and Elsey (eds.), *International Biography of Adult Education*, 533–40. I am particularly indebted to the fine account of Hudson Shaw provided by Professor Marriott.

[50] Maude Royden, *A Threefold Cord* (London, 1947), 35. See also Sheila Fletcher, *Maude Royden* (Oxford, 1989), 47–8. The anonymous benefactor was later revealed to be a Balliol contemporary of Hudson Shaw's, Bolton King. See Hudson Shaw 'To my Unknown Benefactor', 21 Dec. 1883, Royden Papers, Box 222.

He was ordained in 1884 and was a curate in Horsham for the next two years. It was almost inevitable that with his social interests and abilities on the platform Sadler should try and involve him in the extension movement once he became Secretary. He wrote to him in February 1886 offering him an appointment as the first Oxford Staff Lecturer:

We have reached a critical point: the lectures are becoming widely known, the idea is taking root in Oxford and out of it, but we need a staff—I mean a permanent group of trusted Lecturers on whom we can rely for some years of increasingly efficient and practised service, and to whom we can look with confidence for good work and aid in the future extension of the movement.

Sadler held out the inducement of teaching and learning simultaneously: 'The students find help in thinking and guidance in reading from the lecturers, who in turn have an unrivalled opportunity of watching the facts of industrial life from a point of view otherwise inaccessible to them.'[51]

Hudson Shaw accepted, though with reservations. As he recalled much later,

I entered the movement unwillingly, more or less a disbeliever, under pressure from Prof. M. E. Sadler, attracted mainly by the hope held out of close contact with working people and possible opportunity of aiding the ideals of T. H. Green and Arnold Toynbee. My scepticism regarding University Extension disappeared during the first year's work in Lancashire.[52]

He was welcomed immediately in all the great working-class centres on the Oxford circuit. According to Sadler his fame was 'almost mystical' among the working men of the north.[53] He lectured at eight different centres in Manchester for twenty years.[54] At Oldham he lectured for thirteen successive years with an average weekly attendance of 650. His final lectures there drew an audience of over a thousand. He 'won the heads and hearts of thousands of hard-headed Oldhamites, by his strong, simple, homely manner, passionate earnestness and clear grasp of his subject'. He was at Rochdale for nine successive years and at Bolton for seven. At Reading in

[51] M. E. Sadler to Hudson Shaw, 1 Feb. 1886, Royden Papers, Box 222.

[52] G. W. Hudson Shaw, 'The University Extension Movement', Ministry of Reconstruction, Adult Education Committee, Notes No. 75, Public Record Office, RECO 1 894, fo. 1.

[53] Royden, *Threefold Cord*, 34. There is a good description of Hudson Shaw lecturing in Max Leclerc, *Le Role Social des universités* (Paris, 1892) 29–32.

[54] Hudson Shaw, 'University Extension Movement', fo. 2.

1903–4 he drew an average of 1,240 students across two terms.[55]
He also lectured in many of the smaller towns in the Oxford pro-
gramme like Hebden Bridge, Ilkley, Skipton, Kendal and Matlock.
As another Oxford lecturer recalled, over half a century later

In those days Mr Hudson Shaw was living in the Lake District and had
to be home for weekends for his parochial work, so most of his lecturing
was done in the North of England. He was a great favourite with the
working class audiences there, and there is no doubt that he did more
than any man to firmly establish working class centres in that part of the
country. Many such centres invited him year after year. Oldham ... was
the most notable of these. The audience there increased in size year after
year until they reached an average of a thousand for the course.[56]

These efforts were the product of a gruelling routine. According to
Maude Royden, the first woman to give Oxford extension lectures
in the Edwardian period, and eventually, in old age, Hudson Shaw's
third wife,

Hudson would travel all day, lecture in the afternoon, go to the home of
one of his admirers and friends, lecture again in the evening, allow the
class held afterwards to go on as long as students demanded, and go back
to absorbing conversations with host and hostess till nine or ten o'clock,
then he would, exhausted, eat an enormous meal (eat it? bolt it, I should
say), and either continue talking into the small hours or go straight to bed;
either course being equally destructive to his digestion. Hudson enjoyed
this mad way of living ... But he paid for it.[57]

His favourite subjects for lectures were the Renaissance, the history
of seventeenth-century England, and 'Modern Social Reformers' in
which course his admiration for Ruskin could find expression. Indeed, it has been suggested that Hudson Shaw did more than anyone else to spread the notable interest in Ruskin's ideas shown by
many of the leaders of the emergent labour movement at the turn
of the century—in Ruskin's contempt for conventional economics
and the morality of commercial society.[58] Hudson Shaw published

[55] Sir J. A. R. Marriott, 'Hudson Shaw', *Rewley House Papers*, 2/8 (1945), 309;
id., 'G. W. Hudson Shaw', *The Times*, 30 Dec. 1944, p. 6; S. Marriott, 'Shaw',
535; Albert Mansbridge, *Fellow Men: A Gallery of England 1876–1946* (London,
1948), 76–7; *Oldham Industrial Co-operative Record*, 11/19 (July 1913), 223,
quoted in Sheila Rowbotham, ' "Travellers in a Strange Country"; Responses of
Working Class Students to the University Extension Movement 1873–1910', *History Workshop Journal*, 12 (autumn 1981), 72.

[56] George Edens to Maude Royden, March 1952, Royden Papers, Box 222.

[57] Royden, *Threefold Cord*, 43–4.

[58] For evidence of Ruskin's influence on leaders of the Labour Party see 'The
Labour Party and the Books that Helped Make It', *Review of Reviews*, 33/198
(June 1906).

very little: as Stuart Marriott explains, 'Enormous care went into the preparation of the lecture courses, but he resisted all his friends' entreaties to give his work more permanent form. It seems that he felt fully effective only when he was directly addressing an audience.' In 1895 he described his aims: 'to train good citizens, to extend high ideals from the few to the many', and to help form 'a true, cultured, educated democracy'.[59] He combined extension with the Church, holding poor country livings at Thornthwaite, then at South Luffenham in Rutland, and at Old Alderley, Cheshire. At the end of a week's lecturing he returned to parish duties and worship. But when offered the valuable living of Morpeth, worth £1,200 a year, by the earl of Carlisle, he turned it down so that he could continue lecturing.[60] In the same year Balliol elected him to a fellowship which he held until 1898, but it was not well remunerated and did not allow him to reduce his teaching. It was almost inevitable that his health should deteriorate under the strain. John Marriott described him as 'highly temperamental' and he suffered several breakdowns, compounded by personal unhappiness and professional frustration.[61]

Although he was the first Chairman of the Workers' Educational Association in 1903, the change in emphasis in adult education from the grand public lecture to the more intimate and academic tutorial class that the WEA stood for after 1907, reduced his influence in workers' education and provoked his criticism. Hudson Shaw remained loyal to 'the university extension plan and method' which was 'the only really practicable and effective system for adult education in a modern democracy'. In his view, the tutorial class, though it had his 'warmest sympathy' as a method of education, was not a 'superior alternative' to university extension but a 'complementary and specialised department of it. It does not fit the bill. It deals only with a small minority' and therefore was unsuitable for the great task of creating 'a community of trained citizens'. Tutorial classes organized by the WEA did not 'touch the multitude' and appeared unduly narrow in their focus on economics and economic history. Hudson Shaw also opposed the bias of the new movement 'in Socialistic directions': 'University Extension as I knew it was at any rate a free platform and not limited to one Gospel.'[62]

[59] S. Marriott, 'Shaw', 539.
[60] N. A. Jepson, 'Staffing Problems During the Early Years of the Oxford University Extension Movement', *Rewley House Papers*, 3/3 (1954–5), 25.
[61] [J. A. R. Marriott], 'G. W. Hudson Shaw', *The Times*, p. 6. For details of his private life and love for Maude Royden, see Fletcher, *Maude Royden, passim*.
[62] Hudson Shaw, 'University Extension Movement', fos. 4–5.

With the tide running against him, after a serious illness he gave up lecturing in 1912 and devoted his remaining energies to the Church, taking up the Crown living at St Botolph's, Bishopsgate, which he held until 1935. Many recognized his achievement and Sadler expressed it admirably when he wrote to Hudson Shaw in 1909:

For more than twenty years you have been one of the great moving forces for good in English life. Very much of the change which has come over political thought is, in fact, the direct result of your teaching. You have been the link between Ruskin and the labour movement. More than any other man, you have made Ruskin's words live and bear fruit. You have added much of your own. Like all good interpreters, you are yourself a creator of ideals.[63]

Twenty-four years later, Sadler described Hudson Shaw as 'one of the great leaders of my generation'. To a leader of the next generation, Albert Mansbridge, founder of the Workers' Educational Association, Hudson Shaw had been 'a self-sacrificing inspiring force throughout the land'.[64] Another central figure in the history of workers' education, E. S. Cartwright, paid tribute to Hudson Shaw's efforts among the working class at the turn of the century in stimulating the demand for education that was to be met by other, and ultimately more famous figures.

My mind goes back to the old days and the great work you did at Longton. That was a creative time when it was good to be alive. The large and flourishing WEA movement in North Staffordshire owes very much to your guidance and inspiration, and then to Tawney, whom we secured, I always remember, at your suggestion and by your influence. I am often in the Five Towns and can truly say that the work you did there is held in honour and you yourself still warmly remembered by the 'old brigade'.[65]

Hudson Shaw was recruited for Oxford extension by Sadler, but more of his teaching was done for Sadler's successor as Secretary of the Delegacy, John Marriott. Marriott ruled over the Oxford extension empire for a quarter of a century, finally retiring from his position in 1920. In later years he combined the job with a prolific career as a writer on history and politics, and an MP. Indeed, Marriott contended in his memoirs that he had been a politician 'almost from the cradle', by which he meant not just his formal

[63] Sadler to Hudson Shaw, 7 Oct. 1909, Royden Papers, Box 222.
[64] M. E. Sadler to G. W. Hudson Shaw, 10 July 1933; Albert Mansbridge to A. Maude Royden, 26 Jan. 1952, Royden Papers, Box 222.
[65] E. S. Cartwright to G. W. Hudson Shaw, 4 Mar. 1944, Royden Papers, Box 222.

political engagement in parliamentary politics, but his work as an educationalist and lecturer.[66]

Marriott was born in Bowdon, Cheshire in 1859, the son of a solicitor: the sons of the professional middle class, who could not count on a place in the family business or the inheritance of an estate, seem to have been especially drawn to extension lecturing as a career. Educated at Repton and New College, he took a second class in Modern History and then found employment coaching the sons of the aristocracy and gentry through their examinations at Oxford. He was appointed to a lectureship at his undergraduate college and it was during this period that he was caught up in the extension movement: one morning in the spring of 1886 Sadler apparently burst into his room, and with the words 'I want you to go and give a course of lectures at Bath' captured the most prolific extension lecturer of them all. Marriott was ready to be ensnared: 'the whole conception attracted me powerfully. Here was a chance of political work wholly divorced from the environment which too often besmirched politics (in the narrower sense). I had become used to the platform, and found myself at home on it. I knew my subject well, and was conscious of a capacity for speaking and for teaching.'[67] At the end of his life he estimated that he had given approximately ten thousand extension lectures. Indeed, he was still giving them on the eve of the Second World War when he was eighty years old.

His routine in the first years before he became Secretary was punishing. From Saturday until Tuesday morning he was in Oxford, lecturing and tutoring his internal students; the rest of the week was devoted to extension lecturing, so that in an average week he gave perhaps nine lectures and sundry tutorials. 'Hard, indeed, was the work, but I enjoyed it. I found great stimulus in the extraordinary variety of audiences I had to address.' Marriott could charm the 'sealskins'—the middle-class women—in the afternoon, and the workers in the evening, though as a Conservative he steered clear of staunch Liberal strongholds in the industrial north. As he put it, 'I became fairly familiar with most of the cathedral class in Southern England'.[68] He also became familiar with his subject and grew into a respected author and specialist on the history of modern Europe, the diplomacy of the Eastern Question, and the development of the Empire.

[66] Marriott, *Memories of Four Score Years*, 1–4. See also Stuart Marriott, 'John Arthur Ransome Marriott', in Thomas and Elsey (eds.), *International Biography of Adult Education*, 399–408.

[67] J. Marriott, *Memories*, 91–3.   [68] Ibid. 94–5.

As Sadler's successor, Marriott adopted a very different style of leadership. A natural organizer, he won respect and loyalty from his staff for his mixture of firmness and benevolence.[69] Yet beneath the exterior of the slightly pompous patrician there was 'a propagandist pioneer' who had no equal when it came to stirring 'a town or township to start and maintain a "new centre for culture" '.[70] Marriott eventually made his way into national politics, sitting first for Oxford City and then for York between 1917 and 1929. But his parliamentary career came too late, and this devout imperialist and implacable opponent of Home Rule for Ireland was too old for office. He also discovered that the House of Commons does not like to be lectured: his style was too formal and oracular for that particular audience. Marriott was that type of Conservative who presented a paternalistic face to a quiescent working class, but staunchly opposed demands from an assertive labour movement and any form of industrial action. He wrote several inflammatory articles in opposition to trade union action during the Edwardian period which compromised his position in adult education at a time when Oxford was reaching out to renew contact with the organized working class. In his autobiography he recognized that to some working-class students he became 'an obscurantist and reactionary'.[71] Like Hudson Shaw, though for different reasons, Marriott favoured traditional extension lectures that 'catered for all classes' rather than the workers' education that was introduced by Oxford before the First World War. Certainly a new generation of Oxford tutors felt it impossible to work with him and established separate university structures for the new movement, in part to ensure that he could have no influence over their initiatives. And once these new educational structures were in place, and Marriott found his own position to be a more marginal one, it is fair to say that he began to transfer his broadly conceived political interests from education to party politics.

III

So much for the tutors—a diverse group of individualists, attracted to the work for a variety of political and social reasons. What of the students? In a lecture that Sadler delivered in Philadelphia in 1891

[69] 'Sir John Marriott', *The Times*, 8 June 1945, p. 7.
[70] [C. G. R], 'John Arthur Ransome Marriott', *Oxford Magazine*, 21 June 1945, 317–18.   [71] J. Marriott, *Memories*, 139.

he picked out four representative groups from among the students of the extension movement who had most to gain from adult education. There were those with ability but who 'on the very threshold of University life, have been called back by the claims of domestic duty or stopped by sudden loss of means'. There were those intellectually active people 'who cherish the desire of combining with the education of business the education of books'. Third, there were women, deprived of many of the admittedly limited opportunities that then existed in higher education. And finally Sadler turned to the 'great mass of the people, tired by the day's work, fagged by the insistent duties of bread-winning and yet each year more directly charged with the ultimate settlement of great problems, each year feeling a greater need for judgment and for the judgment that comes from knowledge'.[72]

Oxford extension in this phase of its history had only limited success in attracting students from the fourth of these categories, the working class. According to C. R. Ashbee, cast down by the failure to attract artisans to his lectures on architecture and design, 'the audience drive up in their carriages, the footmen wait without, while the young ladies receive culture within'.[73] Of course, there were many centres where the audience was almost entirely composed of workers: places like Bolton, Oldham, Rochdale, Barnsley, Bradford, and Ancoats in Manchester. As might be expected, extension was most successful in working-class centres with a strong co-operative tradition. Thus Oxford had particular success in the three centres of Sowerby, Todmorden, and Hebden Bridge in the Calder Valley. In Hebden Bridge indeed, where the local producer co-operative, the Fustian Co-operative Manufacturing Society, provided the basis, Oxford extension became something of a legend as a succession of gifted tutors—Acland, Lang, Hudson Shaw— lectured there in turn. In the winter of 1888–9 some six hundred working people attended Hudson Shaw's lectures there, one in five of the total population of the town. And working-class audiences once captured were great enthusiasts. In 1886 Hudson Shaw taught a course on English History in Ancoats. He drew an audience of over two hundred, 'chiefly artisans, with a small proportion of clerks, board school teachers, and educated persons from other parts of Manchester'. As he reported to Oxford, 'on the occasion of the

[72] M. E. Sadler, *The Development of University Extension* (Philadelphia, 1892), 8–10.
[73] C. R. Ashbee commenting on his class in Newbury. Oxford University Extension Lecturers' and Examiners' Reports, autumn 1893, Oxford University Archives, DES/R/3/16, fo. 423.

lecture on Sir Thomas More and Utopia nearly the whole audience stayed for the class, and were only got rid of at a late hour by summarily turning off the gas'.[74]

Yet only about a quarter of all students attending lectures came from the working class during the late 1880s and 1890s. Sadler estimated that over three thousand, out of a total of thirteen thousand students in 1887–8, were artisans; in 1892–3 'more than five thousand workmen' attended lectures out of over twenty thousand students.[75] One notable attempt to increase working-class participation in university extension was made by Sadler in August 1893: a conference held in Oxford at the Union Society on 'University Extension and Workingmen' which was chaired by Samuel Barnett, the Warden of Toynbee Hall. Sadler moved the resolution that a 'special effort' be made 'to extend University teaching to our workmen' and Hudson Shaw seconded. But the most important speaker was Tom Mann, a member of the Social Democratic Federation, a leader in the London Dock Strike of 1889, first president of the Dockers' Union, and soon to be Secretary of the new Independent Labour Party. Mann welcomed the aspiration to reach out to the working class and rebuked those 'determined to still monopolise knowledge'. Developing an argument that was to dominate discussion of working-class education in the next decade, he pointed out that 'unless there has been an opportunity for the acquisition of the knowledge which can properly discipline and train and make perfect, how can democracy, even when it becomes powerful, be beneficial to the mass of mankind?' His message was conciliatory: he welcomed a new attitude to the working-class movement in Oxford and Cambridge, and concurred with the desire to reach working-class audiences, for 'it is by education England's difficulties will be solved'.[76]

Working-class students were often deterred by the sheer cost of attendance. In most working-class districts in the early years, attendance at a single lecture might cost 6d and a full course of twelve lectures anywhere from 2s 6d to six shillings. These rates could be prohibitive for working-class budgets. In addition, the local organizing committees tended to be dominated by middle-class activists with the leisure for organizational work and their presence alienated working-class students. As Sadler noted as early as 1888, 'working

[74] Oxford University Extension. Lecturers' and Examiners' Reports 1886–7, Oxford University Archives, DES/R/3/1, fo. 56.

[75] *Annual Report 1887–8*, 5; *Annual Report 1892–3*, 5.

[76] Tom Mann, 'Mr. Tom Mann on University Teaching Among Workmen', *The Oxford University Extension Gazette*, 2/1 (Oct. 1892), 5–7. *The Times*, 6 Aug. 1892, p. 7.

men are attracted to the lectures in large numbers only when the arrangements of the courses are practically in the hands of their own societies'.[77] Hudson Shaw concurred: "Nearly all quite successful Working Class Centres, in my experience, have been those financially supported, and entirely organized, by Co-operative Societies and similar institutions, freely open to their own members, paid for out of common funds."[78] And there was always the problem of sheer fatigue to be overcome. As a member of the Independent Labour Party wrote in 1894,

Imagine reader, if you are one who has never had to face these difficulties, a young man who having finished his ten hours of hard physical labour, rushes home from the mill gates at 6 o'clock to get his tea and change his dress in time for the lecture or class at the evening school. He is tired when he leaves the mill, and has a mile to walk home, and another or more to walk to the school. Add to this the difficulties of study at home, and perhaps the cost of a transit fare from some outside village; see him baffled in obtaining the textbook from the library; and can you wonder that the working classes do not take sufficient interest in Extension work?[79]

There was no exaggeration here. Sadler wrote of a man who had 'organised two classes in Lancashire . . . after 12 hours a day as a secretary to a store'.[80] He reported the cases of a coal miner who walked five miles to and from the lecture before beginning work underground at 10pm and of 'one man employed as a mason at a distance (who) walked sixteen miles rather than miss one lecture'.[81] He reproduced in his annual report for 1887 a letter sent to one of the local centres from a student who had attended two previous courses and sat examinations for one of them:

I came out of work the week Mr Shaw gave his last lecture: by careful management I was able to scrape together threepence per week for Mr Mallett's lectures. I have now no money, and my purpose in writing to you is to enquire if it is possible for you to let me have a ticket for Mr Mackinder's course, and I will pay you as soon as I succeed in obtaining work. I should very much like to attend this course, and writing to ask for a ticket is the only way of my being able to do so.[82]

Those workers and artisans who did attend tended to come from the skilled, organized, upper reaches of their class. As one local

[77] *Annual Report 1887–8*, 15.
[78] Hudson Shaw, 'University Extension Movement', fo. 3.
[79] 'A Member of the Independent Labour Party', 'What the Workman Needs in Education', *Oxford University Extension Gazette*, 5/51 (Dec. 1894), 26.
[80] Sadler to Hudson Shaw, quoted in Grier, *Achievement in Education*, 9–10.
[81] *Annual Report 1885–6*, 10; *Annual Report 1886–7*, 11.
[82] *Annual Report 1886–7*, 11.

organizer expressed it in 1887, 'university extension has as yet only been brought to bear upon the cream of the working classes'.[83] In social background many working-class extension students were rather like the educated, skilled workers and clerks attracted by the ethical socialism of the ILP. 'The literate, politicised worker, or lower-middle-class individual' was not only 'the natural material of the ILP's socialism' as Carl Levy has described, but was naturally attracted also to extension.[84]

Sheila Rowbotham has tried to understand this marginal group in a brilliant evocation of the social and intellectual background of working-class extension students which has considerable implications for the history of the relationship between intellectuals and the working class in Britain. She argues against stereotyping working-class responses, and against seeing their reactions to university extension in simple political and class terms. She provides an emotional portrait of the feelings and beliefs of working men caught up by extension and, through it, given a glimpse of a higher world of learning and thought that often made an uncomfortable contrast with the emotional and intellectual deprivation of the working-class communities from which they came. It is a great strength of Rowbotham's approach that though writing about a class, she nevertheless understands university extension as having profound individual as well as collective impact. She recognizes that in this period university extension 'never came near to a significant penetration of the corporate fastnesses of the working class, but it acted on individual students with a remarkable intensity'.[85]

Rowbotham argues that many sensitive and intelligent students from working-class communities were experiencing the same intellectual and personal upheavals that sent young tutors out from Oxford: that in a very real sense, students and tutors shared a common intellectual perspective. This was clear in matters of religion, where the religious doubt of the dons met 'a corresponding need among workers who might be influenced by free-thought arguments but who were unable emotionally to accept what appeared to be the bleak world of secularism'.[86] Toynbee had noted some years

---

[83] *Report of a Conference in the Examination Schools, Oxford of Representatives of the Local Committees Acting in Concert with the Committee of Delegates of Local Examinations appointed to Establish Lectures and Teaching in Large Towns and of Others Interested in the Extension of University Teaching on April 20 and 21 1887* (Oxford, 1887), 59.

[84] Carl Levy, 'Education and Self-Education: Staffing the Early ILP', in id. (ed.), *Socialism and the Intelligentsia 1880–1914* (London, 1987), 190.

[85] Rowbotham, ' "Travellers" ', 73.   [86] Ibid. 73.

before this, 'an immense spiritual destitution . . . amongst that large body of educated men and women who have parted from the old theology, and yet retain a religious attitude towards life and the world'.[87] For many autodidacts, the void was filled by the imperative to learn and the ethical message of that learning. At the very least, both students and tutors shared a similar quest for something that might remove them all from that 'spiritual destitution'.

In addition, the philosophical idealism that many Oxford tutors carried with them in this period was met by a similar idealism among worker scholars who sought spiritual transcendence through education. Extension helped unlock myriad individual yearnings for the higher life: as Cosmo Lang wrote of his experience of lecturing, 'there was then such a real, often pathetic desire in the breasts of these working men to learn, to reach out to a wider life'.[88] When Tom Mann spoke in Oxford in 1893 he called for the spread of learning among the working class to 'enable those workers to live higher and nobler lives', for they sought nothing less than 'the perfection of human character'.[89] As the *Oldham Industrial Co-operative Record* noted of Hudson Shaw in 1913, he 'carried his audiences from the material to the higher things of life'.[90] They were easily led: according to Robert Halstead, a noted co-operator and extensionist from Hebden Bridge, 'Fortunately for the poor, the highest pleasures of life are not inseparably connected with material possessions. Wealth of intellect has other laws of distribution than material riches, and those who are poor in worldly goods need not succumb to the greater curse of poverty of ideas.'[91] A generation later, the founder of the Workers' Educational Association, Albert Mansbridge, could assert that 'There are miners and factory hands in the North who don't care twopence about increasing their wages or living in bigger houses or wearing finer clothes, but who can discuss Greek history with men like Alfred Zimmern, Greek poetry with men like Gilbert Murray and Greek philosophy with men like W. H. Hadow.'[92] One such was 'a Manchester Socialist', a student in adult education, who was interviewed in 1918. He was

[87] Toynbee quoted in Benjamin Jowett, 'Memoir', in Arnold Toynbee, *Lectures on the Industrial Revolution in England* (London, 1884), p. xxiii.

[88] Lockhart, *Lang*, 48.

[89] Mann, 'Mr Tom Mann on University Teaching', 5, 7.

[90] *Oldham Industrial Co-operative Record*, 11/19 (July 1913), 223, quoted in Rowbotham, ' "Travellers" ', 72.

[91] Robert Halstead, 'Working men and University Extension', *Oxford University Extension Gazette*, 3/32 (May 1893), 109.

[92] Albert Mansbridge quoted in Harold Begbie, *Living Water: Being Chapters from the Romance of the Poor Student* (London, 1918), 187.

Dead against materialism . . . I want to live in my spirit. I want to feel more, and to see more deeply into the truth of things. I want to enjoy my spiritual life. Take away the life of the soul—take away the books, the music, and the plays, and I don't want to live . . . The Socialism of the future is not an economic revolution; it's not the Marxian idea; it's the movement of man's soul towards a more enjoyable existence through and for his reason.[93]

Many working men rejected utilitarian conceptions of education; others went further and subscribed to this wholesale idealism. For such people the appeal of Oxford was obvious: as an article in the *New Statesman* on 'The Place of Oxford in a Democracy' noted later, the adult education movement had been 'marked by a generous, even fervent, appreciation of certain things in university education which have been regarded as characteristic of the older universities'.[94] And idealism did not necessarily compromise their political radicalism. As a miner from Castleford explained, 'I became an enthusiastic member of the [Workers' Educational] Association, losing none of my socialism, but seeing for the first time in my life that the basis of human existence is spiritual'.[95]

As Jonathan Rée has pointed out, for many, their recognition that they came from an impoverished culture that had been deprived of contact with the intellectual life of the nation was a powerful argument in favour of socialism. Indeed, for many worker scholars, self-cultivation was itself a political act, for only the educated could hope to challenge for a redistribution of resources and power. Many also held to the view 'that education makes socialists, because the inadequacy of all non-socialist social fabrics will be evident to any truly educated mind': that education, a good in itself for each individual, would also lead, inevitably, to collective political change because an educated nation could not fail to appreciate and respond to the case for socialism.[96] Such views were held at this time and grew in importance in the next generation with the foundation of the Workers' Educational Association. But the more common response of workers involved in university extension was an individualized one, a complex desire to gain insight and purpose through education, though one that was sometimes inflected with ambivalence towards the institutions and individuals who offered them spiritual liberation.

[93] Ibid. 111.

[94] 'The Place of Oxford in a Democracy', *New Statesman*, 6 Sept. 1913, p. 682.

[95] Begbie, *Living Water*, 136.

[96] Jonathan Rée, 'Socialism and the Educated Working Class', in Levy (ed.), *Socialism and the Intelligentsia*, 211–14.

Rowbotham thus presents evidence and analysis that together amount to a powerful case against a type of crude political interpretation of adult and workers' education. University extension should not be written off as intrinsically bourgeois, as another of the many seductions by which working-class élites were incorporated and disarmed in the mid- and late-nineteenth century. Such arguments are at best insufficient, and in a very real sense, beside the point. It is the burden of Rowbotham's argument that working-class students did not respond to university extension as either militants or collaborators. They responded personally and spiritually, rather than politically, and frequently retained their radicalism even while enjoying Oxford's warm embrace.

The example of one Oxford extension stalwart, the slightly comical but also deeply sympathetic figure of Reuben George may help make this point. George, born in Gloucester in 1864, was a member of the Social Democratic Federation, Labour candidate for Chippenham in the general election of 1918 and the first Labour Mayor of Swindon in 1921. He had a rudimentary education, paying little attention at elementary school, was marked down as 'slow', and was apprenticed at the Gloucester Carriage and Wagon Company until he lost the use of his right hand in an accident when aged twenty-three. He moved to Swindon and took up a job as an insurance agent.[97] At the beginning of the century he had broken with the Liberal Party when he lost confidence in its will to remove 'the wrongs done to mankind' and he helped found the Swindon branch of the SDF. He also broke with the Methodism of his youth: the churches were not doing enough to fight poverty and degradation and they had given support to the Boer War. A pacifist, he attended the occasional Quaker Meeting thereafter.[98] At about the same time he felt 'a yearning for education' and began attending Oxford extension lectures, among them a course delivered by Hudson Shaw at the Swindon Mechanics' Institute in the winter of 1906–7. They were 'my beginning of a new life. It was wonderful what they did for me. I began to feel my own soul within me. I began to see life as I had never seen it before.'[99]

At the end of Hudson Shaw's course he came third in an essay

[97] See Begbie, *Living Water*, ch. 1, 'The Saint Maker'. This presents Reuben George's own account of his life and educational progress.

[98] Reuben George, 'To the Comrades of the WEA', in William Davidson, *Reuben and I* (Swindon, 1922), Reference Library, Central Library, Swindon, Wilts; Nigel J. Gratton, 'Reuben George and the WEA in Swindon', unpublished paper, Swindon Reference Library, L911 (92) GRA (1973), 10.

[99] Begbie, *Living Water*, 26.

competition and won a scholarship to attend the 1907 Oxford Summer Meeting which brought extension students to the university for a brief period of study in residence.[100] He arrived 'uneducated but longing for education'. It was both inspiring and overwhelming: 'Oxford is the greatest spiritual experience of my life. It gave me hope. It showed me the way to a higher life, a newer life, a fuller life.' It was, by his own admission, his formative experience. 'For a man like me . . . to find himself in a place like Oxford, with a lot of other working-men, listening to lectures, and talking over the lectures together afterwards, why, this means hope, and encouragement, and happiness.'[101] Late in his life he recalled 'how we wandered around those old colleges . . . How we met night after night around those majestic pieces of architecture.'[102] He joined the new Workers' Educational Association while in Oxford, returned to help form a branch of it in Swindon in the following year, and, thereafter, took his family on an annual pilgrimage to the alternate Summer Meetings in Oxford and Cambridge. He came to know many of the leading figures in adult education over the next three decades, inviting many of them to speak in Swindon. When Mansbridge visited the town in 1910, he found Reuben George 'full of enthusiasm for the work—bursting to accomplish it. Of such men are movements made.'[103] His open, generous, and childlike manner made him something of a celebrity in the movement in his own right.

Reuben George's account of himself is a heady mixture of idealism and quasi-religious enthusiasm, marked by an almost mystical faith in the powers of education. And at the heart of it lies Oxford. 'I've never wiped Oxford off me. I've got her all round me to this moment. I feel that she is my University, that I've taken a degree there, and that she will be my Alma Mater to the end of my days.'[104] Was this an acute case of false consciousness? Was a humble working man sent spinning by the brief joy of being accepted into the national culture, by the sheer beauty of Oxford, and the kind remarks of the dons? George himself provided the answer. Contact with the university made him, he contended, 'a better Socialist then ever I was before'. In the Social Democratic Federation he had been 'a class socialist talking nonsense'; under the influence of Oxford and the WEA he discovered 'the socialism of man's soul'. He put

[100] Gratton, 'Reuben George', 1.   [101] Begbie, *Living Water*, 27–8.

[102] Reuben George, *'The Path We Trod': Twenty-five Years' Comradeship with the WEA*, repr. from *Swindon Advertiser*, 31 Mar. 1933, Wiltshire Pamphlet No. 103, Swindon Reference Library (Swindon, 1933), 2.

[103] Albert Mansbridge, Journal, 15 Sept. 1910, Mansbridge Papers, British Library, xcvii, Add. Ms. 65292.   [104] Begbie, *Living Water*, 34.

down the newspapers and 'went to the poets for [his] ideas', or more precisely, to Ruskin, William Morris, Shelley, and Blake among others. But there was no diminution of radicalism—'I'd socialise land, shipping, railways, insurance and drink. I'd have municipal theatres, and markets, and trams and lighting.'[105] When he stood for Parliament it was under the slogan 'Down with all that's Up'. And when he became Mayor of Swindon 'he refused to hold the customary service of inauguration at the Parish Church. Instead he had a public meeting at the Swimming Baths to which the Archdeacon was invited as preacher.'[106]

Reuben George was 'something of an eccentric, of great integrity, eventually becoming a local institution in his own right'.[107] A certain degree of caution is required in making any firm generalizations on the basis of his example, therefore. But he does suggest the emotional appeal of extension, and fits exactly into the mould of the early ethical socialists who were attracted to the creed by the promise of 'the new life' it offered, and who believed that socialism would come through education rather than party machines and the ballot box.[108] For them, and for Reuben George, socialism was spiritual rather than material. Reuben George also reminds us that generations of working people did not reject the high culture of the universities; rather, they sought to open and democratize them so that they and their children could have access to that culture as well.

IV

What of the other great constituency of university extension, women? Sadler estimated in 1889 that two-thirds of the students attending Oxford lectures were women.[109] Marriott reflected on the important role that extension played in providing 'a whole generation of women' with a 'liberal training in citizenship' before they won the suffrage in 1918.[110] And Hudson Shaw could say in 1892 that 'if we have done the least thing to help on one of the great modern revolutions

---

[105] Ibid. 29–30.

[106] Gratton, 'Reuben George', 35; 'Reuben George is Dead', repr. from *Swindon Evening Advertiser*, 5 June 1936, Wiltshire Pamphlet No. 8, Swindon Reference Library (Swindon, 1936).

[107] Letter from Mr Trevor Cockbill, Swindon, 7 Feb. 1989.

[108] See Stephen Yeo, 'A New Life: The Religion of Socialism in Britain 1883–1896', *History Workshop Journal* 4 (Autumn 1977), 5–56.

[109] *Annual Report 1889–90.*   [110] J. Marriott, *Memories*, 116.

which the historian of the future will notice, the higher education of the women of England, we have no cause to be ashamed to look our enemies in the face'.[111] University extension was, without doubt, a powerful stimulus to women's education, but, ironically, this singular success for the movement was not appreciated in quite those terms at the time. Stuart, Jowett, and Green had all recognized that extension would be of great assistance to women's higher education but their efforts, and the efforts of those who followed them, tended to be directed at working men. While these efforts were only partially successful before the Edwardian period, extension lectures offered many middle-class women almost their only contact with education beyond the secondary level, and in consequence women came to use the new movement in greater numbers than any other social group and frequently displayed the greatest personal application. As Oxford's first woman lecturer explained, 'A new audience arose out of the middle-class. Women, for whom there were no provincial universities or "higher education" available, created a demand for University Extension lectures. They did not conflict with the working-class demand for women were generally free in the afternoon and men in the evening. They exceeded the working-class constituency in the end.'[112] Almost without seeking them, university adult education found its core constituency; the pattern laid down at the very beginning of the movement, with women predominating, has persisted to the present day.

Again an example may make the point most conclusively, and it is a well-known example: the education of the young Vera Brittain, author of the memoir *Testament of Youth*, which summed the experiences of the generation that came to maturity at the time of the First World War. For the young Vera made her escape from 'provincial young-ladyhood' in Buxton in 1913 as a result of attending a course of lectures delivered by John Marriott in the Buxton Town Hall on the subject of 'Problems of Wealth and Poverty'.[113]

In 1913 Vera Brittain was 'trammelled and trapped' by the 'mean, censorious spirit' of provincialism, an intelligent girl with 'nothing to do and no one to talk to' and desperate to get away—in fact, to go to Oxford like her brother. But her parents were opposed to the scheme until the unlikely intervention of the Secretary of the

---

[111] *The English Universities and the English People. Report of a Conference on the Extension of University Teaching Among Workmen*, Oxford, 3 Aug. 1892 (Oxford, 1892), 14–15.

[112] A. Maude Royden, 'Bid Me Discourse', draft MS of unpub. autobiog., Royden Papers, Box 224, fos. 32–3.

[113] Vera Brittain, *Testament of Youth* (London, 1933), 50–63.

Oxford Delegacy. At Buxton, Marriott apparently 'gave of his vigorous and popular best, but a prophet from heaven could not have impressed his listless and dwindling audience'. This was, Vera wrote in her diary, 'unintellectual Buxton all over'.[114] But she, at least, persevered (though she had missed the first lecture to go to a dance), attending the lectures and classes and dutifully writing essays on 'the Industrial Revolution, the Problem of Distribution, the History of Trade Unionism and the Rise of the Socialist Movement'. They were well received. When Marriott returned her first essay, he told her it was 'an excellent piece of work' while she tried to appear 'as indifferent as I could manage though the inward elation was at bursting point'.[115] On the occasion of Marriott's final lecture, Vera's parents were asked to put him up for the night. According to Vera's diary he 'arrived at five with golf clubs which he very sensibly takes round with him, & which put Daddy off when looking for him on the station, as he "never expected a professor to carry golf clubs!"'.[116] Later that evening, at home after the lecture, Vera spoke openly in front of her parents of her 'longing to go to Oxford' and she 'asked [Marriott's] advice with regard to the first steps to be taken. The genial matter-of-factness with which he gave it seemed to dispel all doubts, and made the customary objections look so trivial that they were hardly ever mentioned again.'[117]

There were many towns like Buxton where extension lecturers found themselves struggling to interest and hold an audience. And there were probably many young women like Vera Brittain for whom Oxford extension offered a lifeline out of social and sexual stereotyping. At the least, such women could hope for some contact through the extension movement, however tenuous, with a wider world of ideas—for a brief escape from the constraints of 'provincial young-ladyhood'. In Vera's case the escape was total: she did go to Oxford to study. And several years later, in 1926, she actually gave a course of extension lectures herself for the Oxford Delegacy on 'Ideals of World Unity' which seems entirely appropriate given the nature of the experiences narrated in her *Testament*.[118] Her account of these events in her life ends with the realization that for Marriott, travelling around the country lecturing and looking out

[114] Vera Brittain, *Chronicle of Youth: Vera Brittain's War Diary 1913–1917*, ed. A. Bishop (London, 1981), 28 (entry for 22 Jan. 1913).
[115] Ibid., 29 (5 Feb. 1913). [116] Ibid., 32 (19 Mar. 1913).
[117] Brittain, *Testament*, 63.
[118] The course was at Westgate-on-Sea and ran from October to December 1926. For Vera Brittain's report on the class, see DES/R/3/56, Oxford University Archives.

for a round of golf, the incidents would soon fade from memory: 'I do not suppose that he ever thought again of our household, or realised in the least how completely his flying visit had altered the atmosphere.'[119]

Another woman whose life was altered by extension was Maude Royden. There had been female extension lecturers in London since 1885 and on the Cambridge circuit since 1893.[120] But when Maude Royden gave her initial extension lecture on 'Shakespeare's Women' at Chester in January 1904 it was the first delivered by a woman at an Oxford centre.[121] Born in 1876, and the youngest of eight children of a Conservative MP and shipowner, she read Modern History at Lady Margaret Hall. After graduating, she worked in the Victoria Women's Settlement in Liverpool, and it was here that her 'point of view began ultimately to change, and with it ultimately my politics'.[122] She came to the attention of Hudson Shaw in 1901 when she was experiencing acute religious turmoil and considering conversion to Roman Catholicism. He persuaded her to remain an Anglican, she became his parish worker, and the two began a long, platonic love affair.[123] Later, Miss Royden was to attain celebrity as a leading suffragist speaker, a preacher, and a pacifist between the two world wars, and one of the first women to campaign for the ordination of women in the Church of England.

Hudson Shaw encouraged her to become an extension lecturer, and bullied the Delegacy into giving her a trial lecture at the 1903 Summer Meeting in Oxford.[124] Her success there led to the formal offer of a lectureship by the Delegacy. But that in itself did not guarantee an invitation from a lecture centre. There were many trivial objections to women lecturers that could be refuted or ignored—that it was inappropriate for a lady or too demanding physically. Far more obstructive was the attitude of many local centres

[119] Brittain, *Testament*, 63.

[120] On London see John Burrows, *University Adult Education in London: A Century of Achievement* (London, 1976), 17. On Cambridge see Kadish, 'The Teaching of Political Economy', 82 n.

[121] Oxford University Extension. Lecturers' and Examiners' Reports 1903–4, Oxford University Archives, DES/R/3/32, fos. 745–50.

[122] Maude Royden, 'A. Maude Royden C. H., D. D.', in Margot Asquith (ed.), *Myself When Young: By Famous Women of To-Day* (London, 1938), 379. See Fletcher, *Maude Royden, passim*.

[123] Her account of the affair can be found in Royden, *Threefold Cord*. Maude Royden married Hudson Shaw, becoming his third wife, in the last weeks of his life.

[124] W. Hudson Shaw, 'A. Maude Royden 1901–1920', *The International Woman Suffrage News* 14/8 (May–June 1920), 130; Royden, 'A. Maude Royden', 377.

(and many women in them) who did not want a female lecturer.[125]
When one local secretary reported on a course of lectures Maude
Royden gave in East Grinstead in 1905, among several reasons
given to explain the poor attendance was 'a strong prejudice against
a woman lecturer'.[126] Miss Royden did manage to establish herself,
and from 1904 to 1910 she was a fixture on the Oxford extension
list, after which she devoted her energies and platform abilities to
the cause of women's suffrage, serving on the executive committee
of the National Union of Women's Suffrage Societies from 1910
and editing its journal, *The Common Cause*. She lectured with success
in genteel county towns and in industrial centres like Preston,
Rochdale, and Bury, usually on Shakespeare.[127] But her sex dogged
her. By 1905 she was due promotion to a higher grade, and thus
entitled to higher fees. But this would make her more expensive to
engage by local centres and only compound her undesirability in
some eyes. Thus Marriott wrote to her to advise her to pass up
promotion:

I think you know how exceedingly anxious I am to obtain employment for
women Lecturers and I am quite sure it is very much to the advantage of
our work to have such Lecturers as yourself upon the Staff, but do what
I will, I seem quite unable to overcome the prejudice which exists in the
vast majority of Extension centres against the engagement of a woman
Lecturer. I am afraid it is true that *certeris paribus* there is hardly a centre
which would accept a woman in preference to a man.[128]

Maude Royden rejected the advice, took her promotion, and her
career as a lecturer flourished. As might be expected, she was a
partisan for women's involvement in extension, whether as students
or teachers. She took heart from the development of the Workers'
Education Association after 1903 and encouraged it to promote the
education of women.[129] She suspected, correctly, that though it gave
rhetorical support to this aspect of the women's cause, its primary
focus was on the education of male workers.[130] And she found that

---

[125] Fletcher, *Maude Royden*, 69–70.
[126] Oxford University Extension. Lecturers' and Examiners' Reports 1904–5,
Oxford University Archives DES/R/3/33, fo. 715.
[127] For reports on her lectures see Oxford University Archives, DES/R/3/32–39.
[128] J. A. R. Marriott to A. M. Royden, 6 Nov. 1905. Secretary's Letter Book,
Oxford University Archives, DES/C/1/1/57, fos. 1–2, cited in Fletcher, *Maude
Royden*, 81.
[129] Maude Royden, 'Women's Work in Education', *The Highway*, 1/1 (Oct.
1908), 4–5 and 'A Chance for Women', ibid., 1/3 (Dec. 1908), 46–7.
[130] See Maude Royden, 'Equality of Opportunity', *The Highway*, 1/4 (Jan. 1909),
62.

the new movement paid little attention to women's suffrage at a time when a majority of working-class men still lacked the vote.[131] Nevertheless, she taught a WEA tutorial class on Shakespeare at Oldham to a group of women cotton spinners. As she recalled,

Owing to the necessity of earning a grant from the education authority, each class had to last two hours. Remembering that my students had been at work all day in the mills and that being mostly married women, they had many other duties as well, I wondered how on earth I was to hold their interest for such a long time, late in the evening. I need not have troubled myself. They not only stayed the course but, at the close of each class, accompanied me down the street to the railway station still arguing and discussing, stood on the platform while I, my head out of the carriage window, continued the class, and made their last contributions to the discussion in shouts above the roar of the train as it pulled out of the station. Can you beat it?[132]

For Maude Royden, as for Vera Brittain, university extension was a conduit to other things. She had fallen into it as a consequence of her involvement with Hudson Shaw rather than chosen it as a vocation. But her deep religiosity and sense of social duty, which had taken her into settlement work after Oxford, were equally well suited to university extension. Her experience in it shows that a movement largely made up of women was not necessarily one designed for them. But lecturing supplied her with a training in speaking and teaching, and so assisted her development into a highly influential Christian, pacifist, and feminist, which brought her fame at the time and gives her the status of a pioneer and role model today. And her success as an Oxford lecturer broke down another barrier—albeit a small one—to women in public life.

v

Vera Brittain went up to Somerville College to read English in 1915. But before that, in 1913, on the basis of her work for Marriott, she won a prize scholarship to attend the Oxford Summer Meeting of that year. No account of university extension would be complete without mention of the Summer Meetings which brought hundreds of extension students to Oxford during the summer vacation, not least because the majority of those who came were women. The idea of bringing groups of extension students to the university to continue and deepen their studies was first tried in a small way in

---

[131] Fletcher, *Maude Royden*, 83.   [132] Royden, 'Bid Me Discourse', fo. 34.

Cambridge in 1884 and 1885 when a handful of working-class students, predominantly Northumberland miners, came for a period of residence in the summer.[133] The first large-scale Summer Meeting, however, was held in Oxford in early August 1888, some nine hundred students attending. Short lecture courses were offered in the mornings, and the evenings were devoted to addresses on literary or scientific subjects. Students took lodgings in the city or secured accommodation in Keble College and the three new women's colleges, Somerville, Lady Margaret Hall and St Hugh's. The Meeting was thrown open to all extension students, whether educated under the auspices of London, Cambridge, or Oxford, and the enthusiasm generated led to the foundation of many new extension centres around the country. As the *Oxford Magazine* reported after the event, 'it would be idle . . . to look for thorough or continuous teaching from so short a residence. But this, we take it, was not the main end in view. The aim of the projectors was rather to arouse interest and to indicate lines of study than to attempt systematic instruction on a large scale.'[134]

In its Oxford form, the Summer Meeting was derived from an American example, the 'chautauqua'. As Sadler later put it, 'the idea of taking the University to the people is English, that of bringing the people together into a vacation university is American'.[135] Chautauqua, a small town beside the lake of the same name in western New York state, was, from 1874, a centre for the education of Methodist ministers, teachers, and church workers. Summer meetings at the Chautauqua Institute, initially on religious subjects, gradually broadened to include a more general curriculum of secular subjects and were then supplemented by correspondence courses during the rest of the year, and so-called home reading. Under the direction of William Rainey Harper, who, when later appointed President of the University of Chicago, helped institutionalize university extension in the United States, the Chautauqua prospered, and other 'chautauquas' were established throughout the country. Indeed, 'chautauqua' became synonymous with 'summer school' in late nineteenth-century America. In England in 1887 a small committee was formed, including among its members Michael Sadler, to organize a 'home reading circle' as pioneered by the original Chautauqua. It was at one of their meetings that the idea of a summer school at an English university was first suggested, apparently

[133] Edwin Welch, *The Peripatetic University: Cambridge Local Lectures 1873–1973* (Cambridge, 1973), 115.
[134] 'University Extension Summer Meeting', *Oxford Magazine*, 17 Oct. 1888, p. 14.   [135] Mackinder and Sadler, *University Extension*, 37.

by Charles Rowley, and Sadler acted upon it with the support of Jowett in the latter's capacity as Vice-Chancellor.[136]

The success of the first Meeting in 1888 was repeated in the following years. In 1889 over a thousand students attended and many stayed on after the Meeting was over for a period of three weeks' supervised private study in Oxford, a division into two parts that became a permanent feature. From 1893 onwards Oxford and Cambridge Summer Meetings were held in alternate years, giving students an opportunity of residing for a short time in each university and hearing the distinguished scholars of the day. The Summer Meetings helped emphasize the unity of the movement, binding together the isolated provincial extension centres. As Sadler explained, 'The local centres do the preparatory work and furnish the constituency for our Summer Meetings; the Summer Meetings in turn have drawn the isolated centres together, have imparted esprit de corps to the students, and have demonstrated the national character of the movement'.[137] In 1888 lecturers included James Murray, the first editor of the *Oxford English Dictionary*, and a famous autodidact himself, and Frederic Harrison, the Positivist and a reminder of an earlier attempt to link Oxford with the new democracy. Murray lectured again two years later, as did Sir Arthur Evans, the archaeologist, and the sociologist, Patrick Geddes. After 1900, lecturers included Asquith, Lloyd George, Sidney Webb, Ramsay MacDonald, and William Beveridge. In time the Meetings came to focus on a theme or subject—a period of history or a particular national culture—that was examined in detail over the ten days of the Meeting in a series of lectures and classes generally held in the Examination Schools. The sheer audacity of the scheme caused scepticism, even contempt. The Summer Meeting became the butt of several comic versifiers in the University.[138] *The Times* described the 1890 Meeting as 'a period of feverish appetite, during which, we fear, a good deal more mental provender is bolted than can possibly be digested'.[139] Yet according to Marriott, as the years went by he was 'embarrassed less by the reluctance of resident teachers to

---

[136] Charles Rowley, *Fifty Years of Work Without Wages* (London, 1912), 215–6; Thomas Kelly, *A History of Adult Education in Great Britain*, 3rd edn. (Liverpool, 1992; first pub. 1970), 228.

[137] Mackinder and Sadler, *University Extension*, 37.

[138] As A. D. Godley of Magdalen College observed in 1888, 'For every train imports a throng/Of sisters, cousins, aunts and nieces,/Who crowd the streets, who storm the Schools,/With love of lectures still unsated.' Quoted in Stuart Marriott, 'Extensionalia: The Fugitive Literature of early Adult Education', *Studies in Adult Education*, 10/1 (Apr. 1978), 52.   [139] *The Times*, 20 Aug. 1890.

lecture at Summer Meetings, than by their eagerness to address the great audiences whom they found more stimulating to themselves and more touchingly eager to absorb knowledge than the average undergraduates'.[140]

Scholarships and bursaries were made available by the Delegacy for students who could not otherwise afford residence in Oxford. In 1890 'among the successful essayists were two carpenters, two clerks, a fustian weaver, an artisan employed in a government dockyard, and three elementary teachers'.[141] Some extension centres raised funds to send up their more deserving students. Other institutions supported their own members: students in 1890 also included working men sponsored by the Central Co-operative Board in Manchester which offered scholarships to its employees and affiliates. As Marriott recalled,

What it meant to an elementary teacher from a country school, or to a Lancashire mill-hand, or a collier from South Wales, to come even for a month under the magic spell of Oxford's beauty, to listen to some of the greatest authorities on history, science, or art, come into daily contact with men and women inspired by similar zeal for higher education, and to exchange ideas with them can be understood only by those who, like myself, were privileged to be their confidants, and to see the leaven visibly working.[142]

The recollection only gains in credibility when we consider the response of Reuben George to this type of contact with Oxford.

Sheila Rowbotham has used the Summer Meetings to demonstrate the peculiar idealism that working-class extensionists brought to the movement. Their reaction to 'the abrupt contrast between the workers' situation and an alternative way of living'—what Carl Levy has termed an 'existential break'—was generally to embrace the University and what it was believed it stood for: learning, culture, the 'higher life'.[143] Their general response to the physical surroundings, the education offered, and the personal freedom they enjoyed for a number of days in Oxford, was one of deep elation. Few were angered by what they saw, or made bitter: for most, in the words of a friend of the leading co-operator and educationalist, Robert Halstead, 'the memory of my visit to Oxford will never die away, it has been one of the chief events of my life'.[144] Rowbotham

---

[140] J. Marriott, *Memories*, 115.   [141] *Annual Report 1889–90*, 2.
[142] Marriott, *Memories*, 106.
[143] Rowbotham, '"Travellers"', 84; Carl Levy, 'Introduction: Historical and Theoretical Themes', in id. (ed.), *Socialism and the Intelligentsia*, 23.
[144] Robert Halstead, 'Impressions of a Summer Meeting', *University Extension Journal*, 5/49 (Oct. 1894), 6.

counsels against cynicism and irony when faced with such testimony; these were the authentic reactions of intelligent and canny working men who were not easily seduced from their roots and beliefs.[145] The Summer Meetings were, without question, important symbols of social solidarity. For a brief period each year the gates of learning were stormed by the underprivileged, and élite institutions could be seen to have recognized wider responsibilities to the community in a literally spectacular fashion. In addition, as dons, middle-class women, and working-class extentionists mixed together, in the words of a Gloucestershire miner who attended the Oxford Meeting in 1892, 'party spirit and class feeling seemed to have melted away, thus beautifully blending us all into one'.[146]

But the Meetings were also important occasions for personal liberation, and the experience of liberation was shared by many who went, ladies as well as working men. Women students also experienced an 'existential break', though it was a break with the constraints of gender and the expectations of home rather than the constraints of class. As Vera Brittain expressed it,

When I did arrive at this Earthly Paradise I was not, strangely enough, in the least disappointed . . . There was a light on my path and a dizzy intoxication in the air; the old buildings in the August sunshine seemed crowned with a golden glory, and I tripped up and down the High Street between St. Hilda's and the Examination Schools on gay feet as airy as my soaring aspirations.[147]

She was particularly fortunate: this was but her introduction to Oxford and higher education. For most students a Summer meeting was a unique, or at best, a brief acquaintance. But it is worth noting that through university extension in this period a handful of students were actually brought to the University to matriculate and take degrees, their talent having been noticed by lecturers on their rounds. Vera Brittain was not, in fact, the first extension student to have found her way to Somerville: much earlier in 1890,

A course of lectures in Zoology recently given by an Oxford lecturer in Devonshire, was attended by a student whose essays convinced the lecturer of her singular powers of accurate and original observation. She was encouraged by the lecturer to undertake a course of systematic study, and at his suggestion became a candidate in the examination for Scholarships at Somerville Hall, where she was elected to the second scholarship.[148]

[145] Rowbotham, ' "Travellers" ', 84.
[146] [Joseph Emes] 'Impressions of a Summer Meeting VIII, By a Gloucestershire Miner', *Oxford University Extension Gazette*, 3/25 (Oct. 1892), 4.
[147] Brittain, *Testament*, 64.   [148] *Annual Report 1889–90*, 2.

The student was Lilian Gould, the daughter of a clergyman, who had been educated at home. The lecturer was E. B. Poulton of Christ Church, and Poulton's wife probably provided the link for she served on the Somerville Council. Miss Gould went on to take a first in Natural Sciences and became Assistant Librarian at the Royal Society.[149]

The story of Joseph Owen, meanwhile, is rather better known. Owen, born in 1871, and 'the son of a working-man co-operator', was a student at some of the extension courses Hudson Shaw gave at Oldham.[150] He had left school at eleven years of age to work half-time as a spinner in a local cotton mill. Hudson Shaw recognized his ability and combined with the Modern History tutor at Balliol, A. L. Smith, to bring Owen and his wife to Oxford.[151] He was coached for Responsions, the university entrance examination which then included compulsory Latin and Greek. Owen passed and was awarded the Brackenbury History Scholarship at Balliol. In 1899 he took a first in Modern History and in the following year was elected a fellow of Pembroke College where he remained until 1908. He then moved on to twenty-five years' service as a member of the schools' inspectorate, specializing in adult education classes. In this Owen set another precedent that many would follow: he not only gained an education from the extension movement but went on to work in the field of adult education himself.[152]

VI

In the generation after 1885, therefore, Oxford extension experienced both successes and failures. The work was established, accomplished tutors were recruited, some of the social aims were met, the university curriculum was expanded and developed, and in terms of crude student numbers, Oxford soon came to surpass the achievements of

[149] I am grateful for the assistance of Joanna Innes and Pauline Adams of Somerville College in identifying Miss Gould.

[150] *Co-operative News*, 7 Dec. 1895, p. 1281.

[151] On Hudson Shaw's role in bringing Owen to Oxford, see Albert Mansbridge to Maude Royden, 26 Jan. 1952 and George Edens to Maude Royden, March 1952, Royden Papers, Box 222.

[152] See H. P. Smith, 'A Note on the Contribution of Balliol to the Making of the Tradition of Extra-Mural Education', uncatalogued MSS, Balliol College, Oxford; 'Adult Students of the University', *Rewley House Papers* (1927), 33; H. P. Smith, 'Adult Students at the University', *Rewley House Papers*, 2/8 (March, 1945), 313; Oxford Extra-Mural Delegacy Annual Report 1957–8, p. 1; *Co-operative News*, 7 Dec. 1895, p. 1281.

Cambridge and London. On the other hand, the group always considered crucial by the movement, the working class, was only reached in certain locations and certain circumstances, and the type of education offered was considered shallow: it might entertain and divert, but only the most disciplined students would really learn from extension. The reality was a long way from the liberal education of working men that Jowett had projected. Because of the failings, it has become customary to dismiss the period and the enterprise: in the view of some, the mid-Victorians may have established the idea of university adult education, but the project was not realized until the Edwardian period and the beginning of the tutorial classes movement. In between, there came a hiatus. The view was encouraged, of course, by those who launched tutorial classes and who wanted to establish a strict demarcation between an academic education for workers and amusement for 'the sealskins'. According to the young G. D. H. Cole, writing in 1912, 'The Extension classes developed into gaping rows of the unoccupied and unemployable middle-class. The unsuccessful husband-hunter and the scholastic blue-stocking took notes assiduously and received prizes and certificates of merit without end; but for education in the wider and truer sense very little was achieved.'[153] It was never as bad as this, but the demarcation was essential if the next generation of adult educators were to establish their credentials with working-class organizations and with the state. Cole's self-conscious and deliberate exaggeration undoubtedly undervalues what was achieved after 1885, and even criticism of a more muted sort is probably untenable if the institutional and financial constraints around university extension are examined. Quite simply, extension did not achieve its aims in the late-Victorian period because it had been forced to adopt the model established by Stuart in the early 1870s.

The essence of the problem was financial. The whole structure depended on local funding and local funding almost alone, leading Hudson Shaw to inveigh against 'our preposterous notions that higher education can ever be self-supporting'.[154] In the five years between 1885 and 1890 local committees managed to raise some £17,800 to fund the work, and the university contributed one tenth of this amount, a further £1,700, to finance the extension office in Oxford. The state contributed nothing.[155] If local committees failed to raise the necessary funds to pay the lecturer's fee and meet all

---

[153] G. D. H. Cole, 'Education and Socialism 12/8/[19]12', G. D. H. Cole Papers, Nuffield College, Oxford, B2/16, fo. 15.

[154] Hudson Shaw, 'University Extension Movement', 3.

[155] Mackinder and Sadler, *University Extension*, 93.

expenses, nothing could be done. The effects were obvious. Few tutors were guaranteed regular work and fewer still were given established positions: retaining them was always difficult, therefore.[156] If the very most that working-class students could be charged for a course of twelve lectures was five shillings, and the average cost of a course was somewhere between £60 and £75, then something in excess of two hundred and fifty tickets had to sold in working-class communities merely to break even.[157]

Sadler discovered immediately 'that the cost of University Lectures is too heavy for the poorer neighbourhoods, which are those where such teaching is most needed'.[158] And this method of funding extension had academic implications also: 'formed without permanent endowment, and acting on at most a temporary guarantee, the Local Committees are bound first to look for courses which will pay their own expenses.'[159] They were bound, in other words, to engage popular tutors with popular subjects: lecture audiences had to be very large to guarantee the funds. Samuel Barnett noted the temptation on the part of local committees 'to offer as lecturers rhetorical teachers who stirred the emotions' rather than the intellect.[160] And to keep up custom it was found necessary to vary the programme each season, so lectures see-sawed between the sciences and arts without system or continuity. As Sadler and Mackinder could see, 'it is want of money which chiefly causes want of educational sequence'.[161] The need to pay the bills at the end of the session made for the shallowness and dilettantism that all decried.

These issues were debated with some vigour at the 1887 conference on extension in Oxford. Hudson Shaw caught the irony of the situation: 'If it is a missionary movement then I take it that the University of Oxford is the first missionary society which ever started forth on its enterprise, and expected the people amongst whom it is to work to pay its expenses . . . The University must make some sacrifice.'[162] But the same arguments that had been raised against Jowett's more substantive schemes of extension in the 1870s were raised again, this time by the Vice-Chancellor and President of St

[156] Annual Report 1885–6, 12; Annual Report 1886–7, 12. Hudson Shaw, 'University Extension Movement', 4.
[157] For an example of the financial constraints that limited the effectiveness of university extension in working class districts, see Alon Kadish, 'University Extension and the Working Classes: The Case of the Northumberland Miners', Historical Research, 60/142 (June 1987), 199.   [158] Annual Report 1885–6, 12.
[159] Annual Report 1887–8, 7.   [160] The Times, 6 Aug. 1892, 7.
[161] Mackinder and Sadler, University Extension, 118.
[162] Report of a Conference in the Examination Schools . . . April 20 and 21 1887, Oxford, 75.

John's, Dr Bellamy—that the university was not wealthy, that even if it was its funds should be spent internally, and that research now had financial priority. 'Our business', he concluded, 'is not to spread learning, but to make learning, and for the funds for spreading it in different towns it is necessary that we should look to others outside.'[163] Acland tried to answer this, asking that the colleges each 'give something like £50 a year' towards extension.[164] And the movement certainly benefited from occasional assistance from colleges, notably Balliol, Christ Church, New College, and All Souls. But the door was closed against any more regular funding from the University.

It was closed against extension by the state, also. For a few years in the early 1890s the so-called whisky money provided a somewhat unlikely source of assistance for extension. At one of those occasional moments in modern British history when governments have become alarmed at the state of skills and applied knowledge among British workers, an excise duty levied on spirits provided funds that the new county councils, recently established, were permitted to use on technical education under the terms of the 1890 Local Taxation Act. Many of them turned to university extension for lecture courses on science and for two or three years Oxford and Cambridge swelled their programmes with relevant courses in many of the counties of England. But the relationship soon declined: the courses were considered expensive, were often at too high a level for the audiences, and the councils came to believe that they could provide a more appropriate service more cheaply for themselves. Several extension lecturers left university service at this point to establish and run local technical education.[165] Thereafter, there was no assistance, either direct or indirect, from central government and only occasional co-operation with local authorities. In 1889 Oxford and Cambridge joined together to form a 'National Committee for Obtaining a Grant-in-aid of University Extension', the said grant to be distributed to the local centres, and the campaign was waged

---

[163] Ibid. 28–9.   [164] Ibid. 45.

[165] See *Report on the Peripatetic Teaching in Scientific and Technical Subjects Carried on in Various County Districts Under the Supervision of the Oxford Delegates for University Extension Acting in Concert with the Technical Instruction Committee of County Councils During the Winter 1891–92* (Oxford, 1892); *Annual Report 1893–4*, 4–5; Welch, *Peripatetic University*, 87–93; Stuart Marriott, 'The Whisky Money and the University Extension Movement: "Golden Opportunity" or "Artificial Stimulus"?', *Journal of Educational Administration and History*, 15 (1983), 7–15.

fitfully until at least the mid-1890s, but without success.[166] As Acland explained to Sadler in 1892, there was little support for state funding when the Universities were doing so little to finance extension themselves:

As to the point you mention involving a State grant (and representation) my feeling has always been that until bodies so wealthy (comparatively) as the colleges make some fairly generous contribution to Women's Educ. and Univ. Exten. (they could easily give £2000 a year between them if they cared to do so to either cause) it is very difficult to get general consent in the House of Commons to a State grant.[167]

Here was the catch: the state would not support extension because the universities would not, and the universities would not because they said they were too poor. It was not until 1924, indeed, that financial assistance was made available for university extension courses by central government.

This merely serves to confirm an earlier conclusion. The form that university extension took from 1873 was not just an unsatisfactory outcome of the process of university reform, as Jowett, Green, and Bryce understood. It also handicapped the movement in practice, limiting its academic achievements and social reach. Acland had tried to circumvent the problems by going directly to working-class institutions and communities, but the approach did not succeed. Sadler then remodelled Oxford extension, but he and his colleagues were immediately and painfully aware that the form of extension they practised militated against the social and educational ends they sought to achieve. Everyone could see the problems, but without funds there was no alternative. The consequence was to force a deviation from the initial and essential aim of Oxford extension—to build an educational and social alliance of dons and workers. From 1885 until the early years of the twentieth century, Oxford extension was locked into a structure of educational provision that made penetration of working-class communities and working-class consciousness much more difficult and contingent.

It is for this reason that we should reject arguments that make a sharp distinction between this phase of university adult education

[166] Mackinder and Sadler, *University Extension*, 127–44. See 'Petition for an Annual Grant by Parliament in aid of University Extension Teaching', in 'Early Papers 1877–97', DES/EP/1/3, fo. 173, Oxford University Archives. The petition called for a central grant of £6,000 annually to subsidize all university extension programmes.

[167] Arthur Acland to M. E. Sadler, Oct. 1892, Sadler Papers 1885–1903, fo. 117.

and the subsequent heroic era, after 1907, when the alliance between universities and the Workers' Educational Association made possible an academic education for working-class students in tutorial classes. It will be shown in the following chapter that the tutorial class evolved out of the extension lecture. Here it is enough to note that the leading figures in university extension recognized the limitations of the education they were providing, projected something very like the tutorial class, and, if they had possessed the means, would have made such classes available to their students. When R. D. Roberts, then Secretary of the London Society for the Extension of University Teaching and later Secretary of the Cambridge Syndicate for Local Lectures, spoke in Oxford in 1887, he called for 'further systematisation of the work', so as to provide a sequential education.

> The Universities must lay down for the students a course of study which will enable them to carry on the work from term to term, each course supplemental to the other, so that at the end of three or four years the students may feel they have gone through a course of study, under the guidance of the University itself, which will give them something which can truly be called a broad education.[168]

Roberts was effectively calling for what became the three-year tutorial class. And two years later Sadler and Mackinder suggested that local committees 'be enabled to supplement their popular courses with others of a tutorial character, more exclusively adapted for small classes of students'.[169] The very terms used tell their own story. This does not diminish the subsequent achievements of Mansbridge, Temple, Tawney, and A. L. Smith who made tutorial classes a reality. Rather, it rehabilitates the reputation of those involved in university extension before them who saw only too well where, how, and why they failed. It brings to mind Jowett's plaint that Oxford would not be able to connect itself to the movement for higher education 'unless by giving some pecuniary assistance'.[170] And it reminds us also of the crucial importance of what was famously called 'the golden stream'—of moderate assistance from the state which made real educational and social achievement possible in the next generation.[171]

[168] *Report of a Conference in the Examination Schools . . . April 20 and 21 1887, Oxford,* 87.   [169] Mackinder and Sadler, *University Extension,* 125.
[170] *University of Oxford Commission 1877: Part I: Minutes of Evidence Taken by the Commissioners,* PP 1881, C. 2868, lvi, 'Evidence of the Rev. Benjamin Jowett, M. A. (Master of Balliol College)'.   [171] See p. 118 below.

4
DONS AND WORKERS 1900–1914

Not the least noteworthy of the developments to strike the future historian of the twentieth century will be . . . the emergence, among the rank and file of the working-class world of the conviction that education may be used as an instrument of social emancipation, and a determination to build up, both through and in addition to the ordinary machinery of public education, an educational movement which is stamped with their own ideals, and the expression of their own experience.[1]

In this way R. H. Tawney explained the developments in workers' education before 1914 in which he, and Oxford, played leading roles. Tawney, writing in 1924, placed emphasis on the determination of workers to build their own educational movement. While this was indeed a crucial determinant of what occurred, the origins of the Workers' Educational Association, its partnership with Oxford and then other British universities, and the development of the tutorial classes movement—the subject of the next two chapters—is a complex story of institutional experimentation and development in which the demand for education from working-class communities was but one of several factors. It is also a story which had considerable implications for the strategy of the British working-class movement at the time, which led to an important debate on the nature of 'workers' education' among the dons and workers involved, and which continues to exercise historians and invite controversy to this day.

The first of several contexts in which to situate the developments after about 1903 is the wider political and social development of the working class itself. The founding of the Labour Representation Committee in 1900, the election of twenty-nine Labour MPs in 1906, and the doubling of trade union membership among British workers from approximately two to four million between 1900 and 1914 were only the most obvious signs of the maturity, growing power, and growing independence of the labour movement in this

---

[1] R. H. Tawney, 'Introduction', in T. W. Price, *The Story of the Workers' Educational Association from 1903 to 1924* (London, 1924), 7–8.

period. Political maturity was not only manifest in the growth of an independent working-class politics; it was also evident in the very nature of working-class communities which, by the end of the nineteenth century, possessed what one historian has called a 'stable and relatively sophisticated' working-class culture.[2] The point was appreciated by the writers of the famous report on *Oxford and Working-Class Education* in 1908 which will figure prominently in this account. As they expressed it,

The genius of English workmen for organization has covered some of the districts of northern England (for example, Lancashire) with a network of institutions, industrial, social, political and religious . . . There are certain towns in which almost every adult appears to a stranger to be connected with half a dozen different associations. It is obvious that the common atmosphere thus created is favourable, like that of an Oxford college, to the dissemination of ideas.[3]

Whether or not the comparison with Oxford was a good one, it was clear to many that this rich associational culture could sustain educational initiatives if of the right sort. As the *1908 Report* (as it was known) went on, 'If a class is formed under the control of members of working-class societies, its influence filters through a hundred different channels, and may leaven a whole town'.[4] As Arthur Greenwood, later deputy leader of the Labour Party, and another of the central figures in workers' education of this period, explained, 'The time was ripe for a development of adult education. A generation of compulsory education had begun to bear fruit, and working class organisations, no longer struggling for mere existence, had become an integral part of the background of working class life.'[5]

It was out of this mature working-class culture at this particular stage that the Workers' Educational Association emerged. As a member of one of the first tutorial classes was to put it much later: 'The more one thinks of the early nineteen hundreds the more strongly one realizes that there was a something "in the air" of which the Association was the culmination and became the rallying

[2] Ross McKibbin, 'Why was there no Marxism in Great Britain?' in id., *The Ideologies of Class: Social Relations in Britain 1880–1950* (Oxford, 1990), 13.

[3] *Oxford and Working-Class Education: Being the Report of a Joint Committee of University and Working-Class Representatives on the Relation of the University to the Higher Education of Workpeople*, 2nd edn. (Oxford, 1909), 58.

[4] Ibid.

[5] Arthur Greenwood, 'Labour and Adult Education', in R. St John Parry (ed.), *Cambridge Essays on Adult Education* (Cambridge, 1920), 120.

point.'[6] Albert Mansbridge, the founder of the WEA, talked of 'the stirring of a vast multitude. Something was happening on all sides of us to the democracy of England. Wherever we went we found this spirit. People were hungry for something. They were reaching out for something.'[7] And Asa Briggs has written more recently of 'a kind of convergence . . . in the early years of the twentieth century' from which the WEA was created.[8] The Association was not just a means of developing working-class interest in higher education and satisfying it, but an organization, with authentic roots in this culture, with which the dons could collaborate. As the history of university extension in the late nineteenth century shows, for Oxford there was always a problem of finding an enthusiastic partner with the loyalty of the working class.

The WEA was founded in May 1903 as the 'Association to Promote the Higher Education of Workingmen': its name was changed two years later at its second annual meeting in Birmingham. Its founder, Albert Mansbridge, was an almost archetypal lower-middle-class scholar who had been involved for some time in the educational activities of the co-operative movement. Born the son of a carpenter in Battersea, he grew up in a family closely involved with the chapel and with co-operation. Mansbridge's own experience illustrated very well the waste of talent in late-Victorian and Edwardian society: though he won a scholarship to Battersea Grammar School he was forced to leave at fourteen because his father would not countenance giving his fourth son the privilege of an education denied to his three elder brothers. Mansbridge eventually became a clerk in the Co-operative Wholesale Society and then, in 1901, a cashier in the Co-operative Permanent Building Society.[9] Here was an almost classic example of one sort of man who had frequented university extension and would be attracted to university tutorial classes after 1908; intelligent, but educationally frustrated, and locked into low-grade white-collar employment.

Mansbridge's three articles in the *University Extension Journal* in early 1903 entitled 'Co-operation, Trade Unionism and University

---

[6] L. V. Gill, 'What can we learn from History?', *The Highway*, 40 (Oct. 1949), 257.

[7] Harold Begbie, *Living Water: Being Chapters from the Romance of the Poor Student* (London, 1918), 182.

[8] Asa Briggs, 'Sixty-Four Years of the WEA', *Workers Education*, 1 (spring/summer 1987), 9.

[9] Bernard Jennings, *Albert Mansbridge and English Adult Education* (Hull, 1976), 3–7.

Extension', set out the terms of a tripartite alliance of these groups.[10] He projected 'an Association, the chief function of which will be to make ready and prepare the Democratic Mind for the ordinary operations of University Extension'.[11] He combined 'evangelical zeal and diplomatic skill' and was able to win the support of the dons for this project without losing the confidence of the working-class movement behind him.[12] It helped that even before he founded his association he was relatively well connected and, as an energetic and deeply religious co-operator, had come to the attention of powerful patrons like Charles Gore, later Bishop of Birmingham. Pre-eminently, he spoke the language of educational idealism which we have already encountered, and which, it has been argued, was an authentic development within the working-class and co-operative movement just as it was, in a different way, in late-Victorian Oxford. The WEA was a product of this spirit. In his first article in 1903 Mansbridge noted that

The appeal of the hour to Trade Unionists and Cooperators is that they make political strokes, promote Bills, register protests, and send deputations to responsible Ministers. The true appeal is that they lift themselves up through higher knowledge to higher works and higher pleasures, which, if responded to, will inevitably bring about right and sound action upon Municipal, National and Imperial affairs.[13]

Later, Mansbridge described 'the old, original faith' of the Association: 'that man is destined, if he would live aright, to develop his mind and body in the power of the spirit, not because it will serve some specific purpose, but because it is the law of his being.'[14] Education was 'spiritual food'.[15] It would lead its votaries 'to the beautiful and the true, where alone citizenship can be realised'.[16] To one contemporary German observer, Werner Picht, Mansbridge 'lays hold of the education question which he identifies with the question of spiritual life, with religious intensity'. This spirituality was especially attractive to the working class élite: 'The WEA is to be understood as the concentrated expression of the endeavour of the English

---

[10] Albert Mansbridge, 'Co-operation, Trade Unionism and University Extension', *University Extension Journal*, 8 (Jan., Mar., Apr. 1903), 53, 85, 118.
[11] Ibid. 118.
[12] Bernard Jennings, 'The Making of the Oxford Report', in Sylvia Harrop (ed.), *Oxford and Working-Class Education*, rev. 2nd edn. (Nottingham, 1987), 26.
[13] Mansbridge, 'Co-operation', 53.
[14] Albert Mansbridge, 'The Beginning of the WEA', *The Highway*, 16/3 (summer 1924), 135.
[15] Harold Begbie, *Living Water*, 187.   [16] Mansbridge, 'Co-operation', 53.

working-class after an intensified spiritual life.' The organization was 'on the way to open the doors of the spiritual world to the intellectual upper stratum of the working-class whose destiny is of decisive importance'.[17] This idealism made Mansbridge's message, and collaboration with him, especially attractive to Oxford. And there is no doubt that he revelled in the attention he received from the great and good, though there is no doubt also, that he was utterly sincere in his convictions and motives. But if he was, in one sense, archetypal of the adult education movement, this clerk with only limited experience of the working class, more lay-preacher than anything else, represented also the new tensions in it. Could the WEA be at one and the same time an agent of spiritual emancipation and an agent of political and social liberation? As Bernard Jennings has suggested, Mansbridge promoted both simultaneously; education was necessary for emancipation, but it was also an emancipation in itself.[18] This may have satisfied one type of student and working-class activist for whom education meant self-development; but the duality was not to all tastes, especially now that workers' education, in the context of a growing and more militant labour movement, was drawing in a new type of class-conscious scholar. The early history of the WEA and the subsequent institutional and ideological division in workers' education after 1909 was to demonstrate a continuous tension between 'cultural purists' and those for whom education was subservient to wider social ends.[19]

The Workers' Educational Association was founded in Oxford at a conference held on 22 August 1903, and 'attended by a large gathering of representatives of co-operative societies, trade unions, and university bodies'.[20] In addition to these, it also depended upon a variety of religious groups, 'particularly adult schools and educational societies attached to churches and chapels'.[21] It rapidly developed into a loose federation of different working-class institutions and individuals. By 1912 it had 110 local branches, 1,879 affiliated

[17] Werner Picht, *Toynbee Hall and the English Settlement Movement*, trans. L. A. Cowell (London, 1914), 182, 186, 205.
[18] Bernard Jennings, *New Lamps for Old? University Adult Education in Retrospect and Prospect* (Hull, 1976), 10.
[19] Roger Fieldhouse, *The Workers' Educational Association: Aims and Achievements 1903–77* (Syracuse, NY, 1977) 58.
[20] T. W. Price, *The Story of the Workers' Educational Association from 1903 to 1924* (London, 1924), 16. See also *The Higher Education of Working Men, Being the Official Report of the Joint Conference Between Co-operators, Trade Unionists, and University Extension Authorities, Held at Oxford, on Saturday, August 22nd 1903* (London, 1903).
[21] Bernard Jennings, *Albert Mansbridge* (Leeds, 1973), 23.

societies and over seven thousand individual members.[22] Its links with the extension movement were evident from the first. The 1903 conference was on the fringe of that year's Summer Meeting, and the chair was taken by the Bishop of Hereford, John Percival, who had played a part in the origins of Oxford extension in the 1870s and in its redirection in 1885. Percival chaired the subsequent Oxford conference of the WEA in 1905, and was present to preach a famous sermon at St Mary's in Oxford during the 1907 Summer Meeting in advance of the conference at which the lines of future development of workers' education were laid down.[23] Indeed, the new association was projected in order to reinvigorate university extension and link it more effectively with the working class: according to the WEA's first historian, 'When the Association was founded, University Extension occupied the chief place in its programme, and it was contemplated that through the Association the field of University Extension would be greatly enlarged'.[24] That was Mansbridge's original intention, though over time it became clear that only a new approach would suffice.

We can get a sense of the way the early Association functioned from a letter written by Mansbridge in 1907 to a highly sceptical and hostile George Lansbury, later leader of the Labour Party, who was evidently intending 'to oppose [the WEA] in Poplar':

Our plan has been to go to any locality and at once to attempt, always with extraordinary success, to federate all working-class and educational organisations for purely educational purposes—in an unsectarian and non-party organisation which must not deal with measures before Parliament, or likely to be before it—but must seek for labour all the education that can be got under the law, and to stimulate a real demand amongst those who at present make no demand.[25]

The contradiction between social emancipation which the WEA also stood for, and professed political neutrality, would not have been lost on Lansbury. He might also have suspected the support for the

[22] Picht, *Toynbee Hall*, 187.

[23] William Temple, *The Life of Bishop Percival* (London, 1921), 277, 282; F. A. Iremonger, *William Temple, Archbishop of Canterbury: His Life and Work* (Oxford, 1948), 74. For Percival's presence at the founding conference in Oxford in 1903, see his letter to Mansbridge, 2 June 1903, Mansbridge Papers, xxi, British Library Add. MS 65215.

[24] Price, *Story of the Workers' Educational Association*, 29.

[25] A. Mansbridge to G. Lansbury, 27 Sept. 1907, in 'R. H. Tawney, Correspondence re Early Tutorial Classes 1907–8' (file), 'Early Tutorial Classes 1907–8' (box), Workers' Educational Association Papers, Temple House, Bethnal Green, London.

new Association emanating from Oxford where a number of dons, among them Sidney Ball of St John's, H. H. Turner of New College, A. L. Smith of Balliol, Hudson Shaw, and also Joseph Owen, by then at Pembroke College, emerged as patrons of the WEA. The particular support of three colleges—Balliol, St John's, and New College—was also noted.[26] The WEA may have begun in Mansbridge's kitchen in Ilford, but in a very real sense its early home was Oxford, and the credibility it won with Oxford dons was crucial to its strategy of winning public acceptance and state funding for its initiatives. Among the dons, Sidney Ball stands out as the most energetic at this stage. He had been noted for his support of working-class causes for many years and had become a sort of personal centre for all types of university activism in education, social service, and socialism. A member of the Fabian Society and 'profoundly interested in all labour questions', Ball was alleged 'to murmur "Religion and the Republic" when the college toast was "Church and King"'.[27]

The reinvigoration of working-class education was also important to another group of dons in Oxford, younger reformers who could use the emerging workers' movement in a wider campaign for the reform of the University. This is another context for the developing relationship of Oxford and workers' education in this period. United in and around the 'Catiline Club', they included Alfred Zimmern of New College, William Temple of Queen's, Richard Livingstone of Corpus Christi, J. L. Myres and W. H. Fyfe, with R. H. Tawney, who was not an Oxford don, but who took up his first university appointment at Glasgow in 1906, lending assistance from outside. Canon Samuel Barnett of Toynbee Hall, for so long a crucial influence in Oxford's political and civic life, had brought the group together. Arthur Acland, though now retired from politics, served as 'the elder statesman of the committee'.[28] Livingstone eventually became President of Corpus Christi College and Vice-Chancellor of Oxford between 1944–7; he maintained an interest in educational reform in general and adult education in particular, and

---

[26] Price, *Story of the Workers' Educational Association*, 18.

[27] Ernest Barker, 'Politics and Political Philosophy', in Oona Howard Ball (ed.), *Sidney Ball: Memories and Impressions of 'An Ideal Don'* (Oxford, 1923), 224; Mary Stocks, *The Workers' Educational Association: The First Fifty Years* (London, 1953), 28.

[28] Janet Howarth, 'The Edwardian Reform Movement' in M. G. Brock and M. C. Curthoys (eds.), *The History of the University of Oxford*, vii, *The Nineteenth Century*, pt. 2 (Oxford, forthcoming). I am grateful to Mrs Howarth who has allowed me to draw on her detailed knowledge of Oxford in this period.

used his influence to promote the cause of residential continuing education in purpose-built centres in the 1940s.[29] Fyfe, another classicist, was a fellow of Merton College and eventually Principal of Aberdeen University.[30] Myres, a classical archaeologist and historian who had worked with Arthur Evans in his youth, was a Student of Christ Church until 1907, and after a brief spell at Liverpool University, returned to the Wykeham Chair of Ancient History in Oxford in 1910, which he held until his retirement.[31]

Temple was to become one of the greatest churchmen of the century and his place in history is secure.[32] But Zimmern is less well remembered. At this time he was an ancient historian whose most important book on *The Greek Commonwealth*, published in 1911, presented fifth-century Athens as a society held together by shared ethics and moral purpose, and in which individual human potential was maximized.[33] Athens was depicted, self-consciously, as a model to be emulated: 'Greek ideas and Greek inspiration' could assist in the great contemporary challenge of 'deepening and extending the range and meaning of Democracy and Citizenship, Liberty and Law'.[34] This was a popular view among Edwardian classicists, and it is not difficult to see what this interpretation of ancient history owed to the influence of Oxford idealism, and how it might have informed and inspired the participation of Zimmern and others like him in adult education.[35] Later, under the impact of the Great War, his focus changed to the cause of international peace. A noted promoter of European amity in the 1920s and protagonist for the League of Nations, from 1930 until 1944 he was the first incumbent of the Montague Burton Chair of International Relations in Oxford.[36] The group also received help from J. A. Spender, one of the members of Acland's Inner Ring in the early 1880s, and editor of the liberal *Westminster Gazette*, which became the organ of the reformers, and Bishop Gore of Birmingham. Gore was a product of Balliol, a former fellow of Trinity, Oxford, a leading Anglo-Catholic,

[29] *Dictionary of National Biography 1951–60*, 648–50. Richard Livingstone, *The Future in Education* (London, 1941).

[30] *Dictionary of National Biography 1961–70*, 409–11.

[31] *Dictionary of National Biography 1951–60*, 762–3.

[32] John Kent, *William Temple: Church, State and Society in Britain* (Cambridge, 1992).

[33] Alfred E. Zimmern, *The Greek Commonwealth: Politics and Economics in Fifth Century Athens* (Oxford, 1911).

[34] Ibid., 2nd edn. (Oxford, 1915), 5.

[35] See Frank M. Turner, *The Greek Heritage in Victorian Britain* (New Haven, 1981), 188–9, 261–2, 441.

[36] *Dictionary of National Biography 1951–60*, 1096–7.

and successively Bishop of Worcester, Birmingham, and Oxford. As the first principal of Pusey House in Oxford (1884–93) he had exercised a profound influence on the religious life of the University; as a Canon of Westminster he had inspired Mansbridge, and he was a friend to the WEA from the first.[37]

The aim of the group, in essence, was to raise academic standards in the University and simultaneously broaden its social range and intake. In other words, they stood for the same things that earnest young Liberals had advocated in the 1850s and 1860s when university extension was first contemplated. Higher research was to be encouraged; the curriculum was to be modernized to include the social sciences; the university was to be subsidized by the colleges (which were to lose much of their autonomy); and clever students from humble backgrounds were to be admitted at the expense of the notorious 'idle pass men'. Entrance examinations to the University were to be reformed to enable a wider range of applicants; scholarships should be awarded to the needy rather than those from privileged backgrounds who had already benefited from private education. Their objectives were expressed by Tawney (under the pen-name 'Lambda') in a series of articles in the *Westminster Gazette* in February and March 1906.[38] Several more anonymous pieces were published in the same newspaper a year later, though this time they were written by Zimmern, Temple, and Livingstone as well as Tawney.[39] And within a few weeks a third series appeared in *The Times* under the title 'Oxford and the Nation'.[40]

Tawney's articles began with the the familiar cry of all university reformers that unless Oxford changed 'she will have abdicated the leadership of English education' within a generation. For Tawney, change meant broadening the social composition of the university and using all funds responsibly to that end. He sought 'a National University . . . accessible to men of humble means' and purged of 'the rich and idle'. He aimed to show that the time had arrived for another 'impartial review of the resources and opportunities of

[37] See G. L. Prentice, *The Life of Charles Gore: A Great Englishman* (London, 1935).

[38] 'Lambda', 'The University and the Nation', *Westminster Gazette*, 15 Feb., 16 Feb., 17 Feb., 23 Feb., 24 Feb., 2 Mar., 3 Mar., 10 Mar. 1906.

[39] [Anon] 'Some Principles of University Reform', *Westminster Gazette*, 22 Feb., 23 Feb., 1 Mar., 2 Mar., 8 Mar., 9 Mar. 1907. See Howarth, 'Edwardian Reform Movement', 9.

[40] 'Oxford and the Nation', *The Times*, 3 Apr. 1907, p. 6; 5 Apr., p. 6; 9 Apr., p. 8; 13 Apr., p. 9; 16 Apr., p. 4; 20 Apr., p. 14; 29 Apr., p. 7; 11 May, p. 20.

Oxford, such as might be made by a Royal Commission'.[41] In subsequent articles on college finance, the relationship of the colleges and the University, the scholarships system, the entrance examination, and on scholarly research, which Tawney wanted to support more actively, he exposed the obstacles that prevented the admission of poor students. And he developed an argument that was to have influence in Oxford over the subsequent initiatives in working-class education: that a university which had always been 'foster-mother to the class which had been dominant in politics, education, and business' now had a duty to 'fresh sections of the community, on whom the responsibilities of education or administration are now devolving'.[42]

The second series of pieces in the *Westminster Gazette* made essentially the same points in terms that were to be repeated almost verbatim when Oxford subsequently responded to this public criticism in the 1908 report, *Oxford and Working-Class Education*.[43] While much space in the third series of articles in *The Times* was devoted to internal reform of the procedures and constitution of the University and colleges, the context of developing national aspirations was not forgotten. As the authors wrote in their first article, 'The educational ideals of the country are in course of rapid growth. It is in essence a movement towards completer employment of human gifts and natural resources for national well-being, and it involves profound changes of method and organization. In this movement Oxford should have a share worthy of her best past.'[44]

Bishop Gore also raised the issue of university reform in a question in the House of Lords in July of the same year, calling for the appointment of a new royal commission 'to inquire into the endowment, government, administration, and teaching of the Universities of Oxford and Cambridge and their constituent colleges, in order to secure the best use of their resources for the benefit of all classes of the community'.[45] As he told the House, 'whatever there is of real

[41] 'Lambda', 'The University and the Nation. I Introductory', *Westminster Gazette*, 15 Feb. 1906, pp. 1–2.

[42] 'The Limitations of the College System', *Westminster Gazette*, 2 Mar. 1906, p. 2.

[43] See, for example, the final article, 'Oxford and the People' in which it is asserted that 'Oxford . . . stands for the contact of ideas with the whole of life', *Westminster Gazette*, 9 Mar. 1907, and compare with *Oxford and Working-Class Education*, 47.   [44] 'Introductory', *The Times*, 3 Apr. 1907, p. 6.

[45] *Parliamentary Debates*, 4th series, clxxviii, 24 July 1907, 1526. See also Jennings, *Albert Mansbridge*, 12–13; Iremonger, *William Temple*, 89; Peter Gordon and John White, *Philosophers as Educational Reformers: The Influence of Idealism on British Educational Thought and Practice* (London, 1979), 126–8. Prentice, *Life of Charles Gore*, 290.

intellectual aspiration and real desire for knowledge, should find its home and instruction in Oxford and Cambridge; and that, and nothing else, should be the real object which the universities manifestly exist to serve'.[46] The reformers hoped that the threat of another Commission would force Oxford into voluntary changes: as Gore explained, 'there is a desire that the Government should intimate an intention of appointing a commission but at the same time should delay its actual appointment for a year or two to give the Universities, as it were, a period of time to reform themselves'.[47] Similar arguments were set down in a letter in *The Times* on the same day that was signed by several of the reformers.[48]

These arguments were repeated for the best part of six years, during which time Oxford and Cambridge were threatened once more with outside investigation by the state. Internal attempts at constitutional reform *were* made, though many of the most controversial aspects of the ancient universities' arrangements remained intact on the eve of the First World War. Partisans for adult and workers' education in Oxford certainly employed the spectre of a commission to extract support for their initiatives out of the University. And Tawney, for one, remained faithful to root-and-branch reform of Oxford. But by 1912 the moment had passed and the idea of an enquiry and legislative reform faded, though it was revived at the end of the First World War.[49] As in the mid-Victorian period, we have to understand Oxford's contribution to working-class education in this period as emerging from a synthesis of attempts at internal university reform and autonomous and independent developments outside the University. Indeed, as the rest of this account will show, in common with the reformers of the mid-nineteenth century, among them Jowett, Green, and Bryce, the would-be reformers of Edwardian Oxford achieved something of what they desired, in that the university extended its provision of educational facilities for the mass of the people through new tutorial classes in harness with the WEA. Yet once again it was an extension at a distance, outside the walls, and often far from Oxford geographically and figuratively: the social base and culture of the university remained narrow and unrepresentative.

The comparison with the mid-Victorian period is also illuminating in another way. For just as the extension movement of the 1860s and 1870s was a response to reforms of Victorian schooling that began to produce men and women with enough education to

---

[46] *Parliamentary Debates*, 24 July 1907, 1530.   [47] Ibid. 1527.
[48] 'The Need of Reform at Oxford', *The Times*, 24 July 1907, p. 10.
[49] Howarth, 'Edwardian Reform Movement', *passim*.

know that they wanted, and would benefit from more of the same, so another context for the emerging tutorial classes movement was the Education Act of 1902. This provided state funds for secondary education for the first time and established local educational authorities with considerable powers which might act as partners in worthwhile voluntary initiatives. The Act opened up the possibility of more than an elementary education for bright working-class children who might progress to the secondary level, and even beyond, on scholarships. More to the point, it ensured the development of a type of student who perhaps stayed on in school to the age of fifteen or sixteen and then took employment in a lower-middle-class job. Such a person had frequently developed the requisite skills and the desire for the type of higher education that would be offered in the new tutorial classes. Many people with some form of secondary education would find their way into adult education in the course of the next generation.[50]

A final context for the developments in working-class education after 1900 was the perceived failure of university extension to reach the working class and provide a sustained and challenging educational experience. As Sidney Ball was to explain in Oxford in 1907, 'that University Extension has not done all that was hoped from it, cannot, I think, be questioned—is, in fact, generally admitted'.[51] Though Oxford extension could boast higher enrolments than ever, there was a general sense of decline: as Picht noted of the extension movement as a whole, 'everywhere there is a falling off ... in the attendance at the discussions following the lectures, in the writing of papers, in the examinations'.[52] We can appreciate many of the problems in university extension by examining the two locations that were to pioneer the new type of adult education after 1908, Longton in the Potteries of North Staffordshire, and Rochdale.

North Staffordshire was not noted for any very developed educational tradition in the later nintenth century, and first Cambridge and then Oxford had laboured in vain to establish extension centres there.[53] But from 1900 one Oxford tutor, A. W. Bateman Brown, who generally lectured on natural science, began to build a following

---

[50] H. P. Smith, *Labour and Learning: Albert Mansbridge, Oxford and the WEA* (Oxford, 1956), 36; W. E. Styler, 'The Report in Retrospect' in S. Harrop (ed.), *Oxford and Working-Class Education* rev. 2nd edn. (Nottingham, 1987), 52.

[51] Sidney Ball, 'What Oxford Can Do for Workpeople', in *Papers Submitted to the National Conference of Working Class and Educational Organisations, held in the Examination Schools, High Street, Oxford, on Saturday, August 10th, 1907* (London, 1907).   [52] Picht, *Toynbee Hall*, 161.

[53] Sir James Mountford, *Keele: An Historical Critique* (London, 1972), 20.

and constituency for higher education focused on Longton. In addition to extension lectures, he began regular classes for the training of uncertificated elementary teachers. He also established a 'Council for the Extension of Higher Education in North Staffordshire' with a view to establishing in the district an extension college modelled on Reading.[54] And then G. W. Hudson Shaw, lecturing after 1905 on, amongst other things, 'The Puritan Revolution' and 'The Life and Teaching of John Ruskin', enjoyed his customary success, further invigorating interest in higher education in the area.[55] Hudson Shaw knew that changes were under discussion and encouraged his students at Longton to apply to Oxford for assistance in arranging a more challenging and more demanding education. In the words of one of them: 'As a result of a particularly stimulating course of History lectures in Autumn 1907 which aroused a live interest in the subject, and a desire to study the subject further, a request was made to the Extension Delegacy on behalf of a group of Extension students, mostly working class, for some means of following up the subject in a more intensive fashion.'[56] The students had been attending Hudson Shaw's lectures on 'Italian Cities' and had run up against the academic limitations of extension; it could not offer them a means of studying a subject in depth.

A similar experience afflicted the worker students of Rochdale. Here, in a town with an especially rich associational culture which had welcomed James Stuart nearly forty years before, working-class education had taken deep root. The Rochdale Education Guild, by now affiliated to the WEA, represented over fifty local organizations (many of them religious groups) and could count on broad local support.[57] A series of extension lectures on literary subjects in 1906 attracted regular working-class audiences in excess of five hundred. But a course in early 1907 on 'Political and Social Problems' drew only about half this amount, which was simultaneously too small a number to break even financially and too large a number for useful discussion after the lecture. As one of the students put it, 'it was obvious that free, unrestricted discussion of economic subjects in a

---

[54] Ibid. 28–9.

[55] R. A. Lowe, 'Some Forerunners of R. H. Tawney's Longton Tutorial Class', *History of Education*, 1/1 (Jan. 1972), 45–50. See also R. A. Lowe, 'Early University Extension Work in North Staffordshire', unpub. paper, Adult Education Reference Library, Rewley House, Oxford, 2(A)(ii)(b).

[56] 'Non-Vocational Adult Education in North Staffordshire', 'Records of the Work in North Staffordshire', Edward Stuart Cartwright Papers, Oxford University Archives. (The memorandum is unsigned and undated, but is probably by Cartwright himself.)   [57] Jennings, *Albert Mansbridge*, 24.

gathering of 200 persons, most of whom wanted to speak, was an impossible proposition'.[58] Here again the students had run up against the rigidities of extension lectures. Thus Mansbridge brought a group of these Rochdale students to the 1907 Summer Meeting to help present a case for change in the way Oxford provided for working-class education.[59] And as part of the campaign already being waged to revive Oxford's extramural provision, they were taken to meet the Dean of Christ Church and Chairman of the Extension Delegacy, Dr T. B. Strong, to impress on him the need for intensive, class-based, and truly academic adult education. Playing his part to perfection, it is said that 'when the Dean raised the problem of cost, one student told him that if he realised how hungry they were for knowledge, he would melt down the college plate to raise the money'.[60]

According to the Delegacy's Annual Report for 1906–7, therefore, 'The past year has in a marked manner revealed the existence of a demand, particularly in working class centres, for more guidance and control on the part of the University, and for more advanced, systematic and continuous instruction in 'humane' subjects than can be afforded by lectures addressed to large and miscellaneous audiences'.[61] All roads now led to Oxford and the Summer Meeting of 1907. The various factors making for a change in the aims and form of workers' education came together here, as was intended by the Delegacy, the WEA, working-class organizations, and sundry interested dons. Over the preceding two or three years there had been considerable discussion about reviving and changing the movement, and those who were to direct it in the future had already hammered out a pretty clear idea of the kind of education necessary and the type of relationship between the University and the Workers' Educational Association they desired. Indeed, as R. A. Lowe has pointed out, something approximating to the tutorial class itself had been tried out already by the London Extension Board with the assistance and encouragement of Samuel Barnett at Toynbee Hall—an important centre for extension lectures in London—after 1900.[62]

[58] Price, *Story of the WEA*, 30.

[59] Stocks, *Workers' Educational Association*, 37–8.

[60] Jennings, *Albert Mansbridge*, 16.

[61] *University of Oxford: Delegacy for the Extension of Teaching Beyond the Limits of the University, Annual Report, 1906–7* (Oxford, 1907), 2.

[62] Lowe, 'Some Forerunners', 43–4. See also Stuart Marriott, 'Oxford and Working-Class Adult Education: A Foundation Myth Re-examined', *History of Education*, 12/4 (1983), 286–7. John Burrows, *University Adult Education in London: A Century of Achievement* (London, 1976), 6–7.

Barnett wanted something that would 'provide far more thorough and systematic teaching than is possible in a course of lectures' and in 1907 Patrick Geddes began such a class in Battersea.[63] But what was now required was the construction and the direction of a coalition of forces to introduce these changes and link together formally the universities and working-class education.

II

That process began at a special 'Joint Conference on Education of Workpeople' under the auspices of the WEA and organized with the assistance of the Extension Delegacy as part of the 1907 Summer Meeting. It was held in the Examination Schools in Oxford on 10 August and over four hundred delegates attended, representing over two hundred organizations.[64] The point of the conference was to win support for the establishment of a 'joint committee' of university figures and representatives of the working class to devise a new type of extramural education. The conference was to give its blessing to this, and solidify the coalition favouring reform of workers' education. The meeting was led-off by two papers from Walter Nield of Oldham, the President of the North Western Co-operative Education Committees' Association, on 'What Workpeople Want Oxford To Do' and from Sidney Ball on 'What Oxford Can Do For Workpeople'. That they bore a resemblance may have had something to do with the fact that Tawney provided suggestions for both authors.[65] Nield concentrated on the provision of scholarships by which 'the best sons of workmen should proceed to Oxford easily' and on the organization of 'reasonably sized classes (under University conditions)' in working-class communities. Responding, Ball set

---

[63] *Ministry of Reconstruction: Adult Education Committee: Final Report*, PP 1919, Cmd. 321, xxviii. 32. See also H. Barnett, *Canon Barnett: His Life, Work and Friends*, 2 vols. (London, 1918) i. 338; Albert Mansbridge, *University Tutorial Classes* (London, 1913), 17.

[64] A. E. Z[immern], 'The Workers At the Summer Meeting', *Oxford Magazine*, 24 Oct. 1907, pp. 23–4.

[65] See the letter from Sidney Ball to Revd Samuel Barnett, 21 Mar. 1907, asking for assistance with his paper. At the bottom is a note in R. H. Tawney's hand: 'S.A.B sent this to Glasgow. I wrote (i) suggestions for Ball (ii) suggestions for Nield. Both used them at the conference from which Tut. Classes started. Ball, not knowing the source of his and Nield's papers, commented with surprise and gratification on the similarity of their tone. R.H.T. 1914.' 'R. H. Tawney: Correspondence re Early Tutorial Classes 1907–8', 'Early Tutorial Classes I', WEA Archives. See also *Papers Submitted to the National Conference ... 1907*.

out a scheme for such classes: 'One or two thoroughly qualified men might be selected for a period of three or five years to organise, in cooperation with local working-class associations, workmen's classes within a certain area: the classes themselves being arranged on a principle of a graduated and continuous curriculum of an Oxford type.'[66]

The conference is usually remembered for two more crucial contributions. The first was from Robert Morant, Permanent Secretary at the Board of Education, who came to offer something more than merely moral support. The Board, he explained, was 'keenly interested' in the new developments taking shape in adult education and would help 'in every way possible'. But he was more specific still: 'What our Department is looking for is guidance from such an association or union as is represented here today, to show us the way in which this particular kind of education can best be furthered; and in particular we believe it is to small classes and solid, earnest work that we can give increasingly of the golden stream.'[67]

But the offer of state funds did not conquer the suspicions of some of the working-class delegates in Oxford: indeed, this in itself may even have excited anxiety among working men who came from communities with deeply engrained distrust for the state and its intrusions. As one of those present later related, the combination of this suspicion on the workers' part and, on the side of the University, of uncertainty 'as to the working class outlook and the precise nature of the working class demand' threatened the outcome of the conference.[68] But a famous speech by James Mactavish, a Scottish-born, self-educated shipwright from the Portsmouth dockyards who later succeeded Mansbridge as General Secretary of the WEA, saved the situation.[69] Mactavish, attending the conference in his capacity as a Labour councillor in Portsmouth, was able to express in impassioned,

[66] W. Nield, 'What Workpeople Want Oxford To Do', in *Papers Submitted to the National Conference . . . 1907* (London, 1907), 7; S. Ball, 'What Oxford Can Do for Workpeople', ibid. 14.

[67] 'Oxford Joint Conference on Education of Workpeople, August 10th 1907', MSS Minute Book, fos. 28–30, WEA Archives, Temple House, Bethnal Green, London. This is a hand-written transcript of all the speeches delivered at the conference. The account in *The Times*, 12 Aug. 1907, which has usually been relied on, is not complete. See also the letter from J. Frank Heath of the Board of Education to Mansbridge, 7 Aug. 1907 in '1907–8 Joint Committee on Tutorial Classes', DES/F/14/1, Oxford University Archives. There is some doubt as to whether Morant attended in person or sent a message that was read to the conference.

[68] Price, *Story of the WEA*, 37.

[69] Ted Mooney, *J. M. Mactavish: General Secretary of the WEA 1916–27: The Man and His Ideas* (Liverpool, 1979).

fervent language the resentments and demands of the working-class delegates while at the same time assenting to the strategy favoured by the WEA and Oxford. It was a skilful performance, perhaps planned in advance with Mansbridge: if a fiercely independent Scottish shipwright could attack the University but still give its plan his qualified blessing, he could draw with him those who doubted Oxford's motives.[70] According to Mansbridge, the speech 'swung the opposition into its place, and won the respect of the Oxford men, who, for the first time, heard in their halls a clear expression of the working-class demand'.[71] It certainly convinced Reuben George, who, long after, recalled the conference and 'the appeal of Mactavish for food—not the crumbs that fell from their master's table'.[72]

Mactavish began by asserting that he was no 'supplicant for [his] class'. Rather, he claimed for them 'the best of all that Oxford has to give . . . as a right'. He questioned 'the true function of a University'—'Is it to train the nation's best men, or to sell its gifts to the rich?' Because Oxford seemed to understand only the latter responsibility, so 'Oxford herself misses her true mission'. He reminded his audience that the new democracy 'will realise itself with or without the assistance of Oxford'; if without, then the university would lose its place in the nation. He turned to the university curriculum and contended that working people needed a new type of history: 'although we are supposed to have no recorded history, without us all history was and is impossible.' He called also for a new economics: 'You cannot expect the people to enthuse over a science which promises them no more than a life of precarious toil.' Rather, they wanted from Oxford 'a science based, not on the acquisitiveness of the individual, but on social utility'. Finally he called on the university to open itself to his class: 'We want Oxford to open wide her doors to the best of our people and take them in.'[73]

Mactavish won the day and the conference supported a resolution to establish a joint committee 'composed of seven persons nominated by the Vice-Chancellor of the University of Oxford and seven persons nominated by the executive of the Workers' Educational Association' to consider 'the best means of carrying into effect the

[70] Smith, *Labour and Learning*, 55.

[71] A. Mansbridge, *University Tutorial Classes*, 26. See also id., *An Adventure in Working-Class Education* (London, 1920), 38.

[72] Reuben George, *'The Path We Trod': Twenty-five Years' Comradeship with the WEA*, Wiltshire Pamphlet 103, p. 3 (reprinted from *The Swindon Advertiser*, 31 March 1933), Swindon Reference Library.

[73] 'Oxford Joint Conference', fos. 36–44 (see n. 67 above).

suggestions made in the two papers read before the conference'.[74] In addition to the formal business of the conference, the vice-president of the National Union of Teachers, W. A. Nicholls, reminded the assembly of the need to expand women's educational opportunities.[75] Philip Snowden, the Labour MP and future Chancellor of the Exchequer, looked to education to cure 'that ignorance and indifference of the work-people' which obstructed social reform.[76] And Bishop Gore gave a summary of his speech before the House of Lords calling for the reform of the old universities which 'should be maintained before all else as places of serious study'.[77] One other contribution is also worth noting; the letter Mansbridge read to the meeting from the Vice-Chancellor, Herbert Warren, President of Magdalen College, who expressed his real interest in 'how to make University teaching accessible in the most helpful form to working men, either by taking it as far as it can be taken, to them in their places of abode, or by bringing those who can come for shorter or longer periods to Oxford'.[78] This was more than a mere courtesy. Warren had been a member of the Extension Delegacy as far back as 1892 and he seems to have been genuinely interested in the alliance between the university and the WEA. His support for the project was important in swinging Oxford behind the new engagement with the working class.[79]

Yet other contributions reveal the latent tensions that were to divide the new movement from both traditional university extension on the one side and a more militant, propagandist form of workers' education on the other. Marriott, who welcomed the participants, could not resist defending his own corner and that of his University, to which he was always fiercely loyal. He tried to argue that Oxford was 'a national institution already' and that 'a very great deal' had already been achieved through university reform, certainly 'more than many people are prepared to admit'.[80] He, at least, was not

[74] *The Times*, 12 Aug. 1907.

[75] 'Oxford Joint Conference', fo. 56 (see n. 67 above).   [76] Ibid., fo. 73.

[77] Ibid., fos. 8–22. For a positive reflection on the conference, see 'Signs of the Times', a final installment of the 'Oxford and the Nation' series, *The Times*, 14 Oct. 1907, p. 14.

[78] T. H. Warren to A. Mansbridge, 5 Aug. 1907, '1907–8 Joint Committee on Tutorial Classes', DES/F/14/1, Oxford University Archives.

[79] In a letter to F. E. Hutchinson, then Secretary of the Delegacy, written a few months before his death, Warren wrote of his pleasure 'that it fell to me as Vice-Chancellor to start the alliance with the WEA', *Rewley House Papers*, 4 (1931), 172. See also Warren's encouraging letter to Tawney, 21 Jan. 1909, expressing his 'best wishes for the work' at Longton and Rochdale, DES/F/2/1/4, Oxford University Archives.   [80] 'Oxford Joint Conference', fo. 3 (see n. 67 above).

about to join a crusade to overturn Oxford. The other great war-horse of extension, Hudson-Shaw, was more outspoken. Evidently stung by Mactavish's assault on the university curriculum he asserted that

Oxford has got no distinct interpretation of either history or economics. If we have a bias, it is that we care not for drum and trumpet history, but the history of the people. My point is that a working-man can get no good from Oxford at all if they (*sic*) are going to dictate to us before they come what they are going to learn... We want to give you everything in our power. But there is one thing we will deny you. We are not, for you or any person in the universe, going to tune our pulpits.[81]

For both these men the new relationships being projected and new types of education under discussion threatened their own hitherto unchallenged positions in university extension. From the other side, meanwhile, Noah Ablett, a South Wales miner and then a student at Ruskin College in Oxford, who was to play a central role in the events there two years later, and to lead the alternative tradition of workers' education which emerged in this period, expressed the enduring suspicions of trade unionists even after Mactavish had said his piece: 'They wonder why the Universities have so suddenly come down to help the workers to emancipate themselves.'[82] And he was not the only participant who questioned the projected alliance of Oxford and the working class. The Barry branch of the Amalgamated Society of Railway Servants sent a representative to the conference and he evidently presented an unfavourable report on the discussions in Oxford on his return. The branch then passed a resolution and communicated it to Mansbridge, contending

That it is inexpedient for the working classes to cultivate a closer relationship with Oxford by University Extension Lectures, or any other methods, until the teachings of the Universities are radically altered, so that a truer view of social questions may be taught, and that it is inadvisable to send workingmen students to colleges unless the curriculum is made suitable for the training of Labour Leaders.[83]

---

[81] Ibid., fo. 63.

[82] Ibid., fo. 64 . On Ablett, see *Dictionary of Labour Biography* (London, 1972–), iii. 1–3, and Richard Lewis, *Leaders and Teachers: Adult Education and the Challenge of Labour in South Wales 1906–1940* (Cardiff, 1993), *passim*.

[83] The resolution was communicated in a letter to Mansbridge dated 16 Dec. 1907. '1907–8 Joint Committee on Tutorial Classes', DES/F/14/1, Oxford University Archives. It was quoted in full and answered in the report on *Oxford and Working-Class Education*, 57–9.

These same suspicions and reservations would spill over in 1909 and divide the movement for workers' education almost at its inception. If the 1907 Oxford conference heralded a new departure in adult education, it also began a process of division and fragmentation within the tradition.

III

The Joint Committee was subsequently established by the Extension Delegacy under a statute passed by the University's Convocation on 27 October 1908. The seven Oxford members who sat on it were Thomas Strong, Dean of Christ Church; Herbert Turner, Savilian Professor of Astronomy from New College; Hastings Lees Smith, Professor of Economics at University College, Bristol; John Marriott; and the three chief protagonists of working-class education in the university, Zimmern, Ball and A. L. Smith. The seven nominated by the WEA included two Labour MPs, C. W. Bowerman and David Shackleton; W. H. Berry from the co-operative movement; Richardson Campbell representing the friendly societies; Alfred Wilkinson, a Labour councillor from Rochdale; Mactavish and Mansbridge.[84] In the event, the Committee's report, *Oxford and Working-Class Education*, often called the *1908 Report*, was written largely by Zimmern and Tawney, with the final draft perfected by Strong who was 'sure to phrase it right for Oxford reading'.[85] It was published in November 1908.

Oxford and Working-Class Education reviewed the whole field of adult education, considered the current commitment to it on the part of Oxford, and presented the case made by working people for access to the university and its educational resources. It outlined the desired programme of tutorial classes, considering such matters as the curriculum and methods of study to be adopted. It considered the admission of working people to the university and in its final chapter it even gave attention to 'the after career of working-class students'. It was hardly an investigative report given that the main recommendations were already clear to the Joint Committee before it began its work. Indeed, it reads rather more as a manifesto for the educational rights of working people and as a plan of action that might be adopted by other voluntary bodies in the future. It was recommended that Oxford university extension should develop

[84] *Oxford and Working-Class Education*, pref.
[85] Quoted in Jennings, *Mansbridge*, 19.

a new emphasis on class work; that each class should meet regularly for at least two years; that classes concentrate on advanced academic work with regular essays and final examinations. The management of the classes was to be the responsibility of local working-class organizations who would choose the subject, choose the tutor, and, to an extent, negotiate over the syllabus.[86] 'We have no fear at all' ran the *Report* 'that were the classes placed, as we recommend, under the direct control of workpeople, in co-operation with University men, they would be used for any but the highest educational ends.'[87] The tutors from Oxford were to be full-time appointees mixing tutorial class teaching with internal university instruction. In addition, the *Report* emphasized that tutorial classes were not a substitute for study at the university, but a preparation for it: 'in the future qualified students from the tutorial classes should be enabled regularly and easily to pass into residence at Oxford, and to continue their studies there.'[88] It was to prove the most difficult to effect of the various recommendations.

The tutorial classes envisaged were to be organized by a new joint standing committee of the Extension Delegacy composed of equal numbers of representatives from Oxford and the WEA—a remarkable example of the University sharing authority with an external agency and, of course, a clean break with the old form of university extension. This had been inevitable from the moment it became clear that Marriott was unsympathetic to the degree of co-operation envisaged between the University and the workers. As negotiations proceeded Marriott became yet more alienated, as his outraged marginalia to a draft copy of the *1908 Report* attest.[89] Mactavish feared that if the Secretary of the Delegacy exerted himself 'he can do a great deal to injure if not entirely spoil our efforts'. Mansbridge, showing his more ruthless side, disagreed: 'He will not be allowed to even put his little finger in the new arrangements.'[90] As A. L. Smith described the denouement, 'After a long debate we told Marriott that a separate secretary was a *sine qua non*, and brought him to acquiescence not altogether ungracefully in this, provided

---

[86] *Oxford and Working-Class Education*, ch. 8, 'Summary of Recommendations'.
[87] Ibid. 58.   [88] Ibid. 88.
[89] See 'Report on Oxford and Working-Class Education 1908. Drafts', DES/F/14/1, Oxford University Archives. See especially the draft of ch. 3 of the 1908 Report on 'The University Extension Movement' marked on the cover 'Private J.A.R.M.'.
[90] Mactavish to Mansbridge, 4 Jan. 1908; Mansbridge to Mactavish 7 Jan. 1908, '1907–8 Joint Committee on Tutorial Classes', DES/F/14/1, Oxford University Archives.

the work of the new Committee should be confined to these tutorial classes'.[91] For the next fifty years the Oxford Extension Delegacy comprised two distinct administrations for tutorial classes and extension lectures. Manoeuvring Marriott into a position of impotence was part of a deliberate policy to make the new administrative structures for working-class education the acknowledged centre of the University's extramural provision. Perhaps it was not just a coincidence that Hudson Shaw suffered a disabling breakdown a few months after the publication of the *1908 Report* and never resumed his work as an extension lecturer.

Certain assumptions in *Oxford and Working-Class Education* are worth noting. At the 1907 conference Philip Snowden had placed emphasis on collective rather than individual advancement—'I would rather have better education given to the masses of the working classes than the best for a few. O God, make no more saints; Elevate the race'[92]—and the *Report* was insistent that this was its aim. In obtaining a university education, it was argued, 'it must not be necessary for workpeople to leave the class in which they were born . . . What they desire is not that men should escape from their class, but that they should remain in it and raise its whole level.'[93] This seems to have been an especially important issue for the representatives of the working class on the committee. At one of its preliminary meetings Shackleton made it clear that though he 'had no desire to bind a student down to his original machine', nevertheless 'the important point was that he should return to his class' and take a position of responsibility within it.[94] At an interesting meeting in Balliol in January 1908 at which members of the Joint Committee, then in session, came before members of the college to explain their project, Mactavish made the same point: 'What the working classes need, is that raising not of individuals, but of the average level; and they look to Oxford, first, to make the highway and get it used; then to train the sons of the people, aye, and their daughters too.'[95] The emphasis on collective goals and social rather than individual advancement was perhaps the most notable and enduring feature of the movement emerging at this time.

[91] A. L. Smith to A. Mansbridge, 16 Oct. 1908, A. L. Smith's Letters, Box 14 'WEA', A. L. Smith Papers, Balliol College, Oxford.

[92] 'Oxford Joint Conference', fo. 77 (see n. 67 above).

[93] *Oxford and Working-Class Education*, 49–50.

[94] Oxford Joint Committee. Minutes of the Meeting held on December 27th and 28th 1907, A. L. Smith Letters, Box 14, 'WEA', 4.

[95] 'Report of a Meeting in Balliol College Hall on Sunday Morning 26 Jan. 1908', A. L. Smith Letters, Box 14, 'WEA', 5–6.

A second theme in the *Report* concerned the need to link Oxford to the class, and the rulers, of the future. Both the University, with its traditional function of educating the governing élite, and the workers, who needed to be prepared for their responsibilities, would lose if a relationship between them could not be established. In the most famous passage of the *Report* it was contended that

The Trade Union secretary and the 'Labour Member' need an Oxford education as much and will use it to as good ends, as the civil servant or the barrister. It seems to us that it would involve a grave loss both to Oxford and to English political life were the close association which has existed between the university and the world of affairs to be broken or impaired on the accession of new classes to power.[96]

The 'need' for education if the working classes were to use power effectively and responsibly was understood on the other side as well. A. D. Lindsay of Balliol, who was to play a leading role in the movement for a generation after the First World War, recalled

talking to the secretary of one of the earliest Oxford tutorial classes in Littleborough, and his surprising me by saying that it was Plato who had made him join a tutorial class. I found on examination that he was referring—not to Plato—but to a passage in Xenophon's *Memorabilia* where Socrates shows a young Athenian ambitious for a political career that he does not know nearly enough for the task he proposes to undertake.

As Lindsay commented, 'able men in the Trade Union Movement found that they were offered power which they had not the knowledge to use'.[97]

In some ways, the case made in favour of educating 'the trade union secretary' is reminiscent of that put forward by university reformers in the 1850s and 1860s when they held that a national university had to open itself up to the sons of the new manufacturing and mercantile classes. But if it may be argued that the 'establishment's embrace' in the mid-Victorian decades undermined the radicalism, independence, culture, and values of the British middle classes and bound them to hitherto alien institutions, with considerable consequences for British economic and political history, then it is not difficult to appreciate the fear that the trade union secretary at Oxford would suffer a similar fate.[98] At the time and since, the

[96] *Oxford and Working-Class Education*, 48.
[97] A. D. Lindsay [Lord Lindsay of Birker], *Universities Quarterly*, 6/1 (Nov. 1951), 84.
[98] On the incorporation of the Victorian middle classes see Martin J. Wiener, *English Culture and the Decline of the Industrial Spirit 1850–1980* (Cambridge, 1981).

charge against *Oxford and Working-Class Education* was that it
effectively provided for the incorporation of leaders of the working
class. There might be little controversy over Shackleton's comment
to the students of Balliol in January 1908 that 'the working class
had now the task of Government laid upon them and wanted to be
taught how to do it'—though some, no doubt, would wonder why
the teaching should come from Oxford. But Shackleton went further: 'It will repay expenditure; for there is in their ranks some
ability and some reasonableness. The best remedy against extreme
views is wider views.'[99] Such comments would have confirmed the
worst fears of many in the working-class movement had they heard
them, and they explain why the *1908 Report* provoked such disagreement. The Joint Committee was evidently aware of this interpretation of its intentions, and the *1908 Report* acknowledged the
suspicion that Oxford was seeking to remove worker scholars from
their class through a process of educational and cultural incorporation. But it attempted to neutralize it by emphasizing the control
that students and their organizations would have over the choice of
tutor and subject-matter. Oxford was 'to co-operate with them in
their efforts to obtain what they want, instead of providing, without
consulting them, what the University thinks they ought to want'.[100]

Like the Workers' Educational Association itself, and perhaps
like the whole of the labour movement at this time, *Oxford and
Working-Class Education* seemed caught between an argument for
wholesale emancipation of the working class and a simultaneous
respect for established institutions and social solidarity. The fundamental continuity with the social outlook of Acland and Toynbee
was evident in the famous comment that 'the education which Oxford
can give, by broadening his knowledge and strengthening his judgement, would make him at once a more efficient servant of his own
society, and a more potent influence on the side of industrial peace'.[101]
Yet the very existence of a report into educational opportunities for
the working class, the evident concern to accommodate the wishes
of the working-class groups involved, the agreement to devolve
control to the students themselves—all this simultaneously suggests
the sincerity and sensitivity of the dons. *Oxford and Working-Class
Education* was an important but flawed document. Perhaps because
it had to satisfy conservative dons as well as proud and class-
conscious workers, it faced in several different directions at once. It

[99] 'Report of a Meeting in Balliol College Hall on Sunday Morning 26 January
1908', A. L. Smith Letters, Box 14, 'WEA', 2–3.
[100] *Oxford and Working-Class Education*, 58.   [101] Ibid. 83.

advocated social emancipation but it was premised on co-operation between classes. It sought to equip the working class for government, but it looked forward to 'industrial peace'. It said that it wanted more working people to study at the University, but it was much more specific in explaining how the new tutorial classes would work in industrial centres in the provinces than in setting out a scheme that would open Oxford itself to the workers. It had no consistent social philosophy, and its ambiguities gave ammunition to all sides, as we shall see.

IV

The first tutorial classes did not wait upon the publication of *Oxford and Working-Class Education*. In January 1908, while the Joint Committee was sitting, two experimental classes began at Longton and Rochdale in response to the representations received from both places to move beyond the constraints of extension lectures. That autumn the new Oxford Tutorial Classes Committee, established by a statute passed by the University's Congregation on 27 October 1908, organized six further tutorial classes and by 1910 Oxford was responsible for a total of thirteen. These were at Longton and Rochdale (where there were two in each town), Chesterfield, Glossop, Littleborough, Oldham, Swindon, Wrexham, Halifax, Hanley, and Huddersfield. Mansbridge judged the Oxford programme at this stage 'a glorious triumph ... Each class has been a success and the tutors are all splendid.'[102] Four years later the Oxford Tutorial Classes Committee was running eighteen classes with a combined total of 367 students.[103] As was always intended, the model pioneered in Oxford spread rapidly to other universities, several of recent foundation, which were beginning to engage in extramural education and which established similar partnerships with the WEA. By 1909 Cambridge, Manchester, Liverpool, Leeds, and Sheffield had all begun tutorial classes.[104] By the end of the 1913–14 session there were fourteen joint committees, some 145 classes and 3,343 students in the new movement. Of universities and university colleges in England and Wales, only Exeter and Southampton had not

[102] A. Mansbridge to A. Zimmern [May 1910], Zimmern MSS, Bodleian Library, Oxford, 12, fo. 152.

[103] 'Memorandum of the Workers' Educational Association', *Royal Commission on Oxford and Cambridge Universities: Appendices to the Report of the Commissioners* (London, HMSO, 1922), 69.   [104] Price, *Story of the WEA*, 38.

yet begun tutorial classes.[105] Out of the 145 classes, just over one half, seventy-four, were in the category of 'Social History and Economics'. Twenty-two were studying modern history, eleven were in sociology, and ten were in political science. There were also seventeen literature classes.[106] It was estimated that 47.5 per cent of the students were from the manual working class.[107]

The whole enterprise depended on energetic fund-raising. Grants from public sources provided a foundation, but in each university the classes were financed by a mixture of central, local, and private financial support. The receipts of the Oxford Tutorial Classes Committee for 1912–13 show an income of £845 from the colleges (rather than the University), £343 from individual donations, £358 in grants from Local Educational Authorities, and £305 from the Board of Education.[108] In the period 1908–14 as a whole, 42 per cent of the income of the Tutorial Classes Committee came from the university and colleges (though mainly from the latter), 21 per cent came from individuals, many of them dons and their friends, 13 per cent from LEAs, and 16 per cent from Board of Education grants. The rest came from local WEA groups and from the students themselves towards their Summer School costs.[109] In the period 1908–19 the largest college donations to the Tutorial Classes Committee were from All Souls (£2,400), New College (£1,670), Magdalen (£1,275), Brasenose (£575), Queen's (£430), and Merton (£350).[110] At the outset, the Rochdale and Longton classes were given central funds, under the terms of the Technical Schools Regulations, at the rate of five shillings per student. This was raised to 8s 6d in the following year. In 1913, further lobbying led to the introduction of special regulations for University Tutorial Classes by the Board of Education, which provided a block grant of £30, or half the tutor's fee, if less, for each class fulfilling certain specified conditions as to attendance and essay work. In 1917 the Board's

[105] Ibid. 45; Thomas Kelly, *A History of Adult Education in Great Britain*, 3rd edn. (Liverpool, 1992; first pub. 1970), 253.

[106] *Ministry of Reconstruction . . . Final Report*, 54. The remaining classes were in 'Philosophy or Psychology' (8); Biology (2) and Economic Geography (1).

[107] Central Joint Committee on Tutorial Classes, Annual Report for 1913, cited in John A. Blyth, *English University Adult Education 1908–1958: The Unique Tradition* (Manchester, 1983), 14.

[108] Smith, *Labour and Learning*, 25; see also 'Report of Committee on Applications by Extension Delegacy', Hebdomadal Council Papers, no. 92, 23 Apr.–27 June 1912, p. 124.

[109] These percentages should be treated as rough approximations only.

[110] *Royal Commission on Oxford and Cambridge Universities: Appendices*, 198.

grant to each class went up to £45.[111] At about that time the Oxford Committee estimated that it expended £70 per class over and above Board of Education grants and purely local sources of income.[112] It paid tutors a fee of £80 for each class for the academic year. In Oxford, the Tutorial Classes Committee was initially located in Acland House, Broad Street. In 1914 it moved to Barnett House (on the corner of Broad and Turl Streets), and this rapidly became a focus for various forms of voluntary and educational activism— a meeting place for the University and social organizations, and a centre for social and economic research.

By 1909 Oxford had established eight tutorial classes in Chester-field, Glossop, Littleborough, Longton, Oldham, Rochdale, Swindon, and Wrexham. The 237 students enrolled in them 'were mainly manual workers, with an intermixture of school teachers and clerks, together with secretaries of working-class organizations'.[113] Fifty-nine per cent of these students were drawn from three groups of trades—engineering, textiles, and building. There were thirty-two clerks and twelve teachers in the classes, as well. All but twenty-one of the students were men, and just over 60 per cent of the whole group were under the age of 34. Indeed, over half the students were between 25 and 34 years of age, which confirms a later description of 'the ordinary tutorial class student' as 'one who has after the elementary school gone to manual work and who after some years of such work desires systematic and higher education'.[114] Perhaps surprisingly, and in sharp contrast to the more recent pattern, only fourteen students were over 45. As the Tutorial Classes Committee explained (though with a touch of exaggeration), 'the personnel of the existing eight Tutorial Classes may be said to be recruited almost entirely from the younger and more energetic members of the manual working-class, who are keenly alive to the civic questions and desire to improve their knowledge of them by impartial study'.[115]

---

[111] Winifred Beaton, 'The Tutorial Class Movement', in G. D. H. Cole *et al.* (eds.), *The WEA Education Year Book 1918* (London, 1918), 255. 'Memorandum by the Central Joint Advisory Committee on Tutorial Classes', *Royal Commission on Oxford and Cambridge Universities: Appendices*, 79.

[112] 'University Tutorial Classes: Tutors' Conference', in *WEA Education Year Book 1918*, 269.

[113] A. Mansbridge and W. Temple, 'Oxford University Tutorial Classes Committee. Report of the First Year's Working', Mansbridge Papers, xxi, British Library Add. MS 65215, fos. 1–3.

[114] 'Report of Committee on Applications by Extension Delegacy', Memorandum A, 1911, Hebdomadal Council Papers, no. 92, 23 Apr.–27 June 1912, 141.

[115] Mansbridge and Temple, 'Report of the First Year's Working', fo. 4.

A great deal of material about the first two Oxford tutorial classes has survived, and as they formed the model for the classes to come, and knowledge of their initial success influenced the Joint Committee in the way it presented its report, they merit detailed consideration. Both were in 'Industrial History', specifically 'The Social, Industrial and Economic History of England, with Special Attention to the Seventeenth, Eighteenth and Nineteenth Centuries'. Economics and economic history were central to the curriculum of the new movement because, above all, the workers 'wanted to know something of the forces which had made them what they were'.[116] Tutorial classes were an exercise in understanding where working-class communities had come from, and also in thinking about where they might be going. A later report by the education inspectorate into Oxford's programme of tutorial classes noted that working-class students 'have been willing to read "economic" history, or "social" history, or "industrial" history in the belief that such special studies would throw light on immediate problems of social life'.[117] As John Dover Wilson explained of the period before the First World War, 'for the majority of adult students in those days, economics was the natural, the inevitable, gateway to knowledge. For any working man of more than average intelligence, what is called "the social problem" had to be tackled first, before anything else, and economics seemed to offer the key to it'.[118]

Both classes were taught by R. H. Tawney, who became one of the great economic historians of the age. He was then living in Glasgow and would leave the city on a Friday morning to arrive at Longton for a class that evening. He would stay the night and then go on for a Saturday afternoon class in Rochdale, returning home on Sunday.[119] Tawney later described a tutorial class as 'the nucleus of a University established in a place where no University exists'.

Thanks to the fact that they are small, tutor and students can meet as friends, discover each other's idiosyncracies, and break down that unintentional system of mutual deception which seems inseparable from any education which relies principally on the formal lecture. It is often before the classes begin and after they end, in discussions round a student's fire, or

[116] Stocks, *Workers' Educational Association*, 46.
[117] *Board of Education: Report by H. M. Inspectors upon University Tutorial Classes under the Supervision of the Joint Committee of the University of Oxford, for the period ending 31st July, 1924* (n.d.), 'Copies of Special Reports, Memoranda etc.', Oxford University Archives, DES/F/2/1/8, folder 3, p. 5.
[118] J. Dover Wilson, 'Adult Education in Yorkshire', *The Journal of Adult Education*, 3/1 (Oct. 1928), 58.
[119] Stocks, *Workers' Educational Association*, 40.

in a walk to and from his home, that the root of the matter is reached both by student and tutor.[120]

At Rochdale, Tawney met a class 'almost, if not entirely, made up of "workmen" in the strictest sense of the term' in the words of the class secretary, L. V. Gill.[121] Another student, T. W. Price, then working at a local bleaching works, was more precise:

There are in the class 12 iron workers, 8 skilled and 4 unskilled, and 3 joiners. All the chief branches of the cotton industry are represented, spinning, weaving, bleaching and finishing. There are also 2 carpet weavers, a wool-sorter, a spindlemaker, a shuttlemaker, a printer, a housepainter, a picture-framer, an accountant's clerk, a cashier, a teacher, 2 journalists, and an insurance agent. Of the lady students one is a clerk, one a dressmaker, one a schoolmistress, and the fourth is a working-man's wife.[122]

Gill wrote to Mansbridge after the first class that 'Tawney captured them right away'. He wrote again, after the second class, to explain that 'it is a case of love at first sight on both sides. His lectures are brilliant, illuminating, simple, lucid, eloquent.'[123] Price apparently 'went home as if I were walking upon air & was so exuberant that my wife wanted to know what was the matter with me'. It was not just that Tawney was 'the right man for teacher . . . we [also] have the right kind of men and women in the class . . . men and women in earnest'. After only two weeks there could be no going back: 'None of us, now that we have become acquainted with Mr. Tawney & his methods, will be contented any longer with the ordinary University Extension lecture; we want lectures that will stimulate us to work, not lectures that are half popular entertainments.'[124] J. W. Henighan, a general labourer, was wonderfully expressive:

At nearly half-past two Gill entered the room followed closely by a young man wearing the gown; he was the much debated tutor . . . Briefly, Tawney stated his opinion of what the class should be, and without more ado

[120] R. H. Tawney, 'An Experiment in Democratic Education', *The Political Quarterly*, May 1914, 74–5.
[121] L. V. Gill to R. H. Tawney, 10 Dec. 1907, 'R. H. Tawney: Correspondence re Early Tutorial Classes 1907–8', 'Early Tutorial Classes', WEA Archives.
[122] 'The Rochdale Tutorial Class', MSS article by T. W. Price dated '1908' with Mansbridge's comment 'by a student who works in the bleaching works', 'Early Tutorial Classes', Box II, exercise book entitled 'Rochdale Class', WEA Archives. (The book comprises letters sent to Mansbridge from the first Rochdale class which he transcribed in his own hand.)
[123] L. V. Gill to A. Mansbridge, 26 Jan. 1908, 2 Feb. 1908, 'Early Tutorial Classes II', 'Rochdale Class'.
[124] T. W. Price to A. Mansbridge, 2 Feb. 1908, ibid.

delved deep into his work. My first impression was of surprise, first at his youth, and secondly at the sweet affable charm of his presence. There was none of the academic manner about him; none of that air which is so inclined to freeze; he was one of us. We had expected the frigid zone; we were landed at the equator. Tawney is not a teacher: he is a man with a soul.[125]

One of the students had taken a Bachelor of Commerce degree from the Victoria University, and he ended a long and reflective letter to Mansbridge with the judgement that 'from the teaching point of view and seriousness of students, I think our class compares favourably with real University work'.[126] But difficulties were inevitable when it came to the contribution that students could make. Henighan advised preparatory instruction in composition before future classes: 'In the case of workmen, essay-writing is the greatest difficulty, so few being able to express their thoughts in writing.'[127]

After the last class of the session, Alfred Wilkinson, a member of the Joint Committee, wrote to Mansbridge to sum up: 'Tawney has captured not only the heads but the hearts of his scholars; if you can get [another] don like him, we can turn England upside down in a few years' time.'[128] Tawney, for his part, also wrote a report on the first session of the Rochdale class which was printed in the local press. He noted the great improvement made by the students over the term and the excellence of the 'first five or six' of them whose work 'was on a level with that in the honour schools of the only Universities with which he is acquainted'. He also took the opportunity to call for improved secondary education on general grounds and so that tutorial class students would have the necessary skills of composition, and for a reduction in overtime so that students would have leisure for study.[129] In his confidential report to the Delegates in Oxford, Tawney emphasized the quality of the best students whose 'power to grasp general ideas and to write forcibly and fluently was most striking'.[130] It is doubtful if he exaggerated their talent: Gill went on to become Secretary of the WEA's North West District and Price became Secretary of the Midlands District

[125] J. W. Henighan to A. Mansbridge, 2 Feb. 1908, ibid.
[126] Fred Hall to A. Mansbridge, 7 March 1908, ibid.
[127] J. Henighan to A. Mansbridge, 14 May 1908, ibid.
[128] A. W. Wilkinson to A. Mansbridge (n.d.), ibid.
[129] 'Tutorial History Class. Mr. R. H. Tawney's Report on the First Session' (press cutting, Rochdale source unknown) in 'Early Tutorial Classes II', 'Rochdale Class'. See also Tawney's report to the Oxford Delegacy on the class, 'Oxford University Extension. Reports of Lecturers, Examiners and Local Committees 1907–1908', Oxford University Archives, DES/R/3/37 fo. 739.   [130] Ibid., fo. 740.

and the Association's first (and best) historian. And one of the two journalists in the class was A. P. Wadsworth, who went on to edit the *Manchester Guardian* and write distinguished histories of the cotton industry. Tawney recalled Wadsworth in an obituary as 'An alarmingly precocious youth of seventeen—Alfie as we called him—whose impish sallies, backed by formidable batteries of recondite information, ensured that the Saturday gatherings of which in the opening decade of the present century he and I were members, should at any rate be kept awake.'[131]

When A. L. Smith wrote to one potential donor to solicit funds for the new tutorial classes he praised the 'remarkable work' produced by the Rochdale students in their first months and offered to show copies of their essays as proof.[132] When Zimmern paid a visit to Rochdale in April 1908 he received 'a royal welcome': 'Price gave me the finest tea I ever had in my life, and we spent a jolly evening at the Club. I was really impressed with the class . . . and Tawney's treatment of the subject is masterly. It was an Oxford lecture in conception and treatment, not a popular lecture at all.'[133]

The examination of students in the Longton class in 1908 was undertaken by L. L. Price, who, long before, had given Oxford extension lectures. He commented that 'the work sent in was of good quality for the most part, showing considerable knowledge . . . It was evident that great interest had been taken and much pains bestowed by the students. Some of the papers were remarkably full and accurate and most exhibited distinct signs of independent thought on the subject.'[134] An official Board of Education inspection of WEA tutorial classes undertaken by J. W. Headlam HMI, and L. T. Hobhouse, the Liberal thinker and sociologist who had been a member of Acland's 'Inner Ring' in the early 1880s in Oxford, was similarly encouraging. Though they doubted the validity of comparisons with undergraduates at Oxford or Cambridge, and though they enumerated the many problems that adult scholars faced, they had met with students 'whose essays compare[d] favourably with

[131] 'Tawney on Wadsworth', *The Highway*, 48 (Jan. 1957), 82. See also R. H. Tawney, 'A Fifty Year's Memory', *Manchester Guardian*, 5 Nov. 1956, p. 4.

[132] A. L. Smith to Lord Balfour of Burleigh, 30 June 1908, A. L. Smith Papers, 'Extra-Mural Work 1907–09'.

[133] A. E. Zimmern to A. Mansbridge, 8 Apr. 1908, '1907–8 Joint Committee on Tutorial Classes', DES/F/14/1, Oxford University Archives. See also 'Report by Mr. Zimmern on the Rochdale Class', Apr. 4 [1908], Cartwright Papers, 'Records of Work in North Staffordshire', Oxford University Archives.

[134] Oxford University Extension. Reports of Lecturers . . . 1907–8, DES/R/3/37, fo. 731. See also Linden West, 'The Tawney Legend Re-examined', *Studies in Adult Education*, 4/2 (Oct. 1972), 112–13.

the best academic work' and who could meet the challenges of the Oxford diploma course in Economics and Political Science (the usual qualification sought by those few adult scholars who did find a place at Oxford) 'without difficulty'. Tutorial class students may have lacked 'the qualities arising out of a general literary education'; but, on the other hand, many of their essays showed 'more maturity of mind and more grip of reality'.[135]

It is evident that many of those involved were concerned to justify the new movement in terms of the standards achieved. And there is little doubt that much of the work, taking into account the educational background of the students, was impressive. Nevertheless one senses exaggeration in some of the claims made, notably A. L. Smith's characteristically generous assessment that 25 per cent of the essays written were as good as the work done by men who obtained first class honours in Modern History at Oxford.[136] In addition, it may be more than coincidental that almost all the examiners and inspectors in these early years seem to have had some long-standing connections with the movement or could have been expected to sympathize with it. Truly dispassionate observers seem to have been kept at arm's length.

The Longton Class was rather different in social composition from that at Rochdale 'being representative of all sections of . . . the middle and working classes' and as such was undoubtedly more like the majority of tutorial classes to follow.[137] It comprised 'a gardener, a plumber, a potter's thrower, a potter's decorator, a basket-maker, a miner, a mechanic, a baker, several clerks, a librarian, a grocer, a miller's agent, a railway agent, a clothier, insurance collectors, and elementary school teachers'.[138] In fact there were seventeen of the last category among a total of 38 in the class. One of the students later described the class as 'a cross-section of many callings and activities'.[139] The *1908 Report*, in reproducing the

---

[135] *Special Report on Certain Tutorial Classes in Connection with the Workers' Educational Association'* (J. W. Headlam HMI and Professor L. T. Hobhouse), Board of Education, Special Reports, No.2. (n.d [1910]).

[136] Mansbridge, *An Adventure*, 40.

[137] On the socially mixed nature of Cambridge tutorial classes and their recruitment from the ranks of clerks, teachers, and the lower middle class generally, see Edwin Welch, *The Peripatetic University: Cambridge Local Lectures 1873–1973* (Cambridge, 1973), 112.

[138] Report of the Local Secretary, W. T. Cope, in Oxford University Extension. Reports of Lecturers . . . 1907–8, DES/R/3/37, fo. 735. See also 'Reports on Tutorial Classes', *Oxford and Working-Class Education*, 105.

[139] A. Emery, 'In the Early Tutorial Classes, (1) Longton', *The Highway*, 44 (Apr. 1953), 253.

report of the class secretary, referred to this mix as 'ideal', reinforcing the perception that some of those who were ostensibly investigating specifically 'working-class education' also favoured the integration of the social classes through adult education.[140] Certainly the Longton class was unrepresentative of the local employment and class structure, but, as Tawney himself explained, the social divisions within the class were more apparent than real: 'Teachers, elementary and secondary, are often the children of work-people and marry them; while their salaries are so low as to place them, at any rate at first, in an economic position inferior to that of many artisans.'[141] A similar point was made in the first report of the Tutorial Classes Committee by Mansbridge and Temple: the clerks and shop assistants enrolled in the earliest classes were 'not usually classified as "workpeople" ', but the majority of them still 'belonged to working-class families'.[142] These comments may serve as a useful reminder that many students in lower-middle-class occupations who came to extension lectures or tutorial classes had not broken their links with the working class, and did not enjoy better living conditions. It is also worth noting the presence in the class at Longton of a knot of seasoned campaigners from the local branch of the Social Democratic Federation: this may explain why Tawney was warned against 'setting up a den of iniquity' when he met one local public official to discuss a venue for the class.[143]

At Longton, as in Rochdale, Tawney won universal acclaim: 'The lecturer was the right man in the right place and is evidently experienced in dealing with audiences of workpeople. He was lucid and eminently pure-minded in his treatment of the subject, and possessed the faculty of being able to capture and hold the interest of the class.'[144] But the surviving sources on the Longton class are rather more honest and detailed on the problems encountered. The class secretary, Edward Stuart Cartwright, wrote candidly to Mansbridge in November 1909 to explain them:

We are trying hard here to keep the class up to a high level. There are several of the newer members who find the subject very stiff owing chiefly

[140] Ibid.

[141] Oxford University Extension. Reports of Lecturers . . . 1907–8, Oxford University Archives DES/R/3/37, fo. 732.

[142] Mansbridge and Temple, 'Report of the First Year's Working', fo. 4.

[143] H. P. Smith, 'A Tutorial Class Makes History', *Adult Education*, 31/4 (spring 1959), 271–3.

[144] Report of the Local Secretary, W. T. Cope, in Oxford University Extension. Report of Lecturers . . . 1907–8, Oxford University Archives, DES/R/3/37, fo. 735. See also 'Reports on Tutorial Classes', *Oxford and Working-Class Education*, 105.

to their defective preliminary education...One thing this has brought home to me, personally—how very difficult and distasteful the mere physical act of writing is to a miner or a potter. I can see this is a very big initial obstacle to surmount. I felt weary in spirit last night when it was brought home to me what spade work had to be done before the Tutorial Classes movement can begin its work proper.[145]

Because most of the students 'had little practise in composition' Tawney himself did not 'think it wise to press them too hard to write papers'.[146] A few months later Cartwright identified the greatest difficulty as 'the unstable conditions of life of the ordinary industrial student, with sometimes long and sometimes irregular hours of work, and the uncertainty of employment'.[147] Zimmern, writing about workers' education in North Staffordshire in 1914, itemized 'the ravages of overtime, the anxieties of unemployment, the suspicions of foremen and managers, the difficulties of obtaining quiet for reading and writing' as enemies of the working-class student.[148] Headlam and Hobhouse related that one student they encountered, 'in order to get a time when the house was quiet for working in ...went to bed at seven, got up at midnight, worked for two hours, and then went to bed again'.[149]

One of the students in Tawney's class in Wrexham expressed the frustrations of worker students in a letter written to Mansbridge to ask leave to withdraw from the group:

Having had practically no education I am handicapped at every point, the rules of grammar, composition, punctuation, and the sequence of historical persons and events are so absent from my knowledge as though they did not exist; for instance, I could not at the present moment say who was Queen Victoria's father, nor who preceded her in the monarchy and when I hear such names as William of Orange, Pitt and Sir Walter Raleigh, I don't know until I search for their history whether they were Primates, Pirates, Peers or Premiers. Of course, until I joined the Economics class I

[145] Cartwright to A. Mansbridge, 9 Nov. 1909, DES/F/2/1/4, Oxford University Archives.
[146] Oxford University Extension. Reports of Lecturers...1907–8, DES/R/3/37, fo. 732.
[147] 'Longton Tutorial Class. Report for Session 1909–10', p. 3, Cartwright Papers, 'Records of Work in North Staffordshire' (Box), Oxford University Archives. See also Cartwright's report as local secretary for 1908–9 in Oxford University Extension. Reports of Lecturers...1908–9, DES/R/3/38, fo. 564.
[148] A. Zimmern, 'Education and the Working Class', *The Round Table: A Quarterly Review of the Politics of the British Empire*, 14 (March 1914), 264.
[149] *Special Report on Certain Tutorial Classes* (Headlam and Hobhouse), 6. See also their remarks on the chronic problem of providing books for the classes, ibid. 7–8.

had never found it necessary to know anything about them because my life had been spent in a sphere in which the only important thing seemed to be the devising of some scheme whereby one could escape from what seemed to be the inevitable end of one's fellow workers, viz., poverty and that old British institution, the workhouse.[150]

Another poignant letter of resignation from a student in a later Oxford tutorial class at Littleborough set down the health problems of a husband and wife who 'both go to the Mill', thus presenting another set of difficulties that militated against workers' education—chronic medical conditions that afflicted many of the manual working class.[151]

Reports on the first Oxford tutorial classes give graphic insight into the disabling effects of fatigue, unemployment, poor housing, illness, and poverty that disfigured working-class life in the first years of the century. The first annual report on Oxford's tutorial classes gave an example of a student in Tawney's Longton class who worked for 626 hours in nine weeks between February and April 1909, and concluded that 'the long hours of labour' was the 'greatest single obstacle to the extension of adult education'.[152] Tawney's own reports on his classes in 1909–10 inveighed against the 'systematic misuse' of overtime by some employers: 'A very promising student in one of my classes has worked from 6 a.m. to 9 p.m. every day from October to March, with the result that even when he can attend the class he is too worn out to read or do the requisite number of essays.'[153] The class secretary at Littleborough in the same year noted the 'most discouraging effect' of unemployment on the students: 'their minds have never been free from worry and depressing thoughts of the morrow.'[154] At Longton in 1908, eight students ceased to attend the class between the beginning of the term in October and Christmas, and 'the chief reason was unemployment'.[155] One tutor apparently 'watched individual students, who began work with enthusiasm and capacity, gradually sink through unemployment into a state of mental despondency and

[150] C. B. Caldecott to A. Mansbridge, 26 Dec. 1909, Tutorial Classes Committee Correspondence, Oxford University Archives DES/F/2/1/10. For Mansbridge's less than sympathetic response, see A. Mansbridge to C. B. Caldecott, 30 Dec. 1909, DES/F/2/1/10.

[151] J. M. Vaughan to J. A. S. Walkden (class secretary at Littleborough), 16 Sept. 1909, Tutorial Classes Committee Early Papers, i, DES/F/2/1/1.

[152] Mansbridge and Temple, 'Report of the First Year's Working', fo. 7.

[153] *Oxford University Extension Delegacy: Tutorial Classes Committee: Annual Report 1909–10*, 8. [154] Ibid. 13.

[155] Mansbridge and Temple, 'Report of the First Year's Working', fo. 5 n.

distress in which every thought of education gradually disappeared before the question, "How shall I earn a living tomorrow?" [156] In such circumstances tutors also functioned as social workers. F. W. Kolthammer of Brasenose (who changed his name to Cuthbertson during the First World War) was teaching Oxford classes in Chesterfield, Glossop, Hanley, Huddersfield, and Oldham in 1910. He recorded that: 'For one man, keen and hard working, I found permanent employment on a Labour Exchange; for another (a political victim, turned out of home as well as from work) I have found jobbing work and may soon find permanent employment; another I sent to Fircroft [College] for educational improvement till chances improved. In some cases I have not been able to help; emigration was the refuge.' [157]

The problems were offset by the mutual support, cameraderie, and sheer enthusiasm which usually developed. At Rochdale, for example, after the Saturday afternoon class, Tawney used to have tea and spend the evening at the home of one of the students 'and on these occasions other members of the class would crowd into the house to the limits of accommodation—and even beyond—and the discussion would often go on until the early hours of the morning'. [158] It was the same at Longton. Cartwright recalled a particular scene:

The class meeting is over, and we sit at ease, taking tea and biscuits . . . Talk ranges free and wide—problems of philosophy, evolution, politics, literature. Then R. H. T. reads to us Walt Whitman's 'When Lilacs Last in the Dooryard Bloom'd'; this moves a student to give us his favourite passage from the same source: 'Pioneers! O, Pioneers!' Another follows, quoting from a poem from Matthew Arnold that evidently has bitten him . . . And for some of us as we sit listening, a new door opens. [159]

That was written in 1929 and it echoes what Cartwright wrote after three years of work in Longton in 1911: 'The tutorial class has made for something more than mental training, it has made for the development of the human spirit; and for many of us opened the door to a wider and deeper life.' [160] Once again it is only the

---

[156] Ibid., fo. 9.

[157] *Oxford University Extension Delegacy: Tutorial Classes Committee: Annual Report 1909–10*, 15.

[158] Price, *Story of the WEA*, 33–4.

[159] [E. S. Cartwright] 'Looking Backwards: A Tutorial Class Anniversary. By an Old Student', *Rewley House Papers*, 2 (1929), 72–3.

[160] E. S. Cartwright, 'Longton Tutorial Class: Report on the Work of the Past Session and also Since the Commencement', 10 Apr. 1911, p. 2, Cartwright Papers, 'Records of Work in North Staffordshire' (Box), Oxford University Archives.

language of personal transcendence and idealism that can capture the experience of learning for these adult scholars. Tutorial classes may have provided the tools for the social emancipation of a class; they continued to offer students personal and emotional liberation, as well.

Yet the consciousness of collective endeavour and collective advancement was profound. There was no contradiction between personal enrichment and the social project that was intended by this new movement. *Oxford and Working-Class Education* had insisted that a general elevation of the working class was the movement's goal. The WEA named its magazine *The Highway* to emphasize its mission to construct a broad path 'along which the average man and woman can travel towards a larger life' rather than an 'educational ladder' by which the lucky or talented few could escape their origins.[161] The early students rejected the idea that three years of study in a tutorial class should end in individual qualifications and 'testamurs' for the successful.[162] And the students in the original tutorial classes were also resistant to the idea that some of their number might qualify for scholarships to study at Oxford, even though this was an explicit aim in *Oxford and Working-Class Education*. The Rochdale class rejected the idea of three of its members going to the University in 1910. In the following year Herbert Turner visited both Rochdale and Longton to reassess the mood and found that the majority of students, especially at Rochdale, were still against the idea of prize scholarships for the best. Turner quoted one Rochdale student to give a flavour of their opinions:

Workers have as much right in Oxford as anyone, but not in ones and twos...Present proposition bad. We who have never had a fortnight's holiday in our lives have suddenly dangled before us the chance of a year or two at Oxford, which one is to get & another not. Tell the Committee straight we absolutely refuse this offer, thanking them for nothing.[163]

But opinion at Longton had been more divided, and in 1913 the class wrote to the Tutorial Classes Committee in Oxford to endorse the idea of scholarships, though only under specific conditions. Longton students remained against the idea of prizes for the few in principle, but they 'would not have the same objection to a student proceeding to the university with the definite object of becoming a

---

[161] Price, *Story of the WEA*, 45.
[162] Beaton, 'Tutorial Class Movement', 256.
[163] 'Professor Turner's Report on his visit to Longton and Rochdale, Jan 1911', DES/F/2/1/8, Oxford University Archives, 6.

Tutorial Class teacher'.[164] Even this was controversial, however, and met with 'vigorous opposition within the WEA'.[165] Nevertheless, funds were found to bring Albert Emery, a potter, and Maud Griffiths, an elementary schoolteacher, to Balliol and St Hilda's Hall respectively in October 1913.[166] Emery lacked classical languages and did not read for a degree but spent three years studying Modern History under A. L. Smith before he took up tutorial class teaching in Sheffield. Later he became a tutor for the Oxford Committee and went back to the Potteries, where he taught until the 1950s. As a colleague wrote in 1949, 'Old Emery was a constant reminder of the ability of one of their own to make his university training available to industrial workers'.[167] Griffiths, meanwhile, passed the University Diploma in Economics and Political Science with a distinction, and then took up employment as a social worker at Bourneville, the Cadbury company town, in the absence of any openings in adult education.[168]

That these two adult scholars did go to Oxford is less significant than the rejection of individual advancement as a goal of the movement by the students themselves. Over time this position softened, certainly, but it is worth considering it as another reason why less was achieved in bringing working people to the University than in taking tutorial classes out to them. There were obvious problems associated with the admission of adult scholars, among them dealing with a curriculum that placed such weight on attainment in subjects utterly alien to workers, coping with the demands of written examinations, translating adult students to an entirely unfamiliar culture for three years, and funding the residence of students without means. When, in 1912, the Tutorial Classes Committee applied to the University for an annual subvention, a committee of the Hebdomadal Council reported in favour of promoting tutorial classes and summer school residence, but, on grounds of expense, against bringing working people into residence in the University. More good could be done with the money by subsidizing short

[164] H. Jenkins and W. Morries to the Oxford Tutorial Classes Committee, 21 Feb. 1913, in 'Report on University Scholarships Held by Tutorial Class Students', Nov. 1916, p. 1, DES/F/2/2/3.

[165] Howarth, 'Edwardian Reform Movement', 41.

[166] See A. E. Zimmern to A. Mansbridge, 19 Aug. 1913, Mansbridge Papers, lxiiiA, Add. MS 65257, fo. 34.

[167] J. W. Campbell to H. P. Smith, 11 Oct. 1949, DES/F/10/3/1, J. W. Campbell, Staff Tutor's File, Oxford University Archives.

[168] *Report on University Scholarships Held by Tutorial Class Students, Nov. 1916*, 6–14.

periods of university study and regular class work than scholarships.[169] And this was a position that the Joint Committee accepted and approved, notwithstanding the opposition of Tawney himself.[170] It submitted evidence to the Council that the majority of students consulted in several Oxford classes 'expressed a hope that the Committee would devote its energies rather to developing the Summer Classes and making it possible by means of scholarships for more students to attend them, than to bringing a few students up to the University for a regular course of two or three years'. Yet it was also hoped 'that it should be possible to meet the case of exceptional individuals', notably those who might be educated to become tutors themselves.[171]

But to these practical and financial considerations must be added lingering opposition to the very idea that some students might gain more from the movement than others. And allied to this was a deep suspicion of the very criteria applied by the universities in choosing the most deserving and able students. When William Temple came before the Royal Commission on Oxford and Cambridge in 1920 to give evidence in his capacity as President of the WEA, he explained the feeling in the movement, 'that the method of selecting [adult scholars] ought to be quite special in these cases; they should be chosen, as far as possible, by the class itself rather than the University authorities, because of our extreme desire to keep out from the work in those classes anything of the competitive spirit'.[172] The collective good took precedence over individual advantage; the ethos was co-operative rather than competitive. As such, the early workers' education movement was overtly opposed to the fundamental philosophy of the national educational system.

Perhaps the finest example of the camaraderie and the collective endeavour of the early tutorial class students was the North Staffordshire Miners' Higher Education Movement, started in 1911 by the students of the first Longton class. It was an evangelizing

[169] 'Report of the Committee on Applications by Extension Delegacy', Hebdomadal Council Papers, no. 92, 23 Apr.–27 June 1912, 125. The Tutorial Classes Committee asked for £522 and the Hebdomadal Council agreed to provide £400 per annum, but the state of university finances would not allow any payment at all in 1912–3. See Ibid., pp. lxiv–lxv, 138, 239, 271.

[170] 'Report of the Committee on Applications by the Extension Delegacy', Memorandum B, Apr. 1912, pp. 145–6. On Tawney's opposition, see below pp. 156–7.

[171] 'Report of Committee on Applications by Extension Delegacy', 144–6.

[172] 'Evidence of the Workers' Educational Association represented by Canon Temple', 18 June 1920, Royal Commission on Oxford and Cambridge Universities, Bodleian Library, MS Top Oxon b 109, fo. 575.

movement, intended to bring adult education to the isolated mining communities to the north and west of the Potteries.[173] As Zimmern explained in 1914,

These villages are for the most part difficult to reach and are thus removed from all contact with the ordinary opportunities of civilization. The university tutorial class students three years ago discerned in these semi-industrial villages a great field for missionary work, and as this coincided in point of time with a demand for higher education which came from the miners themselves, the two parties were quickly brought together and a new educational movement set on foot.[174]

It started with a meeting at the Stoke School of Mining in May 1911 which brought together members of the Longton tutorial class and representatives from some twenty neighbouring mining villages. Tawney gave an address on 'Higher Education Considered Apart From Industrial Training'.[175] Cartwright, joint secretary of the scheme for its duration, wrote to Oxford to appeal for assistance and described the project as 'the education of a whole coalfield'.[176] The Longton tutorial class students organized it and were themselves the tutors, passing on the knowledge and insight they were gaining from Tawney to other workers.[177] Eight of the ten 'class leaders' in the first year were students from the Longton class—a miner, a colliery weighman, a potter's engineman, a potter's decorator, a railway telegraphist, an elementary schoolteacher, a secretary, and a clerk. They included Cartwright, Albert Emery, and Maud Griffiths, and they all remained members of Tawney's tutorial class while going out themselves and teaching.[178] After the first year, students from other tutorial classes that were beginning or in process in the Potteries assisted and shared the work. It was not successful in all locations, but the first classes reached approximately two hundred students and by 1916–17 the Movement was serving 650 students in twenty-seven centres.[179] In 1921 the Movement voluntarily merged into the newly established North Staffordshire District of the WEA. Seven years before that Zimmern related that he had attended a

---

[173] See R. A. Lowe, 'The North Staffordshire Miners' Higher Education Movement', *Educational Review*, 22/3 (June 1970), 263–77. See also *Ministry of Reconstruction: Adult Education Committee: Final Report*, 296–309.

[174] Zimmern, 'Education and the Working Class', 267.

[175] H. P. Smith, 'Edward Stuart Cartwright. A Note on his Work for Adult Education', *Rewley House Papers*, 3/1 (1949–50), 20.

[176] Quoted in Smith, *Labour and Learning*, 30.

[177] Cartwright, 'Looking Backwards', 69–70.

[178] Smith, 'Cartwright', 19.

[179] Lowe, 'North Staffordshire Miners', 267–8.

lecture given to 'an audience of miners in a village schoolroom on one of the ridges overlooking this vale of smoke'. The lecturer, 'a distinguished student of sixteenth century England' (and hence almost certainly Tawney) had apparently mused that if Erasmus himself had returned to Britain 'to meet his fellow scholars' and to 'investigate the revival of humanism in the England of today' he would have been directed to visit the Potteries.[180]

v

He might also have been directed towards the WEA Summer School which was first held in Balliol in 1910 and quickly became a national focus for tutorial class students. From 1903 WEA students had been attending the extension Summer Meetings in increasing numbers. They formed a distinct social group at these, and once tutorial classes had begun, a distinct group educationally as well, for they required a more intensive academic experience than could be provided under the format of a Summer Meeting. The idea of a separate WEA summer school designed to build on the work done during the year in tutorial classes, came out of a dinner party held by A. L. Smith in Balliol during the 1909 Summer Meeting for leaders in the new movement like Mansbridge and Zimmern, and students like Gill, Price, and Reuben George of Swindon.[181] Its organization fell to Price of Rochdale and Kolthammer of Oxford, and in the following year some eighty-seven students came into residence during July and August. As the *Annual Report* for 1910 explained,

The original plan for this experiment included an idea of (i) Getting hold of scattered students who had shown enthusiasm for any particular subject, and capacity to pursue that subject further; and (ii) Bringing to such students some permanent benefit by clearing up their difficulties, directing them to the best sources, and giving them the stimulus of personal contact with authoritative representatives in each subject.[182]

There were no tuition charges, though students paid for their train fares and board and lodging in the town or in college rooms. For most, the week in Oxford was their annual holiday. They were sent reading lists in advance and once in Oxford attended lectures each

---

[180] Zimmern, 'Education', 263–4. [181] Price, *Story of the WEA*, 48–9.
[182] *Oxford University Extension Delegacy: Tutorial Classes Committee: Report Including Accounts on the Second Year's Work to September 30 1910* (Oxford, 1910), 40.

morning, had two or three individual tutorials each week, and wrote two weekly essays. In 1910 most of the teaching fell to Kolthammer, Tawney, R. V. Lennard and a young fellow of Balliol, A. D. Lindsay. But the Summer School soon came to the attention of many more sympathetic dons who offered their services. In 1914, for example, the lecturers and tutors included half the historical talent of early twentieth century Britain—G. N. Clark, G. D. H. Cole, Lewis Namier, David Ogg, A. L. Smith, A. D. Lindsay, Keith Feiling, Ernest Barker, and R. W. Seton-Watson. Many rather more unlikely figures also lent support and made donations to the cause of residential working-class education in Oxford. Mansbridge depicted Sir William Anson, the Warden of All Souls and also the Unionist MP for Oxford University 'near to midnight, keeping time to "Auld Lang Syne" with hands clasping those of the burly trade unionists on either side of him'.[183]

The reponses of working-class students to Oxford were varied. Some simply revelled at being in the University; more made appreciative and thoughtful comments about the lasting effects of the academic work on them.[184] George Brown, later the deputy leader of the Labour Party, remembered 'with pride' the Balliol Summer School he attended somewhat later in the 1930s, and explained that the pride came 'from the studies one was enabled to do there'.[185] Others responded as missionaries: 'we will do anything to get other workers interested, so that there will be a greater demand in the future for a fuller and freer education.'[186] Indeed one student wrote in 1911 that he was 'hoping to be able to read some papers on Plato's *Republic* to the clubs in our district':[187] perhaps Zimmern's story about the new humanism in the Potteries was not that farfetched after all. Yet some of the comments articulated a complex amalgam of the aspirations and frustrations of worker students who lacked the means either for self-development or social advance. According to one student who attended in 1911,

The young man who has never had to rough it, and is studying merely for the sake of obtaining a degree, or for position, would scarcely study with equal earnestness and determination to one who has suffered in contact with the world, who is conscious of the existence of evils, and knows that

[183] Mansbridge quoted in Smith, *Labour and Learning*, 45.
[184] *Oxford University Extension Delegacy* ... (see n. 182), 31–59; *Report on the Working of the Summer Classes held during the Long Vacation at Oxford in Balliol College and New College* (Oxford, 1912).
[185] George Brown, *In My Way* (London, 1971), 29.
[186] *Oxford University Extension Delegacy* ... (see n. 182), 55.
[187] *Report on the Working of the Summer Classes*, 18.

it is only by personal effort at higher education that he may be of any use in overcoming those evils. Such men exist among the workers; they have minds full of practical knowledge, but are unable to reveal the contents of those minds, either by word of mouth or by pen.[188]

An article in *The Highway* on the 1911 Summer School described very well the ambivalence of some of the students who manifested 'a strange admixture of humility and pride'. Those who came to Oxford offered 'generous submission to authority', but held fast 'by a wilful revolt against [social] conditions'. Oxford simultaneously gave 'mellower comprehension, and [made] acquiescence more impossible than before'. The author picked out one particular worker from a linoleum factory in Lancashire to make his point: 'Such men come to Oxford, and rejoice in its mental discipline, but their intolerance of injustice is not weakened but strengthened.'[189] Once again we are being warned off any simplistic association of Oxford and incorporation, and any crude association between university adult education and a weakening of radicalism. It was possible to admire the University and the culture it represented without falling victim to it.

This seems to have been true of Albert Emery, who would eventually study at the University and then teach adult classes in his native Potteries into the 1950s. He first visited Oxford to attend the 1909 Summer Meeting. On returning to Fenton, Staffordshire, he set down his reflections on the experience in a letter to Zimmern:

Coming back to this 'city of dreadful night', with its smoke wreathes curling up from its myriad chimneys, with its squalid streets and oppressing gloom, where the noise of the machine drowns the cry of the helpless, and the cancer of modern industrialism is laid bare, and contrasting it with 'the city of dreaming spires', the heart turns sick, and the brain reels, and one wonders if there is not some way of ridding England of these miniature hells, some broad highway along which this degraded mass of toiling humanity may pass to a higher ideal, a higher mode of life, a nobler purpose.

Oxford was associated with a higher calling and with a physical as well as a spiritual transcendence in the mind of yet another worker-scholar. Yet Oxford had not seduced him: 'Zimmern,' he continued, 'Oxford has made me a worse rebel than I was before.'[190] The

---

[188] Ibid. 49–50.
[189] R. L. Jones, 'The Invasion of a University', *The Highway*, 3/35 (Aug. 1911), 173.
[190] A. Emery to A. Zimmern, 23 Aug. 1909, Zimmern MSS, Bodleian Library, Oxford, 12, fos. 63–5.

working men who came to the Summer Meetings did not forget who they were, as William Temple found out on a famous occasion at the 1912 Summer School. He had preached at St Mary's in the morning, acceded to the request of some of the students that he answer their questions on religion, and he spent a heroic four hours after dinner in the hall at Balliol, fielding questions about Christianity and the Church from a gathering of workers that 'was critical if not actually hostile'.[191]

Mansbridge wrote of 'a general labourer and an ardent socialist [who] could not restrain his tears as, standing upon New College Tower, he gazed on the incomparable beauty of Oxford. "I want my comrades to see this," he said.' Mansbridge took him to mean that 'he would strive with all his power to make the dingy, gloomy, crowded town in which he lived as near to the ideal of beauty as ever it was in his power to do'.[192] But another and similar story gives reason to doubt this interpretation. In the early 1930s the young Frank Pickstock, later Deputy Director of the Oxford Extra-Mural Delegacy and Labour Mayor of Oxford, came for a week to the Balliol Summer School. He used to relate that he was in tears in the train back to Stoke when the week was over, and that he cried because he had never seen such a place as Oxford and could not bear to leave it and return to the ugliness of the Potteries.[193] Pickstock's honesty, so like Emery's response a generation before, rings true: for many working-class students, Oxford was confusing and disorientating. It may or may not have affected their politics, but it invariably affected them emotionally and aesthetically. Margaret Cole once wondered aloud about 'the influence of the Summer School, that peculiarly Anglo-Saxon combination of holiday-making, sociability, and more-or-less intellectual effort, on the development of British radical thought'.[194] One suspects that the answer to her query would be rather more complex than she appreciated.

IV

As the recruitment of tutors for the Summer School suggests, the tutorial classes movement and the alliance with the Workers'

---

[191] Iremonger, *Temple*, 84; A. Mansbridge, *Fellow Men: A Gallery of England 1876–1946* (London, 1948), 49.

[192] A. Mansbridge, *The Older Universities of England* (London, 1923), 185.

[193] I am grateful to Douglas Hewitt who first told me this story which he had heard from Frank Pickstock himself.

[194] Margaret Cole, *Growing Up Into Revolution* (London, 1949), 117.

Educational Association quickened interest in adult education in Oxford and brought into the movement a new generation of dons to match the new generation of students. A. D. Lindsay began lecturing in 1910, became a member of the Tutorial Classes Committee in the following year and served on it until 1948. W. G. S. Adams, Warden of All Souls between 1933 and 1945, joined the committee in 1913 and remained a member until his retirement. Another of the new enthusiasts, William Temple, a fellow of Queen's College, a future Archbishop of Canterbury, and one of the Joint Secretaries of the Tutorial Classes Committee between 1908 and 1910, had almost been born and bred for the movement. Like several of those who came into extension lecturing in the 1880s, he had been educated at Rugby, went up to Balliol, where he took a double first, and was President of the Union in his final year as an undergraduate, 1904. His father, Archbishop Frederick Temple, in association with Sir Thomas Dyke Acland, father of Arthur Acland, had long before been a pioneer of the Oxford local examinations, a milestone on the road to university extension. It is said that William was drawn into the movement when he attended the 1905 meeting of the WEA in Oxford out of respect for his former headmaster, Bishop Percival, who was in the chair.[195] And to cap it all, he married a niece of Arthur Acland, linking once again the Acland and Temple families. Temple was accustomed to university extension by birth, education, and connection, and from 1908 to 1924 he was President of the WEA. He remained involved in the WEA and committed to working-class higher education all his life.[196]

An entirely different kind of don who came into the movement at this stage was G. D. H. Cole. He later recalled that just after taking his degree at Oxford (and just before he took up a prize fellowship at Magdalen College) 'I first linked up with the Workers' Educational Association. My first contact with it was at the Oxford WEA Summer School' where, in 1912, he lectured on Rousseau.[197] It seems that he was 'led . . . WEAwards' by the combined influence of A. L. Smith and A. D. Lindsay.[198] In a speech he gave in 1938

[195] R. H. Tawney, 'William Temple. An Appreciation', *The Highway*, 36 (Jan. 1945), 44. [196] Iremonger, *Temple*, 73–89.
[197] G. D. H. Cole, 'Recollections of Workers' Education', G. D. H. Cole Papers, Nuffield College, Oxford, A1/24/9/1–4.
[198] See Cole to Lady Lindsay, 'Thursday' 1952: 'I was one of the many who as undergraduates got inspiration from him: indeed, he started me off on my course as a political theorist and, with A.L. [Smith], led me WEAwards, with consequences momentous to me.' Papers of A. D. Lindsay, Keele University Archives, L/231. I am grateful to Brian Harrison for this reference.

Cole recalled his motives at the time: 'I felt I should be doing something in which I should come into really close contact with people who wanted to learn, that I should be free to adapt my methods to their needs, and that I should learn a great deal myself in the process.'[199] Cole had been a socialist since his teenage years and his reading of William Morris, and he cut a figure in University journalism and politics after he went up to Balliol in 1908.[200] Working-class education obviously appealed to a young man attracted to a voluntaristic and communitarian form of socialism, and when Cole discovered a passable model of the good society at Balliol in 1912, he was enraptured. 'It was', he wrote, 'a stirring and encouraging experience.'[201]

His initial responses were set down in a paper written while the Summer School was still in progress in August 1912 and subsequently read to the Oxford Fabian Society, entitled 'Socialism and Education'.[202] Cole sought to define the 'ideal of working class education', the extent to which it was attainable 'in the existing colleges and associations engaged in promoting it', and to discuss the relationship of education to political activism and political change.[203] Cole defined the 'three root principles' of 'successful adult education': 'it must teach what the learner wants, in an impartial spirit, and from a philosophical standpoint.'[204] He associated these principles with what he had seen and experienced at Balliol and the essay thus became in Cole's words, 'a plea on behalf of the WEA'; indeed, it amounted to 'a complete vindication of the aims and methods of the WEA'.[205] He praised the Association's educational practices, notably its rejection of examinations, and he was particularly impressed by the general ability of the students: 'Perhaps the most encouraging feature of the present is that so far there have been revealed, not a few geniuses standing above a dead level of mediocrity, but a high average level of keenness and intelligence.'[206]

In a subsequent article on the Summer School, published in 1913, Cole continued to enthuse over the ability of the students. He discussed the problems that prevented workers from coming to Oxford

---

[199] Speech to a conference of the British Institute of Adult Education, Sept. 1938. TS in Working-Class Education file, Cole Papers, A1/24/10/1–7.

[200] See A. W. Wright, *G. D. H. Cole and Socialist Democracy* (Oxford, 1979), 13–31.

[201] G. D. H. Cole, 'An Oxford Summer School', *The Blue Book*, 1/5 (March 1913), 389.

[202] G. D. H. Cole, 'Socialism and Education 12/8/[19]12', Cole Papers, B2/16.

[203] Ibid., fo. 6.   [204] Ibid., fo. 12. See also fo. 19.

[205] Ibid., fos. 18, 23.   [206] Ibid., fos. 13, 20.

for any length of time. But he commended the compromise of tutorial classes through the winter and 'friendly intercourse and individual tuition' in Oxford in the summer. He rejected 'the mania' for
comparing standards in the movement with those at Oxford, and he
looked forward to the movement 'doing its own work' in its own
way. Above all, Cole responded, as Oxford always did, to the
idealism he found in the worker-scholars who 'come to the classes,
not with any idea of material advancement—for the WEA has none
to offer—not with an eye to results—for the WEA does not judge
by results—but from a real desire for knowledge and understanding
of the world in which we live'. He warmed to a movement which
understood education as 'the fostering of spiritual growth'. And in
a great peroration he concluded from his brief acquaintance with
the movement that 'the rising force of labour is finding its spiritual
equipment, its ideas and *droit prolétarién*, defined and formulated
by its own unselfish and philosophic endeavour'. This probably tells
us rather more about the nature of socialism in Edwardian Oxford
than about adult education. Evidently Green's ideas and Toynbee's
rhetoric continued to exert their influence.[207]

Cole's thus far brief experience of adult education formed a theme
in his first book, *The World of Labour*, also published in 1913.[208]
He pictured the new adult education movement building a cadre of
leaders for the workers, and forming 'a type of man ... capable of
understanding the working class, and remaining of it, even if his
standards rose higher than those of his fellows'.[209] *The World of
Labour* was Cole's first expression of the ideas of Guild Socialism,
that fascinating synthesis of workers' control of industry with democratic participation, voluntarism, communitarianism, and fellowship.
These ideas dominated the next decade of Cole's life as he tried to
put before the labour movement an alternative to the state
collectivism of Fabianism, the industrial militancy of syndicalism,
and the conformity of traditional parliamentarianism.[210] It would be
too much to argue that his experiences at Balliol in 1912 were a
milestone on the road to the Guild idea. But contact with workers'
education in 1912 came just as Cole grew disillusioned with the

[207] Cole, 'Oxford Summer School', 389–96.
[208] G. D. H. Cole, *The World of Labour: A Discussion of the Present and Future
of Trade Unionism* (London, 1913), 16–18.   [209] Ibid. 384.
[210] For a discussion of Cole's early political thought see J. M. Winter, *Socialism
and the Challenge of War: Ideas and Politics in Britain 1912–18* (London, 1974),
chs. 4, 5, pp. 99–149; A. W. Wright, 'From Fabianism to Guild Socialism: The
Early Political Thought of G. D. H. Cole', *Bulletin of the Society for the Study of
Labour History*, 32 (spring 1976), 23–5.

reformism and *étatism* of the Fabians which began to seem to him to be lacking in spirit, imagination, creativity, and will—the very qualities he had found in the socialism of Morris, touched by romanticism and utopianism, and to which he remained deeply attracted. Indeed, the paper he composed on 'Socialism and Education' while the WEA Summer School was in session in Balliol, was explicitly critical of Fabianism 'for its failure to understand the centrality of working-class education for the development of consciousness'.[211] He argued that spiritual growth was every bit as important as material advance to the labour movement and that Fabianism, in its neglect of the former had also neglected the primary means to this spiritual development, working-class education.[212] In his postscript to the piece he offered as his apology for writing it 'that we [the Fabians] have so clearly failed to do our duty'. He hoped 'to encourage Fabians generally, and especially in Oxford, to take up the [educational] questions for themselves'.[213] Three years later he resigned from the Fabian Society, critical of the Webbs' narrow focus on legislation and administration as 'the cure of all social ills', though he later rejoined.[214]

To Cole, the experience of fellowship with worker scholars engaged in the simultaneous projects of self-improvement and collective advance demonstrated the limitations of a socialist political strategy that had not engaged directly with the working class, but which supposedly acted on its behalf. The summer school in Balliol must have also seemed like a model of the 'Guild' society to which he was moving at this time. This explains his enthusiasm at that moment in 1912 and his subsequent engagement with working-class education. Cole taught tutorial classes for Oxford and London University through the First World War and went on to become Director of Tutorial Classes in London between 1922 and 1925. It was during this period that he played a leading role in bringing together the WEA and the tutorial classes movement with the trade unions, and creating the Workers' Educational Trade Union Committee (WETUC).[215] After his return to Oxford in 1925 as university reader in economics with a fellowship at University College, he

[211] Wright, *Cole and Socialist Democracy*, 23. G. D. H. Cole, 'Socialism and Education', 12 Aug. 1912, Cole Papers.
[212] Cole, 'Socialism and Education', fos. 24–7.   [213] Ibid., fo. 30.
[214] G. D. H. Cole, 'Recent Developments in the British Labour Movement', *American Economic Review*, 8/3 (Sept. 1918), 492, quoted in Winter, *Socialism*, 139.
[215] Margaret Cole, *The Life of G. D. H. Cole* (London, 1971) 106.

continued to teach tutorial classes for several years, but was probably more influential in spreading interest in adult education among students in interwar Oxford than as a tutor.[216] In the 1930s and 1940s he served on the Oxford Extra-Mural Delegacy. Throughout his academic career, and in all the twists and turns of his social and political thinking, the education of the labour movement as the essential precondition for winning, holding, and using power, was an article of faith for him.[217]

The new movement also drew its personnel from among the students. Given the emphasis in the WEA and in *Oxford and Working-Class Education* on democratic control of the class and syllabus and on the active participation of students in the organization of their education, it was to be expected that people of ability and resourcefulness would emerge to take a wider share in the work. More to the point, perhaps, many of the students were already used to organizational work in unions, friendly societies, the co-operative movement, and other forms of adult education, and many of those who were not when they joined a class were similarly involved by the time they left it. As a founder member of the tutorial class at Tunstall in North Staffordshire explained of his enrolment in 1913, 'I was then a young man craving for some method and opportunity of acquiring knowledge to enable me to give service in trade union, politics and public affairs'.[218] Henry Clay, later the first Warden of Nuffield College, Oxford was an early tutor of tutorial classes after a period as warden of a settlement house in Sheffield. He noted in 1910 that most of his students in Halifax were 'active political workers, nine are engaged in Sunday school and Adult school teaching, and one member has been sent to Holloway Gaol three times for attempting to present petitions to Mr. Asquith'—was a suffragette in other words.[219] A survey in 1918 by the Tutorial Classes Committee in Oxford found that 64 per cent of students were taking part in some form of voluntary work in connection with trade unions, co-operative societies, local authorities, political and religious bodies, and in the adult education movement itself.[220] Tutorial

---

[216] G. D. H. Cole, 'The Tutor', *The Highway*, 44 (Apr. 1953), 282; Hugh Gaitskell, 'At Oxford in the Twenties', in Asa Briggs and John Saville (eds.), *Essays in Labour History: In Memory of G. D. H. Cole* (London, 1960), 15.

[217] Wright, *Cole and Socialist Democracy*, 89, 144–6.

[218] J. A. Mack, *The History of Tunstall II Tutorial Class 1913–34* (Stoke-on-Trent, 1935), 25.

[219] *Tutorial Classes Committee Annual Report 1909–10*, 22.

[220] *Ministry of Reconstruction: Adult Education Committee: Final Report*, PP 1919, Cmd. 321, xxviii. 58.

classes drew on an activist élite of the working class and trained others to take their place within it. As Tawney explained in 1938 in the preface to a book designed to publicize the public achievements of WEA students, 'A considerable proportion of the members of WEA classes join them under the impulse of a social motive. A considerable proportion use the knowledge acquired in them to serve the cause of their fellow workers, either in voluntary organizations or on public bodies.'[221]

From the first classes, Gill and Price of Rochdale, who showed considerable ability, went swiftly into senior positions in the WEA, and Edward Stuart Cartwright, the class secretary from Longton, went to Oxford to be Organizing Secretary of the Tutorial Classes Committee in January 1912. He remained in Oxford for over thirty years until his retirement in 1945. No one did more than he to realize the goals set down in *Oxford and Working-Class Education*. As Tawney wrote in his obituary of Cartwright, he carried the new Oxford initiative 'from infancy to maturity, piloted it through two world wars, and turned it from an interesting experiment into a triumphant reality'.[222] He was exactly Cole's new 'type of man' who could lead the working class without being of it.

Cartwright, often known as 'E.S.C.', was born in 1876.[223] The son of a clerk, he also worked as a clerk in the service of the borough of Longton where he lived. He was a gifted student, and in the succession of extension courses held in Longton after 1900 that focused interest in higher education locally, he won a string of distinctions in the final examinations. Ernest Barker, indeed, after reading one of his scripts, thought that if he wanted to try for Oxford 'he would have quite a good chance of winning a history scholarship'. But Cartwright was more than just a clever student; he was also, as *The Highway* put it in 1911, 'an organizer of quite extraordinary ability and power of work'.[224] After a course on astronomy at Longton in 1902 the Oxford tutor, J. A. Hardcastle, was evidently surprised by his success there and yet his relative failure nearby in Stoke during the same session, and he put it down

---

[221] R. H. Tawney, 'Preface', in *The Adult Student as Citizen: A Record of Service by WEA Students Past and Present* (London, 1938), 4.

[222] R. H. Tawney, 'Mr. E. S. Cartwright: A Leader of the Adult Education Movement', *Manchester Guardian*, 16 Aug. 1950, p. 3.

[223] The following remarks on Cartwright draw on the portrait of him presented in Smith, Cartwright, *passim*.

[224] Oxford University Extension: Reports of Lecturers, Examiners and Local Committees 1907–8, Oxford University Archives, DES/R/3/37, fo. 52; *The Highway*, 4/39 (Nov. 1911).

to 'the personal energy of Mr. E. S. Cartwright . . . I am not sure of the regulations about S[ummer] M[eeting] scholarships, but he deserves recognition both as a student and a worker in the cause.'[225] Indeed the sudden emergence of Longton as a genuine centre for higher education may well have owed everything to Cartwright's work. Once in Oxford, he oversaw the programme of tutorial classes and made the annual Balliol Summer School into a national focus of the adult education movement.

Mary Stocks called Cartwright 'a host in himself on the side of working-class education. His whole personality was aflame with enthusiasm for it and delight in it.'[226] But an Oxford tutor who probably knew him better, and who knew the region of his birth intimately, was more accurate in his description of the modesty and 'shy genius' of a 'dapper' man who 'exercised the creative touch by stealth'.[227] Another colleague paid tribute to his 'quiet, unobtrusive, but pervasive way of putting people at their ease'.[228] George Wigg, later a Labour MP and Cabinet minister, came to know Cartwright well, first when Wigg was an honorary Area Organizer for the WEA in Kent in the early 1930s (while Wigg was in the army) and then between 1935 and 1940 when he was District Secretary of the WEA in North Staffordshire. Wigg admired greatly the 'stalwart, saintly secretary' of the Tutorial Classes Committee in Oxford: ' "E.S.", diffident and dedicated, lived for the ideal of an England made homogeneous and great by, to quote him, "the seeping through of responsibility based on knowledge" '.[229] Cartwright was one of those 'self-educated . . . new men and women of socialism's voluntary associations' described by Carl Levy, whose activism led them to enter 'the white-collar world' and who experienced thereby a host of changes in their terms of employment, work-time discipline, and geographical and social mobility. This is where he belongs sociologically.[230] Indeed, it was the very fact of this social translation that gave him his role in the adult education movement as an intermediary trusted by all. Cartwright was 'an interpreter of Oxford to those outside its gates. He stood for Oxford to a whole generation

[225] Oxford University Extension: Lecturers' and Examiners' Reports 1902–3, DES/R/3/31, fo. 223.
[226] Stocks, *Workers' Educational Association*, 38.
[227] Cecil Scrimgeour, *Personalities and Partners in the North Staffordshire WEA District, 1921–1971* (Stoke-on-Trent, 1972), 4.
[228] Smith, 'Cartwright', 12.
[229] George Wigg, *George Wigg* (London, 1972), 81.
[230] Carl Levy, 'Introduction', in id., *Socialism and the Intelligentsia 1880–1914* (London, 1987), 23.

of students who passed through the Tutorial Classes and the Summer School.' And in the other direction, Cartwright interpreted the WEA and working-class education generally to the University.[231]

But even Cartwright would have deferred to his close friend R. H. Tawney when it came to winning the confidence of both sides in the new movement. At one of the meetings of the Joint Committee responsible for *Oxford and Working-Class Education*, Mactavish had 'raised the question of the character and standpoint of the teachers. He said they must be men capable of approaching the subjects they taught from the working-class point of view . . . there was too little common language and sympathy between lecturers and working-class audiences.'[232] It was Tawney's achievement that he was able to find the common language and the sympathy to make the first classes so successful and thus set a standard and a model for the movement to follow.

Like Temple, his friend from boyhood, Tawney was educated at Rugby and Balliol. He graduated in 1903 with a second in Greats and went to live for three years at the University's settlement, Toynbee Hall, in Whitechapel, taking on the position there of Secretary of the Children's Country Holiday Fund. At Toynbee Hall, observing and investigating the lives of the poor, he came to reject Samuel Barnett's traditional Christian piety and evangelism. Although Tawney remained loyal to Christian values throughout his life (indeed, there are those who place Christianity ahead of socialism in Tawney's outlook and commitments)[233] he began to understand that these values could be relevant and realizable only in a society which had been altered so as to respect social justice and fairness. One way to alter society was through education. Tawney gave several classes at Toynbee Hall, some of which were on social and industrial issues. In 1905 he joined the WEA and was elected to its executive committee in a matter of months. And in 1906, as if he were Edward Hallin from Mrs Humphry Ward's *Marcella* come alive, he wrote to his future brother-in-law, William Beveridge, to explain that 'teaching in an industrial town is just what I want ultimately to do'.[234] As Terrill has put it, Tawney 'had come to

[231] Smith, 'Cartwright', 24.
[232] 'Oxford Joint Committee. Minutes of the Meeting held on December 27th and 28th 1907', A. L. Smith's Letters, Box 14, 'WEA', 3.
[233] I owe this insight to Dr Gerald Aylmer who was one of Tawney's last postgraduate research students.
[234] Quoted in J. M. Winter, 'R. H. Tawney's Early Political Thought', *Past and Present*, 47 (May 1970), 73.

think that education, not charity, was what workers needed'.[235]
After a brief period teaching economics at Glasgow University, his
Oxford contacts and involvement in the negotiations leading up to
the launch of tutorial classes won him the chance to teach the first
groups. And their success led to a formal appointment. At the first
meeting of the Tutorial Classes Committee in November 1908 it
was resolved: 'That Mr. R. H. Tawney, B.A., Balliol, be appointed
as a teacher under the Committee, to take, if possible, five classes;
the Committee to be responsible for £200 annual payment to Mr.
Tawney, and for Mr. Tawney to reside and lecture in Oxford in the
summer term.'[236] Tawney taught tutorial classes for Oxford for the
next six years. Most were on economic and industrial history, but
he also gave classes on seventeenth-century political history, economic
theory, and local government.

Beatrice Webb, who knew him well, described him as 'a scholar,
a saint and a social reformer'.[237] But that was written in the 1930s.
At this stage he was also a young man with a career to build who
stood out for a permanent position teaching Oxford's tutorial classes.
Letters to Mansbridge in early 1908 suggest how cussed and demanding he could be in the pursuit of secure university employment
and status.[238] He wanted to teach tutorial classes and be given an
official position within the university as well; he would not be fobbed
off delivering 'lectures in Oxford of an unofficial kind'.[239]

Tawney was also among the more militant and impatient of the
leaders of working-class education. While others put their energies
into building the infrastructure and spirit of this movement, Tawney
did not deviate from the position he set out in 1906 when writing
anonymously in *The Westminster Gazette*: that provision for working-

---

[235] Ross Terrill, *R. H. Tawney and His Times: Socialism as Fellowship* (London, 1974), 37.

[236] 'Tutorial Classes Committee: Minutes of First Meeting', 'Extra Mural Work 1907–09', A. L. Smith Papers.

[237] Beatrice Webb, *Diary of Beatrice Webb*, iv, 1924–43, ed. N. and J. Macken-zie (London, 1985), 360 (entry for 8 Dec. 1935).

[238] See a series of letters from Mansbridge trying to soothe Tawney's anxieties over his position and career. Mansbridge to Tawney, 10, 28, 29, 30 Jan.; 27, 31 Mar.; 6 Apr. 1908, 'R. H. Tawney: Correspondence re Early Tutorial Classes 1907–8', Early Tutorial Classes I (box), WEA Archives. See also Mansbridge to A. L. Smith, 29 Jan. 1908, 'Extra-Mural Work 1907–09', A. L. Smith Papers.

[239] R. H. Tawney to Mansbridge, 6 Apr. 1908, '1907–8 Joint Committee on Tutorial Classes, DES/F/14/1, Oxford University Archives. During the Hilary and Trinity terms 1909, Tawney lectured in Balliol on 'The History of the English Poor Law'.

class students and communities was to go hand in hand with the reform of the ancient universities. He continued to press for a Royal Commission to investigate the finances and social composition of Oxford and Cambridge, and, as some remarkable letters to Mansbridge in the autumn of 1912 demonstrate, he took it upon himself to goad the WEA to pursue this course in parallel with its strictly educational work.

Tawney wanted the WEA 'to take risks' and 'to be willing to face anger at the Universities'. He wanted to see the Association 'stepping boldly forward and not merely asking for a Commission to inquire, but specifying in outline the abuses which need inquiry'. The Association's annual meeting should pass a resolution decrying such attempts at reform as had so far been made in Oxford; the *Highway* should 'commit itself to a forward policy'. To Tawney, the object of the WEA was 'not to be popular with all parties but to speak for those who can't speak for themselves, and the more unpleasant that is, the more readily it should do it'. It was necessary to take the initiative because, in Tawney's view,

Oxford at least is sinking back into the bad old ways. Class prejudice is as strong there as ever (naturally it is not shown to you). Workpeople who go there for the summer school accept kindness when they ought to demand justice. Can you honestly say you think that the great system of educational and social privilege of which Oxford is the symbol is nearer being shaken than it was when the Oxford Report was presented? I cannot . . .[240]

The real object for Tawney was to open Oxford so that working people could study within the University. Even while teaching tutorial classes and extolling their virtues in public, he regarded them as insufficient for the educational needs of the workers and as all too easily provided by a University that remained fundamentally unchanged by their existence. In a subsequent letter to Mansbridge he reminded him of the recommendation of the *1908 Report*: 'that Tutorial Classes were only a step towards throwing open the University & not a substitute for it'. Oxford was content to 'throw crumbs to labour in the shape of Tutorial Classes' and the annual Summer School: the initiatives since 1907 were 'a sort of "fire insurance" ' for the University. Indeed, it was 'becoming a settled doctrine at the Universities that Tutorial classes exhaust their responsibilities'. Hence the Oxford Joint Committee should demand

[240] R. H. Tawney to Mansbridge, 21 Sept. 1912, Mansbridge Papers, xxii, Add. MS 62516, fos. 89–93. I am grateful to Janet Howarth of St Hilda's College, Oxford, who drew these letters to my attention.

a reduction in the cost of student living and a reform of the scholarship system to channel assistance to poorer students.[241] As he explained in a third letter, calling on the WEA to press the prime minister, Asquith, for a Royal Commission, 'directly we let educational authorities think we are almost satisfied, our day is over'.[242] Conciliation, as Tawney called it, had not succeeded. Pressure should be applied because Oxford was vulnerable. As he wrote to Mansbridge in exasperation, 'Don't you yet understand that Oxford started Tutorial Classes because it was *afraid*?'[243]

The accuracy of this comment may be open to some doubt. These letters had a purpose: Tawney was trying to stiffen the sinew of a man noted for his gentleness and emollience, and who was, as Tawney hinted in his first letter, rather too easily impressed by Oxford's charm and 'good manners'.[244] It could as well be argued that Oxford assisted the tutorial classes movement thanks to the well-orchestrated campaign of a handful of mainly younger, reforming dons, supported by the vague goodwill of rather more sympathetic onlookers. The evidence does not suggest that fear alone inspired Oxford's patronage of the new movement; indeed, a better word might be prudence. The enthusiasm of a minority met with the enlightened self-interest of considerably more dons, who recognized the merit in being seen to support the educational democracy, but showed no very great willingness to change the settled structures of the University and devote considerable resources to the project. This was exactly the response of the university authorities to university extension in the 1880s and 1890s, after all, and it would have been unrealistic to have expected attitudes to have changed rapidly, notwithstanding the *Oxford Report* and the establishment of the Joint Committee. Moreover, as we have seen, Tawney's own students in the first tutorial classes were suspicious of scholarships to Oxford for just a few of their number: the movement was feeling towards a collective ethic of education, which in other respects Tawney supported. And Tawney's putative assault upon his own university would have alienated Oxford from the movement for working-class education at a time when University and college finance, as well as good will, were crucial to it.[245]

Tawney's impatience, as expressed in these letters, and his continued campaign for extensive institutional reform of the universities, mark him out from many of his colleagues in the movement

[241] Ibid., 10 Oct. 1912, fos. 79–82.   [242] Ibid., 15 Oct. 1912, fo. 98.
[243] Ibid., 21 Sept. 1912, fo. 92.   [244] Ibid., fo. 90.
[245] Howarth, 'Edwardian Reform Movement', 41.

who seemed somewhat more willing to accept and use what was offered. Later images of him as a benign and statesmanlike intellectual father-figure to the labour movement have tended to obscure the impatient radical of the Edwardian period. But unlike other critics of the WEA's strategy, however, Tawney did not reject the partnership with the universities which he had himself helped to construct. Indeed, it was in these years and through these new forms of adult education that, as Terrill has suggested, Tawney 'found himself'.[246] His so-called *Commonplace Book*, a mixture of his ethical and social reflections and his observations of the working-class life he encountered as a tutor between 1912 and 1914 (when he volunteered as a private in the Manchester regiment), gives an insight into the way in which working-class education provided a basis for the development of his mature social philosophy.[247]

Intriguingly, Tawney's point of departure in the *Commonplace Book* was Toynbee's question of the early 1880s—what have been the results for the people of a century and more of industrialization? As Tawney expressed it in May 1912, 'For the last 100 years man's command over nature has been steadily increasing. How far does the increase in resources which this brings about result in increasing prosperity in all classes, irrespective of legislation and social arrangements?'[248] Yet Tawney's major preoccupations as they emerge from these jottings are moral rather than material in so far as he believed that the material injustices of his society were the result of moral failings. As he put it in June 1912, 'The industrial problem is a moral problem of learning as a community to reprobate certain courses of action and approve others'.[249] If this were true, then it followed that only a change in beliefs, in values, in spirit would lead to a more equal and just society. If, as he believed, 'modern society is sick through the absence of a moral ideal', then it could not be cured by political means.[250] Other socialists, notably the Edwardian Fabians, who trusted to politics and to the manipulation of mechanisms of reform—to instrumentalities—were misguided.

This is where I think the Fabians are inclined to go wrong. They seem to think that you can trick statesmen into a good course of action, without changing their principles, and that by taking sufficient thought society can add several cubits to its stature. It can't, as long as it lives on the same spiritual diet. No amount of cleverness will get figs off thistles. What I

[246] See Terrill, *Tawney*, 31.

[247] R. H. Tawney, *R. H. Tawney's Commonplace Book*, ed. J. M. Winter and D. M. Joslin (Cambridge, 1972).

[248] Ibid. 8.   [249] Ibid. 12.   [250] Ibid., 9 (6 May 1912).

want to do is to get clear in my mind what these moral assumptions or principles are, and then to put others in their place.[251]

Tawney joined the Fabian Society in 1906 and the Independent Labour Party three years later. For Tawney as for Cole (though in different ways) Fabianism helped form his ideas through a critical engagement with its aims and ends. Cole rejected Fabianism because it could not liberate individuals and transform society: it offered merely a better means of administering existing structures. To Tawney, socialism meant 'a shift in human attitudes or no change at all',[252] and Fabianism could not offer this. Tawney was in many ways reminiscent of the early socialists in Britain of the 1880s and 1890s who manifested a quasi-religious dedication to their political creed and eschewed electoral politics because it would routinize and deaden the spirit. Like missionaries, they believed in 'making socialists' by speaking, debating, and educating, the better to build a socialist society with the sincere convictions of the people at its base. Stephen Yeo has argued that this approach was lost after 1900 as socialism became synonymous with the Labour Party and was subordinated to building a political machine, winning elections, and, as in the case of the Fabians, permeating the structures of the state.[253] In Tawney it seems to have lived on. His opposition to Fabianism had no personal side to it, certainly: he dedicated *Equality* to the Webbs. But Beatrice Webb could see the differences between them and appreciated the special character of Tawney's prescriptions for a better world. As she wrote in her diary at a time when Tawney was thinking of trying to enter politics in the 1930s, 'His task is that of a discoverer and an expounder of the new faith (economics based on service of man rather than the exploitation of man by man) not that of a manoeuvrer or politician or even an administrator'.[254]

There was indeed something saintly about Tawney and, as Raymond Williams suggested, it is difficult 'to disagree with the humanity of his arguments'. But there are grounds for scepticism about Tawney's methods. Williams questioned whether men could be persuaded to make 'a moral choice' as Tawney hoped, and questioned also just how easy it would then be to reform society in practice along lines laid down by these beneficent choices: 'the

---

[251] Ibid., 46 (2 Dec. 1912).
[252] Winter, 'Tawney's Early Political Thought', 88.
[253] Stephen Yeo, 'A New Life: The Religion of Socialism in Britain, 1883–1896', *History Workshop Journal*, 4 (Autumn 1977), 5–56.
[254] Quoted in Terrill, *Tawney*, 76.

analysis, while decent, is likely to seem lacking in depth.' Tawney 'sought to humanize the modern system of society on its own best terms'. That involved an assumption that men and women could be persuaded to see the world through Tawney's eyes and would comply with the principles of the moral reformation Tawney sought. This, as Williams noted with some justice, was a mark of his limitations as a political thinker.[255]

To Tawney, the process of persuasion depended on education: only by education could the moral reformation be achieved. Indeed, we can go further: it was in adult education specifically that Tawney, like the younger Cole, met and himself helped shape, an example of the good society—the tutorial class. The class was a functioning example of fellowship, equality, and democracy and it also gave to its members the opportunity for spiritual self-realization. The experience of adult education gave Tawney 'his model of the socialist society'.[256] As Jay Winter has put it, 'These classes were voluntary groupings of men and women who came together out of their belief in a moral principle—the pursuit of knowledge, which was in Tawney's view one of the gifts of God'.[257] Indeed, Tawney wrote in his *Commonplace Book* that people should 'think of knowledge, like religion, as transcending all differences of class and wealth . . . in the eye of learning, as in the eye of God, all men are equal because all are infinitely small'.[258] But Tawney did not lack a certain realism: if we judge him only by his private musings we are likely to present this great economic historian and student of the origins of capitalism whose lifelong academic project was to understand the rise of materialism, as a thoroughgoing idealist alone. But there were limits to his moralizing: as he wrote on the first essay he received from Cartwright, who was to become his lifelong friend, 'Our problem at the present day is to put economic activity in proper relation to the other elements of human life. But if we forget the economic motive altogether and overlook the material conditions on which the production of wealth depends, we become mere sentimentalists and dreamers.'[259]

---

[255] R. Williams, *Culture and Society 1780–1950*, 3rd edn. (Harmondsworth, 1963), 219, 223.

[256] Norman Dennis and A. H. Halsey, *English Ethical Socialism: Thomas More to R. H. Tawney* (Oxford, 1988), 155.

[257] Winter, 'Tawney's Early Political Thought', 74–5. See also A. W. Wright, *R. H. Tawney* (Manchester, 1987), 6.

[258] Tawney, *Commonplace Book*, 43 (30 Oct. 1912).

[259] The essay answered the following question: 'If you were going to devote six months to the study of Economics, what branch should you select, and why; and how should you set about it?' Cartwright argued lucidly that he would 'choose for

Teaching tutorial classes helped fix Tawney's convictions and suggested a lifelong vocation as teacher, therefore. The classes themselves gave him insight into the values and organization of the kind of society he was seeking to create. They also provided an education in the life of the working class for the tutor himself. The *Commonplace Book* contains anecdotes and details about the employment and the attitudes of his students. And Tawney pressed his students to provide him with information on wages, piece-rates, hours, conditions, and household budgets.[260] He, in turn, peppered his reports to the Oxford Committee with details of their difficulties and their exploitation. In 1912 he published his first important work of economic history, *The Agrarian Problem in the Sixteenth Century*, which was written to provide his classes with a textbook. Here he acknowledged his debt 'to the members of the Tutorial Classes conducted by Oxford University, with whom for the last four years it has been my privilege to be a fellow-worker. The friendly smitings of weavers, potters, miners, and engineers, have taught me much about the problems of political and economic science which cannot easily be learned from books.'[261]

It was not the only book to emerge out of the early Oxford tutorial classes; nor was Tawney the only tutor to have learnt as he taught. In a textbook on economics published in 1916 Henry Clay also paid tribute to his students' 'wide and diverse industrial experience' and to their criticisms of the views he put before them.[262] Late in his life Tawney reflected that if he 'were asked where I received the best part of my own education, I should reply, not at school or college, but in the days when as a young, inexperienced

study that branch of Economics which deals with Social Conditions and at the same time should look forward to the realization of Ruskin's noble ideal when other ideas of wealth than mere possessive ones may hold sway in economic thought'. E. S. Cartwright Papers, 17 Feb. 1908, Oxford University Archive DES/ F/13/7.

[260] See several letters from his students responding to Tawney's requests for information in the box 'R. H. Tawney: Correspondence, various papers, press cuttings', WEA archive. See also the weekly budgets supplied by his students in 'Essays of Students of Early Tutorial Classes, Including Rochdale and Longton', in Early Tutorial Classes I (box), WEA archive.

[261] R. H. Tawney, *The Agrarian Problem in the Sixteenth Century* (London, 1912), p. ix.

[262] Henry Clay, *Economics: An Introduction for the General Reader* (London, 1916), p. x. Other books emerging from Oxford tutorial classes included G. D. H. Cole, *Social Theory* (London, 1920) and Ivor Brown, *English Political Theory* (London, 1920). See 'Memorandum by the Association of Tutorial Class Tutors', *Royal Commission on Oxford and Cambridge Universities: Appendices to the Report of the Commission* (London, HMSO, 1922), 73–4.

and conceited teacher of Tutorial Classes, I underwent, week by week, a series of friendly, but effective deflations at the hands of the students composing them.'[263] He not only learned from his students; he managed also to achieve that personal integration into working-class communities that had eluded him in a very different social context at Toynbee Hall. As Gill wrote in his class secretary's report from Rochdale in 1910, their tutor had 'established for himself a position in the town especially among Labour men, and his withdrawal from Rochdale would be looked upon as a calamity by a far larger circle than the members of the class'.[264] Learning from his students was all part of the essential equality of tutor and student in the tutorial class. It also appealed to a man who was an instinctive democrat and who looked forward, in the words of the *1908 Report*, to 'the development of a democratic education and of an educated democracy'.[265] As Tawney told the people of Rochdale in 1910, 'In the past, education had been supplied too much by churches, philanthropic institutions, and a group of benevolent officials at Whitehall. It should be supplied by the people for the people.'[266] But should it also be supplied for the people by the University of Oxford? There were some in the labour movement who thought not.

[263] R. H. Tawney, 'The WEA and Adult Education', in id., *The Radical Tradition: Twelve Essays on Politics, Education and Literature* (London, 1964), 82.

[264] *Tutorial Classes Committee Annual Report 1909–10*, 2.

[265] *Oxford and Working-Class Education*, 85.

[266] 'Workers and Education: Mr. Tawney's Appeal to Organised Labour', *Rochdale Observer*, 14 Apr. 1910, quoted in Sheila Rowbotham, ' "Travellers in a Strange Country"; Responses of Working-Class Students to the University Extension Movement 1873–1910', *History Workshop Journal*, 12 (autumn 1981), 88.

5

THE DEBATE ON WORKING-CLASS EDUCATION

I

'Oxford is a poison.' Thus wrote Ramsay MacDonald to Albert Mansbridge on 4 December 1908, soon after the publication of *Oxford and Working-Class Education*. MacDonald had published a critical review of the *1908 Report* in *The Labour Leader* a few days before; Mansbridge had then written a letter of remonstrance to him, and now MacDonald filled out his views on the alliance of workpeople and the university.

I want my people to feel a sense of self-respect so strong and so proud as to be protected by its own inner merit from fawning before dons, deans or anybody else. Those of us who have experienced life, are quite as educated, in the best sense of the word, as those who have read books. My idea of the working man is that he should have both experiences, but he really cannot have them unless he retains a pride in his own genuine roughness, and capacity for looking on realities, even if they are humble and simple. Tawney is an excellent fellow, and will be the very last to impart Oxford culture and Oxford views of life to our people, but, as I explained to him, what I feel is that his work will be very much better done if it had not residence at Oxford as an aim. You cannot re-create Oxford by an infusion of workingmen. Oxford will re-create workingmen. Oxford is a settled social organism. The pilgrims you send to it have not that character. Therefore, Oxford will assimulate (*sic*) them, not they Oxford. That is the sociological weakness of your report . . . My point of view is that of one who believes there can be no progress of any kind unless it issues from a sound democratic mind. Not only are the people good enough, but they are the only good, and everything that takes them away from their internal sources of power and culture is bad.[1]

Here encapsulated are all the arguments that were and have been raised against the alliance of dons and workers. At issue was a dilemma that has faced a succession of groups excluded from full acceptance in modern British society, notably the nonconformist

---

[1] J. Ramsay MacDonald to A. Mansbridge, 4 Dec. 1908, Tutorial Classes Committee Early Papers, vol. 1, DES/F/2/1/1, Oxford University Archives.

religious denominations in the nineteenth century as well as workers in the early twentieth century: should Oxford, standing for the dominant national culture, be ignored, or should the excluded seek a place in the cultural metropolis the better to signal their existence and self-confidence, and yet risk incorporation by established institutions? MacDonald did not merely fear incorporation; he was arguing that the labour movement's greatest strength was its own internal resources. There was some philistinism in his argument, but also a fierce class-pride at the heart of a powerful case powerfully expressed: we must set aside the irony that the letter was written by a future Labour prime minister whose supposed fondness for the establishment is held to have led to his 'betrayal' of the movement in August 1931.

In MacDonald's original article he had warned the labour movement to 'be very careful before committing themselves to such a scheme'. He feared that the WEA was 'in grave danger in allowing itself to become a sort of medium for Oxford culture . . . inoculating the more intelligent sections of the working-class'. He contended that working people should attend their own educational institutions 'built up by men who know working-class life and who are full of the spirit, not of academic democracy but of Democracy'. And he turned the argument of the Oxford reformers on its head: they had wanted to reform the university by associating it with the life of the nation and arranging for an infusion of working-class talent. MacDonald argued that the process of reform had to come first: 'Oxford must be changed before the working-class will be benefited by any culture it can impart to them.'[2] Other Labour periodicals were also critical. *Justice*, the organ of the Social Democratic Federation, questioned whether the Labour members of the Joint Committee were really representative of the movement.[3] *The New Age*, a journal dedicated to the ideas of Guild Socialism, agreed with MacDonald that Labour should ignore the *1908 Report* because it deserved 'a more richly varied education than is served out at these institutions for the training of young gentlemen'.[4]

In response to MacDonald's article the correspondence flowed thick and fast: *The Labour Leader* noted that no other topic it had covered in recent times 'evoked so many desperately long letters', most of them from WEA partisans encouraged by Mansbridge.[5] The

[2] J. Ramsay MacDonald, 'Oxford and the Democracy', *The Labour Leader: A Weekly Journal of Socialism, Trade Unionism and Politics* (27 Nov. 1908), 757.
[3] Henry Atkins, 'Oxford and Working-Class Education', *Justice*, 25/1, 301 (19 Dec. 1908), 6–7.   [4] *The New Age*, 3 Dec. 1908, p. 103.
[5] *The Labour Leader*, 11 Dec. 1908, p. 792.

evidently remarkable Vicar of Tilty in Essex, E. G. Maxted, agreed with MacDonald and described the WEA as 'an organisation cleverly managed by certain members of the possessing classes' which had been established to divert the working-class movement from a policy of 'complete socialization of the universities'.[6] Letters from Mansbridge, Mactavish, T. W. Price, and Reuben George made predictable points about Oxford's goodwill, the role of the WEA, and the role of labour representatives on the Joint Committee.[7] But another correspondent cogently expressed the opposite of MacDonald's strategy; that labour had to take the commanding heights of culture rather than build an alternative and separate culture of its own:

From Oxford and Cambridge come the men who are to run our Empire, sit in our Parliaments, practise in our courts, lecture from our pulpits, dominate our Civil Service. I submit that they represent a sphere of influence which Labour has to conquer. 'The Oxford point of view' is what Oxford men make it, and if working-men are sent in sufficient numbers the point of view will change. We do not want a Labour University. We want the old and newer universities of the country transformed till they become national universities, democratically controlled.[8]

Oxford could not be ignored; so it would have to be taken. If Labour wanted to govern, the movement would have to control the institutions where power was located and exercised. The idea of a national university, which to Mark Pattison had meant one in which all creeds and classes were represented, had now been altered to denote one controlled by the new democracy. Here was one answer to MacDonald.

II

The issues of strategy, content, and control of workers' education which animated this exchange of views were at the heart of an almost simultaneous controversy within Oxford itself in the immediate aftermath of publication of the *1908 Report*—the famous strike and secession at Ruskin College. The affair not only dramatized the divisions within the labour movement over workers' education;

---

[6] Ibid., 4 Dec. 1908, p. 770.   [7] Ibid., 4, 11 Dec. 1908, pp. 770, 786.

[8] Archibald Ramage in a letter in *The Labour Leader* (4 Dec. 1908), 770. For other letters to Mansbridge expressing concern about the reaction to the 1908 Report, see Tutorial Classes Committee Early Papers, i, DES/F/2/1/1, Oxford University Archives.

it also prompted the development of a different tradition from the Oxford–WEA alliance. The events at Ruskin have generally been explained in terms of the students' commitment to 'independent working class education' in the face of attempts to undermine the independence of the college on the part of the University. Their commitment to independence cannot be questioned or criticized; it was an entirely legitimate and strategically credible response to the growing demand for education in the working class, and entirely consonant with the position MacDonald was articulating. But it is less clear whether Oxford really did menace Ruskin's autonomy, and whether the University can really be said to have caused the secession of the students and their supporters into the Plebs League and the Labour Colleges movement. It is also doubtful if the ideology of this new movement was ever capable of carrying the working class with it.

Ruskin Hall had been founded in 1899 as a college for working men by the combination of a wealthy American philanthropist, Walter Vrooman, and a young American Progressive (in the American sense of that term), Charles Beard. Beard had a celebrated career ahead of him as one of the greatest and also one most controversial of American historians. Fittingly, classes began at 14 St Giles which was leased from Balliol and which had been the home of T. H. Green.[9] When George Bernard Shaw was approached by Beard to deliver a lecture at the new foundation, his response was on similar lines to MacDonald:

My first impulse on hearing of the Ruskin Hall project was to ask Mr Vrooman what on earth he wanted to send workmen to Oxford for? . . . A workman ought to have a vulgar prejudice against Oxford . . . In short, if a workman asked me whether he should endeavour to put in a few terms at Ruskin Hall, I should strongly advise him not to unless he wanted to do exactly what you deplore—that is, change himself from a workman into a schoolman.[10]

The college was designed to provide for the general education of working men 'in science, history and modern languages, and generally in the duties of a citizen, and in practical industrial work'.[11]

[9] On the early history of Ruskin College see Harold Pollins, *The History of Ruskin College* (Oxford, 1984) and Paul Yorke, *Ruskin College 1899–1909*, Ruskin Students' Labour History Pamphlets, no. 1 (Oxford, 1977).

[10] George Bernard Shaw to Charles Beard, 1 May 1899, 'Ruskin College Strike', i, fo. 15, Ruskin College Library, Oxford. (The two volumes of papers entitled 'Ruskin College Strike' are composed of materials collected by the Principal of Ruskin, Dennis Hird, and are sometimes referred to as 'Dennis Hird's Papers'.)

[11] 'Memorandum and Articles of Association of Ruskin Hall Incorporated, 11 June 1900', cited in Yorke, *Ruskin College*, 3.

And perhaps because it offered this broad academic education it attracted a very miscellaneous group of students in its first years, only some of whom could qualify as 'workers'. But from 1903 the proportion of working-class students, and among them trade unionists, increased. By 1907 more than half its funds came from unions, while most of the rest came from individual donors.[12] And with this shift towards a student body of young, class-conscious workers came attendant problems within the college which antedate any hint of university 'imperialism' and were the chief cause in themselves of the 1909 secession.

As early as 1905 there were disputes about the curriculum, especially over the teaching of economics. The arrival in 1908 of an inexperienced new tutor in economics, H. Sanderson Furniss, who was judged to be too orthodox by some of the students, only made the situation worse.[13] There were also disputes over the place of Marx in the syllabus: some of the students wanted more Marxism and, led by Noah Ablett, who made the most notable dissenting speech at the Oxford conference in August 1907, they organized their own classes in the subject.[14] There were divisions within the staff and between some of the staff and the students, some of which were personal and some of which were political. There were misgivings about the college's governance and the role on its governing Council and Executive Committee of Oxford dons and sympathetic well-wishers who were suspicious of socialism. There were also problems over discipline, the issue that was used as grounds for the dismissal of the Principal, Dennis Hird, in March 1909, and which precipitated the student strike.[15] The relatively frequent fracas and fisticuffs between Ruskin students and undergraduates from the University, which seem to have generally taken place in full public view at the Martyr's Memorial in St Giles, did not add to harmony and, understandably, seemed to some members of the college's Council to project the wrong image of Ruskin.[16] Taken together, 'the disagreements that emerged were not simply over minor issues related to day-to-day administration of the college, but fundamental disagreements over the type of college Ruskin ought to be'.[17] The

---

[12] Pollins, *History of Ruskin College*, 17.

[13] Richard Lewis, *Leaders and Teachers: Adult Education and the Challenge of Labour in South Wales 1906–1940* (Cardiff, 1993), 59.

[14] Ibid. 62; see also Stuart Macintyre, *A Proletarian Science: Marxism in Britain 1917–33* (Cambridge, 1980), 74.

[15] Yorke, *Ruskin College*, 24–35; Pollins, *History of Ruskin College*, 20–3; Bernard Jennings, 'Revolting Students: The Ruskin College Dispute 1908–9', *Studies in Adult Education*, 9/1 (Apr. 1977), 1, 6.

[16] Yorke, *Ruskin College*, 25–6.   [17] Ibid. 34.

Plebs League was later to maintain that it was formed to counter the attempt of the University to control Ruskin as set out in *Oxford and Working-Class Education*: it seems more likely that the *1908 Report* was used by the Plebs to justify a secession that had been developing over several years and for several reasons.

There can be no doubt that the University did want to develop closer links with Ruskin. As early as 1905, members of the Extension Delegacy were considering in informal discussions how to assist the college and bring it into communication with the University without threatening its autonomy.[18] In his address to the 1907 conference, Sidney Ball noted that Ruskin was 'being drawn into nearer relations with the Oxford Colleges'. He saw Ruskin as 'the nucleus for the education of working-men at Oxford itself. Here the working classes have an instrument ready to their hand, and here the University has an organisation at its very door, inviting it to organise or assist in the organisation of definite courses of study for workingmen qualified to take advantage of them.'[19]

It was only to be expected that the subsequent investigation into the links between Oxford and the working class would touch on Ruskin in some way, not least because five members of the Joint Committee—Bowerman, Shackleton, W. H. Berry, Ball and Lees-Smith—were on the Ruskin College Council. But what emerged from the Joint Committee's discussions of Ruskin and its place in the new relationships being established, and from the *1908 Report* itself, was respect for its independence and a set of very modest proposals which, arguably, derived from an entirely honest desire to widen opportunities for Ruskin students. A briefing paper on Ruskin, drawn up for the Joint Committee, which discussed Ruskin's possible role in any scheme to bring students to Oxford, showed evident concern for the college's independence and special function, and appreciated the sensitivity of its relations with the University:

Whether scholarships offered under any scheme of the Joint Committee should be tenable at Ruskin College depends upon the principle on which such scholarships are to be awarded. Ruskin College must be regarded primarily as a place of training for men who will return to their handicrafts and may take part in the work of labour organizations, and of local

[18] Stuart Marriott, 'Oxford and Working-Class Education: A Foundation Myth Re-Examined', *History of Education*, 12/4 (1983), 290–1.

[19] Sidney Ball, 'What Oxford can do for Workpeople', in *Papers Submitted to the National Conference of Working Class and Educational Organisations, held in the Examination Schools, High Street, Oxford, on Saturday, August 10th, 1907*, 13–15.

authorities. The College cannot be used as a hostel for students who are taking the general course of University education.[20]

Ruskin took up but a small part of *Oxford and Working-Class Education*. In discussing residence in Oxford for working-class students, the *Report* counselled against restricting them to Ruskin, for that would give the impression that 'it is the wish of Oxford to put them off with some kind of unofficial recognition, and to confine the ordinary Colleges to men of other social classes'.[21] It went on to make two formal recommendations. First, that a year's residence at Ruskin and satisfactory work during that time should be accepted by the University as meeting the standard required to begin work on Oxford's Diploma in Economics and Political Science. Second, 'that under any scheme of scholarships or exhibitions for workingmen' devised by the Joint Committee, some of these should be tenable by second-year students at Ruskin to allow them to study there for the University Diploma.[22] The basic aim was to make it possible for Ruskin students to study in the college on a university course: the first recommendation laid down a qualifying standard they had to attain, the second offered financial assistance to enable students at Ruskin to take the Diploma.

According to one historian, 'The Oxford Report appeared making definite propositions for the transformation of Ruskin College into an institution preparatory for university studies, effectively therefore under university control'.[23] It was apparently intended to transform 'its whole ethos and purpose'.[24] According to another, this was 'an attempt to make [the] college into something of a preparatory school by means of which the working-class élite could enter the University of Oxford'.[25] These judgements are difficult to substantiate. There is no evidence of such downright motives in the relevant archives, rather the reverse in fact, and certainly no indication in the *1908 Report* itself that Ruskin was to be 'transformed'. These

---

[20] 'Notes for the Consideration of the Joint Committee of the University and the Workers' Educational Association on the Possible Relations between Ruskin College and the University', in '1907–8 Joint Committee on Tutorial Classes', DES/F/14/1, Oxford University Archives. Brian Simon, who has used this document in his account of the strike and secession at Ruskin, evidently interprets it in a different way. See Brian Simon, *Education and the Labour Movement 1870–1920* (London, 1974), 320 n.
[21] *Oxford and Working-Class Education*, 2nd edn. (Oxford, 1909), 77.
[22] Ibid. 89–90.   [23] Simon, *Education and the Labour Movement*, p. 321.
[24] Ibid. 317.
[25] Chushichi Tsuzuki, 'Anglo-Marxism and Working-Class Education', in Jay Winter (ed.), *The Working Class in Modern British History* (Cambridge, 1983), 187.

were modest suggestions only, in no way mandating action, that an independent institution such as Ruskin might or might not adopt. It is difficult to sustain an argument that the University wanted to 'control' Ruskin on the basis of some permissive recommendations affecting the syllabus there. Furthermore, to assert that this amounted to an attack on Ruskin's 'ethos and purpose' is to beg questions about the identity of the college at this time: it was just because Ruskin had no agreed 'ethos and purpose' after several years of internal discord that the controversy arose. And as Hastings Lees-Smith, later a Labour MP and Postmaster General in the Labour government of 1929, tried to explain to a special 'Conference of Delegates from the Trade Unions and Co-operative Societies which had financially supported the College' in October 1909, the Ruskin Executive Committee, which he chaired, would have been inviting all sorts of problems if they had really intended 'attaching Ruskin to the University':

All that would happen would be that whereas we now stand on our own feet, we should then come under the control of the University; the move-ment of the College would be blocked, because every departure, every forward step, would have to receive the consent not only of progressive members [of the university] . . . but of the most reactionary elements. Surely this is a matter of common sense to see that the Executive Committee would stand to gain nothing by any closer connection with the University?[26]

This is not to dismiss the misgivings of some of the Ruskin stu-dents, however. According to one handbill put out by them at the end of March 1909, the 'Oxford and Working-Class Educational Committee . . . seeks to establish a definite connection between Ox-ford University and Ruskin College, making the latter a sort of half-way house'.[27] They had legitimate fears that if the recommendations in the *1908 Report* were enacted, then teaching at the college would become conformable with teaching in the University and Ruskin would lose its identity. As the secessionists explained in their famous pamphlet, *The Burning Question of Education*, 'If these diplomas were founded, then the teaching at Ruskin College must become identical with the teaching of the University, and Ruskin

---

[26] *The Democratic Control of Ruskin College, Oxford* (Leicester, 1909), 7–8. ('Verbatim Report of Speeches . . . Made by the Chairman of the Executive Com-mittee, Professor H. B. Lees-Smith, MA, at the Conference of Delegates from the Trade Unions and Co-operative Societies which had financially supported the College, held at Oxford on Saturday, October 30th, 1909'.)

[27] 'Ruskin College: Enforced Resignation of Mr. Dennis Hird' (March 26, 1909), 'Ruskin College Strike', i, fo. 85.

College must become only a means to enter the University'.[28] 'Must' and 'only' are too strong: it does not seem to have been envisaged that the whole college should follow a university syllabus, only that some students with the requisite qualifications *might* take the Diploma course. But whatever was intended, the recommendations evidently exacerbated tensions in the college that already existed between those who wanted workers' education based on Marxism, and those who favoured a broader and more orthodox curriculum, and between those who saw Ruskin as educating socialists, and those who saw it as educating working men. For some of the students it was a contradiction in terms that 'a Labour College . . . was controlled by University Dons, private individuals, and a few non-representative Labour leaders'. In their view, 'A Labour College must be devoted to a particular training of men, already conversant with Labour difficulties, and who have already proved their ability in local spheres on working-class activity'.[29] Above all, a Labour college must be independent: 'The mission of the workers cannot be committed for achievement to those above them in economic position: it must be self-accomplished'.[30]

The subsequent events are well known. In October 1908, just before the *Report* was published, the students formed the Plebs League in order 'to bring about a more satisfactory connection of Ruskin College with the Labour Movement'.[31] They took their name 'from a brochure written by the American socialist, Daniel De Leon, entitled *Two Pages from Roman History*'.[32] In the following month the college's Executive Committee established an enquiry into the administration of Ruskin, and in March 1909, when the enquiry was completed, asked for the Principal's resignation.[33] It was at this point that all fifty-four students went on strike in order to win Hird's reinstatement. The strike continued until September 1909 when twenty-seven of the students, with the support of ex-students and some trade unions, set up a rival Central Labour College in rented accommodation in Oxford, and began organizing local study groups around the country. They included Arthur Jenkins, later a Labour MP, and father of the present Chancellor of the University

[28] W. H. Seed (ed.), *The Burning Question of Education: Being an Account of the Ruskin College Dispute, its Causes and Consequences* (Oxford, 1909), 14.

[29] Ibid. 6, 8.   [30] Ibid. 20–1.   [31] Ibid. 15.

[32] Yorke, *Ruskin College*, 34. Daniel De Leon, *Two Pages from Roman History. I. Plebs leaders and labor leaders. II. The Warning of the Gracchi* (New York, 1903).

[33] The report of the subcommittee of the Ruskin Executive can be found in 'Ruskin College Strike', i, fo. 69.

of Oxford, Roy Jenkins.[34] Twenty-three 'loyal' students returned to Ruskin, and the college reopened to teach them. From 1910 Ruskin students began to sit for the University Diploma in Economics and Political Science and attend university lectures. Ruskin itself remained institutionally independent from the University, as it is still today.[35]

A little-known account of these events from one who was a participant may serve to give a flavour of what happened. Sidney Ball, a member of the Ruskin Council, was no neutral, certainly, but his letter to Ramsay MacDonald in early April 1909 presents an interesting explanation of the disputes at the college. As Ball saw it,

The present students, with Hird at their head, made an open & determined attempt to convert the College into (politically speaking) a denominational institution, & to substitute for the educational authority constituted by the Charter a purely political authority. This is, I think, not an unfair way of putting it. They were no doubt recruited to this movement, which materialized into a Plebs League & a Plebs Magazine, by our attempt to put a limit to street propaganda & more particularly by a suspicion of designs upon the independence and integrity of the College & its curriculum on the part of the University, or at any rate, the serving members of the Council, & in this, I think they regarded themselves confirmed by the report of the Oxford & Working Class educat. Committee. There is no *real* ground for this view . . .

Ball recounted another grievance: 'that the teaching of economics was too orthodox & not the pure economics of Marx which is what the students desire for their consumption and nothing else.' He accepted that 'there was some ground for this', and explained that the enquiry instituted by the Executive Committee 'reported in favour of some change & of a considerably less "academic" method and doctrine'. Though the Ruskin Council did not think much of Hird's version of Sociology and though 'a rather tactless attempt was made to interfere with it', the subject was popular with the students, and Ball explained that he 'had no difficulty in maintaining freedom of teaching'.

Ball seems to have blamed Hird for the problems at the college, for he had

made no secret of his desire to let the students have their own way in everything & has continually refused to support us in any kind of general discipline whatsoever . . . He has in fact been the leader of the revolt. I don't respect him the less for this, & have a good deal of sympathy with the point of view of both Hird & the men, but it was absolutely a deadlock.

[34] Roy Jenkins, *A Life at the Centre* (London, 1991; repr. 1992), 5–6.
[35] For accounts of the strike, see Pollins, *History of Ruskin College*, 18–20; Yorke, *Ruskin College*, 27, 36–7.

We were there to administer an institution framed by charter on 'non-party' lines, & were quite willing to put as liberal interpretation as we could on the connexion beween the College & the 'labour movement' (though there is no reference to this in the charter). We had to draw the line at the point Hird & the present students had reached.

Ball seems to have made a distinction between the issues of personality, discipline, and control which had caused the breach at Ruskin, and which had motivated the enquiry and Hird's dismissal, and his personal political distaste for the brand of socialism that the Principal and many of the students there espoused—though such distinctions, in the nature of things, are easily blurred. He complained that 'the ruling sentiment at R.C. just now is "class-consciousness"', which he evidently disliked, and he ended his account to MacDonald with a more personal reflection: 'Entre nous, the present students seem to be rather "rotters"—& not to be doing or likely to do much good to the movement, & Hird's Socialism is much too much of the SDF type & kind of which I have no objection (*sic*)—but as a ruling passion it does seem to me rather sterile.'

Ball's letter may be taken to represent the view of the affair of those Oxford 'friends of labour' involved in workers' education. The account is neither vindictive nor especially self-righteous. Ball showed a fair-minded willingness to give ground where a good case was made, as over the teaching of Economics and Sociology. He expressed some sympathy with the students' views, and he emphasized that matters of discipline and Hird's maverick behaviour brought things to a head. He admitted that his own politics were very different from those espoused by some members of Ruskin, though he made it clear that these were differences of strategy and timing as much as ideology: as he explained to MacDonald, 'I don't myself think things are ripe for a purely socialist College'. The overall tone of the letter is apologetic and even betrays some embarrassment: this is not the stuff of a deliberate political witch-hunt.[36]

One historian who has tried to get to the bottom of the events at Ruskin has concluded that 'an early casualty was the truth'.[37] A rather spectacular example of this may suffice to make the point: the infamous visit to Ruskin of the Chancellor of Oxford, Lord Curzon, formerly Viceroy to India, on 11 November 1907, while he was gathering evidence for his personal investigation into the state of the University and its reform. An account of this has appeared

[36] S. Ball to J. Ramsay MacDonald, 6 Apr. 1909, MacDonald Papers, Party Correspondence 1909, Public Record Office, London PRO 30/69 1153, fo. 14–5. I am grateful to Janet Howarth of St Hilda's College, Oxford, who alerted me to the existence of this letter.   [37] Jennings, 'Revolting Students', 11.

in several works on the period because, in the version recorded, it seems to encapsulate the struggle that Ruskin students fought against Oxford's 'imperialism'.[38] Yet the account as presented is probably a fabrication. Curzon certainly did go to Ruskin on the stated day as part of a whole series of visits he was making to institutions in Oxford. And in the received version which is taken from *The Burning Question of Education*, he was given a hostile reception. He was depicted at the centre of a ring of students: 'Autocratic disdain and the suggestion of a power feudal in character, seemed stamped on his countenance.' Curzon apparently 'sounded the note of a loose affiliation' of Ruskin to the University. His offer was answered by Hird, the Principal, who 'in substance' said

My Lord, when you speak of Ruskin College you are not referring merely to this institution in Oxford, for this is only the branch of a great democratic movement that has its roots all over the country. To ask Ruskin College to come into closer contact with the University is to ask the great democracy whose foundation is the Labour Movement, a democracy that in the near future will come into its own, and when it does will bring great changes in its wake. As he concluded the burst of applause that emanated from the students seemed to herald the dawn of the day to which Mr Hird had referred. Without another word Lord Curzon turned on his heel and walked out, followed by the remainder of the lecturing staff, who looked very far from pleased.[39]

It is a magnificent account for which there is no verification. Several press reports of what took place provide summaries of Curzon's address, including, in one case, his honest references to the students' 'lurking suspicion' of contact with the University. But they make no reference at all to a withdrawal by the Chancellor, and if Hird's speech is mentioned there is no hint of discord.[40] According to *The Oxford Times*, indeed, 'In thanking the Chancellor for his visit, the Principal said it was marvellous what progress the college had made since its establishment. They felt it was important that there should be a real friendship between educated persons and all well-wishers of their country and themselves. [Applause].'[41]

Those students who remained loyal to the College put out their own version of events in a pamphlet and called the Plebs' account

[38] See for example, Simon, *Education and the Labour Movement*, 320–1; W. W. Craik, *The Central Labour College 1909–29* (London, 1964), 50–1; J. P. M. Millar, *The Labour College Movement* (London, 1979), 4–5.
[39] Seed (ed.), *The Burning Question*, 10–11.
[40] 'Lord Curzon and Ruskin College', *The Times*, 12 Nov. 1907, p. 8; *Oxford Times*, 16 Nov. 1907, pp. 3, 7; *Oxford Magazine*, 21 Nov. 1907, p. 89.
[41] *Oxford Times*, 16 Nov. 1907, p. 3.

'a sheer invention'. Hird merely thanked Curzon for his visit 'and indulged in the usual courtesies of such an occasion', and the press did not print his inflammatory speech because it was never made: 'No reporter having heard the statements alleged to have been made by Mr Hird, the Plebs College people proceeded to construct a speech for him two years after its alleged delivery.'[42] There exists also a typewritten memorandum in the Ruskin College archives in which someone who was present also disputes the Plebs' account. Hird did make a speech, according to this account, but not the one published by the Plebs, and the 'description of Lord Curzon's visit' is called 'a vile invention'.[43]

Curzon, imperial proconsul and University Chancellor was an obvious target and a fine symbol of what the secessionists argued was at issue. He may have attracted especial attention in their account of events because of his remarks on working-class students and Oxford in the book he published in early 1909, while the conflict in Ruskin was at its most intense, on *Principles and Methods of University Reform*, which set out his views on the changes Oxford then required. In a chapter on 'the admission of poor men' he went much further than the *1908 Report* and argued for a separate working men's college inside the University, which 'could exist side by side, and without risk of competition, with Ruskin College', to which the best tutorial class students would proceed 'in order to carry their training to its logical conclusion'.[44] Curzon stated that his remarks 'were in print' before the problems at Ruskin became public knowledge and he denied that they were influenced by events there.[45] Whether this was, or was not, the case, he commented upon the 'danger that a Working-men's College, outside the University, and subject neither to its influences nor its discipline, may develop into a club dominated by the narrow views of particular political or economic schools'.[46] Though Curzon was explicit that his scheme did not involve Ruskin, his ideas may have exacerbated fears of a university putsch against its independence. Subsequently, Hebdomadal

[42] *Ruskin College and Working-Class Education: Its Trials: A History of the Dispute: Future Development of the College* (n.d. [1909]) ('Issued by the Committee of Ruskin College Students'), 16. (The pamphlet can be found in 'Ruskin College Strike', ii, fo. 143, Ruskin College Library.)

[43] 'Lord Curzon's visit', unattrib. typed memo (n.d.) in loose-leaf file 'Ruskin College 1909', Ruskin College Library. Paul Yorke believes that this memo was written by Ruskin's General Secretary, Bertram Wilson. See Yorke, *Ruskin College*, 35.

[44] Lord Curzon, *Principles and Methods of University Reform: Being a Letter Addressed to the University of Oxford* (Oxford, 1909), 65.

[45] Ibid. 58 n.   [46] Ibid. 63.

Council rejected his suggestion of a separate workers' college inside the University.[47] Curzon's book, and his remarks on working-class education, have not always found a place in the account of the Ruskin secession. And the seceding students were probably wise to concentrate their fire on the official University report from the Joint Committee rather than the purely personal opinions of the Chancellor. Nevertheless, it seems probable that Curzon's remarks, when published in 1909, gave further ammunition to the case for independent working-class education, and that his special place in the received account of events, if fabricated, was a response to the threat he seemed to pose.

The suspicion of fabrication only increases with the knowledge that A. L. Smith of Balliol was apparently also misquoted by the Plebs. Smith had made a private visit to Ruskin in 1907 and depending on the account consulted, he either came to sound out the College about a 'sort of loose affiliation' to the University as the Plebs recorded it, or to discover 'whether he could do anything from inside the University which would help the students at Ruskin College without undermining their independence,' as the loyal students recalled.[48] When the Plebs account was brought to Smith's attention he apparently countered that when he made his visit he had gone 'out of [his] way to say that [he] had not the slightest intention, wish, or desire, that Ruskin College should in any way be identified with the University'.[49] It cannot be asserted that the Plebs' accounts of the meetings with Curzon and Smith are false because there is insufficient impartial evidence available. But the existence of contrary accounts, even from interested parties, at least throws considerable doubt on the received version.

Does all this matter? Not much, perhaps; these are but details in a small story of institutional friction. Yet the received version of Curzon's visit to Ruskin is something of a set-piece known to many. And the fact that the seceding students may have had to fabricate evidence of the University's imperialism, and rope such a patently honest and generous figure as A. L. Smith into the plot, suggests again that they may have felt the need to justify actions that had their roots in divisions within Ruskin itself. Certainly fabrication came easily to the early Plebs: at one point Ablett concocted a

[47] H. P. Smith, *Labour and Learning: Albert Mansbridge, Oxford and the WEA* (Oxford, 1956), 56.

[48] Seed (ed.), *The Burning Question*, 10; *Ruskin College and Working-Class Education*, 17.

[49] *Ruskin College and Working-Class Education*, 17; see also Yorke, *Ruskin College*, 35; [Bertram Wilson?] 'Lord Curzon's visit'.

preposterous fiction that Lord Winterstoke, heir to the Wills tobacco fortune, was proposing to give Ruskin £10,000 if it compromised its independence and diluted its politics.[50]

Whatever the details of the Ruskin dispute, the arguments deployed by the Plebs League deserve respect. They were articulated by a range of Labour opinion, expressed sincere convictions, and represented one position, albeit that of a minority, in a much wider debate over Labour's strategy in these years. The early numbers of *Plebs*, the Plebs League's magazine, explained their differences with Oxford. In the first number in February 1909 they called for 'the education of the workers in the interests of the workers'.[51] In the second, a month later, they described the *1908 Report* as an attempt by the University to influence working-class leaders 'with the ideas of a class above them, so that their interests may become identical with the interests of that class'.[52] And in the third, they presented another version of MacDonald's argument:

No working-class student can undergo a University education and come through it untainted . . . University life is the breeding ground of reaction. It incites by its very nature towards breaking away from working-class aspirations . . . [Oxford University] is the place where men are taught to govern, it is the governing class who control it, it is they who decide what shall be taught and how it shall be taught and as the interests of these people are in direct anatagonism to the interests of the workers, it is sheer folly to think that any good can come of sending any of their number there.[53]

The Plebs were quite open about the subordination of education to politics. Their constitution spelled out their aim: 'To develop and increase the class-consciousness of the workers, by propaganda and education, in order to aid them to destroy wage-slavery and to win power.'[54] In their eyes university tutorial classes were simply a covert form of liberal, establishment propagandizing, and they derided the WEA for claiming that the education it provided was ideologically neutral. This was not a mere confrontation between education and propagandism, but between people who believed that knowledge—and educational institutions—could be separated from ideology, and others who believed that they could not.

These positions did not alter in the subsequent years of friction and acrimony between the WEA and the universities on one side, and the Labour College movement on the other. To the Plebs, the

[50] Lewis, *Leaders and Teachers*, 73.   [51] *Plebs*, 1/1 (Feb. 1909), 4.
[52] *Plebs*, 1/2 (Mar. 1909), 22–3.   [53] *Plebs*, 1/3 (Apr. 1909), 44.
[54] 'The Constitution of the Plebs League', *Plebs*, 16 (1924), 162.

WEA's alliance with Oxford and the universities, and its acceptance of state funds, had compromised it fatally.[55] As Tawney recalled much later, 'the Association was alternately denounced as a socialist intrigue and a capitalist conspiracy'.[56] Thus the Plebs attempted to build something else. The Central Labour College, which was financed largely by two unions with strong syndicalist traditions, the Amalgamated Society of Railway Servants (later the National Union of Railwaymen) and the South Wales Miners' Federation, moved from Oxford to London in 1911. And the Plebs League undertook workers' education with considerable success on Clydeside, in the North East, in Lancashire and Yorkshire and especially in South Wales, 'forming branches of the League and promoting local labour colleges and evening classes'.[57] The Central Labour College provided training for tutors; the Plebs League and its journal, *Plebs*, held the movement together. To co-ordinate the movement as it expanded after the First World War, the National Council of Labour Colleges was established in 1921.[58] In the early 1920s the WEA, through its industrial arm established in 1919, the Workers' Educational Trade Union Committee, and the NCLC, were locked in competition to win the agreement of the Trades' Union Congress and of individual unions to provide their members with education.[59] And in 1926–7 the NCLC classes enjoyed a peak enrolment of over thirty-one thousand students.[60] Thereafter, the movement experienced a steady decline, and in 1929 the Central Labour College was forced to close. Frequent disruptions there had alienated the trade unions, and peculation by leading officers of the college deterred potential donors. The college had also come into conflict with the NCLC over the distribution of the movement's resources. But probably the most important reason for its demise was the loss of the financial support of the South Wales Miners' Federation after the miners' defeat in 1926–7.[61] The NCLC and the Plebs League, meanwhile, were locked in an 'internecine conflict' over the leadership and strategy of the general secretary of the former, J. P. M. Millar.[62]

[55] Geoff Brown, 'Independence and Incorporation: The Labour College Movement and the Workers' Educational Association Before the Second World War', in Jane L. Thompson (ed.), *Adult Education for a Change* (London, 1980), 114–15.
[56] R. H. Tawney, 'Mansbridge', *The Highway*, 44 (Nov. 1952), 44.
[57] Macintyre, *A Proletarian Science*, 74–5.
[58] Simon, *Education and the Labour Movement*, 325–41.
[59] Brian Simon, 'The Struggle for Hegemony, 1920–1926', in id. (ed.), *The Search for Enlightenment: The Working Class and Adult Education in the Twentieth Century* (London, 1990), 15–70.
[60] Macintyre, *A Proletarian Science*, 78; Lewis, *Leaders and Teachers*, 177.
[61] Lewis, *Leaders and Teachers*, 156–67.   [62] Ibid. 79–81.

Political conflict and factionalism weakened the organization in the late 1920s and early 1930s, therefore, and by 1937–8 enrolments had fallen to only thirteen thousand.[63] Ironically, in the 1940s and 1950s the NCLC and the journal *Plebs* 'became the voice of the more extreme right-wing in the labour movement'.[64]

How should the history of the dispute at Ruskin College and the subsequent division in working-class education be interpreted? There are so many claims and counter-claims in material on the strike, and the events themselves were played out in such a feverish atmosphere of mutual suspicion, that it is almost impossible to be sure of the accuracy of any account. Broadly, it would seem that disputes within the college were leading some students towards the idea of independent working-class education before the University began to consider its future relationship with Ruskin. The students had legitimate grounds for concern about the outcome of Oxford's review of facilities for working-class education, but exaggerated the threat to Ruskin's autonomy, probably intentionally. In this way they could justify their actions more easily and, they hoped, call on broader support in the labour movement.

If we place the Plebs in the context of the wider debate about the aims and means of workers' education, it is clear that their critique of the Oxford–WEA partnership and their distrust of the universities and state was only more virulent rather than substantively different from the critiques of more mainstream Labour figures. But it can be argued that the decline of their movement over time only showed how unrealistic and generally unappealing was their commitment to an education in the principles of Marxism. That they failed to win the workers in large numbers may be taken to illustrate the impossibility of combining education with propaganda and at the same time reaching a broad constituency. In 1918 Mactavish referred to 'the policy of class-conscious isolation pursued by the Plebs League'.[65] There certainly is a sense in which the Plebs were caught in a ghetto of their own making: they offered an education which only those already converted to the faith would find attractive. The difference in approach between the two movements is captured in one tale told by an Oxford tutor in Lincoln, Alice Cameron. Apparently one of her students had left her class to join another one started locally by the Plebs League. 'When I met this man in the road soon after and asked him how he liked it, "Oh,

---

[63] Simon, 'The Struggle for Hegemony', 63.   [64] Ibid. 64.

[65] J. M. Mactavish, 'The WEA: Its Propaganda, Organisation and Method', in G. D. H. Cole *et al.* (eds.), *WEA Yearbook 1918* (London, 1918), 332.

it's all right," he replied; "but I must confess that nobody asks me, as you used to do, 'What do *you* think, Mr Heath?'"'.[66]

The WEA could at least claim that in appealing to a varied student body it had the chance to make new converts for the labour movement. On the other hand, the relative durability of the WEA over the decades was only bought at the expense of its commitment to working-class education. It became a general voluntary educational association for adults, in which role it achieved (and still achieves) a very great deal. The WEA may have grown in numbers and influence after 1908, but after the Second World War it ceased to be any sort of vehicle for the radical social change envisaged by some of its founders. Perhaps the answer is not to compare the two traditions, in which comparison the weaknesses of both become all too evident, but to treat them, as G. D. H. Cole did, as entirely separate and distinct.

In a paper Cole wrote in 1936 he called the conflict between the two movements 'a pretty senseless affair'. This was because their intentions were different. To Cole, 'The N.C.L.C., proclaiming Marxist principles and announcing that it could "promise to be candid, but not impartial", was in effect a propagandist body, running elementary classes as an adjunct to the propaganda work of the Labour Movement. As a good socialist, I had no quarrel with it. The more people it could attract, the better I was pleased.'[67] The WEA, conversely, 'had deliberately set out to do, not propaganda, but education aiming at letting students see all sides of a question, and at leaving them to make up their own minds.' Cole had no quarrel with the NCLC, though he was aggrieved that it had a quarrel with him. Indeed, he 'did not at all deny the usefulness of a kind of education that set out for the acceptance of certain beliefs in an intelligent way.' But he chose for himself a different course: 'to help students towards a fuller appreciation of life, to equip them for facing and solving some of its problems for themselves, and therewith to run the risk of some of them ending up with convictions very different from those which their tutor might hold to be right or true'. This was entirely in keeping with the mixed motives of Oxford extension from its foundation and as expressed in *Oxford and Working-Class Education*. Cole evidently hoped that a WEA education would assist social emancipation, but he also recognized that education had other, more personal and, arguably, more important functions. He wrote

[66] Alice Cameron, 'Lindsay and the Tutorial Classes', A. D. Lindsay Papers, Keele University Archives, File L 174.

[67] G. D. H. Cole, 'Recollections of Workers' Education', handwritten MSS, G. D. H. Cole Papers, Nuffield College, Oxford, A1/24/9/1–4.

1. Arthur Johnson, the first Oxford
Extension Lecturer

2. Arnold Toynbee

3. Professor T. H. Green

4. Michael Sadler

5. Arthur Acland and 'The Inner Ring', 1883. Cosmo Lang is standing at the extreme left of the group as we see it. L. T. Hobhouse is sitting on the left in the front row. Arthur Acland is sitting in the very centre of the group. To the left of him, as we see it, sits Bolton King, who was G. W. Hudson Shaw's anonymous benefactor. To the right of Acland is Michael Sadler. Next to Sadler is J. A. Spender, later the editor of the

6. The First Oxford Summer Meeting, 1888. Michael Sadler, wearing a gown and square, is at the front of the group.

7. The 1891 Summer Meeting gathered in Balliol College

8. A close-up from the 1891 Summer Meeting. From left to right the following may be seen: John Marriott, Benjamin Jowett, Sir William Markby (sitting) who is flanked by Michael Sadler and G. W. Hudson Shaw standing behind him, and W. A. S. Hewins.

9. J. A. R. Marriott

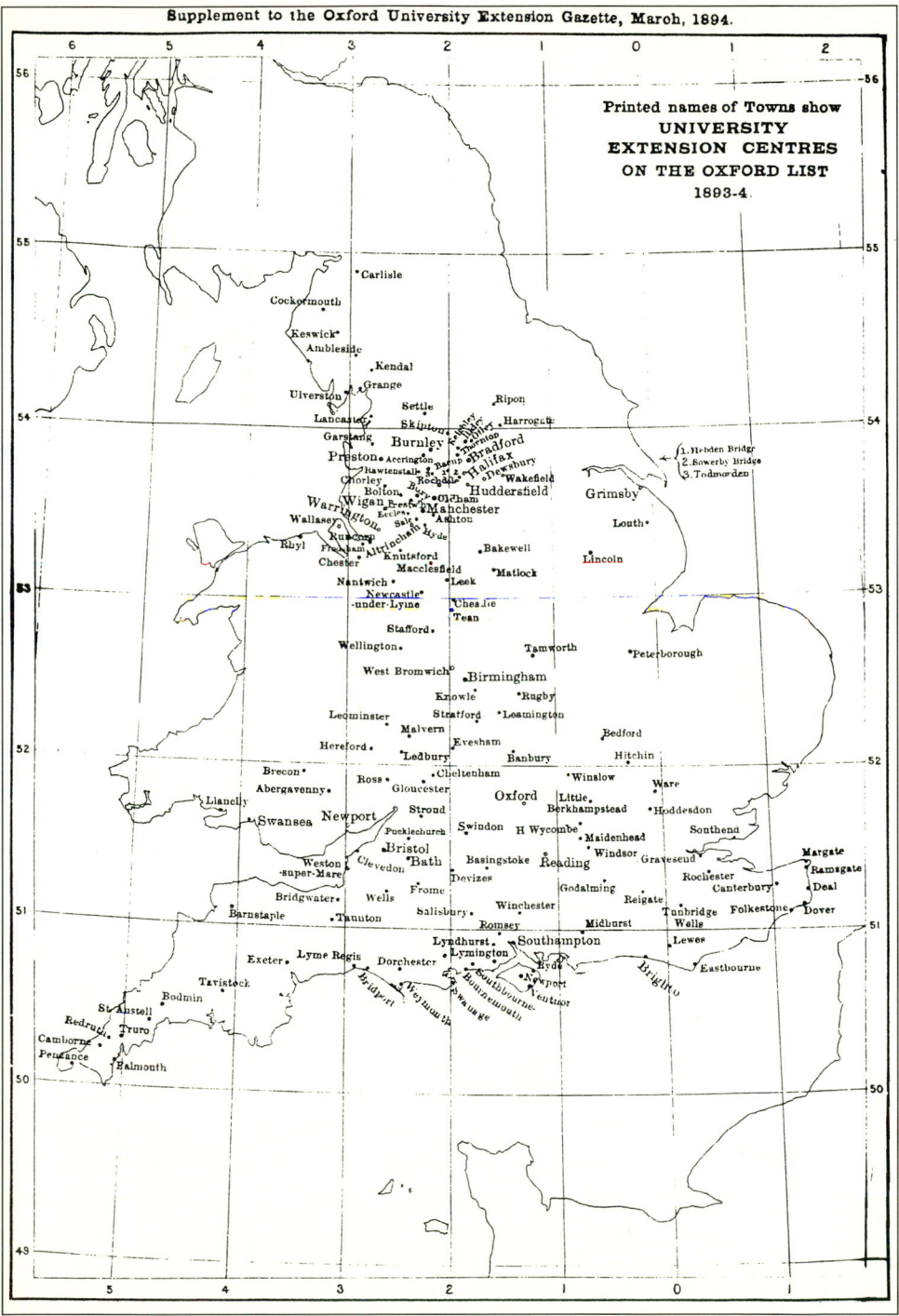

10. University Extension Centres on the Oxford List 1893–4

11. Tutors at the 1909 Summer Meeting. Back row, left to right: K. H. Vickers, Revd R. Baym, A. W. Bateman Brown, Revd W. H. Draper, J. T. Mills. Middle row, sitting, left

12. The Joint Committee of Oxford University and Working-Class Representatives, 1909. Left to Right. Back row, standing: Sidney Ball and J. A. R. Marriott. Middle Row, standing: A. Wilkinson, W. H. Berry, Professor H. H. Turner, J. M. Mactavish, Hastings Lees-Smith, Richardson Campbell. Front Row, sitting: C. W. Bowerman, A. E. Zimmern, D. G. Shackleton, Herbert Warren (Vice-Chancellor of Oxford), T. B. Strong, Albert Mansbridge, A. L. Smith.

13. R. H. Tawney and the Rochdale class in Industrial History, 21 March 1908

Oxford University Extension Delegacy.

BOROUGH OF LONGTON.

THE EDUCATION COMMITTEE HAVE PLEASURE IN ANNOUNCING THAT ARRANGEMENTS HAVE BEEN MADE FOR AN

ORGANIZED UNIVERSITY COURSE

OF

24 Weekly Tutorial Classes,

TO BE HELD ON CONSECUTIVE

FRIDAY EVENINGS, Oct. 2nd to Dec. 18th, 1908, and January 15th to April 2nd, 1909 (inclusive),

FROM 7·30 TO 9·30 P.M., AT THE

SUTHERLAND INSTITUTE,
STONE ROAD, LONGTON.

SUBJECT :—

The Industrial and Economic History of England
in the 18th & 19th Centuries.

TUTOR :—

Mr. R. H. Tawney, B.A.,
BALLIOL COLLEGE, OXFORD.

Special attention will be given to the Industrial Revolution of the 18th Century, its Causes and Effects.

Fee for the whole course - 2/6.

As this Class is intended for serious Students, and in order to comply with the conditions laid down by the University, each Student will be expected to attend the Class regularly, and to do the Homework, which will not be onerous, and which will consist of the necessary reading, and also of writing a Fortnightly Paper to be set by the Tutor. At the end of the Course an Examination will be held for those Students who have complied with the conditions, on the result of which the University will award to successful Students a valuable certificate or diploma.

Text Book :—TOWNSEND WARNER'S LANDMARKS OF ENGLISH INDUSTRIAL HISTORY.

The University will provide a small Library for the use of Students. Eligible Students will be admitted in order of application until the Class is full.

Scholarships to the Summer Meeting of Extension Students at Oxford University in 1908, will be open to members of this Class.

FOR ADMISSION TO CLASS AND FOR FURTHER PARTICULARS, APPLY TO:—

W. T. COPE,
Secretary to the Education Committee.
COURT HOUSE, LONGTON.

SEPTEMBER, 1908.

HUGHES & HARBER, LTD., THE ROYAL PRESS, LONGTON.

14. Handbill for the first Oxford Tutorial Class in Longton, 1908

15. R. H. Tawney and the Chesterfield Tutorial Class [1910?]

16. A WEA Dinner Party in Balliol at the 1909 Oxford Summer Meeting. This group met to set up the annual WEA–Oxford summer school. Left to right, standing: R. V. Lennard, the hon. George Collier, F. W. Kolthammer, A. L. Smith, C. S. Buxton, Alfred Zimmern, William Temple, G. W. Hudson Shaw. Left to right, sitting: Albert Mansbridge, T. W. Price, L. V. Gill, Reuben George.

17. The WEA Summer School in Balliol [1912?]. G. D. H. Cole is sitting in the centre of the group, his arms folded, his hair parted in the middle. E. S. C. Cartwright of Long-

18. A. D. Lindsay, E. S. C. Cartwright, and Albert Mansbridge at the 1912 WEA Summer School

19. North Staffordshire Miners at the Balliol Summer School, 1954. Raymond Williams is standing at the extreme right of the back row.

that he was 'happiest and, I feel, most useful when I am teaching after the WEA manner' and it seems likely that his identity and commitment as a professional scholar and teacher made it impossible for him to do anything but provide a balanced and objective education for his students.[68] This was certainly true of another eminent Labour intellectual involved in adult education between the wars, Harold Laski. He may have taught for the Plebs League and the NCLC, and he was not as outspokenly opposed to their aims as other middle-class socialists at work in adult education, but he was also more comfortable in the open, liberal atmosphere of the WEA.[69] As Cole expressed it, 'However strongly I may hold an opinion when I am teaching, I feel a strong repugnance to ramming it down my students' throats. I like trying to state the other side as well as I can; and I am sure my students get most out of me when I teach in that way.'[70]

Cole held these opinions when a young man as well as when a mature don. He was editor of a magazine called *The Oxford Reformer* while an undergraduate, and his editorial in February 1910 opposed the Ruskin secession because those involved had forgotten that 'the best interests of the students are served not by deliberate instruction in party propaganda, but by fair and unbiased economic education'.[71] Noting 'in the more extreme Socialist and Labour newspapers, violent denunciations both of Ruskin College and of the Workers' Educational Association', in his essay on 'Socialism and Education' in 1912 he was ironic: 'Are we to take the young and promising Trade Unionist, and instil mechanically as much of the pure Marxian doctrine as we can force into his head? Are we to say to him that if he will not be a Marxian he is a traitor to his class and shall have no education at all?'[72] He defended a traditional conception of education as a means of promoting 'growth in the learner'; it must be 'broad and human'. He rejected 'propagandism'.[73] Tutors had to come before students 'as impartial counsellors. Our business is to show others how to make up their own minds, not to make their minds up for them.'[74] Socialism could only be won 'by taking on every occasion the path of freedom rather

[68] A. W. Wright, *G. D. H. Cole and Socialist Democracy* (Oxford, 1979), 145.

[69] Isaac Kramnick and Barry Sheerman, *Harold Laski: A Life on the Left* (London, 1993), 182.

[70] Cole, 'Recollections of Workers' Education'.

[71] Quoted in Wright, *Cole and Socialist Democracy*, 18.

[72] G. D. H. Cole, 'Socialism and Education 12/8/[19]12', Cole Papers, B2/16, fo. 5.

[73] Ibid. fo. 6.   [74] Ibid. fo. 11

than that of control'.[75] Later, when giving evidence to the Education Committee of the TUC in 1923, and explaining the differences between the two traditions of workers' education, Cole described himself as a 'Socialist and a Marxian' who wanted his students 'to believe what I hold to be true; but I try to keep my own bias under, and to draw them to make their own decisions; even against my view of the truth. The Labour Colleges have a different method.'[76]

Tawney was in agreement. Late in his life, in 1953, at a time when the issue of political bias in adult education was once more causing problems for the movement, he recalled that, 'As a teacher of Tutorial Classes, I never felt tempted to engage in propaganda. A doubtless very improper conceit persuaded me that the world, when enlightened, would agree with me. I thought, therefore, that the longest way round was the shortest way home and that my job was to promote enlightenment.'[77] The comment reminds us that, as Jonathan Rée has pointed out, to many in the movement, 'enlightenment' implied socialism: that a fair and dispassionate analysis of society and economy must inevitably result in the acceptance of socialism, not only as a more just social system, but also as a more economically efficient one as well.[78] The tutor did not have to indoctrinate, merely explain.

Cole's distinction between the projects of the WEA and the NCLC is important because it illustrates a point that is often missed. These were not alternative projects as sometimes presented by historians, but different projects. The Plebs certainly articulated the same criticisms as other Labour figures of the link between Oxford and the WEA. But they did not themselves create the alternative that these Labour figures projected. The specifically Marxist education they offered was arguably even further removed from the needs of the labour movement as interpreted by MacDonald in 1908 than that embodied in *Oxford and Working-Class Education*. Among a working-class that for economic, cultural, and ideological reasons was resistant to, or simply untouched by Marxism, the Plebs' solution to workers' education was always likely to arouse suspicions and end in failure. MacDonald had not written to Mansbridge to

[75] Ibid. fo. 17.

[76] Trades Union Congress Education Committee Minutes, 5 May 1923, quoted in Clive Griggs, *The Trade Union Congress and the Struggle for Education 1868–1925* (Lewes, 1983), 193.

[77] R. H. Tawney, 'The WEA and Adult Education', in id., *The Radical Tradition: Twelve Essays on Politics, Education and Literature* (London, 1964), 82–93.

[78] Jonathan Rée, 'Socialism and the Educated Working-Class', in Carl Levy (ed.), *Socialism and the Intelligentsia 1880–1914* (London, 1987), 214.

call for a specifically socialist education; he had written to question the way in which the WEA had chosen to deliver its message in alliance with the educational establishment. The alternative MacDonald envisaged was not Marxist and class-conscious, but an education coming from the people, for 'they are the only good, and everything that takes them away from their internal sources of power and culture is bad'.[79] Arguably the Plebs were as far removed from the people and their culture in Edwardian England as were the dons of Oxford. A *real alternative* to the WEA–Oxford alliance might have involved the creation of an authentically working-class educational association, with roots in working-class communities, offering a broad education, but independent of outside influences and the state, and establishing classes and colleges for itself. This seems to have been in MacDonald's mind when he wrote of 'educational institutions built up by men who know working-class life'.[80] But the Plebs and Labour Colleges movement were something else, were 'aggressively Marxian in outlook and teaching' as Cole put it in 1918, and thus alien to mainstream labour traditions in Britain.[81]

III

Cole's distinction between the WEA and the NCLC and the points flowing from it have been overlooked by those historians who in recent years have resurrected the debates on workers' education from the early twentieth century as a means of criticizing the dominant tradition of adult education coming out of the *1908 Report*. Stuart Macintyre, though careful not to 'impugn the honesty' of Tawney and his fellow workers, presents the development of university adult education nevertheless 'as an integral aspect of social policy', designed to marginalize and eradicate other forms of working-class knowledge and understanding, especially Marxism.[82] According to Roger Fieldhouse,

The adult education movement was welcomed by the establishment as a bulwark against revolutionism, a moderating influence and a form of social control. It helped to channel and reduce pressures and conflict, neutralise class antagonism and integrate the working class into British society—just like its 'partner', the Labour Party . . . It attracted potential working class

[79] MacDonald to Mansbridge, 4 Dec. 1908.
[80] MacDonald, 'Oxford and the Democracy', 757.
[81] G. D. H. Cole, 'Trade Unionism and Education', in id. *et al.* (eds.), *WEA Education Year Book 1918*, 371.
[82] Macintyre, *Proletarian Science*, 89–90.

activists and leaders by its radical image, but diverted them from the communist or revolutionary politics to which they might otherwise have been drawn.[83]

The essentials of the case are here set down and the argument is premised on a belief that without the unholy alliance of the WEA and 'the establishment' a very different type of workers' education would have emerged. According to Professor Fieldhouse, 'The WEA played a significant part in restricting the promulgation of Marxist theory among the British working class ... it is arguable that the WEA's chief influence on the working class was not that it seduced many of its leaders and activists from loyalty to their class, but that it encouraged them to think in terms of non-Marxist politics.'[84] But where is the evidence that the British working class would, in other circumstances, have been drawn to a more militant politics? Professor Fieldhouse himself cites work demonstrating, in his own words, 'that Marxism did not penetrate very far, or greatly influence English political thought' and this long-appreciated feature of the national culture, or rather, this absence, has been analysed and explained in recent years.[85]

As McKibbin has argued, the British workforce in the early twentieth century was fragmented and localized in small units of production and had little of the type of collective social and political identity that might have sustained a Marxist working-class party. Its culture was as likely to encourage pigeon-fancying and sport as politics and, indeed, workers' education. In working-class communities there was little of the social and political alienation that often motivated Continental socialists. British workers were loyal monarchists and keen parliamentarians and they had been granted a unique freedom from state intervention in their relationships with their employers: the state did not menace them. Nor did they show an inclination to follow any but men like themselves at the head of their movement: there was no place for a middle-class socialist leadership

[83] Roger Fieldhouse, 'Conformity and Contradiction in English Responsible Body Adult Education 1925–1950', *Studies in the Education of Adults*, 17/2 (Oct. 1985), 123; id., 'The Ideology of English Adult Education Teaching 1925–1950', *Studies in Adult Education*, 15 (Sept. 1983), 29–30; id., 'The 1908 Report: Antidote to Class Struggle?', in Sylvia Harrop (ed.), *Oxford and Working-Class Education* (Nottingham, 1987), 40–1. See also Anne Phillips and Tim Putnam, 'Education for Emancipation: The Movement for Independent Working-Class Education 1908–1928', *Capital and Class*, 10 (spring 1980), 21–2.

[84] Roger Fieldhouse, *The Workers' Educational Association: Aims and Achievements 1903–1977* (Syracuse, NY, 1977), 33–4.

[85] Fieldhouse, 'The 1908 Report', 46, n. 23.

within the Edwardian Labour Party.[86] Indeed, the Party actively excluded 'a programmatic socialism and any candidate who ventured to stand as a "socialist", which was understandable given that '"socialism" meant little, if anything to most working men in Edwardian Britain'.[87]

There was never a viable Marxist alternative to the tradition of British Labourism, in other words, and that tradition—nonideological, consensual, parliamentary, and democratic—seems actually to have been summed in the outlook and project of the WEA. The very contradictions and confusions in the social aspirations of the dons and their worker allies—did they seek greater working-class participation and opportunity within a cohesive society, or did they believe in Labour's control of politics, economy, and culture?—seem to match exactly the contradictions in the British labour movement more generally. The desire to win for the workers their educational rights without rending the social fabric is entirely consonant with the outlook of Labour at this time. In alliance with the universities the working classes received what they had always wanted—recognition of their right to the educational resources of the nation and access to the national culture.

Professor Fieldhouse is working with a model of what would or perhaps what *should* have happened without Oxford's embrace. But there is little evidence that Marxist politics and Marxist adult education were attractive to the working class; rather the reverse, in fact. Indeed in 1923, in an ironic inversion of events at Ruskin in 1909, students at the Central Labour College actually complained about the concentration on Marx to the exclusion of anything else, and demanded a broader curriculum, access to other authors, and training in useful skills.[88]

The problems with Professor Fieldhouse's argument are evident in his discussion of the suggested curriculum for tutorial classes that was appended by the Joint Committee to the *1908 Report*. He is critical of the reliance in the specimen courses on economics, history, and politics on 'Liberal and Fabian writers' and of the 'predominantly Fabian ... approach' overall, and suggests that the curriculum was designed to exclude Marxism.[89] Where Marx *was* included in the suggested syllabus for an economics class, *Capital* was only an optional text to be read 'if many members of the class have socialistic views' and it was to be balanced by Böhm-Bawerk's

[86] Ross McKibbin, 'Why was there no Marxism in Great Britain?', in id., *The Ideologies of Class: Social Relations in Britain 1880–1950* (Oxford, 1990) 1–41.
[87] Ibid. 1, 31.   [88] Lewis, *Leaders and Teachers*, 157–8.
[89] Fieldhouse, 'The 1908 Report', 45–7.

critique of Marxist economics.[90] But the omission of Marx from the syllabus does not necessarily imply that the Joint Committee was anti-Marxist. It may more reasonably be suggested that this merely confirms the relative unimportance of Marx and Marxism in Edwardian Britain. The tradition was merely irrelevant to the interests of the students and teachers and to the questions of the moment as they understood them.

Liberalism and Fabianism were the very stuff of Edwardian politics on the other hand. As A. W. Wright has put it, the political and intellectual 'world before 1914 . . . was a very Fabian world, not only in terms of the consolidation of Fabian ideas, but also in the apparent triumph of permeation via the New Liberalism'.[91] Many of the students had probably been Liberal voters or supporters in the very recent past, after all; many, perhaps, were still. Cole's disillusion with Fabianism from about 1912 and Tawney's private dialogue with the strategy of the Webbs in his *Commonplace Book* demonstrate that the ideas of the Fabians were central to political debate on the left, whether or not they won support. As it happens, even Albert Mansbridge believed that a tutorial class in economics should have 'access to the opinions of all the economic writers, the orthodox equally with the unorthodox. No class, for example, can afford to disregard either Marshall or Marx.'[92] And even if Professor Fieldhouse *is* correct—if the aim on the part of a committee including several prominent figures from the labour movement, really was to exclude consideration of Marxism—then that in itself is significant. What price a Marxist alternative to the Liberal/Fabian ethos of the WEA when Marxism had so few friends among the working class?

This is not to dismiss the argument that the *1908 Report* and the tradition that developed from it altered the class-consciousness and politics of individuals. Alfred Zimmern recalled 'a student of a tutorial class who wanted a social revolution; he really wanted it quite badly; but at the end of the class he was working with a tremendous will for townplanning in his own district. He hadn't ceased to be a social reformer.'[93] Zimmern saw this transformation as an indication of political maturity and approved; it could also be interpreted as an example of the way in which liberal adult education smoothed out the rough edges of radicalism. It certainly raises questions about

[90] See *Oxford and Working-Class Education*, 'Appendix VII: Courses of Study. Economics', 111.   [91] Wright, *Cole and Socialist Democracy*, 13.
[92] A. Mansbridge, *University Tutorial Classes* (London, 1913), 119.
[93] Harold Begbie, *Living Water: Being Chapters from the Romance of the Poor Student* (London, 1918), 169.

the effect of this form of working-class education, and it would be unbalanced to ignore such evidence and its implications. But it is surely inappropriate to apply a reductive interpretation of deliberate manipulation of the working class through the WEA and universities to the complex and haphazard process of institutional development in this period. Politicians and civil servants may have come to see in time that the tutorial classes movement was a guarantor of social cohesion.[94] And the story is told of a 'member of a Senior Common Room who voted for a colleague's proposal to grant £50 towards the work of tutorial classes, on the ground that it might be wise to "placate the brigands"'.[95] But it is difficult to find evidence to back the contention that, in the Edwardian period, 'support for the WEA . . . was part of a well-established strategy to contain and subordinate working class politics'.[96] If it was, exactly who was pulling the strings? At what level of government or in which Senior Common Room had it been decided to use the WEA in this way? There can be no doubt that the movement was essentially moderate in its politics and outlook, as convinced of the need for social solidarity as social emancipation. But this was never the consequence of any 'strategy', merely the outcome of the attitudes and the convictions that both dons and workers brought with them into the new alliance.

The resort to arguments based upon the concept of 'social control', meanwhile, is a sure sign of imprecision. As Stedman Jones has pointed out, such a general concept is most unhelpful in explaining the dynamics of specific historical situations. It is also a kind of tautology: societies are made up of myriad power-relations between superordinates and subordinates, and thus almost every conceivable social and political relationship may be explained in terms of the catch-all, 'social control'. Someone or something may always be said to 'control' another, but after this is said, there is a need to be clear how that control was exercised, in what circumstances, and how 'social control' in one situation differs from 'social control' in another.[97] Moreover, *Oxford and Working-Class Education* simply does not read as an exercise in 'social control'. Why share power in this new movement with working-class organizations and representatives on joint committees if that was the aim?

[94] Fieldhouse, 'The 1908 Report', 45–6.
[95] F. A. Iremonger, *William Temple, Archbishop of Canterbury: His Life and Letters* (Oxford, 1948), 75. [96] Fieldhouse, 'The 1908 Report', 40.
[97] G. Stedman Jones, 'Class Expression versus Social Control? A Critique of Recent Trends in the Social History of Leisure', *History Workshop Journal*, 4 (autumn 1977), 163–70: 164.

Why even offer 'to give a controlling voice in the selection of a teacher' to the students?[98] Why present the tutorial class as a model of democratic participation? Why 'attach great importance to the principle of the direct representation' of working-class organizations, if, according to Professor Fieldhouse, 'one of the main objectives of the Report was to secure University control of the education of the leading members of the working class'?[99]

Professor Fieldhouse is particularly hard on the dons who apparently saw in the WEA 'an ideal opportunity for acquiring a veneer of working-class participation and support without risking any fundamental upheavals'.[100] They may not have wanted the latter, it is true, but it is difficult to draw the conclusion from the history of Oxford's engagement in adult and working-class education dating from Green and Toynbee to Tawney and Cole that it was only a 'veneer' that was required. To reach working-class communities was the very animating impulse of the whole movement from the 1870s. The alliance of dons and workers is treated by Professor Fieldhouse as aberrant, when it was in keeping with the traditions of the British labour movement. In the 1860s and 1870s the Positivists had provided the strategy, publicity, and arguments that won legal recognition and social acceptance for British trade unions. In the first half of the twentieth century the Fabian Society supplied guidance and ideas to the Labour Party even if it had little to do with the party's formation and organization. By the 1940s and 1950s Labour was led largely by the products of an Oxford education. It is true that the Edwardian Labour Party was led by the same sort of men who supported it and voted for it. But it would be difficult indeed to argue that each of these relationships was diversionary; the very recurrence of associations between the working class and the educated, progressive middle class, suggests that they were axiomatic to the movement. Above all, there is at the heart of this kind of argument a type of condescension towards thousands of working people who were apparently duped into becoming the fools of the establishment when they attended WEA classes or went to the Balliol Summer School. Whatever they might have gained personally from the experience, and whatever view they took of the movement they had joined, they were apparently being corralled into an ideological and political dead-end. At the heart of such an approach there is a fundamental lack of respect for the choices and the aims of the students themselves.

[98] *Oxford and Working-Class Education*, 58.
[99] Ibid. 148; Fieldhouse, 'The 1908 Report', 41.
[100] Fieldhouse, *Workers' Educational Association*, 7–8.

Many of those aims were educational rather than political. As this book argues, we cannot reduce adult and workers' education to a political project in which the educational experience of students is of merely secondary importance. The majority of students wanted access to educational resources previously denied them before they wanted anything else, and they sought in education a personal and spiritual transcendence. Even so, it cannot be argued that a liberal education of the sort offered by Oxford and the WEA was either apolitical or opposed to political commitment, given the recognition of many working-class students that the acquisition of skills and an objective knowledge of the society they lived in were prerequisites for changing it. It is interesting to note that after the Plebs secession, Labour College classes were organized in Rochdale in competition with the WEA tutorial classes that began in the town. But L. V. Gill wrote to Oxford to explain that the WEA had not lost many students to its new local rival and he emphasized that 'the whole affair has really strengthened our movement, having led men to re-examine the WEA position and attitude, and to decide that partisan education is undesirable even for strong party men'.[101] Confirming long-held convictions was a poor training for the battle against political opponents to come. Indeed, using WEA students as examples, Jonathan Rose has argued, *pace* Fieldhouse, that the WEA often liberated people from everyday commercial culture, and radicalized them. Rather than turning students into passive upholders of dominant values, education in the WEA created, as was intended, restless, critical, vigilant, and civic-minded people who sought local and national influence.[102]

In short, the alliance of Oxford and the WEA was neither diversionary nor aberrant but consistent with the aims of those who had founded the extension movement on the one side and with the social and educational aspirations of an élite of working people on the other. MacDonald's strictures in 1908 could not be ignored, and focused attention on the problems of such an alliance. But the 'alternative' offered by the Ruskin secessionists and the movement they founded, though impressive in itself, was no alternative at all for the mainstream of the labour movement, because it neither offered the impartial education students wanted and required, nor emanated from a political tradition with deep roots in most working-class communities. And many activists in the labour movement questioned the strategy of building alternative institutions and traditions when

[101] Quoted in Jennings, 'Revolting Students', 14.
[102] Jonathan Rose, 'The Workers in the Workers' Educational Association 1903–1950', *Albion*, 21/4 (winter 1989), 602–8.

the political imperative of the age seemed to point to winning access to, and control of, national institutions. In 1897 the Trades' Union Congress resolved 'that the workers . . . should not be satisfied until the highest educational advantages which the country affords are within reach of all'.[103] In 1900 the members of the Shoreditch branch of the Social Democratic Federation protested at the foundation of an independent workers' college, Ruskin Hall, in Oxford: 'Oxford and Cambridge and other endowed seats of learning were the rightful inheritance of the people, and . . . to attach themselves to any other educational institution would be to give their acquiescence to this deprivation of their rights'.[104] A TUC deputation to the Board of Education in 1910 that sought an enquiry into the use of educational endowments explained 'that workpeople are not going to rest until the finances of Universities are right and true and sound, and so arranged that every child of high capacity and true character shall have an opportunity to continue his studies in them for the benefit of the whole community'.[105] And as H. H. Turner wrote to Alfred Zimmern after his visits to the Longton and Rochdale tutorial classes in early 1911, 'What the workers want is that the doors of Colleges should not be closed to them. They may find ultimately that they are better off outside: but they want to verify that for themselves.'[106]

[103] '1897 TUC Education Resolution', in Griggs, *The Trade Union Congress*, 259.

[104] Quoted in Jonathan Rée, *Proletarian Philosophers: Problems in Socialist Culture in Britain, 1900–1940* (Oxford, 1984), 19.

[105] 'Notes for the Deputation to the President of the Board of Education on March 17th 1910', Mansbridge Papers, Add. MS 65215.

[106] H. H. Turner to A. Zimmern, 15 Feb. 1911, Zimmern MSS, Bodleian Library, Oxford, 12, fo. 5.

6

ADULT EDUCATION IN WAR AND PEACE, 1914–1945

I

In the late summers of 1914 and 1939 the Oxford Delegacy found itself planning for a new academic year as war was declared. Peripatetic educational programmes, administratively complex and dependent on the goodwill and contributions of many separate institutions and individuals, were particularly vulnerable to disruption and it is hardly surprising that uncertainty pervaded the correspondence and reports of the early months of both wars. Yet in the course of the conflicts, adult education found a role for itself. After 1939, university adult education in general and Oxford's extramural classes in particular, experienced expansion and innovation and made an interesting contribution to the war effort at home and among combatants. The tradition of an education for citizenship, intrinsic to Oxford's conception of the tasks of adult and workers' education since the late nineteenth century, was especially relevant in the 1940s, and Oxford lecturers found themselves part of a broadly based movement for social change that they helped on where they could. The experience of the First World War was rather different; educationally, the achievements were of a lesser order, though not inconsiderable. But after 1916 the enthusiasts for adult education in Oxford were themselves architects of the changing public mood in campaigns of general educational advance on the one hand, and for the recognition by the state of the special claims of adult education, on the other. Indeed, there is a sense in which the last two years of the First World War and the first year of peace after it were a climacteric for the movement and for the specific conception of the place of adult education in a democratic community as understood in Oxford.

The first effect of the declaration of war on 4 August 1914 was physical: the Delegacy lost its home when the Examination Schools were requisitioned as a military hospital. Queen's College came to its aid, making rooms available for the duration of the war, after which it was temporarily transferred 'to two huts in the quadrangle of the Examination Schools'.[1] Once the initial euphoria, and the disruption of August 1914 had passed, only 22 out of 103 local centres for Oxford extension lectures cancelled their arrangements.[2] At Chatham, two tutorial classes due to begin work in September had to be suspended 'as most of the students were employed in the Dockyard, and were working day and night'.[3] At Glossop, a tutorial class of thirty manual workers was reduced to a dozen students inside two years.[4] Enlistment in the armed forces, overtime in war work, restrictions on petrol, blackouts, and, in the south-east, air raids, deterred students and disrupted courses.[5] Total student numbers for extension lectures fell from over twelve thousand in 1913–14 to seven and a half thousand three years later in 1916–17, and 103 centres were reduced to 53. Over the same period the number of Oxford tutorial classes had fallen from eighteen to ten. Ironically, the session that began in the autumn of 1918, as the war drew to its convulsive close, proved 'the most difficult of the five' wartime years. Less than nine thousand attended Oxford courses, and the winter of 1918–19 'was probably the most distracting the movement has experienced'.[6] The combination of the Armistice, the influenza epidemics of that winter, the general election in December 1918, and the local elections in the following spring, disrupted the programme at regular intervals. Survival was in itself an achievement: 'the system has withstood the strain' as the Delegacy's annual report for 1918–19 put it. But there was also scope for innovation. With Tawney away on war service and unable to conduct his classes in North Staffordshire, F. W. Cuthbertson (Kolthammer) went to live in the district through the winter of 1915–16 and kept things going—a first informal experiment in the system of 'resident tutors' that Oxford and other extramural departments would develop after the war.[7] In the same year, the Tutorial Classes Committee organized the Kettering Women's Class, most of whose members were drawn from a local clothing factory, which began to study European History.[8] The class numbered twenty-three, of whom nineteen were working women with an average age of about 25. 'None of them had had any education since leaving the elementary school

[1] *University of Oxford: Delegacy for the Extension of Teaching Beyond the Limits of the University: Annual Report 1919–20*, 3.
[2] Ibid., *1914–15*, 1.
[3] *Oxford University Extension Delegacy: Tutorial Classes Committee: Annual Report 1914–15*, 1.
[4] Ibid., *1915–16*, 4.   [5] *Delegacy Annual Report 1916–17*, 2.
[6] *Tutorial Classes Committee Report 1918–19*, 4.
[7] Ibid., *1915–16*, 5.   [8] *Delegacy Annual Report 1916–17*, 6.

at thirteen, and most of them were overcome at the mere thought of writing an essay.'[9] By the end of the war some of the Delegacy's lecturers were also engaged in the first attempts at forces' education, an enterprise that gained in urgency and official support as troop morale began to fall in 1917. Voluntary bodies, notably the YMCA, had taken the lead in organizing lectures and classes for units in Britain and abroad, and Oxford had representatives on the overseeing committee and at work among British troops at home, in Europe and the Middle East.[10] Oxford lecturers who taught soldiers in France in early 1917, for example, included E. B. Poulton and H. H. Turner.[11] The precedent was to be developed more systematically after 1939. As A. L. Smith was to put it, 'The war itself, its issues and problems, the Army life itself with its atmosphere of new interests and strong common feeling, have created a new educational opportunity'.[12]

With lecturers and tutors engaged in the services or on war-related work, there were opportunities for new teachers as well. One of these was the young T. S. Eliot, recently married, the author of a first volume of poems, *Prufrock and Other Observations*, and in need of income.[13] He had spent the academic year 1914–15 studying in Oxford, and in early 1916 he approached the Delegacy with the offer of various courses on French writing and criticism. He was despatched to Ilkley in the autumn of that year to give six lectures on Modern French Literature, a dauntingly severe course which, as Eliot explained to one of his Harvard professors, was actually 'on Social, Philosophical and Religious Problems in Contemporary France'. Eliot had devised a long and complex reading list, running from Rousseau to Ezra Pound. He admitted himself that the course was 'difficult and involved' but was critical of the

---

[9] *Ministry of Reconstruction Adult Education Committee Final Report*, PP 1919, Cmd. 321, xxvii. 256.

[10] Ibid. 338–42; Thomas Kelly, *A History of Adult Education in Great Britain*, 1st edn. (Liverpool, 1970), 304–7; *Delegacy Annual Report 1917–18*, 2–3. S. P. Mackenzie, *Politics and Military Morale: Current Affairs and Citizenship Education in the British Army 1914–1950* (Oxford, 1992), 1–17.

[11] 'Memorandum Re Special Lectures in France, Jan.–Mar. 1917', Ministry of Reconstruction, Adult Education Committee, Public Record Office, RECO 1 897.

[12] 'Covering Letter from the Chairman to the Prime Minister', *Adult Education Committee, Final Report*, 7. On education in the armed forces during the First World War see 'Education in the Army', *Second Interim Report of the Adult Education Committee of the Ministry of Reconstruction*, PP 1918, Cd. 9225, ix.

[13] See Robert Schuchard, 'T. S. Eliot as an Extension Lecturer' (2pts.), *Review of English Studies*, NS 25 (1974), 163–73, 292–304.

students who attended classes after his lectures for their passivity.[14] The class secretary, in excusing an evident failure, drew attention to the practical problems of putting on the course during wartime, though she too, found the subject 'difficult'.[15] With the Battle of the Somme still in bloody progress it is indeed 'difficult' to know what Eliot's audience made of lectures on French romanticism and the reaction to it. Eliot had high hopes before he set out for Yorkshire: 'If I can establish myself in this Oxford Extension Lecturing I shall abandon teaching, and shall also have a clear six months a year for whatever else I wish to do.'[16] However, the tutor, the subject, the circumstances, and the students were ill-matched, and this was the only class the young poet taught for the Oxford Delegacy. But Eliot had better luck with the University of London Extension Board: in the autumn of 1916 he also began a three-year tutorial class in Modern English Literature at Southall, mainly composed of elementary schoolteachers, which was much more successful. As he wrote to his father, 'The class is very keen and very appreciative, and very anxious to learn and to think. These people are the most hopeful sign in England, to me.'[17] He was evidently impressed by his students' selflessness, contrasting their 'disinterested . . . devotion to study and thought' to American educational attitudes.[18] Indeed, in view of what he was writing at the time and his subsequent conservatism and cultural élitism, Eliot's generous praise for his students in his correspondence from this period is not without significance.[19] It substantiates John Carey's argument that the contempt for ordinary people expressed by several of the great imaginative writers of this period was based on ignorance. Because they had no contact with the workers or the clerks, they could imagine them as an undifferentiated and uncivilized mass; close up, it was possible to recognize their humanity and individuality. Sadly, his spell teaching a tutorial class does not seem to have had lasting impact on Eliot's social attitudes.[20]

Eliot's failure in Ilkley demonstrates the point that, at this time,

[14] Lecturer's Reports, Oxford University Archives, DES/R/3/46, fo. 55.
[15] Local Secretary's Report, Oxford University Archives, DES/R/3/46, fo. 56.
[16] T. S. Eliot to Professor J. H. Woods, 7 Sept. 1916, in Valerie Eliot (ed.), *The Letters of T. S. Eliot*, i, *1898–1922* (London, 1988).
[17] T. S. Eliot to Henry Ware Eliot, 1 Mar. 1917, ibid. 161.
[18] T. S. Eliot to Charlotte Eliot Smith (sister), 21 Mar. 1917, ibid. 166.
[19] See also T. S. Eliot to Eleanor Hinckley, 23 Mar. 1917, ibid. 168.
[20] Eliot's uncharacteristically generous response to his students is noted by John Carey, *The Intellectuals and the Masses: Pride and Prejudice among the Literary Intelligentsia 1880–1939* (London, 1992), 16.

lecturers and tutors were far more successful when responding to public interest in the origins of the conflict and in the domestic and international issues it raised. In September 1915 Arthur Greenwood, then a tutorial class tutor for Leeds University and chairman of the Yorkshire WEA, and later an MP, Cabinet minister and deputy leader of the Labour Party, gave a talk on 'Education, Citizenship and the War' at the Stoke School of Mining in a lecture series arranged jointly by the Oxford Tutorial Classes Committee and the North Staffordshire Miners' Higher Education Movement. Greenwood believed that

Education was the most vital necessity the country should keep going during the war. Shells were not the only thing to win the war. Education was quite as important. Purposeful action, the realization of the difficulties in the way of the country, the necessity of knowing what it all means and where we are driving, were absolutely essential if we were to prosecute the war successfully.[21]

Marriott wrote to all extension lecturers encouraging them to adapt 'to the conditions of the moment. This does not mean that all lectures must be on war subjects, but it does mean that lecturers must have regard to the prevailing atmosphere.'[22] Much later he recollected that 'propaganda in the narrower sense was not within our proper province. But we substituted for our usual lecture subjects, courses which had a direct bearing on the war, its antecedents and issues.'[23] Yet looking at press accounts of extension lectures given during the war, it is clear that many lecturers presented a fiercely patriotic and anti-German case, and were engaged in an 'educational' campaign very unlike that called for by Greenwood.[24] There were conventional assaults on German militarism and tyranny. There were variations, at least until late 1917, on the theme of 'our plucky Russian allies'. One lecturer in the Hereford Town Hall pictured Russia 'defending the liberty of Europe and . . . fighting for justice and righteousness'.[25] Another gave 'some delightfully informing glimpses of the character and life of the Russian peasant' at the Town Hall in Hove.[26] The same lecturer also offered six lectures on

[21] *The Staffordshire Sentinel,* 18 Sept. 1915.
[22] Cyclostyled letter bound with the *Delegacy Annual Report 1914–15* in the Oxford University Archives.
[23] J. A. R. Marriott, *Memories of Four Score Years* (London, 1946), 153.
[24] The following examples are taken from the volume entitled 'Press Cuttings 1915–22', DES/PC/1/3, Oxford University Archives. Most of the cuttings concern Marriott's lectures.
[25] Mr Rothay Reynolds MA, *Hereford Times,* 5 Feb. 1916.
[26] Mr R. H. U. Bloor, BA, *The Brighton Herald,* 19 Nov. 1915.

'William Shakespeare as an English Patriot' at Bournemouth. And there were suitably martial or patriotic courses on subjects like 'English Naval History' and 'Britain and her Colonies'. Marriott himself seems to have had little doubt about his role in wartime; despite his protestations of neutrality, his expositions presented his own view of the justice of the British cause in 'a crusade—a holy war' against a foe who would 'put back the civilisation of the world for centuries'.[27]

The attitude of the tutorial classes movement was rather different, however. Temple's presidential message to the Workers' Educational Association in October 1914 stressed the need to create 'a fully informed democracy' during the war and refused to 'assume conclusions and then look for evidence by which we can support them'.[28] Men and women, as he later wrote, were to 'form their own judgments' about the conflict.[29] The WEA would not present any particular view of the war and consequently attracted accusations of pacifism and pro-Germanism, not least because it refused to condemn conscientious objectors.[30] A. L. Smith, who believed in the struggle, set out to combat in print and on the platform 'the disturbing lack of enthusiasm for the war' that he found in sections of the WEA.[31] The cross-currents within the organization, and the buffeting it received from outside sources during the war, were clear in the curious, opaque, and contradictory section of its annual report for 1915 entitled 'The WEA and the Great War'. This declared that 'there could only be one purpose' for the movement during wartime: 'to help and to strengthen England and her overseas Dominions'. In terms redolent of the 'Prussianism' many believed they had gone to war to combat, it was asserted that 'every organization should be ready to subordinate itself to the supreme need of the State in a critical hour'. But those who read on were informed that the association stood for 'calm and wise study of the forces

[27] *Bournemouth Visitors' Directory*, 27 March 1915. This is drawn from a lecture that was part of a series Marriott gave at the Co-operative Hall, Winton on 'The Great European War'.
[28] William Temple's Presidential Message in *The Highway* in Oct. 1914, quoted in Mary Stocks, *The Workers' Educational Association. The First Fifty Years* (London, 1953), 65.
[29] William Temple, 'Leading Facts in the History of the Workers' Educational Association', in G. D. H. Cole *et al.* (eds.), *The WEA Education Year Book 1918* (London, 1918), 326.
[30] T. W. Price, *The Story of the Workers' Educational Association from 1903 to 1924* (London, 1924), 59–60.
[31] Stuart Wallace, *War and the Image of Germany: British Academics 1914–18* (Edinburgh, 1988), 168.

which move men and nations' and that 'freedom of discussion and fearlessness in pursuing it has been through all these trying months the well-approved practice of the Association'.[32]

Many Oxford tutorial classes, already at work on three-year programmes on economics or social history, saw these out before turning to subjects connected with the war. When they did so, the approach was academic and the focus was as likely to be domestic as international. At Bournemouth in 1916 Cole, who was initially opposed to the war, devised a two-part course on 'Comparative Institutions' that brilliantly harnessed immediate issues and concerns to formal education. It first examined the political systems and recent history of all the principal combatant nations, ending with consideration of future means for maintaining international peace. It then considered in similar fashion the white dominions and foremost dependencies of the Empire, ending with a final class on 'Suggestions for a new Government of the Empire' that anticipated the rise of nationalism at the end of the conflict.[33] In the following year Cole offered a course on 'Social, Economic and Political Reconstruction' of a sort that became common at the end of the war, analysing the problems of the moment and likely issues of the future, from demobilization and industrial relations, through economic and social policy, to politics and the franchise. During the conflict Cole was continually reminding those in the labour movement who would listen, that victory would not solve the outstanding industrial and social problems—that class struggle should continue even while workers supported the national cause against Germany.[34] As he recognized, and as recent historians have confirmed, 'We shall be faced after the war not so much with absolutely new problems as with old problems greatly intensified'. His course was designed to emphasize 'the continuity of a development which the war has served rather to accelerate than to interrupt'.[35]

[32] *Workers' Educational Association: Twelfth Annual Report* (London, 1915), 6–7.

[33] G. D. H. Cole, *Syllabus of a Course of Classes on Comparative Institutions* (Oxford, 1917), 'Oxford University Tutorial Classes Committee Syllabuses 1912–1921, A–C', DES/SB/2/1/1, Oxford University Archives.

[34] J. M. Winter, *Socialism and the Challenge of War: Ideas and Politics in Britain 1912–18* (London, 1974), 121–3.

[35] *Syllabus of a Course of Lectures on Social, Economic and Political Reconstruction* (Oxford, 1917), DES/SB/2/1/1. See also 'Syllabus of a Short Course of Lectures by H. Clay M.A.' on 'Economic and Social Problems Raised by the War', DES/SB/2/1/1.

II

Explaining the origins of the war and inviting consideration of its outcome was one obvious function of the adult education movement as a whole after 1914. The war also prompted reflection on what the movement had itself achieved in the preceding decade. In sombre and dissatisfied mood, Zimmern wrote to Mansbridge in the summer of 1915 complaining that the the WEA had 'lost some of its ideal quality'. The Association had become 'too Fabian . . . too administrative'; it lacked direction and policy, and could point to few achievements.

We are not yet a working-class University, our students are comparatively few of them doing Honours work, we are not doing much to improve the national system of education in accordance with our Annual Meeting resolutions. We have secured rather the names than the real support of most of our affiliated working class bodies. We are not really democratic either in our Central [administration], our Districts or our Branches, even our rank and file are not yet anything like 'an educated democracy'. All this is true. We have fallen short, that is both in our practical educational policy and in our scholarly aspirations and it is these shortcomings which have 'found us out' in the testing time of war.[36]

But the 'testing time of war', though it prompted this type of self-criticism, also offered opportunities for would-be reformers, as hitherto accepted principles were questioned, institutions remodelled, and practices adapted to meet the new national need. Zimmern continued to have faith: he continued to 'believe in the powers and capacities of ordinary underprivileged people, and especially in the inherited gifts and future destiny of the English working class'. Nevertheless there was work to be done: 'what we have to do is to make English people believe in education'.[37] One way of achieving this was to take advantage of the more open and flexible attitudes in wartime to lead and direct public opinion and government towards social reform in general, and better educational provision in particular.

Tawney had fought as a volunteer in the war, turned down a commission, and had been seriously wounded on the first day of the Somme. Soon after his recovery, at the end of November 1916, he joined with Zimmern, J. W. Mallon, a WEA stalwart who would later become Warden of Toynbee Hall, and others, in drafting a

[36] A. E. Zimmern to A. Mansbridge, 25 Aug. 1915, Mansbridge Papers, lxiiiA, British Library Add. MS 65257, fos. 48–53.
[37] A. E. Zimmern to Mrs Mansbridge, 29 Aug. 1915, ibid., fo. 57.

memorandum calling for an intensification of the war effort through the process of democratization: only by liberating the energies of the people could victory be secured. The memorandum blamed the 'poison of social prejudice and class interests' for national failure in wartime, noted the baleful influence of the regular officer class who were now leading a citizens' army, and called for more governmental direction of the war effort. The memorandum was drafted with the assistance of Lloyd George, who was then Minister of Munitions, but who was, within days, to oust Asquith and become prime minister.[38] A few weeks later Tawney returned to the theme in an anonymous article entitled 'Democracy or Defeat'. A nation, argued Tawney, 'cannot be the champion of the supremacy of the moral law in international affairs unless it is willing to submit its domestic conduct to the same criterion . . . It cannot fight for freedom against the crooked ways of kings, unless it has rallied all the social forces which make for freedom within itself to its side.' He called for an end to war profiteering, increased taxation on large incomes and luxuries, and greater state involvement in economic and social life: 'it is for democracy to plan the economic and social organization, by which a war for democracy is to be carried on.' He also observed that 'it is only by means of something like an internal revolution that a war of principles' could be fought.[39]

In a letter Tawney wrote to A. L. Smith, now Master of Balliol, at the end of 1917, we may catch some recognition on his part of the opportunity apparently then presenting itself. He noted the general disillusion with the war: 'I doubt if one could get a hearing at a working class meeting if one spoke on the principles at stake. One would be laughed down.' He explained military failure in terms of the inability to harness the energies and commitment of the people: 'This war seems to have caught us halfway in transition to democracy. We have not the kind of strength Germany has. Nor have we the kind of strength we should have if the mass of the working people felt that this war was their war, not an enterprise for which their rulers want their arms but not their minds and hearts.' And he criticized the 'intellectual direction and leadership' of the war, noting that 'one cannot expect a respect for intelligence in an emergency, if one has not cultivated it before the emergency arose'. The war, in other words, exemplified the wasted potential of the nation, and showed how an inadequate and exclusive social and political system

[38] Thomas Jones, *Whitehall Diaries*, ed. R. K. Middlemas, i, 1916–1925 (London, 1969), 28 Nov. 1916, pp. 2–3.

[39] [R. H. Tawney] 'Democracy or Defeat. By a Soldier', *The Welsh Outlook*, 4/37 (Jan. 1917), 9, 11.

limited national power. But in demonstrating the worst features of British society it made the case for reform that much more urgent and credible. To Tawney, there appeared an immediate need, and an opportunity, to harness popular energy through political democratization and education.[40]

Smith agreed, interpreting the opportunity that war presented in terms of the idealist tradition that had helped form him in Balliol. The spirit and achievements of wartime were evidence of what might be possible in a renewed society dedicated to collective welfare. Thus, 'the time has come to meet the old, narrow, exploded form of individualism in English thought by definitely developing that other aspect of life which is conveyed in the words Co-operation, Community, Corporateness.'[41] And he pointed to an example of such co-operation in the ethos of working-class education, 'where they do not compete with each other but work as a group together'.[42] When Smith gave his opening address in July 1917 to the members of the Ministry of Reconstruction's Adult Education Committee, which did as much as any agency at this time to lay down a framework for civic participation, he sensed the moment:

Englishmen are now in an extremely rare and unprecedented mood of open-mindedness, willing to believe that they have been wrong in the past, and ready to put their house in order. After the South African war the country was in a similar mood, but it was transient and quickly passed away; in the present case, it is our duty to utilize the opportunities while they exist.

As Smith explained, 'we are on a sort of rising wave of the movement'.[43]

This was adult education's climacteric, the moment when its historic mission seemed most relevant to the needs of the nation; when its long-standing aim of increasing provision and accessibility seemed close to realization; when it seemed possible that its special claims would be recognized by the state. 'Reconstruction', the key domestic theme from 1916, could best be achieved if the movement's civic culture was promoted by the state and used as a guide for institutional reform throughout society and government. The movement was expectant. The WEA's unique *Education Year Book* for 1918 was

[40] R. H. Tawney to A. L. Smith, 27 Dec. 1917, Letters to A. L. Smith, Box 12 (T), A. L. Smith Papers, Balliol College, Oxford.
[41] A. L. Smith, *The Christian Attitude to War*, Oxford Pamphlets (Oxford, 1915), 16. [42] Ibid. 17.
[43] 'Chairman's Address at the Opening Meeting' [of the Adult Education Committee of the Ministry of Reconstruction], 11 July 1917, Public Record Office, RECO 1 897.

a compendious manifesto for change in every area of education. Edited by Cole, Mactavish, Tawney, Temple and Zimmern, it was designed 'to set people thinking about educational questions and to increase the desire for educational progress' and it was premised on the belief 'that no phase of Reconstruction so much demands attention as Education'.[44] Harold Begbie, a campaigning journalist and writer with a social conscience and a noted talent for sympathy that made him a gifted listener, went so far as to produce a book in 1918 specifically about the adult education movement. It was designed 'to convince the sceptical and to persuade the indifferent that there is a craving in the mind of our working-classes for the noblest benefits of education'.[45] The book was based on interviews 'gathered in the course of a recent tour through industrial England'. Some were with easily identifiable figures like Mansbridge, Zimmern, and Reuben George. Most of those interviewed remain anonymous, but many in turn told a similar story of spiritual satisfaction and developing social awareness since coming into the movement. As the Oxford Tutorial Classes Committee explained the mood two years later: 'The intellectual ferment caused by the War, the growth of new democratic ideals, the extension of the franchise and the reform of the educational system, all indicate the likelihood of an increasing demand by adults for humane education, which in the interests of good citizenship must be met.'[46]

The expectancy that flowed through the adult education movement from 1916 developed into two separate educational campaigns with roots in Oxford. The first of these, a campaign for a general educational advance that led to the 1918 Education Act, was launched at a national conference in Balliol in July 1916 sponsored by the WEA, and held soon after Smith became Master. Over three days an agenda for reform was prepared. The school leaving age was to go up to 14, and half-time education below that age was to be abolished. After 14, there was to be a compulsory system of continuation education, mixing work and schooling. Full-time secondary education beyond 14 was to be encouraged where possible. Teachers should be better trained and remunerated; class sizes were to be reduced; physical education was to be 'a necessary part of

[44] 'Editorial Preface', *WEA Education Year Book 1918*. The *Year Book* was also edited by Arnold Freeman.

[45] Harold Begbie, *Living Water: Being Chapters from the Romance of the Poor Student* (London, 1918), 7–8.

[46] See 'Royal Commission on the Universities of Oxford and Cambridge. Memorandum by the Tutorial Classes Committee of the University of Oxford 9 April 1920', Oxford University Archives DES/F/14/2, p. 6.

education', and the school medical service was to be developed further. Finally, higher education was to be made more accessible.[47] With this established, Zimmern, Cartwright, W. G. S. Adams (soon to become Lloyd George's private secretary), and above all, Smith himself, took to the road and addressed many meetings and conferences in the cause of educational reform.[48] At the British Association in Newcastle, Smith called for 'the co-operation of democracy and intelligence. In the future we must have an educated democracy.'[49] At the annual Conference of Educational Associations he warned that unless the nation 'made proper use of our opportunities we should not be, in the sense we wished, victors in this war'.[50] At the Southwark Diocesan Conference he criticized the existing 'fragments' of an educational system and 'the amount of talent that was thrown away'.[51] At a conference at Barnett House on the future of secondary education he called for 'a great educational campaign'.[52] The campaign Smith envisaged took advantage of a growing concern 'to improve national efficiency and competitiveness prevalent from the summer of 1916'.[53] It brought together many different groups, and the public enthusiasm for educational reconstruction thus generated gave H. A. L. Fisher at the Board of Education, newly appointed by Lloyd George, the opportunity to formulate legislative proposals which did indeed raise the school leaving age to 14 and introduced continuation schools for day-release pupils. The Act also introduced state scholarships for study at university. To create something more than the fragments of an educational system, the 1918 Education Act called upon local education authorities to formulate complete schemes of education from nursery provision upwards, though postwar economies were to put paid to several of the planned improvements.[54]

[47] F. W. Goldstone, MP, 'National Union Notes', *Times Educational Supplement*, 14 Sept. 1916, p. 129.

[48] John A. Taylor, 'The Making of the 1919 Report', in *The 1919 Report: The Final and Interim Reports of the Adult Education Committee of the Ministry of Reconstruction 1918–1919* (Nottingham, 1980), 27. John Jones, *Balliol College: A History 1263–1939* (Oxford, 1988), 256.

[49] *The Times*, 7 Sept. 1916, p. 6.

[50] *The Times*, 2 Jan. 1917, p. 12.

[51] *Times Educational Supplement*, 8 Feb. 1917, p. 50.

[52] *The Times*, 13 Nov. 1916, p. 5.

[53] Arthur Marwick, *The Deluge: British Society and the First World War* (London, 1965), 243.

[54] On the 1918 Education Act see Lawrence Andrews, *The Education Act 1918* (London, 1976) and Gerald Bernbaum, *Social Change and the Schools 1918–1944* (London, 1967).

Pushing forward the cause of specifically adult education, mean-while, demanded a different approach—not the management of a public campaign, but the use and manipulation of the bureaucratic structures established to oversee the planning of postwar recon-struction. Asquith had made weak attempts at organizing this from March 1916, but reconstruction was much enhanced, or so it seemed, after Lloyd George became prime minister nine months later.[55] A revitalized Reconstruction Committee (subsequently transformed into the Ministry of Reconstruction in mid-1917) appointed an Educa-tion Panel whose members 'were closely involved with adult educa-tion'.[56] With the Board of Education at work on the new education bill there was limited scope for investigation into schooling. In these circumstances a special committee was projected 'to enquire into the provision for and possibility of adult education among working men and women and to make recommendations'. And this commit-tee in turn was largely composed of people active in, or sympathetic to, adult education. At its centre, the work was carried out by Smith, Tawney, Cartwright, and Arthur Greenwood.[57] Bernard Jennings has written of the 'incestuous tendencies' within the adult education movement and the emergence of a 'network' of activists including 'Mansbridge, Temple, Greenwood, Tawney, Alfred Zimmern, Haldane, A. L. Smith and the latter's successor at Balliol, A. D. Lindsay'.[58] Oxford was one of the experiences and influences linking this network together, and the *1919 Report* was shaped by one of the network's subgroups. Opportunities had presented them-selves, in other words, and this nexus had taken advantage of them. In keeping with Oxford's leadership of the movement for a genera-tion and more, the views of a small group of Oxford tutors and administrators were to be dominant in the subsequent deliberations. Mansbridge, noting that 'Oxford is so powerful already' and that 'Oxford men seem so prominent in educational matters', actually suggested that, on grounds of balance, the chairman of the Adult Education Committee should come from Cambridge.[59] In the event he came from Balliol: A. L. Smith was invited to take the lead. Eight

[55] Marwick, *The Deluge*, 239.

[56] Taylor, 'Making of the 1919 Report', 28.

[57] Ibid. 33. See the file on the composition and terms of reference of the com-mittee in the Ministry of Reconstruction Papers, Public Record Office, RECO 1 669.

[58] Bernard Jennings, 'The Reception of the Report', in *The 1919 Report* (Not-tingham, 1980), 43.

[59] A. Mansbridge to W. G. S. Adams, 19 Apr. 1917, Mansbridge Papers, Add. MS 65195, i, fo. 1.

of the twelve plenary meetings of the committee between July 1917 and February 1918 were actually held in Balliol.[60] Indeed, 'it used to be said by Mrs A. L. Smith that the very paths in Balliol quad were made by "A.L." and Cartwright as they walked and talked over the problems of their work during composition of the 1919 Report.'[61]

The *Final Report of the Adult Education Committee of the Ministry of Reconstruction*, published in November 1919 and known as the *1919 Report* has often been considered the most important text on British adult education. It attempted a comprehensive survey of past, present, and future in specifically liberal adult education: technical and vocational education were not part of the committee's remit. The *Report* was not the fruit of long and searching investigation; rather, the committee, with much in common, drew on their experience to make their case. At the very first meeting they were thus able to discuss and provisionally agree a series of resolutions that formed the basis of all subsequent deliberation: for example, that 'the community, through various channels, both public and voluntary, should make adequate provision for adult education'; 'that industrial conditions and the physical environment are such as to place very great obstacles in the way of adult education'; 'that extra-mural work should be regarded as an integral part of university work'.[62] It is evident that the spirit and ethos of the joint tutorial class was always uppermost in the committee's collective outlook; its members displayed a firm commitment to a concept of adult education as 'an inseparable aspect of citizenship' that should prepare men and women 'for the exercise of public spirit in their social relations'[63]. In Smith's covering letter to Lloyd George he laid down some of the principles on which the Committee's conclusions were based: that 'the goal of all education must be citizenship' and that 'there is latent in the mass of our people a capacity beyond what was recognized, a capacity to rise to the conception of great issues'. In consequence, adult education was more than 'a luxury for a few exceptional persons here and there' but was 'a permanent

---

[60] 'Covering Letter from the Chairman to the Prime Minister', in *Ministry of Reconstruction: Adult Education Committee: Final Report*, PP 1919, Cmd. 321, xxvii. 8. See 'Adult Education Committee—Proceedings', Ministry of Reconstruction Papers, Public Record Office, RECO 1 895.

[61] H. P. Smith, 'A Tutorial Class Makes History', *Adult Education*, 31/4 (spring 1959), 271–80.

[62] 'Proceedings of the First Meeting, 11–12 July 1917, Balliol College', RECO 1 895.

[63] *Adult Education Committee, Final Report*, 5, 57.

national necessity' and should be 'both universal and lifelong'.[64] In the words of the Committee's thirty-second resolution, 'the main purpose of Adult Education is to enable a man to fit himself for life, and in a civilised community to fit himself for his place as a member of that community'.[65]

To understand the *Final Report of 1919*, and, indeed, the climacteric of these years in the movement more widely, it is necessary also to know something of the Committee's *Interim Report on Industrial and Social Conditions in Relation to Adult Education*, published in the preceding year. The committee here set down the failings of the old society that had to be addressed and removed if the civic culture they projected was to flourish. Its purpose was to indicate those 'changes in industrial organization' necessary if public education was to develop.[66] As Arthur Greenwood privately explained, 'The main argument of the Report is that responsible citizenship and higher standards of intellectual and social life are impossible so long as the industrial and social conditions prevailing before the war, remain'.[67] In large measure it was a humanitarian assault on industrialism's effects on the bodies, minds, and communities of working people. Its style was indignant, personal, sometimes utopian; the *Interim Report* reads like a catalogue of the social ills that impressionable tutors, without previous experience of working-class life, had encountered and written about in their reports back to Oxford before 1914. It called for a statutory reduction in working hours, for the regulation of overtime, for an end to shift-work, and for regular holidays for workers. In passages that seemed to owe their inspiration to Ruskin and Morris, the *Report* presented a 'fundamental criticism that the present industrial system offers little opportunity for the satisfaction of the intellectual, social and artistic impulses'.[68] It suggested that monotonous work be shared out on the factory floor, that workers alternate their tasks, that education help raise public taste and standards of craftsmanship.[69] 'Industry' it asserted 'exists for man, not man for industry... Material progress is of value only insofar as it assists towards the

---

[64] Ibid. 4–6.

[65] 'Proceedings of the Eighth Meeting, 10–11 April 1918, Balliol College', RECO 1 895.

[66] *Ministry of Reconstruction: Adult Education Committee: Interim Report on Industrial and Social Conditions in Relation to Adult Education*, PP 1918, Cmd. 9107, ix. 3.

[67] A. Greenwood to V. Nash, 14 May 1918, RECO 1 887.

[68] *Min. of Reconstruction: Adult Education Committee: Interim Report*, ix. 20.

[69] Ibid. 14–15, 20–1.

realization of human possibilities.'[70] It also played upon the theme of social solidarity, developing the ideas of *Oxford and Working-Class Education* in this respect but using them more obviously as powerful arguments—indeed, threats—against inertia: to 'stand still' and do nothing about social conditions would invite 'civil dissension at home'.[71]

In the *Interim Report* the adult education movement linked itself to wider social aims, for the movement was, as Tawney wrote subsequently, 'the expression in the sphere of education of ideals which find their other applications in the efforts to raise the level, not only of education but of industrial society and social organization'.[72] There is a very real sense that at this particular moment the leaders of the movement believed they spoke for all progressive opinion seeking social change and the 'reconstruction' of society. This was no doubt presumptuous and also naïve: adult education could only be a relatively minor aspect of the social reforms then being discussed. But there is no better evidence of the ambitions that many invested in adult education than the *Interim Report*. In so far as adult education would gain from a more humane society, the *Report*'s authors felt able to call for its creation. The *Interim Report* thus embodied the view held by several influential leaders of the early Labour Party that state action to improve living and working conditions was the precondition 'to ethical self-fulfilment and participation in public life'.[73]

It is not surprising that the *Interim Report* was controversial: there is more than one file in the Public Record Office which includes letters and memoranda between the Home Office and Ministry of Reconstruction over the question of whether it should have been published without full consultation with other departments affected by its proposals, and hence the inevitable dilution of its message. The Home Secretary, Sir George Cave, apparently believed that the report's 'proposals on industrial matters' were 'outside the scope of their reference'. But the Minister of Reconstruction, Christopher Addison, mounted a robust and successful defence of the report and the decision to publish it in its original form. He found it 'difficult to hold that a Committee appointed "to consider the possibilities of adult education" were travelling beyond their province in devoting attention in the first place to the limitations of these possibilities

---

[70] Ibid. 20, 27.   [71] Ibid. 29.

[72] *Adult Education Committee, Final Report*, 31.

[73] Jose Harris, 'Political Thought and the Welfare State 1870–1914: An Intellectual Framework for British Social Policy', *Past and Present*, 135 (1992), 133.

imposed by the industrial conditions under which very large numbers of the adult working-class live'.[74]

The Committee also paid attention to the particular difficulties of women, devoting a section of the *Final Report* to their educational needs at a time when it was hoped that the social and political gains that women had made during the war years would encourage greater participation in adult education.[75] A subcommittee, chaired by Mrs Huws Davies, who was, among other things, a tutorial class teacher in London, sent out a questionnaire to establish the extent of provision for, and enrolment by, women in various forms of adult education.[76] While war conditions had obviously affected participation, pushing up the relative proportions of women in adult education classes, the responses gave some basis for calculations. The subcommittee estimated that women comprised 'between half and three-quarters' of extension lecture audiences, and noted that, with the men called away, between 1912–13 and 1917–18, the proportion of women in all tutorial classes had risen from 16.5 per cent to 39 per cent. In the latter year, 1,014 out of 2,586 students in tutorial classes were women.[77] The secretary of the Wolverhampton extension centre estimated that 'out of an audience of about 400, two-thirds are women . . . The average age would be about thirty. The audience consists of home and voluntary workers, teachers, shop assistants & clerks. Equal proportions of married & single women.' The secretary at Mold gave a similar picture: 'Women of all ages attend, and of many occupations, but generally speaking, those who have attended a secondary school, & are now employed as clerks, school teachers, or in shops, are the large majority. I doubt if the work touches the average working man's wife at all, though one or two may occasionally come in.'[78]

Women's adult education remained the domain of the respectable and leisured classes. The committee concluded that the involvement of working-class women in the movement was prohibited by household duties, tradition, and prejudice against women learning for its own sake. It was also noted that where an interest in education did

[74] See the letter from Edward Troop, undersecretary of state at the Home Office, to the Secretary of the Ministry of Reconstruction, 9 July 1918, and the response from Vaughan Nash dated 8 Aug. 1918, RECO 1 673. See also the letter of R. R. Bannatyne at the Home Office to H. Eustace Davies at the Ministry of Reconstruction, 27 June 1918, RECO 1 887.

[75] *Adult Education Committee, Final Report*, 255.

[76] For responses to the questionnaire from a variety of adult education centres and organizations, see RECO 1 886.

[77] *Adult Education Committee, Final Report*, 256.   [78] RECO 1 886.

exist among working women, it 'has usually been aroused by connection with some propagandist or political organization' like the women's co-operative guilds, or the Women's Labour League. In a pattern similar to that of working-class men, in other words, adult education was especially attractive to women already engaged in social and political activism, and by definition, therefore, somewhat out of the ordinary. Neither the average working man, nor the average working man's wife, had yet experienced a need for adult education.[79] In a subsequent essay, published soon after the *1919 Report* appeared, Mrs Davies logically extended the approach taken in the committee's *Interim Report* to call for social and domestic reforms— better houses, modern bathrooms, medical care for mothers, and the assistance of other family members with the domestic routine— so that women would be able to participate in adult education.[80]

The *Final Report* was, overall, a far more circumspect document than the *Interim Report*. It developed several premises as the basis for its recommendations for university adult education, though its investigations and suggestions covered all types of liberal provision. First, adult education was conceptualized as distinct: even though the authors of the *Report* were linked to a movement for general educational improvement, they developed the argument that however good other forms of education might be, adult education had specific social and communal ends that made it indispensable in a democratic community.[81] It was not advocated to deal with the faults in elementary and secondary provision; it was *sui generis*. It was no 'temporary makeshift or stopgap, but a normal part of the educational provision of a democratic community'.[82] Adult education was necessary for a critical, discerning citizenry, able 'to form an independent judgement'; it fulfilled the individual's desire for knowledge for its own sake; it would also help establish 'a better social order'.[83] The *Report* was premised also on a new image of the university which was to become more flexible, adaptive, and representative. A university should be a 'natural meeting place for all who have the desire and capacity for advanced study' and the breadth of experience and diversity this would encourage would help sustain a richer intellectual life and closer links with the community.[84]

The fundamental recommendation in regard to university adult

[79] *Adult Education Committee, Final Report*, 259, 261.

[80] Mrs Huws Davies, 'Women and Adult Education' in R. St John Parry (ed.), *Cambridge Essays on Adult Education* (Cambridge, 1920), 151.

[81] Wiltshire, 'A General Introduction to the Report', in *The 1919 Report*, 12–13.   [82] *Adult Education Committee, Final Report*, 50.

[83] Ibid. 52, 53, 57.   [84] Ibid. 102.

education was that 'the provision of a liberal education for adults should be regarded by universities as a normal and necessary part of their functions'.[85] All types of extramural education should be eligible for government grants, and universities, assisted by national and local authorities, were recommended to spend more in absolute and proportionate terms on adult education. They should employ an adequate staff of tutors and lecturers and pay them better. They should develop the system of 'residential tutors' in areas where they carried out extramural work, and promote the establishment of colleges in these districts. They should also devise ways of bringing more adult students to the universities for periods of residence and study.[86] And given that all these suggestions were designed to regularize the status of university adult education and give it parity with provision for undergraduate and postgraduate studies, the committee recommended that 'there should be established at each university a department of extramural adult education with an academic head'.[87] They imagined such departments as 'the eyes and ears of the universities. They would be concerned, to use a convenient metaphor, with questions of foreign policy. They would report on the needs of new types of student, on the value of novel educational experiments, on the possibility of extending the influence of the Universities into fields which as yet they have not touched.'[88] It was a prescient description of the modern extramural department.

III

The *Final Report of the Adult Education Committee* was published a year after the end of the war. It coincided, therefore, with the rapid decline of political and public interest in 'Reconstruction' that blighted all projects for social renewal. The *Report*, like many other schemes and suggestions, fell foul of the combination of the 'hard-faced men' in a conservative House of Commons hostile to public expenditure; sudden economic downturn and the enforced economies of 1920; an absence of enthusiasm for its recommendations in the Board of Education; and, overall, the absence of any strategy for the implementation of social change on the part of the coalition government.[89] Nothing was done, in other words. Its publication

---

[85] Ibid. 169.   [86] Ibid. 169–70.   [87] Ibid. 98–9.   [88] Ibid. 99–100.
[89] Philip Abrams, 'The Failure of Social Reform: 1918–1920', *Past and Present*, 24 (1963), 43–64. See also Wiltshire, 'General Introduction to the Report', 22–3; Taylor, 'Making of the 1919 Report', 34; Jennings, 'Reception of the Report', 39–41.

received relatively little attention from the press, and public interest faded. 'Never again did adult education move into so central a position on the political stage.'[90] This may be true, but it does not mean that the *Report* was some sort of failure. For those already involved with adult education, and armed with Arthur Greenwood's digest of its proposals, it validated their engagement and inspired them with a plan for the future.[91] Immediate implementation was impossible, but the *Report* served as a guide to the formulation of policy and as a standard to aim at in succeeding years. As Greenwood had written prophetically to Mansbridge in June 1917 before the committee had begun work, 'It may turn out to be able to point the way to big developments in the future'.[92] The *1919 Report* focused the thinking of the adult education movement on what was desirable, and it also permeated the planning of the Board of Education, local education authorities, universities, and voluntary agencies.

This was nowhere more evident than in Oxford itself. The *1919 Report* was published as a new Royal Commission on Oxford and Cambridge began its work of investigation.[93] Adult education was one theme in the Asquith Commission's deliberations, and the influence of the *1919 Report* was clear in the evidence the Commission accumulated and in its recommendations. The Asquith Commission's report actually began its discussion of extramural education by paying its respects to the work of the Adult Education Committee whose earlier report 'has been so strongly approved'.[94] The Tutorial Classes Committee submitted a memorandum that cited the *1919 Report* liberally and which presented a set of future aims replicating the *Report*'s recommendations. The chief claim was for financial assistance to facilitate expansion: 41 per cent of the Committee's total expenditure of £22,800 since 1908 had come 'from some fourteen or fifteen sources within the University' which, in the nature of things, could not always be relied on. A further 24 per cent of expenditure had come from miscellaneous sources—

[90] Brian Harrison, 'Oxford and the Labour Movement', *Twentieth Century British History*, 2/3 (1991), 234.

[91] Arthur Greenwood, *The Education of the Citizen: Being a Summary of the Proposals of the Adult Education Committee* (London, 1920).

[92] A. Greenwood to A. Mansbridge, 25 June 1917, Mansbridge Papers, Add. MS 65195, i, fo. 6.

[93] See John Prest, 'The Asquith Commission, 1919–1922', in Brian Harrison (ed.), *The History of the University of Oxford*, viii, *The Twentieth Century* (Oxford, 1994), 27–43.

[94] *Royal Commission on Oxford and Cambridge Universities, Report*, PP 1922, Cmd. x. 1588, 120.

donations, subscriptions, receipts from the Summer School, and so forth. Only just over a third of its income had come from public sources—21 per cent from Board of Education grants and 14 per cent from local educational authorities.[95] The Committee needed a secure income and more of it. As the memorandum put it, 'the extra-mural work of the University should be regarded as much a part of its educational function as its intra-mural work is. From this it would follow that the University should make regular and adequate financial provision from time to time for its extra-mural work.'[96] The WEA echoed the call for regular and dependable finance.[97] The Labour Party asked for an extension of extramural work in both universities, an increase in the number of working-class children admitted to them, and suggested special 'one year courses for adults' at Oxford and Cambridge, including 'teachers, trade union officials, co-operators and municipal civil servants'.[98]

In its report, published in 1922, the Asquith Commission endorsed many of these educational and financial claims. It accepted the central contention of the *1919 Report* that adult education was integral to the functions of each university. Extramural education should be 'part of the normal and necessary work of a University'. It should be accorded 'improved status in the Universities, effective machinery for the work of expansion, ample funds, and an increasing supply of highly qualified and enthusiastic teachers'.[99] It recommended that Oxford and Cambridge establish Extra-Mural Boards to oversee lectures and classes in accordance with the *1919 Report's* recommendation to establish university extramural departments. In each case, the board should consist of separate committees for tutorial classes and extension lectures.[100] In 1924 Oxford established such a Delegacy for Extra-Mural Studies. In addition to the usual grants for tutorial classes, the Asquith Commission recommended also that each university receive £6,000 annually from the Board of Education to support adult education, including the education of mature students studying inside the walls.[101] It favoured

[95] 'Memorandum by the Tutorial Classes Committee of the University of Oxford, 9 Apr. 1920', Oxford University Archives DES/F/14/2, p. 4.

[96] Ibid. 7.

[97] See 'Evidence of the Workers' Educational Association Presented by Canon Temple, June 18 1920', Royal Commission on Oxford and Cambridge Universities, Bodleian Library, MS Top Oxon b 109, fo. 563.

[98] Memoranda by the Labour Party and WEA, *Royal Commission on Oxford and Cambridge Universities: Appendices to the Report of the Commissioners* (London, HMSO, 1922), 60–71.

[99] *Royal Commission on Oxford and Cambridge Universities, Report*, 123–4.

[100] Ibid. 129.   [101] Ibid. 128.

continuing with the experiment of resident tutors and also suggested joint intra/extramural appointments of staff who would teach both adults and undergraduates.[102] Extramural education required 'an increased number of teachers with high qualifications, adequate pay and assured prospects'.[103] The *1919 Report* had set an agenda and provided a range of answers that the Commission followed without demur.

The Commission also recommended 'the establishment of a Centre or House for Extra-Mural Students, in as central a position as possible, at both Universities, consisting of the necessary offices and of accommodation for the existing libraries, and for students wishing to read or write there'.[104] Five years later, in 1927, Oxford purchased Rewley House in Wellington Square for the purpose. Built in 1873 as a convent school, St Anne's Rewley, it had been used as a furniture warehouse since 1903. The building provided space for a library, common room, and two lecture halls in addition to offices.[105] It also provided a name with long academic associations; Rewley Abbey, to the west of the city, had been founded in 1280 by Edmund, second earl of Cornwall, as a 'studium' where Cistercian monks could live while studying in the University. And Wellington Square, laid out in the 1820s, was a fitting location: the boarding houses and small hotels that lined it, had been used to accommodate students at Summer Meetings and Summer Schools, and were host to the distinct community of WEA students when they came to Oxford in the first years of the century. Mansbridge had lodged at No. 40 during the 1907 conference and Zimmern described the informal meeting in his rooms that then took place:

Most branches of education were represented: Whitehall (which sat on the window-sill), Cambridge in the person of a Fellow of Trinity, the Oxford professoriate and the elementary teacher; there was capital in the shape of a London banker, and there was labour galore (in both sexes) . . . Wellington Square is not perhaps the place a romance-writer would select for his vision of Utopia; but that night at least it seemed a 'centre of intellectual aspirations of the whole community'.[106]

---

[102] Ibid. 130. See R. H. Tawney's advocacy of joint appointments in his oral evidence to the Commission on 21 Sept. 1921, Bodleian Library. MS Top Oxon b. 109, fo. 533.
[103] *Royal Commission on Oxford and Cambridge Universities, Report*, 239.
[104] Ibid. 130.
[105] 'Rewley House', *Rewley House Papers*, 1 (1927), 5; 'Rewley House—A New Oxford Foundation', *Rewley House Papers*, 3 (1961–2), 49.
[106] A. E. Z[immern], 'The Workers at the Summer Meeting', *Oxford Magazine*, 24 Oct. 1907, pp. 23–4.

Mansbridge was present again to open Rewley House formally in December 1927. He recalled the same gathering in August 1907 and then, in characteristic style, referred to the new building as 'the material expression of that spiritual and intellectual enterprise which has united us in the boundless area of learning'.[107]

But the 'boundless area of learning' was contracting, metaphorically and physically. Indeed, the possession of an institutional focus in Oxford and a new status within the University marks the 1920s as a watershed in this story. For fifty years Oxford, like Cambridge, played on a national stage, and (unlike Cambridge in this) affected to speak for the adult education movement as a whole. But bricks and mortar in Oxford signified a gradual change in focus and a reduction in ambition, though this would not be evident until the late 1940s. From the 1920s onwards, Oxford's project in adult education was as much concerned to win an accepted place among the regular functions of the University as to promote a national educational crusade irrespective of its institutional position within Oxford itself. If the *1919 Report* was some sort of climax in the history of the movement, and of Oxford's influence within it, the national role that Oxford had always attempted to play in the promotion of its distinctive conception of adult education was no longer available or, arguably, necessary. By the end of the 1920s extramural departments had been established at Nottingham (the first, dating from 1922), Exeter, Bristol, Hull, Southampton, Birmingham, and Leicester Universities.[108] They were often small, underresourced, and marginal, but their existence made it presumptuous for any single institution to speak for 'university adult education'. More generally (and perhaps controversially), although the middle decades of the twentieth century were witness to Oxford's undiminished national influence through the personnel of politics, so many of whom had been educated at the University, nevertheless the slow decline in the University's cultural and political ascendancy from late-Victorian and Edwardian heights was also underway. Adult education was part of this process.

The crucial issue was territory. In 1924 a report by the education inspectorate on Oxford's tutorial classes found it 'remarkable' in view of the developing programmes of other universities 'that in the latest session Oxford classes are still to be found, not only in Staffordshire (seven classes) and Kent (four classes) but in Chesterfield,

---

[107] 'Address of Albert Mansbridge on the Opening of Rewley House, 3 Dec. 1927', in 'Mansbridge and Rewley House—A Flashback', *Rewley House Papers*, 3 (1961–2), 46, 48.

[108] Kelly, *History of Adult Education*, 269.

Leeds, Lincoln, and Kettering as well as nearer home in Oxford-shire'.[109] During the First World War practical and financial difficulties and the absence of tutors led the Tutorial Classes Committee to give up several of its centres, notably in Yorkshire and Lancashire. And in the significant expansion in the number of tutorial classes in the North and Midlands after the war, which was led by the civic universities, Oxford played only a minor role. Between 1914–15 and 1919–20 the programme of tutorial classes administered by the joint committees of the universities of Leeds and Sheffield rose from 13 and 10 classes respectively to 28 and 23. In the same period Oxford's programme actually declined from 16 tutorial classes to 14.[110] It was losing ground to local universities in distant industrial regions while its own immediate hinterland did not contain the sort of working-class communities for which the joint tutorial class had been devised. As the inspectorate noted in 1924, 'In recent years the chief advance in other parts of the country has taken place in a number of compact districts organized from a local centre. The problem for the Oxford Committee is very much more difficult.'[111]

In the course of the 1920s and 1930s many extension lecture centres also passed to neighbouring universities. At a national conference in 1923 it was accepted that local extension committees might retain their links with the two old universities if they wished. In such circumstances local universities were 'to refrain from soliciting applications for lectures'. But the new universities were given freedom to respond to specific requests directed to them for lectures from local centres previously linked to Oxford or Cambridge. And they were to have a 'free hand' to organize courses in new centres in their adjoining regions.[112] Before 1914 university adult education was dominated by Oxford, Cambridge, and London: on the eve of the Second World War these universities 'were responsible for only about two-fifths of the total provision, the remainder being shared among seventeen universities and colleges'.[113] Oxford's geographical

[109] *Board of Education: Report of H.M. Inspectors upon University Tutorial Classes under the Supervision of the Joint Committee of the University of Oxford for the period ending 31 July, 1924* (n.d.), Oxford University Archives, 'Copies of Special Reports, Memoranda etc . . .' DES/F/2/1/8, folder 3, p. 1.

[110] 'Memorandum by the Central Joint Advisory Committee on Tutorial Classes', *Royal Commission on Oxford and Cambridge: Appendices* 77.

[111] *Board of Education: Report by H.M. Inspectors . . . 1924*, 3.

[112] See 'Adaptation of Scheme OE/3/441 of the University of Bristol. Adopted at Conference of U[niversity] E[xtension] Representatives, London, July 11, 1923, As a Basis of Future Discussion', Oxford University Extension Committee Minutes, Oxford University Archives, DES/M/1/5, fo. 328. See also Extension Committee Minutes, 30 Nov. 1923, fo. 320.

[113] Kelly, *History of Adult Education*, 271.

responsibilities narrowed to the three counties surrounding the university—Oxfordshire, Buckinghamshire, and Berkshire—and to an assortment of far-flung territories 'that could be explained in terms of history rather than defended on grounds of convenience and efficiency'.[114] These included North Staffordshire, Kent, East Sussex, the city of Lincoln, and other anomalies like Swindon, Chipping Camden, Heaton Moor, and Mold. All would be ceded to the postwar generation of new universities in the 1960s and 1970s. Oxford and Cambridge could fall back on pioneering traditions for their moral authority but they were no longer dominant forces. Even though the civic universities tended to promote the same educational philosophy through the same methods, the pattern of provision became more diverse, new traditions were established, and student loyalties were transferred to other institutions.

These changes, at least before the onset of the Slump, took place in a peculiarly benign regime for adult education. Before departing to become Warden of New College, Fisher at the Board of Education managed to win exemption for liberal adult education from the notorious Geddes Axe on public expenditure.[115] It is not surprising that 'adult education . . . enjoyed unique favours from high-placed friends', however: on his appointment Fisher had written to Temple to encourage the WEA and had added that 'I shall want to help you in any way possible'.[116] Here is more evidence of the 'incestuous network' in action. Thus in 1922–3 rather than a cut, there was actually an increase in expenditure on adult education of some 20 per cent. Then in 1924 the first minority Labour government introduced new and generous regulations for adult education which allowed universities and other designated recipients of public funds, the so-called responsible bodies including the WEA, to claim grant for extension lectures in addition to tutorial classes.[117] And when these regulations were reviewed after five years the second Labour administration was in power. On both occasions the President of the Board of Education, Sir Charles Trevelyan, dealt kindly with the movement.[118]

There were problems none the less. Blyth notes a decline in the creativity of the tutorial classes movement in the 1930s: the university scholars of the first phase had moved on and their successors

---

[114] *Department for External Studies Annual Report 1974–5* (Oxford, 1975), 1.

[115] John A. Blyth, *English University Adult Education 1908–1958: The Unique Tradition* (Manchester, 1983), 50; Stocks, *Workers' Educational Association*, 94.

[116] Blyth, *English University Adult Education*, 89; F. A. Iremonger, *William Temple, Archbishop of Canterbury. His Life and Letters* (Oxford, 1948), 86.

[117] Kelly, *History of Adult Education*, 268.

[118] Blyth, *Adult Education*, 89.

lacked their imagination and zeal, and had now to deal with detailed official regulations and a consequent growth in bureaucracy.[119] But perhaps this was inevitable. The work was now routine rather than consciously innovatory and pioneering; that, after all, was what the *1919 Report* had always intended. There were inevitable organizational problems also: in Oxford's case, the difficulty of working with an inefficient and constantly changing WEA infrastructure in Kent.[120] And during the 1920s came recognition that the movement was failing to reach the mass of the working class. In 1919–20, out of 5,482 students in all tutorial classes (317 of whom were taught under Oxford's programme) the two largest occupational categories were teachers (823) and clerks (767). Skilled manual workers were present in large numbers, certainly, but at the other end of the scale there were only 33 students classified as 'labourers'.[121] In a piece on the future of the WEA written in 1928, Tawney, now President of the Association in succession to Temple, lamented that working-class organizations were 'crippled and stultified because they still too often refuse to take seriously the business of ensuring that educational facilities are available to their members'.[122] But then, as the Chairman of the North Staffordshire District of the WEA pointed out in the following year, most of the working class had no reason to want further education. They did 'not look back on their school days either with pride or pleasure' but had left school 'with a decided distaste for pseudo-education and education methods, and this fact has made the work of the WEA and kindred institutions very much more difficult than it ought to be'.[123] Adult education might be *sui generis,* but it was still dependent on the quality of learning lower down the educational system.

At some stage in the mid-1920s the movement seems to have ceased to speak and write of 'working-class education' and substituted

[119] Ibid. 100–1.

[120] See 'The WEA in Kent, Nov. 1928', p. 13, Archives of the South-Eastern District of the Workers' Educational Association, Rochester, Kent. (This document seems to have been written for the Oxford Tutorial Classes Committee, probably by E. S. Cartwright.)

[121] 'Memorandum by the Central Joint Advisory Committee on Tutorial Classes', 78.

[122] R. H. Tawney, 'The Future of the Workers' Educational Association', *The Highway*, 21 (Oct. 1928), 4.

[123] George Carpentier, 'Chairman's Address to the Annual Meeting', 'Annual Report of the North Staffordshire District of the Workers' Educational Association 1928–29', p. 2, Archives of the North Staffs District of the WEA, Cartwright House, Broad Street, Hanley, Staffordshire.

'adult education' instead.[124] By 1923–4 it was noticeable that the number of tutorial classes in literature nationally, some 78, was very close to the number in economics, 81; this in itself was no bad thing, but it did suggest changing and perhaps diminishing political priorities in the movement.[125] The inspectors who reported on Oxford's tutorial class programme in 1924 were evidently concerned, on purely educational grounds, that the traditional adult curriculum should be broadened; they wanted the students to be challenged with new material that had no relation to their immediate social context. Thus they welcomed the decline of economic history in Oxford classes and its replacement by other forms of historical study and other subjects altogether. In 1913–14, all 18 Oxford tutorial classes were at work on aspects of economic history: by 1923–4 only 4 of 19 'followed the beaten track of Economics and Industrial History'.[126] There was a tension, in other words, between the development of the curriculum and the political imperatives of the movement, and such changes in emphasis entailed losses as well as gains. But some of the changes could only be welcomed: as the proportion of working-class men in tutorial classes declined, so women came to fill their place. In 1912 women comprised not quite 14 per cent of tutorial class students nationally. By 1922 this proportion had climbed to 32 per cent and on the eve of the Second World War, to 43 per cent.[127]

Another success, albeit on a very modest scale, was the introduction of a scheme to bring adult students to Oxford to study for undergraduate degrees, starting in 1925. This had been recommended in the *Reports* of 1908 and 1919; it was also recommended by the Asquith Commission which hoped that the new Delegacy would secure entrance to Oxford of 'poor students of maturer years who are intellectually qualified for a University training in some special branch of study, but need special facilities to enable them to come into residence'.[128] It was suggested that traditional entrance examinations be dispensed with; colleges should rely instead on recommendations from tutorial class tutors.[129] In the first year the four

[124] H. P. Smith, 'Adult Education in England', in the Papers of A. D. Lindsay, Keele University Archives, L. 174.

[125] H. D. Hughes, 'A General Introduction to the Year Book', in Cole *et al.* (eds.), *WEA Education Year Book 1918* (Nottingham, 1981 repr.; first pub. 1918), 9.

[126] *Board of Education: Report of H.M. Inspectors ... 1924*, 4–7.

[127] Jonathan Rose, 'The Workers in the Workers' Educational Association 1903–1950', *Albion*, 21/4 (winter 1989), 601.

[128] *Royal Commission on Oxford and Cambridge, Report* x. 243.

[129] Ibid. 162.

scholarships available were awarded to two engine-fitters, a rail-wayman, and a cocoa-maker. In 1926 they went to a coal miner, a machine-turner, a dockyard engine-fitter, and a blacksmith. In 1927, when there were 328 applications, they went to a potter's saggarmaker, an ironmoulder, a civil servant, and two clerks.[130] The selected adult scholars, with a record of study behind them, were exempted from Responsions and granted 'senior standing' which allowed them to read for an honours degree in two years. Between 1925 and 1941 some seventy-one adult students recommended by the Delegacy matriculated in Oxford, and three-quarters of them could claim only to have had an elementary education.[131] Most were in receipt of Delegacy scholarships; in some cases the Delegacy recommended adult students who had financial support from other institutions.

The Oxford scheme, and others like it at Cambridge and London, offered almost the only route to university in the interwar period for mature students. There were other working-class students at the University in this period who had come through grammar schools on scholarships, 'but it now became possible for the first time for young men and women who had left school at fourteen, who had spent several years in industry, and who had come to feel the need for further education, to take an Honours course at Oxford as adult students'.[132] Many of the 'Delegacy Scholars' were drawn from Oxford tutorial classes; others were put forward by trade unions, co-operative societies, and other branches of the labour movement who contributed to their upkeep. Their numbers expanded rapidly at the end of the Second World War so that in the late 1940s and early 1950s forty or so adult students were taking Oxford degrees each year. The scheme continued until 1961 by which time Mature State Studentships awarded by the Ministry of Education and financial assistance for mature students from local educational authorities had made late entry into higher education somewhat easier and reduced the significance of Oxford's financial contribution.[133]

---

[130] 'Adult Students at the University', *Rewley House Papers*, 1 (1927), 33. See also E. S. Cartwright, 'The Extra-Mural Student at the University', *Journal of Adult Education*, 3/1 (Oct. 1928), 60–70. (A 'saggar' is the clay box in which pottery is packed for baking.)

[131] W. J. Lunn, 'Adult Scholars at Oxford Since the War', *Rewley House Papers*, 3/2 (1953), 66–9.

[132] Henry Sanderson Furniss, *Memories of Sixty Years* (London, 1931), 213–14. (In 1925 Sanderson Furniss retired as Principal of Ruskin College and became 'supervisor' to the adult scholars, providing them with pastoral guidance while they were in Oxford.)

[133] *Delegacy for Extra-Mural Studies: Annual Report 1960–61*, 3.

Delegacy Scholars included George Woodcock, who came up in 1931, took a first in PPE at New College and rose through the Trades' Union Congress to become its General Secretary; Frank Pickstock, who read PPE at Queen's College between 1935–7 and later returned to make his career in adult education in the Oxford Delegacy; and Fred Mulley, the son of a general labourer, who read PPE at Christ Church after the Second World War and went on to senior positions in the Wilson and Callaghan Cabinets of the 1970s as Secretary of State for Education and Science (1975–6) and then for Defence (1976–9). Generally, and as *Oxford and Working-Class Education* had hoped, these adult scholars left the University for work in trade unions or in adult education.

IV

In a report on university tutorial classes in May 1922 the education inspectorate estimated that 'at least 80 per cent of the members of tutorial classes are connected with the Labour Party'. They speculated 'that the close connection with Labour circles' had kept out many potential students with a different politics. On the other hand, they recognized that the WEA had brought into adult education many 'working men and women who are actively connected with trade unionism and Labour politics' but who would have ignored it otherwise.[134] In the years immediately following the First World War adult education became more closely associated with the labour movement than before, with interesting implications for the relationship between dons and workers. In earlier stages of the movement, adult education had brought students and dons into contact with the working class and their institutions and so assisted in the social education of both parties. But relatively few lecturers had followed Acland's example and used this contact as a conduit into politics. After 1918, however, the identification of adult education with the labour movement at the moment of its political maturity offered greater opportunities than before for the making of Labour careers. It was still difficult for those not born into the working class to find a position in the Labour Party. But the Party was beginning to shed the authentic labourism of the Edwardian period. During and especially just after the First World War, an

---

[134] *Board of Education: H.M. Inspector's Report on University Tutorial Classes 26 May 1922*, Reports and Memoranda, ii, no. 49, Oxford University Archives DES/F/2/1/8.

influx of intellectuals was absorbed in organizations like the War Emergency Committee, the Labour Research Department and the Party's new advisory committees on which Sidney Webb, Tawney, and Cole played influential roles.[135] Harold Laski, educated before the First World War at New College, threw his energies equally into the Labour Party and workers' education in the 1920s, helping to found the British Institute of Adult Education.[136] And adult education was one of the routes into the interwar Labour Party for other middle-class intellectuals, as the interlocking cases of Hugh Gaitskell, Evan Durbin, Dick Crossman, and Lord and Lady Longford (Frank Pakenham and Elizabeth Harman) attest.

If 'the first major turning point' in the life of Hugh Gaitskell, leader of the Labour Party between 1955 and his death in 1963, was the General Strike, the second was the year he spent, fresh out of Oxford and at the prompting of G. D. H. Cole, teaching tutorial classes for the Extra-Mural Department at Nottingham University.[137] Gaitskell was a Wyckhamist at New College, intermittently studying for the new school of Politics, Philosophy, and Economics, and coasting to a second. But the Strike, in which he served as Margaret Cole's driver on trips to and from London, brought him into contact with Labour-supporting circles in Oxford and more particularly with Douglas Cole.[138] Gaitskell was tutored by Cole in his final year for a special subject on 'Labour movements' and he became an early member of the famous 'Cole Group', which had begun life as the University strike committee in 1926 and which met regularly in Oxford for political discussion and planning thereafter.[139] Morally engaged and now notably more serious, Gaitskell worked for a first, which he duly took in the summer of 1927.[140] Over dinner in Soho, Cole then suggested that he either consider research into the history of the Chartist movement or try his hand at adult education in Nottingham. 'Having heard Douglas talk about the WEA I had sometimes wondered if I could do this sort of job but thought it probably beyond me. Yet there I was being offered a start at once.

[135] Winter, *Socialism and the Challenge of War*, 141–2, 272–3.

[136] Isaac Kramnick and Barry Sheerman, *Harold Laski: A Life on the Left* (London, 1993), 180–2.

[137] Philip M. Williams, *Hugh Gaitskell: A Political Biography* (London, 1979), 16, 22; see also John Betjeman, 'School Days and After', in W. T. Rodgers (ed.), *Hugh Gaitskell 1906–63* (London, 1964), 15–18.

[138] Margaret Cole, 'Discovering the Labour Movement' in Rodgers (ed.), *Gaitskell*, 32.

[139] On Cole's influence on the young Gaitskell, see Maurice Bowra, 'Oxford in the Nineteen Twenties' in Rodgers (ed.), *Gaitskell*, 24.

[140] Williams, *Gaitskell*, 18–22.

I plumped for it, and on the strength of Douglas' recommendation got the Nottingham post. It was my experiences there—especially in the coalfields—which were to turn me later towards active politics.'[141] Gaitskell recalled Cole once saying to him 'that WEA tutors were in many respects the true missionaries of today—doing the kind of job which at one time the churches used to do'.[142]

Like many before him, working-class living conditions shocked Gaitskell, though he took up the work at a particularly critical moment.[143] Disillusion was rife among the miners following the collapse of the coal strike. The blacklisting of strikers who remained loyal to the Nottinghamshire Miners' Association and the tensions caused by the breakaway 'Spencer Union' only added to the bitterness and ill will. Most of Gaitskell's students in his four classes were unemployed miners, and they apparently gave their inexperienced and stuttering tutor 'a hammering' at first, though he won their respect in time. During the year he came 'to know working-class people as well as working-class conditions' for the first time. Deeply impressed by the communal loyalties in the towns and villages he visited, 'often he said later that it was those miners who made him a Socialist'.[144] The experience was brief because in the following year, 1928, he was offered a position in the Economics Department at University College, London. But its effects endured: when the economic historian Michael Postan first met him soon after his move to London, it was evident that it 'had bitten deeply into him'.[145] Perhaps for this reason he continued to teach WEA classes at Shoreditch, Eltham, and Gravesend. Having shown him the working class at first hand, and given him confidence to meet and mix with workers, adult education now provided a route into Labour politics. In the course of his teaching Gaitskell met and impressed the WEA organizer for Kent, George Dexter, who was also chairmen of the Chatham Labour Party. By 1932 Gaitskell had been adopted as parliamentary candidate for the constituency. He stood unsuccessfully in Chatham in the 1935 general election.[146]

Gaitskell's closest friend, Evan Durbin, was similarly involved in adult education. The earnest son of a Baptist minister and product of a radical Liberal background, described by Margaret Cole as 'a person of austere mind as well as great kindness of heart', Durbin

---

[141] Hugh Gaitskell, 'At Oxford in the Twenties', in Asa Briggs and John Saville (eds.), *Essays in Labour History: In Memory of G. D. H. Cole* (London, 1960), 16. [142] Ibid. 15.

[143] M. Cole, 'Labour Movement', 39. [144] Williams, *Gaitskell*, 22–7.

[145] Michael Postan, 'Political and Intellectual Progress', in Rodgers (ed.), *Gaitskell*, 55. [146] Ibid. 48–9.

went up to New College at the same time as Gaitskell, though he took a first degree in zoology before taking a second degree in PPE.[147] He left Oxford in 1929, spent a year teaching economics with Gaitskell at University College, and then moved on to a post at the London School of Economics in 1930.[148] For over a decade he gave extension lectures for the Oxford Delegacy, first on 'The Economic Problems of Today' in the winter of 1929–30 in Gnosall and Uttoxeter and subsequently between 1937 and 1939 on international affairs in places as far afield as Burnley, Oldham, High Wycombe, Haywards Heath, Brighton, and Glossop. In 1943, when he was personal assistant to the deputy prime minister, Attlee, Durbin gave a final Oxford course on 'reconstruction problems' in Brighton.[149] In a wartime pamphlet published a year earlier on 'The British Social Tradition' he wrote of having found his 'spiritual home' lecturing for the WEA 'in the Town Hall at Uttoxeter, the Town Hall at Oldham, the Public Library at Burnley and the Town Hall at Glossop'.[150] Durbin had first been a Labour candidate at East Grinstead in the 1931 election and he fought the 1935 election as candidate for Gillingham, adjoining Gaitskell's constituency, with 'a very candid, very educational, very WEA type of campaign'.[151] It did him no good, however, though in 1945 he was elected for Edmonton in London. He was a leading spirit among socialist intellectuals like Douglas Jay, Colin Clark, and Gaitskell whose work in the 1930s in the New Fabian Research Bureau, which had been founded by Cole in 1931, and for the Labour Party's policy committees, overseen by Hugh Dalton, began the process of planning for a future Labour government and assimilating the new Keynesian economics into party policy. Durbin also left a famous and influential text on *The Politics of Democratic Socialism* as his political legacy.[152] His death by drowning in heroic circumstances in September 1948 ended what would surely have been a considerable political career. At the outset, he was pictured by Elizabeth Longford as 'a leading light' at the 1930 Balliol Summer School, 'a natural teacher

---

[147] M. Cole, 'Labour Movement', 40.

[148] On Durbin see Elizabeth Durbin, *New Jerusalems: The Labour Party and the Economics of Democratic Socialism* (London, 1985).

[149] Durbin's courses, like those of all the tutors and lecturers for the Oxford Extra-Mural Delegacy, were listed at the end of each of the Delegacy's annual reports.

[150] E. F. M. Durbin, *What Have We To Defend? A Brief Critical Examination of the British Social Tradition* (London, 1942), 89; Elizabeth Durbin, *New Jerusalems*, 96.   [151] Williams, *Gaitskell*, 73–4.

[152] E. F. M. Durbin, *The Politics of Democratic Socialism: An Essay on Social Policy* (London, 1940).

and a wonderfully human companion' who helped draw her into adult education and who made youthful claims to speak for the working class 'with an engagingly unjustified authority'.[153]

The case of Frank Pakenham, on the other hand, was rather different, for he was a Conservative, when, in 1929, two years after graduating, A. D. Lindsay and Cartwright sent him to North Staffordshire to teach tutorial classes.[154] Pakenham, like Henry Brooke of Balliol, later a Conservative Home Secretary, was one of the 'Tory show-pieces' apparently engaged by the Tutorial Classes Committee to allay accusations of political bias.[155] Rather like Cosmo Lang in the 1880s, Pakenham had set out to equip himself 'for a [Conservative] political career' and wanted 'to live under working-class conditions'. But the experience of teaching two classes on 'Political Theory' at Fenton and Longton was formative and transforming. He 'drifted rapidly leftwards in the winter of 1929' and 'after a few months in Stoke [his] political outlook was never the same again'.[156] Contact with his students and their socialism 'diluted' Pakenham's Conservatism; he had discovered 'a world of working men and women passionately seeking education but at the same time politically conscious and full of pity, indignation and sardonic wit'.[157] His best student in the economics class at Longton was Doris Robinson, described by Elizabeth Longford 'as a chair-bound cripple in constant pain who nevertheless had powers of literary, even poetic, perception that went far beyond economics'.[158] Pakenham taught for another year in the Potteries, beginning a class on Economics at Longton in 1930–1. His full political conversion took several years, after which he went on to a career as a minister in four Labour administrations.

During his two years as a tutor he also began a relationship with his future wife, Elizabeth Harman, whom he married in 1931. She was from a high-minded Oxford, Unitarian family and she studied English at Lady Margaret Hall between 1927 and 1930. Soon after her final examinations she was encouraged by Pakenham and Durbin to join them as a tutor at the Balliol Summer School.[159] Never had she spent 'a more fulfilling week. I loved the work, the workers and the odd collection of tutors.' She was especially impressed by 'the dynamic, high-spirited workers of North Staffordshire'.[160] Though a

[153] Elizabeth Longford, *The Pebbled Shore* (London, 1986), 100.
[154] Lord Pakenham, *Born to Believe: An Autobiography* (London, 1953), 59. Peter Stanford, *Lord Longford: A Life* (London, 1994), 72–3.
[155] Longford, *Pebbled Shore*, 100.
[156] Pakenham, *Born to Believe*, 59–60.   [157] Ibid. 66.
[158] Longford, *Pebbled Shore*, 99.   [159] Ibid. 95–6.   [160] Ibid. 99–100.

graduate in English, she taught economics at the Summer School (in accordance with the movement's motto of 'learn while you teach') and that autumn began a tutorial class in the Potteries. She decided to live in the area and lodged in the home of the WEA District Secretary, Ted Hobson. She found North Staffordshire 'an alienated society . . . once a community of proud, prosperous craftsmen, now on the dole through no fault of their own'.[161] But like so many Oxford tutors before her, she warmed to the idealism of her students. They believed 'that mind triumphed over matter, however much it was cramped and stunted by the system. And the system itself would, of course, soon be abolished. There was much optimism interwoven with hardship.'[162] She immersed herself in the life of her students: 'The working-class ethos of Stoke became my own. I saw with their eyes, ate with their appetites, sensed life with their antennae.'[163] Before contact with the WEA she had 'no party political interests whatever'. But she became 'a socialist early in her time in the Potteries'.[164] She joined the Stone Labour Party and was actually a nominee for Labour candidate in the constituency at the 1931 general election, though in the event she was not adopted.[165] Later she contested Cheltenham and Oxford as Labour parliamentary candidate in 1935 and 1950 respectively.

Finally there was Richard Crossman—Labour minister, editor of the *New Statesman*, wit, raconteur, and political diarist of the future—who was everywhere in the mid- and late-1930s. He began giving extension lectures in 1935–6 with a course at Princes Risborough entitled 'Can Democracy Survive?' and one at Hanley on Hitler's rise to power. But his affair with Zita Baker, the wife of a colleague, led to the loss of his fellowship at New College in 1937, and for three years he gave classes and lectures for the Delegacy full-time until claimed for war work in the Psychological Warfare Division, SHAEF, in 1940.[166] From Bolton and Burnley, through Longton and Wolverhampton, to Folkestone and Reigate (and in many more locations as well) Crossman was in demand and 'his lecturing schedule was punishing'.[167] He had spent a year in Germany in 1930–1 after graduating with a double first, and he knew something of Hitler and National Socialism close up. Courses

---

[161] Ibid. 107.   [162] Ibid. 100.   [163] Ibid. 117.
[164] Ibid. 108; Pakenham, *Born to Believe*, 64.
[165] Longford, *Pebbled Shore*, 118.
[166] Anthony Howard (ed.), 'Introduction', in Richard Crossman, *The Crossman Diaries: Selections from the Diaries of a Cabinet Minister 1964–1970* (London, 1979), 13–16.
[167] Anthony Howard, *Crossman: The Pursuit of Power* (London, 1990), 70.

on 'Germany Since the War' and 'Whither Europe?' met the needs of the hour and paid Crossman's bills at a difficult stage in his life. They also left an indelible impression on Crossman: his WEA classes were 'enormously important' to him.[168] As he wrote in his diary in 1967: 'Ever since I was a young don I've believed in the WEA, in training the mass of the people for responsibility, for self-government and I've been convinced that if we could use education for that purpose we would be able to substitute genuine social democracy for oligarchy.'[169] He paid tribute to the influence of Tawney and Lindsay in this; they had taught him 'that social democracy consists of giving people a chance to decide for themselves—that's the essence of it'.[170] And in so far as Tawney, Smith, and Lindsay probably prized self-government and democracy above socialism, Crossman was correct. Crossman's motives were not entirely pure, of course; as an ambitious man looking for a way into Labour politics he had apparently first gone up to the Potteries to give a course of lectures at Hanley Town Hall in the hope of putting himself forward for a safe Labour seat in the district.[171] Whatever his aims, when he left the employ of the Oxford Delegacy, tribute was paid to 'his grasp of his subject, the brilliance of his presentation' and 'his intense personal interest in the cause of Adult Education', all of which 'delighted and stimulated his audiences'.[172] And contact with the miners and potters of North Staffordshire left him with an abiding concern for those who suffered from the respiratory diseases associated with both trades.[173]

Each of these vignettes is different. Crossman turned to adult education in the hope of a political career; Gaitskell found his way into politics as an unexpected outcome of experiences as a WEA tutor. Pakenham took up lecturing when a confirmed Conservative; his close friend Durbin was already a socialist. Crossman and Durbin were extension lecturers, honing their platform style before large audiences; Gaitskell and Pakenham taught tutorial classes. But there are links none the less. All four men were educated at New College in the mid- and late-1920s and give further evidence of that college's long-standing links with the adult education movement. H. A. L. Fisher, who had been taught by Green at Balliol, had returned to New College as Warden in 1925 and he remained there until

---

[168] Tam Dalyell, *Dick Crossman: A Portrait* (London, 1989), 31.
[169] Richard Crossman, *The Diaries of a Cabinet Minister* (London, 1976) ii. 627, 31 Dec. 1967.
[170] Ibid., ii. 50, 24 Sept. 1966.   [171] Dalyell, *Crossman*, 31.
[172] *Oxford Extra-Mural Delegacy Annual Report 1940–41*, 3.
[173] Dalyell, *Crossman*, 31.

1940. The moral and intellectual tradition he embodied, and his influence in favour of progressive politics and the service of the community, must have played a part in forming the group.[174] All four came under the influence of an older figure in the adult education movement, certainly: Gaitskell and Durbin were inspired in the work by Cole; Pakenham and Crossman by Lindsay. This pattern was common, of course: in the 1880s Sadler and the Inner Ring had been inspired by Acland. But it was especially notable during the interwar years. Harold Marks was taught by Cole as an undergraduate at University College, Oxford, and was later a member of the education inspectorate specializing in adult education. He recalls lunching with Cole at his home in Hendon, discussing his future with his former tutor, and Cole there and then making a telephone call to Cartwright in Oxford that sent Marks up to Stoke and five years of tutorial class teaching.[175] Bridget Hill recalls Tawney telling her about his experiences in North Staffordshire when teaching her during the Second World War at the London School of Economics. She was thus inspired to become an Oxford tutor and teach there herself from late 1944.[176]

Through adult education Gaitskell, Durbin, Pakenham, Harman, and Crossman came to learn something more about the life of the working class, and in this the adult tutors who came to maturity in the 1930s were no different from those who went out to teach and discover for themselves in the 1880s or 1900s. It is not clear that the adult education movement had broad influence among Oxford students in the 1920s and 1930s; from the nature of these case histories it would seem that young men and women often fell in with the movement by chance. Certainly the guide to 'Red Oxford' written in 1930, and John Parker's recollections of 'Oxford Politics in the Late Twenties' make no mention of the links between socialist politics in the University and adult education outside it.[177] But for a favoured few, contact with the Oxford Delegacy, or the prompting of their tutors and friends, opened up an entirely new set of experiences and possibilities.

[174] Kramnick and Sheerman, *Laski*, 50–1.

[175] Tape-recorded Interview with Mr Harold Marks, Belsize Park, London, 30 Sept. 1992.

[176] Discussion with Bridget Hill, Rewley House, Oxford, 2 May 1989.

[177] M. P. Ashley and C. T. Saunders, *Red Oxford* (Oxford, 1930); John Parker, 'Oxford Politics in the Late Twenties', *The Political Quarterly*, 45/2 (April–June 1974), 216–31.

V

Tutors in the 1930s were also held together by two compelling issues which came to dominate the curriculum of extramural education; first the Slump and then the rise of Fascism. It was assumed at first that the unemployed would naturally be attracted to education, not only as a way of filling time, but also out of a desire to understand their predicament in the context of the international economic crisis. The WEA expected to play a more pronounced role in such circumstances. The assumption was false. As a cabinet-maker and WEA member from Birmingham had told Harold Begbie more than a decade before, 'A period of unemployment knocks all the study out of one, especially when one has the responsibility of a wife and family. No one knows except by experience the degrading influence of the fear of insecurity.'[178] In the eloquent words of the annual report of the North Staffordshire District of the WEA for 1932–3,

Prolonged unemployment and depression is bound to affect a Movement like our own more than financially. The people who find themselves denied the conventional means of commanding the respect of others in society by earning a living are not likely to seek knowledge for its own sake or pursue truths which to them are meaningless. The basis of our Movement in the past in North Staffordshire has been the men and women who were proud of their craftsmanship, sure of their social worth, who valued their working-class birthright, eager in their search for knowledge and truth, and sincere in their desire for a social order which would be nearer to their conception of the good life. These are becoming fewer; the craftsman is being replaced by the machine-minder, and the morale of all working-class organizations is being ruined by unemployment. Many are losing faith and hope.[179]

A reduction in government grant made the situation more difficult still, though in North Staffordshire assistance from the Miners' Welfare Fund allowed WEA educational work to continue in mining areas.

The experience was similar in many parts of the country. A. J. Allaway, a tutor for the Manchester extramural department, recorded the response to one of his visits to the Rossendale Valley in the early 1930s: 'What is Manchester thinking about in sending a man to the Valley at a time like this? How can they expect people to be interested in attending classes when things are so bad?'[180] The work was even

[178] Begbie, *Living Water*, 76.
[179] 'Annual Report of the North Staffordshire District of the WEA 1932–3,' 6.
[180] Quoted in Blyth, *Adult Education*, 92.

affected in the south-east of England. Cuts in the grant to the WEA South-Eastern District meant a reduction in its educational programme in the early 1930s.[181] And the District lamented the 'extremely small' number of the unemployed who had joined classes for free: 'Various reports were given on what branches had tried to do to interest unemployed men and women. It was generally agreed that most of the efforts in this direction had been far from the success which was anticipated.'[182] On the other hand, WEA lectures did provide a stimulus in some centres like Ashford, Canterbury, and Herne Bay for 'the formation of unemployment committees' and centres for the unemployed.[183] A recent review of the social and psychological effects of unemployment in the 1930s has questioned the accepted model of progressive personal degeneration without work, and suggested that there is little evidence in Britain of a 'rapid decline in the associational capacity of the unemployed'. It has also been argued that working-class habits and lifestyles did not change much under the impact of unemployment: 'the way people managed unemployment was very largely determined by the life they led before they became unemployed.'[184] In so far as the WEA in the south-east could not attract the unemployed to adult education, this may be correct: those who had never been touched by the movement simply remained aloof. But these arguments do not seem to be substantiated by evidence from the adult education movement in other, and especially industrial regions. The evidence from North Staffordshire suggests very strongly that unemployment demoralized many previously active students: centres there where the WEA 'could normally have looked forward to a steady expansion of educational work [were] finding it a hard struggle to keep going at all'.[185] John A. Mack, teaching a tutorial class in philosophy at Tunstall in the mid-1930s noted the destablizing effects on his students of 'the

[181] 'Workers' Educational Association South Eastern District, Annual Report, 1931–2', Minute Books, WEA South-Eastern District, Rochester, Kent.

[182] 'Minutes of the District Council Meeting held at the Technical Institute, Ashford, 10 February 1934', Minute Books, WEA South-Eastern District, Rochester, Kent.

[183] *Adult Education in Kent and East Sussex* (WEA South-Eastern District, 1945), 34. (This is a pamphlet reviewing the history of the WEA in the South-East in the library, Rewley House, Oxford.)

[184] Ross McKibbin, 'The "Social Psychology" of Unemployment in Inter-war Britain', in id., *The Ideologies of Class: Social Relations in Britain 1880–1950* (Oxford, 1990), 257.

[185] 'Annual Report of the North Staffordshire District of the WEA 1932–3,' p. 1.

great depression, the political crises, and the general confusion of the past five years'.[186]

The response to the Slump on the part of the WEA, Oxford and other universities, was to co-operate in the organization of a variety of different types of course, many of them taking the form of short, intense conferences, to explain the economic collapse. Taking the example of the WEA South Eastern District, in the winter of 1930–1 the Workers' Educational Trade Union Committee organized two weekend conferences at Hastings and Rochester respectively: the first on 'Finance and Banking' was led by Frank Pakenham and the second on 'The Political and Economic Future of Great Britain' by G. D. H. Cole and C. R. Morris. Barbara Wootton also led a day-school at Gillingham during that winter on 'Industry and the Monetary System'. In the following winter Evan Durbin gave lectures at a day-school in Tunbridge Wells on 'The World Economic Crisis'; Hugh Gaitskell took part in a day-school at East Grinstead on 'The Gold Standard'; and Reg Bassett lectured at a day-school for the unemployed in Chatham on the causes of their worklessness. These events were not subsidized by government grant; the unemployed attended without charge, and tutors gave their services *gratis*.[187]

For three or four years in the early 1930s many Oxford tutors were engaged explaining the economic crisis to varied audiences in traditional and new types of course. Then, very quickly, the focus switched to international affairs. There was an intimation of this in the annual report of the North Staffordshire WEA for 1933. It was explained that arrangements for the District to hold a summer school that August at the Labour College in Düsseldorf had been cancelled 'in view of the political condition in Germany'. Following the Enabling Law of March 1933 and the systematic intimidation and imprisonment of German socialists and trade unionists, the decision was inevitable.[188] In the same year the 'marked interest in subjects which call for treatment on an international scale' was noted by the Oxford Delegacy.[189] Day schools in the South Eastern District during 1933–4 included A. L. Rowse lecturing at Maidstone on

[186] John A. Mack, *The History of Tunstall II Tutorial Class 1913–1934* (Stoke-on-Trent, 1935), 47.

[187] These examples are drawn from the annual reports (in typescript) of the South-Eastern District of the WEA, WEA South-Eastern District, Rochester, Kent.

[188] 'Annual Report of the North Staffordshire District of the WEA 1932–3', p. 2.

[189] *Annual Report of the Oxford Extra-Mural Delegacy 1932–3*, 8.

'Fascism'. In the following year at Canterbury Durbin and Crossman led conferences on respectively, the New Deal in America and 'The Inner Conflict in Germany since the Nazi Revolution', and Seton-Watson went to Chatham to lecture on 'Central European Problems'. In 1935–6, Kingsley Martin led a day-school in Brighton on 'The League and Abyssinia' and Margaret Cole lectured on the Soviet Union at Canterbury. In 1938 WETUC organized residential week-ends in the District at which first Crossman and then the refugee economist Karl Polanyi, who taught for the Oxford Delegacy in the late 1930s before moving on to a post teaching economics in the University of Chicago, led programmes on the crisis across Europe. In early 1935 Crossman had given a series of extension lectures on 'Germany Since the War' in the Examination Schools in Oxford which attracted an audience of eight hundred, the majority of them residents in the town rather than members of the University.[190] From 1937 several German academic refugees were giving classes for the Delegacy and explaining Fascism from personal experience. They included Heinz (Henry) Koeppler, who was not a jew, but who had left Germany in 1933 'because he could not stand Hitler or the Nazis'.[191] At the Balliol Summer School in 1938 it was taken to be 'a sign of the times' that a third of the students in residence chose to work on international relations.[192] And in the autumn of that year the new classes of the 1938–9 session 'were in the process of formation when they were caught by the sudden impact of the Munich crisis' and the fear of imminent war.[193] In the late summer of the following year it was for real.

Tawney had written in the first chapter of the *1919 Report* on the history of adult education that it could not 'be interpreted in iso-lation from the interests and pre-occupations which form the back-ground to the intellectual activities of each generation'.[194] That was almost a truism, of course. Up to the point at which he wrote it, the movement had been focused on the social emancipation of the working class and the role that dons and intellectuals more generally might play in that process. It was always affected by contemporary politics and concerns of the moment, but the essence of the movement

[190] 'Notes and News', *Rewley House Papers*, 1 (1935), 366; Howard, *Crossman*, 57.

[191] A. J. P. Taylor, *A Personal History* (London, 1983), 171. Koeppler was later assistant under-secretary of state at the Foreign and Commonwealth Office, 1975–7.

[192] *Annual Report of the Oxford Extra-Mural Delegacy 1937–8*, 4.

[193] Ibid., 1938–9, 4.

[194] *Adult Education Committee, Final Report*, 9.

was a process of collective self-discovery, often through the study of subjects like history, economics, and politics, that would assist the self-understanding of working-class scholars and their organizations. And in this respect the educational themes of the movement, the subjects that it made its own, were not directly linked to the ebb and flow of events beyond it. The task for the WEA on its foundation was to help students understand their social position and then change it; for this, attention to issues of the moment was less important than a deeper understanding of economic theory or, say, labour history. But in the 1930s, under the pressure of events, the focus began to change.

This is to not to argue that a growing interest in international issues was a diversion for the movement. In the interwar period the British left was often preoccupied with the problems of the League of Nations and international humanitarian issues, and figures like Zimmern, Crossman, and Durbin brought them to the attention of the adult education movement. In the postwar period, Thomas Hodgkin, the Secretary of the Oxford Extra-Mural Delegacy, and those he brought into the movement, were to link adult education in Oxford to developments in the communist and developing, post-colonial, worlds. Internationalism was not new or aberrant, therefore. From the late 1920s the movement could not but address the interlocking economic and international crises, and this did not necessarily involve any loss of educational purpose. Quite the reverse, in fact, for it was probably easier to teach economics and economic history with the Slump in progress and the examples to hand in every newspaper, than in other and more stable circumstances. Nevertheless the almost irresistible force of events that commanded the movement's attention in the 1930s probably altered its educational aim and role significantly. From a focus in the early tutorial classes on who the students were, where their communities had come from, and how they could understand the systems by which they lived so as to change them, adult education moved towards a more imme-diate function, that of explaining current events. This was entirely appropriate and beneficial, but it was different in kind from the earlier project in the movement. Though it is hazardous to gener-alize, if the 1920s gave rise to an organizational watershed for Ox-ford and the extramural movement as a whole, the 1930s saw the beginnings of an educational change as well, which has continued to the present. Understanding the flow of events, an essentially re-active process, began to take the place of the analysis of the inter-connections between the individual, the community, the nation, and the state.

VI

Explaining immediate circumstances was the central theme of adult education during the Second World War. In November 1939 Tawney envisaged 'a demand for lectures, study circles and conferences on the causes of the breakdown; the countries most directly concerned in it; the nature of the settlement by which it should be followed; the possibility and methods of averting a similar catastrophe'. He asked also for thinking on 'the changes required to make political democracy more of a reality, and to put the economic system in its proper place as the servant of the public'.[195] This was the agenda of the war years. Whereas consideration of reconstruction only began some two years into the Great War, the theme was being broached from the outset of the Second World War and would become a dominant interest from 1942. In that year A. D. Lindsay gave an address to a conference of service personnel arranged by the University and set out a complementary set of aims for the education of combatants. 'In a citizen army' he contended,

it does matter enormously that men should, as Cromwell said, know what they are fighting for and love what they know. They should be encouraged to learn more about the cause and encouraged to discuss it. It is only a belief that this time we shall have an England in which our children can grow up into healthy and useful citizens that will enable them to put the last ounce into the struggle.[196]

The certainty of combat in a just cause, unlike the ambivalent position of the WEA after 1914; the belief that an education in citizenship could contribute to that cause; the hope that victory would be accompanied by social improvement—these were the concerns that directed the work of the Oxford Delegacy in helping to create the distinctive social and political spirit of the 1940s.

Several extension lecture centres cancelled their courses in the autumn of 1939 and only twenty-six were given in some 22 locations.[197] But only one tutorial class failed to meet and by 1940–1 the Tutorial Classes Committee was responsible for a record number of fifty-one classes.[198] The programme increased throughout the war years. In 1938 Oxford tutorial classes enrolled 1,050 students and

[195] R. H. Tawney, 'The Workers' Educational Association in Wartime', *The Highway*, 32 (Nov. 1939), 4–6.
[196] A. D. Lindsay, 'The Education of a Citizen Army', *Rewley House Papers*, 2/5 (1942), 198.
[197] *Annual Report of the Oxford Extra-Mural Delegacy 1939–40*, 2
[198] Ibid., 1940–1, 5.

in 1944 the comparable figure in sixty-eight classes was 2,467. The south-east had particular and obvious problems early in the war with invasion a possibility, and the Battle of Britain and then the Blitz rendering any communal functions difficult if not dangerous. But by 1943 the WEA District was reporting an amount of work 'well above that of any pre-war year'.[199] In North Staffordshire the number of tutorial classes went up from fifteen in 1938 to twenty-one in 1942, and in the same period the number of one-year and short courses rose from 47 to 82.[200] The expansion testified to widespread interest in the issues Tawney had picked out and to extra financial assistance provided by central government, local authorities, and various Oxford colleges. In the case of All Souls, for example, the annual grant of £250 for tutorial classes went up to £600 and the college provided an additional £300 each year for the Delegacy's work in forces' education.[201] At a national level, 'the regulations of the Board of Education were modified to meet war conditions and were generously interpreted'.[202] And after the passage of the 1944 Education Act the new Ministry of Education increased further the funds for adult education. The adaptation of the Oxford programme fell to Cartwright, who delayed his retirement until 1945, and L. K. Hindmarsh, the Secretary of the Delegacy. Their working conditions in Rewley House were rather cramped. The Delegacy served as an academic and social centre for Ruskin College, which had been requisitioned as a maternity hospital. Its library was open to students of Westfield College of the University of London which had moved to Oxford. It provided a temporary home for the Central Advisory Council for Education in HM Forces after its London offices were bombed. And most poignantly of all, the Delegacy offered accommodation for the Oxford branch of the League of Nations Union and the chance, no doubt, to contemplate the wreck of collective security on which its members had pinned their interwar hopes in the (relative) quiet of Rewley House.[203]

In addition to tutorial classes the Delegacy undertook 'experimental work' and 'pioneer work' so-called. Its 'Review of the War Years' noted work done with 'Civil Defence, National Fire Service,

[199] 'Annual Report of the South-Eastern District of the WEA, 1942–3'.
[200] 'Memorandum on the Development of Adult Education in North Staffordshire After the War', North Staffs. Advisory Committee on Adult Education, app., p. 13, WEA South-Eastern District, Rochester, Kent.
[201] *Annual Report of the Oxford Extra-Mural Delegacy 1939–40*, 5.
[202] A. D. Lindsay and T. L. Hodgkin, 'Review of the War Years', in *Annual Report of the Oxford Extra-Mural Delegacy 1944–5*, 17.
[203] 'Notes and News', *Rewley House Papers*, 2 (1940), 116.

Land Army, Munition Workers, Firewatchers groups etc'.[204] Collaborating closely with the WEA in this, tutors went into factories, canteens, clubs, and the like to give occasional lectures and to lead discussions. There was 'a constant adaptation of peacetime methods to meet war-time conditions', assisted by the new Ministry of Education's grant aid for these 'courses of a less formal character' at the end of the war.[205] To one Staff Tutor, Thomas Hodgkin, who became Secretary of the Delegacy in 1945, the great opportunity of the war years was to get at 'the vast body of men and women who up to the present have been outside the educational movement' through such means. He noted in an article in 1941 that people were asking questions

not only in regard to the problems of education, industrial organization, food supply and prices, which make an immediate impact upon their own lives, but also in regard to the remoter, more fundamental problems of the war: How did it arise? When is it going to end? What sort of situation are we going to have to face after it is over? Is there any means whereby we can ensure that similar wars don't occur in the future?

The opportunities 'for an educational movement which regards its function as essentially a struggle against complacency' were obvious. Its task was 'to stimulate a questioning attitude of mind among the people of this country towards the problems of the world in which they live, and to help them to acquire the grasp of facts and methods of approach which will enable them to solve these problems for themselves'.[206] This probably summed the collective aspirations of the Oxford Delegacy, and caught the popular mood. Another Oxford tutor noted in 1943 'the awakening of a broader social and political consciousness throughout the country'.[207] The enthusiasm that greeted publication of the Beveridge Report in late 1942 was the authentic expression of this consciousness and adult education played its part in sustaining it and developing it. In Lincoln, for example, still part of Oxford's extramural responsibilities, the Delegacy and WEA launched three separate classes to discuss the Report's vision of the future.[208] And Cecil Scrimgeour, District Chairman of the WEA in North Staffordshire and later a

[204] Lindsay and Hodgkin, 'Review of the War Years', 17.
[205] *Annual Report of the Oxford Extra-Mural Delegacy 1941–2*, 1.
[206] T. L. Hodgkin, 'Some War-Time Developments in Adult Education', *Rewley House Papers*, 2/4 (1941), 141–5.
[207] 'An Oxford Staff Tutor', 'The Place of Education in War-Workers' Hostels', *Rewley House Papers*, 2 (1943), 223.
[208] 'M.L.', 'The Work and Progress of a WEA Branch', *Rewley House Papers*, 2 (1946), 379.

Staff Tutor in Literature for Oxford, recalled that every tutor 'carried in his knapsack copies of the Beveridge Report and Mr Butler's White Paper on Educational Reconstruction, for those documents not only embodied the general hopes but provided first-rate texts to start discussion from'.[209] Indeed, from 1942 there was a 'campaign of conferences, public meetings, deputations, publications—reminiscent of the 1917–18 agitation but with a larger force of public opinion behind it and riper experience to direct it' which ended with the passage of the Butler Education Act in August 1944, and in which the WEA and adult educationists were fully engaged.[210] The Act recognized adult education as part of the national educational system and charged local education authorities with the duty of ensuring its adequate provision. Their schemes of further education had to be submitted to, and vetted by, the Ministry of Education. In addition, direct Ministry grants to extramural departments and voluntary bodies under the new regulations issued at the time of the 1944 Act were paid for the programme as a whole, rather than for each class separately, and were set at a more generous level than before. University adult education prompted, and responded to the public mood in the early 1940s in a way that it had probably never done before nor has done since, and was rewarded in turn. As Lindsay and Hodgkin put it, the war created an 'intellectual ferment' and 'the efforts of those involved in adult education met with a keener response than in times of peace'.[211]

Civilian education was only a part of the story. The Second World War also saw an educational campaign directed at the armed forces in which Oxford and especially Lindsay played their part. Army education, tried for the first time at the end of the First World War, had fallen victim to peacetime spending cuts in the early 1920s, and was 'on the brink of final extinction' in 1939.[212] The WEA was the first organization to understand the role that education might play in a civilian army if and when war came.[213] And Lindsay played a pivotal role in the winter of 1939–40 in convincing the military and civil authorities to design and introduce a scheme. In December 1939 he wrote impatiently to George Adams at All Souls to request assistance: 'We are taking the line that Oxford ought to go ahead at once to show people what can be done, and not wait until all these co-ordinating bodies have called all their conferences and done

[209] Cecil Scrimgeour, *Fifty Years A-Growing: A History of the North Staffordshire District, the Workers' Educational Association 1921–1971* (Stoke-on-Trent, 1973), 62.   [210] Stocks, *Workers' Educational Association*, 131.
[211] Lindsay and Hodgkin, 'Review of the War Years', 16.
[212] Mackenzie, *Politics and Military Morale*, 56.   [213] Ibid. 58–61.

everything through the proper channels and in due course.'[214] In a letter to *The Times* a few weeks later, calling for a comprehensive scheme of army education, Lindsay wrote that

> The army at home is bored. It is an Army of men accustomed to adult education and to discussion. In the last war when this kind of scheme was eventually adopted it proved an immediate and enormous success. In the intervening years adult education in this country has progressed by leaps and bounds, and the success of a scheme of this kind should be even greater now. From the experimental work which has been already done it is clear that there is (1) a great demand for single lectures by men who are authorities on such subjects as foreign affairs, history, exploration, literature and economics; (2) a great demand for short courses of about four lectures in places where men are stationed for periods of two months or more.[215]

A conference in London in December 1939 had established an academic Central Advisory Council for Adult Education in HM Forces to co-ordinate forces education with the Army Education Corps. Lindsay was made its vice-chairman. In the following month Oxford and Reading Universities set up a Regional Committee (which Lindsay chaired) including representatives from the Board of Education, local education authorities, the WEA, other voluntary bodies, and the armed forces themselves, to provide courses and lectures for units stationed in Oxford's extramural area. Similar regional commitees, twenty-three in all, were created across the country, with universities providing administrative support and academic direction.[216] The Oxford Committee began establishing a panel of lecturers, and in what remained of the academic year 1939–40, some 240 lectures 'mainly devoted to explaining the background of the war' were delivered to 77 units. Thereafter the project expanded rapidly. In 1941–2 the Oxford Delegacy, on behalf of the regional committee, arranged, or its own staff gave, over seven thousand forces' lectures. In each of the two succeeding years (1942–3 and 1943–4) the figure was in excess of thirteen thousand. To take an example, in 1940–1 the Oxford Committee was responsible for 58 single lectures to service personnel in North Staffordshire; in 1942–3 the number was nearly thirteen hundred, and there were a further

---

[214] A. D. Lindsay to W. G. S. Adams, 18 Dec. 1939, 'Papers relating to adult education in the forces, 1939–45', 198 L, Lindsay Papers, Keele.

[215] *The Times*, 9 Feb. 1940, p. 6.

[216] Lindsay and Hodgkin, 'Review of the War Years', 16; *Annual Report of the Oxford Extra-Mural Delegacy 1939–40*, 9–10; Kelly, *History of Adult Education*, 323–6; Drusilla Scott, *A. D. Lindsay: A Biography* (Oxford, 1971), 277–82.

157 short courses of instruction.[217] The Delegacy also arranged short residential courses for officers in Oxford, usually in Balliol or St Hilda's, to assist them 'in giving talks to their men on the bulletins issued by the Army Bureau of Current Affairs (A.B.C.A)'.[218]

Forces' education during the Second World War has, of course, passed into modern folklore. The purpose was serious, the discussion sometimes intense. There were many 'anxious corporals' in servicemen's camps during the war 'who asked questions about the sort of world we would go back to', including among them the present author's father.[219] There were many more, as well, who showed little interest, or who looked on an hour's discussion as time saved from other duties. But it was also an arena for the unexpected and comical: A. J. P. Taylor, who had returned to Oxford as a fellow of Magdalen in 1938, 'went out three or four nights a week throughout the war' to address the troops under the auspices of the Oxford Committee, and he found it 'great fun'—though he was sure that the men 'liked hearing what was going on in the world and how we had got where we were'.[220] Tutors were despatched to units at short notice, often driven through the blackout by the Women's Voluntary Service (WVS) to they knew not where, and might have to begin a discussion with a handful of servicemen, or face an audience of hundreds. One experienced Oxford Staff Tutor enumerated the difficulties:

In one discussion a questioner explained that his views of Balkan politics had profited from private conversations with King Carol of Rumania; in another, the lecturer, who had relied at one point on the evidence of a well-known writer on diplomacy was informed that the writer's son was in the audience; in a third, where discussion turned on British tariff policy, the most persistent questioner had been a highly placed officer in the Inland Revenue.[221]

But 'talking politics' was unfamiliar to the armed forces and not always welcome. As Lindsay wrote to Margery Allingham, 'The distance between the army officer and those Workers' Educational Association people is, to start with, immense. Some of our troubles come from that distance.'[222] One lecturer recalled a particularly

[217] 'Memorandum on the Development of Adult Education in North Staffordshire After the War', p. 6.

[218] *Annual Report of the Oxford Extra-Mural Delegacy 1941–2*, 6; Mackenzie, *Politics and Military Morale*, 96.

[219] Richard Hoggart, 'The All-Important Minority', *The Guardian*, 26 Sept. 1968, p. 12. Hoggart is quoting Arthur Koestler.

[220] Taylor, *Personal History*, 152.

[221] G. E. Fasnacht, 'Education in H.M. Forces: A Lecturer's Impressions', *Rewley House Papers*, 2/4 (1941), 146.   [222] Scott, *Lindsay*, 282.

'bleak session' before a cowed audience 'under the eye of a ferocious R[egimental] S[ergeant] M[ajor]'.[223] It had been exactly the same in the Great War. The *1919 Report* noted 'the mingled astonishment and scepticism' at first of the military authorities at the prospect of army education, and recorded the response of an earlier sergeant-major to the news that a battalion was about to parade for a history lesson: 'History? History won't kill Germans.'[224] Many officers were sympathetic to army education if it could lift troop morale, but shared none of the wider social and political aims of the lecturers, many of whom came from the prewar adult education movement and looked on the enterprise as an opportunity to instil the men with the values of that movement. There were many complaints from the military that army education too often meant, as they heard it, philo-Sovietism and socialist politics. To try to minimize problems, the Central Advisory Council issued guidelines to lecturers and tutors that set down rules to which 'they must conform'. They had to avoid criticizing specific military operations and the 'Government's higher direction of the war'. They 'should promote mutual confidence, not suspicion or mistrust'. The crucial point was to 'bear in mind that [the lecturer's] task is education and not propaganda'.[225]

Many Conservative politicians, Churchill included, looked askance at forces' education as some sort of diversion of military energies spreading subversion through the ranks. More likely, as Lindsay hinted, it helped kill some time: war, as Alun Lewis told us, is a slow business.[226] And it may also have kept the troops a little happier.[227] It has sometimes been argued that the Army Bureau of Current Affairs and forces' education in general, won the services vote for the Labour Party in the 1945 election—that, as Churchill put it himself, the army had 'a big say' in his defeat. Historians have dismissed the idea: the votes cast by service personnel, only 1.7 million out of a total of twenty-five million, were not enough to account for the large majority Attlee won, and the assumption that the armed forces were indoctrinated by visiting lecturers misreads the authentic popular mood of the 1940s and undervalues the

---

[223] W. E. Moore, 'E. H. Birchall', *Rewley House Papers,* 4/1 (1962–3), 43–4.
[224] *Final Report of the Adult Education Committee,* 343.
[225] 'Central Advisory Council for Adult Education in H.M. Forces. Memorandum to Lecturers and Tutors', typescript in 'Papers relating to adult education in the Forces 1939–45', 198 L, Lindsay Papers.
[226] The reference is to Alun Lewis's poem 'All Day It Has Rained . . .', written in 1942.   [227] Mackenzie, *Politics and Military Morale,* 190.

essentially radicalizing experience of fighting a war.[228] The mood of the early 1940s had developed spontaneously in reaction, whether justly or not, to the perceived failures of interwar Conservatism. Adult education merely worked with the grain, helping soldiers and civilians to find answers to questions they had asked without prompting. It was itself a part of the new spirit rather than a cause of it. Nevertheless the 1945 election was the moment of its political triumph. According to Mary Stocks, fourteen members of the Labour government, including the Chancellor of the Exchequer, Dalton, were either WEA tutors, former tutors or members of the WEA Executive, and fifty-six 'active WEA adherents' sat on the back benches.[229] Margaret Cole put it higher: over a hundred of the Labour MPs 'had been trained as tutors or students in the adult education movement'. In North Staffordshire alone, five of the region's Labour MPs were products of the WEA. George Wigg, elected for Dudley, had been the local District Secretary; Stephen Swingler (Stafford) and Harold Davies (Leek) had served as WEA tutors in the 1930s and lectured to the armed forces during the war; Albert Davies (Burslem) had been involved in the Miners' Higher Education Movement, and had come up through the WEA; and Dr Barnett Stross (Hanley) was an active patron of the local branches. It was a remarkable tribute to the social and political impact of workers' education in the Potteries, which had functioned for two generations as a focus for working-class aspirations.[230] If knowledge was to lead to power, if adult education was designed to give working people the analytical tools and confidence with which to change their society, then the 1945 election could only be interpreted by the movement in one way—as a culmination of its long emancipatory project and tradition.

VII

From the First to the Second World Wars two figures were at the centre of the adult education movement in Oxford and in Britain as

---

[228] Paul Addison, *The Road to 1945* (London, 1975), 145–51; Alan Sked and Chris Cook, *Post-War Britain: A Political History*, 2nd edn. (Harmondsworth, 1984), 17–19; David Childs, *Britain Since 1945*, 2nd edn. (London, 1986), 12–13; Mackenzie, *Politics and Military Morale*, 178.

[229] Cited in Blyth, *Adult Education*, 169.

[230] Margaret Cole, *Growing Up Into Revolution* (London, 1949), 118; Scrimgeour, *Fifty Years A-Growing*, 73.

a whole—A. L. Smith and A. D. (Sandie) Lindsay, successive Masters of Balliol. Arthur Lionel Smith has generally been neglected in surveys of adult education, perhaps because in comparison with his successor, his style was rather less flamboyant.[231] Born in 1850 into a middle-class family—his father, who died when Smith was a child, was a civil engineer—he was a little too young to have been touched by the university liberalism that moved many of the founders of the adult education tradition in the universities in the 1850s and 1860s. Indeed, he seems to have owed little to political inspiration of any sort in his involvement with the movement. First a fellow of Trinity College from 1874 and then a fellow of Balliol from 1882, he was the very model of a college tutor in modern history, immersed in the education of his students and the rituals of college life. He was a great teacher, certainly. But there was a strain of the intellectually unorthodox to him also, touched as he was both by Green's idealism and Comtean positivism with its ambition to unite the sciences of man and society.[232]

He was not untouched by adult education either, as his role in bringing Joseph Owen to Oxford and preparing him for entrance to Balliol suggests. But it was only in the early years of the new century that Smith engaged fully with the movement, though at a formative juncture in its history. From his membership of the 1907 Joint Committee until his death in 1924, adult education and tutorial classes in particular, were a consuming passion. Smith's 'sympathy, humour, and generosity won him the loyalty and affection of many generations of undergraduates'.[233] Those same qualities seem to explain his interest in adult education. Unlike Sidney Ball, another 'ideal don' of the same generation, but one who had been long associated with progressive causes and the labour movement, Smith seems to have been moved more by personal than political motives.[234] He warmed to the worker students he met, instinctively believed in giving them a fair chance, and judged that the moment was right for the University to take a lead. He was, it is true, an avowed democrat, talking often of the need to democratize education, as society more generally. He meant by this, increasing participation,

---

[231] It is also the case that there is no good biography of Smith. The account by Mrs A. L. Smith, *Arthur Lionel Smith: Master of Balliol (1916–1924): A Biography and some Reminiscences by his Wife* (London, 1928) is essentially concerned with personal matters.

[232] Alon Kadish, *The Oxford Economists in the Late Nineteenth Century* (Oxford, 1982), 36.   [233] 'A. L. Smith', *Dictionary of National Biography*.

[234] The reference is to Oona Ball's edited tribute to her husband published as *Sidney Ball: Memories and Impressions of 'An Ideal Don'* (Oxford, 1923).

opening up institutions to the less favoured, nurturing talent from wherever it came. But the democratic impulse seems to have sprung from his character and instinct rather than from formal political engagement.

Smith endeared himself to the movement and there are many stories of his kindnesses and good humour. The most famous concerns a young miner who apparently arrived at Balliol for the WEA Summer School and immediately met 'a rather shaggy, friendly-looking man' whom he mistook for a worker like himself. ' "This is the sort of place my mates and I are going to smash," said the miner. "Well," answered A. L. Smith, "let me show you round and tell you its history. You'll be able to smash it so much better, once you know." '[235] One of Harold Begbie's interviewees, 'the passionate student' who had lost a leg as a teenager working on the railways, affectionately recalled his arguments and wrangles with Smith till late into the night during the week he spent in Balliol.[236] At the 1915 Summer School Smith so inspired one Kent village schoolmaster from Ham Street, A. A. Farrer, that he returned home and started in the same year a federation of village study groups which developed into the original Kent District of the WEA.[237]

But Smith had other talents, also: according to Tawney, he 'combined . . . the power of imaginatively grasping large ends with a realistic appreciation of the practical means needed to give them effect'.[238] According to Cartwright, indeed, 'The late Master was no theorist; his touchstone in regard to any plan was "Does it work?" ' He could organize and persuade, therefore. As a member of the original Joint Committee in 1907–8, as Chairman of the Tutorial Classes Committee, when lecturing all over the country from 1916 in support of educational renewal, and as Chairman of the Adult Education Committee that produced the *1919 Report*, he was, in the words of Henry Clay, 'the great ambassador for the WEA in the academic world'.[239] Tawney went further: Smith 'was by far the most

---

[235] H. P. Smith, *Labour and Learning: Albert Mansbridge, Oxford and the WEA* (Oxford, 1956), 83.   [236] Begbie, *Living Water*, 166.
[237] 'The WEA in Kent, Nov. 1928', WEA South-Eastern District Archives, p. 1. 'Extracts from a thesis on "Adult Education in Kent" by H. L. Baker, May 1931', Rewley House Adult Education Reference Library, Box 2 (A) (ii) b, 13–15.
[238] R. H. Tawney, 'In Memoriam: The Master of Balliol', *The Highway*, 16/3 (summer 1924), 146.
[239] 'Adult Education Movement. Honouring Pioneers in North Staffs. Late Master of Balliol and Mr. H. Jenkins', repr. from *Staffordshire Sentinel*, 11 Jan. 1927, WEA North Staffordshire District Archive. Cartwright and Clay paid tribute to Smith at a ceremony in the New Council Chambers, Hanley.

representative and influential of the academic leaders connected with adult education in the last twenty years'.[240]

The same might have been written of Smith's successor as Master of Balliol and Chairman of the Tutorial Classes Committee in Oxford, Alexander Dunlop Lindsay. He was born in Glasgow in 1879 and had a singular presbyterian upbringing in a cosmopolitan, lively, and socially conscious household. His father, T. D. Lindsay, was an eminent historian of the Reformation and Principal of the Glasgow Free Church College. His mother, Anna Dunlop, was the daughter of a Liberal MP. Lindsay was educated first at Glasgow University, and then at University College, Oxford. From 1902–1906 he taught philosophy at Glasgow, Edinburgh, and Manchester universities and he was then elected fellow and Classical Tutor at Balliol. The consuming passion of his career, despite many other honours and campaigns, was adult education, to which, in the words of his daughter, 'he gave his heart'.[241] He began extension lecturing at Manchester in 1904 and he came back to Oxford in 1906 just as the new alliance of the University with the WEA was taking shape. Indeed 'it is impossible to understand at all what Lindsay stood for without understanding his devotion to the WEA.'[242] In 1910 he taught 'Recent Political Theory' at the first Summer School; in 1911 he was made a joint secretary of the Tutorial Classes Committee, succeeding William Temple.

Lindsay had imbibed the same Oxford idealism that had moved many of those who began adult education in the University in the 1880s. He wrote several works on Kant and provided a preface to an edition of Green's *Lectures on the Principles of Political Obligation* in 1910, and in so far as idealism predisposed its adherents to an interest in adult education it may be said to have played a role in Lindsay's case. But his interest in it was also more personal: he was attracted to the kinds of people he met in the WEA and at the Summer School. With them he could be at his ease. As if to make the point, a portrait of John Elkin, a miner and a member of the original Longton Tutorial Class, who became a good friend of Lindsay, was presented to him at the twenty-first anniversary celebration of the Longton class in 1930, and it hung for many years in the Master's Lodgings at Balliol.[243] Lindsay was attracted also, as

---

[240] Tawney, 'In Memoriam', 146.   [241] Scott, *Lindsay*, 63.
[242] Ibid. 128.
[243] 'Presentation of the portrait of Mr. J. Elkin to the Master of Balliol', 27 Nov. 1930. Handbill in the E. S. Cartwright Papers, 'Records of Work in North Staffordshire', Oxford University Archives. See also Smith, *Labour and Learning*, 21. The portrait was returned to the Longton branch of the WEA by the then Master

were so many young tutors, by the sheer experience of working-class students and by their collective endeavour in their communities and trade unions.[244] Because Lindsay so respected this experience and the wisdom of adult students, he recommended the challenge of adult teaching for all dons: they would thus be forced to provide clear expositions of their ideas to their classes, and would have to substantiate assertions before quizzical adults that undergraduates accepted far more readily. At the end of the First World War (a large part of which was spent by Lindsay in France where he became Deputy Controller of Labour) he actually thought of trying to persuade Smith to allow as many Balliol tutors as possible to be employed 'half on college work and half on WEA'.[245] And through the interwar period, as we have seen, he encouraged many students to try their hand as tutorial class teachers.

In Lindsay's case there was also a particular attraction to adult education. He was especially interested in the type of questions that working-class students were asking—large, important questions about the organization of society and individual purpose within it, questions to which Lindsay's broad and generous nature was instinctively drawn.[246] Lindsay left several legacies to Oxford: as Vice-Chancellor in the mid-1930s he helped stabilize the University's finances, expand Oxford sciences, and establish Nuffield College. But perhaps his most influential initiative was his role in the introduction of the new course of 'Modern Greats'—Politics, Philosophy, and Economics—in 1922. The course was an expression of his educational ideas; in PPE he hoped to create a curriculum relevant to modern issues, yet able to develop general understanding and 'power of judgment'. In Lindsay's mind the new course was an antidote to the increasing specialization in university education which he deprecated.

When he went to be first Principal of the new University College of North Staffordshire (now Keele University) at the end of his life, Lindsay was a partisan for the common foundation year of general university studies that the university pioneered. His interest in adult education flowed from this educational philosophy: he admired the way the movement united academic learning with work, community, the solution of immediate problems, and the contemplation of greater ones. Lindsay looked askance at 'the separation of intellectual

---

of Balliol, Christopher Hill, at a special ceremony in 1968. It was at first hung in Tawney House, the local adult education centre in Longton. It now hangs in the District Offices of the WEA at Cartwright House, Hanley. See Eve Rowley, *A History of the WEA in Longton* (Stoke-on-Trent, 1988), 10.

[244] Scott, *Lindsay*, 71.   [245] Ibid. 87.   [246] Ibid. 70.

development from all-round development of the individual'; at 'the separation of the "intelligentsia" from ordinary life'.[247] These views were derived *from* his experience of adult education, but the instincts of a generalist who believed that the philosophy he taught should assist people in controlling and developing their lives, attracted him *to* the movement from the first. 'He found in the best of the Tutorial Class students the power of judgment, the sense of proportion, the understanding of essentials, which seemed to him the real goal of education.'[248] And he tried to transfer this spirit and outlook back to the University itself in helping design the School of Politics, Philosophy, and Economics so as to prepare the products of Oxford for the new challenges of public life. Not surprisingly, Lindsay was at odds with the academic development of philosophy in his own lifetime, and made his mark as a teacher rather than a scholar.[249]

Lindsay is remembered as an annual fixture at the Balliol Summer School. 'He loved *to be about,* with time for casual meeting and talk, and here he was always infinitely accessible and ready to discuss.'[250] According to Alice Cameron, one of his students from Somerville College whom Lindsay sent off to teach tutorial classes in philosophy,

It was at the Balliol Summer School that I first saw something of Lindsay's way of lecturing and discussing with the working men from various places who attended it, including potters from Stoke, miners from South Wales, engineers from Lincoln . . . His spirit seemed to pervade all the 'School' in their formal and informal studies, their work and play. The first thing which struck me was the *respect* for the workers which marked his attitude in all he said and did. This was based, I believe, not merely in the idea expressed in the words he so often quoted—'The poorest he that is in England hath a life to live as the greatest he'—but on his respect for the skill and craftsmanship of the artisan. Such respect was not unique in Oxford, where it inspired men like Cole and Tawney to join the Labour Movement and give it of their best, but Lindsay's respect seemed to have a certain personal quality which made his style of approach infinitely winning to the shy and awkward men who filled the Balliol Common Room those summer days.[251]

Lindsay was another instinctive democrat, and was always fascinated by the ideas expressed in the Putney Debates of 1647. He

[247] Ibid. 348–9.   [248] Ibid. 129.
[249] Sir James Mountford, *Keele: An Historical Critique* (London, 1972), 42.
[250] Scott, *Lindsay*, 127.
[251] Alice Cameron, 'Lindsay and the Tutorial Classes', typescript in file L 174, A. D. Lindsay Papers. See also Scott, *Lindsay*, 72.

wrote an introduction to them for an edition published in 1935, and when he looked at the army of the 1940s he formed the impression, no doubt fancifully, 'that there had never been an army in England which discussed like this one since that famous Puritan Army which produced the Putney Debates and laid the foundations of modern democracy'.[252] His favourite line about 'the poorest he' was uttered at Putney by the army Leveller, Colonel Thomas Rainsborough. As Christopher Hill has put it, echoing another of Lindsay's heroes, Cromwell (who was, of course, on the other side at Putney), Lindsay had a 'profound sense of the dignity and equality of all human beings, or at least of all human beings who had the root of the matter in them'.[253] For Lindsay, as for A. L. Smith, 'democracy meant a way of living'.[254] His dedication to it was instinctive, certainly, but it was also derived from his Christianity. In this he was not unlike Tawney. And from this belief in the democratic way of life—participatory, representative, tolerant, consensual—came also his commitment to adult education. As he told a WEA group in the 1920s, 'Adult education is not the process of teaching adults what they ought to have known when they were young, it is education in the ideals and practice of democracy'.[255] In his book on *The Modern Democratic State*, published in 1943, he expressed a reverence for 'free associations' which were the essence of democracy. Churches, universities, trade unions, and above all, the WEA, summed the democratic spirit for Lindsay, and this explains why, as a statesman for extramural education he passionately defended the role within it of voluntary bodies like the WEA. He was able to persuade a whole range of authorities and institutions to fund the Association without demanding supervisory control.[256] This was more than clever policy and self-interest: Lindsay honestly believed in the moral superiority of self-governing voluntary associations. Adult education was an example of democracy at work. In turn, it would help create in Britain 'the educated democracy' that he and many others in the movement wished to see.

Lindsay apparently said that he 'had imbibed the true spirit of the Jowett tradition' from A. L. Smith.[257] He was conscious of the

[252] Ibid. 282. See A. D. Lindsay, 'Foreword' to A. S. P. Woodhouse (ed.), *Puritanism and Liberty* (London, 1935).

[253] Christopher Hill, 'A. D. Lindsay', *Dictionary of National Biography 1950–60*, 641. For Lindsay's discussion of Rainsborough's idea, see A. D. Lindsay, *The Essentials of Democracy* (London, 1929), 13.

[254] W. B. Gallie, *A New University: A. D. Lindsay and the Keele Experiment* (London, 1960), 42.   [255] Scott, *Lindsay*, 101.

[256] Sir Charles Morris, 'Lindsay of Balliol', *Rewley House Papers*, 3/2 (1953), 9.

[257] Scott, *Lindsay*, 107.

Balliol tradition he had inherited and so were others. Perhaps the most famous episode of Lindsay's life occurred when he stood against the Conservative candidate, Quintin Hogg (Lord Hailsham), as an Independent Anti-Munich candidate (who had the backing of both the Labour and Liberal parties) in the Oxford city by-election of October 1938. After the election, which Lindsay lost narrowly, Michael Sadler, now retired from the Mastership of University College, wrote to Lindsay's wife to congratulate them both for making a stand against the appeasement of Hitler and the betrayal of the Czechs:

It was in the tradition of Balliol that you and he did what you have done. T. H. Green seeking election to the Oxford City Council; Arnold Toynbee risking his life those winter evenings in London; and the Master's courage and sense of duty in challenging the policy and extenuations of some of his most influential friends, are three great public services which men of my age will always associate gratefully with Balliol.[258]

But Lindsay was more than a college man in an honourable (if here, a slightly artificial) tradition. The long Oxford affinity with North Staffordshire was especially important to him, and he spent considerable periods in the Potteries and came to know and respect the area and its people. For this reason the portrait of him in John Betjeman's *Summoned by Bells,* though gently sympathetic, is also inaccurate:

> While Sandy Lindsay from his lodge looks down,
> Dreaming of Adult Education where
> The pottery chimneys flare
> On lost potential firsts in some less favoured town.

When Lindsay dreamt of adult education it was an altogether more vigorous image of men and women in their own communities learning and discussing so that they might become better and more insightful citizens, leaders in the institutions they had themselves created. As Alice Cameron pointed out, it was not just 'the lost potential firsts' that concerned him but the 'less academic talents' and the waste of that innate wisdom in so many people 'which he valued most of all'.[259] And did Lindsay really consider Longton and Hanley and Stoke 'less favoured towns'? At the end of his life he rejected retirement and chose to go to the Potteries to oversee the establishment of a local university at Keele, one of the joint aims of Oxford and the people of North Staffordshire since A. W. Bateman Brown had gone to lecture there at the beginning of the century.

[258] Ibid. 256.   [259] Ibid. 73.

Lindsay was no saint. He liked getting his own way and his self-righteousness irritated enemies and colleagues alike who did not assume with such confidence that they had found the correct moral line. He was a national figure involved in so many projects that academics, especially other philosophers who looked askance at his criticisms of their work, mistrusted him for his enthusiasm and his preaching—though there was too much of the don about him to win the full confidence of politicians.[260] Nevertheless, he was an adviser on education to the Labour Party and TUC, and from 1945 a Labour peer as Lord Lindsay of Birker. He was not 'a great scholar' as an editorial in the *Manchester Guardian*, perhaps by Tawney, pointed out at his death, 'But he was a great administrator of scholarship, a great educator. He brought into the academic world a profound sense of social conscience; he was perhaps the most representative voice in the world of the thoughtful, practical idealism of the moderate left.'[261] That final phrase—'the thoughtful, practical idealism of the moderate left'—may be said to sum the Oxford tradition of adult education from Jowett, Green, and Toynbee, through Tawney and Temple (and perhaps even Cole), to Gaitskell and Durbin and Lindsay himself. Lindsay was perhaps its last great exponent in Oxford.

[260] Gallie, *New University*, 9.
[261] *Manchester Guardian*, Mar. 19 1952, p. 6.

7
THE END OF THE TRADITION: OXFORD AND ADULT EDUCATION SINCE 1945

I

Writing the history of university adult education after 1945 is considerably more difficult than for any preceding period. In recent decades the ideals of the movement have become less clear; it has been subject to complex external pressures preventing it from determining its development for itself; indeed, the very idea of a movement has dissipated as liberal adult education has fragmented into many different types of provision and provider, and vocational education has grown to challenge it as the basic function of continuing education. In the past generation the educational and political tradition that this book describes has declined, if it has not expired, as the social and educational conditions that promoted it in the late nineteenth and early twentieth centuries have changed, in some cases beyond recognition. The relative affluence of the postwar period, the corresponding increase in time for leisure, the development of television and the mass-media, the broadening of opportunities in schools and higher education, have all dictated changes in the nature and purpose of adult education. As Tawney recognized in 1947: 'All movements, and particularly our own, have to reckon with the mentality of a generation which, while it starts life with a better preparation than in the past, has many more means of occupying its leisure, many more claims on the time of its more active members, and greatly increased sources of information and recreation.'[1]

Above all, the disappearance of established working-class communities, institutions, and traditions—indeed the gradual decline of a self-conscious working class itself—and changes in the nature of academic life, have altered, if not destroyed the fundamental relationship between dons and workers. That association was premised on the development by the mid-Victorian period of an established and mature working-class culture and a corresponding political will

[1] R. H. Tawney, 'Programme for Action: A Speech Delivered to the Annual Conference 1947', *The Highway*, 39 (Nov. 1947), 3.

to see an expansion in working-class opportunities. For nearly a century the relationship held; objective social conditions were relatively stable, at least in comparison with conditions since the 1950s, and educational traditions took root. The labour movement strove for power; the dons saw themselves as helping that process forward. But its achievement in 1945 left a movement, whose self-identity depended on the concept of political advance, with new problems. How could it sustain itself, let alone build on its achievements, when its aims appeared to have been realized? How could it continue to motivate its members and students when Labour politics had turned into the less glamorous and often more controversial enterprise of administering a declining economy and appeasing powerful interests opposed to Labour in government? And the difficulty was more fundamental still at a social level: how could the movement for workers' education and the relationship between dons and workers be sustained, when, from the early 1950s, as Eric Hobsbawm has pointed out, 'the forward march of Labour' had been halted for sociological reasons—because of the decline of the working class as an occupational and social category under the impact of technological and cultural change and limited social mobility?[2] The social context in which the 'great tradition' of tutorial classes, the WEA, and the alliance with the universities had been established half a century before, was simply dissolving. This was apparent to many in the movement, but especially evident in Oxford as, often reluctantly, it divested itself of responsibility for extramural provision in outlying areas after the war, and turned to work in the immediately contiguous three home counties of Buckinghamshire, Berkshire, and Oxfordshire. The tutorial classes movement had not been designed for such communities, and from the 1950s predominantly middle-class groups from them needed a different type of education. In a very real sense the tradition of adult education as developed by Oxford came to an end in 1962 when responsibility for adult education in North Staffordshire, the scene of so may fruitful collaborations between dons and workers after 1900, passed to Keele University.

Few of these problems were appreciated in 1945, it is true. There was an understandable belief that the successes of wartime could be developed further and in 1943 the Oxford Extra-Mural Delegacy set up a committee to advise on ways to do this.[3] At the new Nuffield College a similar review was attempted as part of a wider

---

[2] Eric Hobsbawm, 'The Forward March of Labour Halted?', in Martin Jacques and Francis Mulhern (eds.), *The Forward March of Labour Halted?* (London, 1981), 1–19. [3] *Oxford Extra-Mural Delegacy Annual Report 1942–3*, 3.

investigation into postwar education policy, and a committee including Lindsay, Cartwright, Henry Clay, and Elizabeth Pakenham
produced a report in 1946 on the implications of the Butler Education
Act for 'the further education of men and women'.[4] The success of
short, intensive courses for service personnel during the war led to
a widespread interest in developing facilities for residential education in the movement as a whole. The Oxford Delegacy collaborated with the WEA and the various local education authorities in
North Staffordshire at the end of the war in establishing the Wedgwood Memorial College at Barlaston Hall in Barlaston as a centre
for such work. The Tutorial Classes Committee paid the salary of
the Warden, and its resident tutors in the District taught many of the
courses there. The College was formally opened in July 1947 by the
President of Corpus Christi College and then Vice-Chancellor, Sir
Richard Livingstone, who had played a role forty years before in
the original alliance of Oxford and the WEA.[5] Indeed, at the war's
end, with the intention of applying 'the lessons and experience of
the war years to the opportunities of peace', the Oxford Delegacy
made an unprecedented appointment of six new full-time members
of the academic staff.[6] This was in line with the pattern in almost all
extramural departments. The University Grants Committee effectively
tripled the funds it provided for university adult education between
1945 and 1951 and in consequence the number of grant-aided full-
time extramural tutors rose over the same period from 43 to 260.[7]
Judged by the level of student enrolments the optimism was well
founded: the late 1940s saw a continuation of wartime expansion.
In 1945–6 the Oxford Tutorial Classes Committee organized 71
tutorial classes for 1,312 students and 111 short-term (usually year-
long) or 'experimental' courses with just over two thousand students attending them. In the following year the combined total of
students enrolled on all courses under the Committee was nearly
four thousand. Enrolments continued to increase up to a peak in
1950, after which the rate of increase slackened somewhat. But in
the mid-1950s student numbers were substantially higher than they

[4] *The Further Education of Men and Women: A Task of the 1944 Education
Act* (Nuffield College) (London, 1946).
[5] *Oxford Extra-Mural Delegacy Annual Report 1946–7*, 3. Cecil Scrimgeour,
*Fifty Years A-Growing: A History of the North Staffordshire District, the Workers'
Educational Association 1921–1971* (Stoke-on-Trent, 1973), 71. *Wedgwood Memo-
rial College: Barlaston Hall: First Annual Report 1945–6* (Hanley, 1946), 5–6.
[6] *Oxford Extra-Mural Delegacy Annual Report 1944–5*, 6.
[7] John A. Blyth, *English University Adult Education 1908–1958: The Unique
Tradition* (Manchester, 1983), 171, 222, 278. Alan Bullock, 'The Universities and
Adult Education', *The Highway* (May–Sept. 1952), 1.

had been before the Second World War, and the trend since has been upward. Though precise comparisons with the past are impossible because the University has given up responsibility for outlying areas over time, and though there have been exceptions to the trend, notably the sharp (though temporary) fall in student numbers at the time of the economic downturn in the mid-1970s, nevertheless demand for university adult education in Oxford and its surrounding region has steadily increased through the postwar period.

Yet a growth in numbers could not offset deep-seated anxiety in Oxford and in the movement as a whole about its future. It was one thing to get more students into a classroom but what should they be taught and to what end? As Raymond Williams was later to observe, 'the whole problem was not whether the message would be accepted or rejected or modified but . . . what the message should be'.[8] In the last months of his life, at the end of 1951, Lindsay considered 'the whole problem of adult education in the changed circumstances of the present time'. He feared that many of those previously brought into the movement were now proceeding, and would in future proceed, via grammar schools, to university, and be lost to the movement. He recognized that the election of a Labour government in 1945, and the implementation of its programme of nationalization and state welfare, had altered the political context of adult education. Given that 'the drive and pressure' of the early WEA was essentially political in inspiration, Lindsay wondered if it would be possible to maintain the educational momentum without the same motive. Finally, Lindsay could intuit the educational consequences for the movement of social change: was the WEA in future to be 'the working class body concerned with problems of working class education' in a society in which the working class, as a distinct economic, social, and cultural entity was losing its identity, or should it seek 'responsibility for all forms of adult education'?[9]

Ten years later an editorial in the *Oxford Magazine* went further, indeed rather too far. 'The heroic days of the WEA are over' it announced, 'and the dreams of R. H. Tawney and A. L. Smith have in a sense been realised'. It was contended 'that the WEA has lost its old *raison d'être*' because the 'great reservoir' of the educationally disadvantaged had been drained by increasing opportunities. The decrease of manual workers as a proportion of total students

[8] Raymond Williams, 'Adult Education and Social Change' in *Adult Education and Social Change: Lectures and Reminiscences in Honour of Tony McLean* (WEA South Eastern District, 1983), 21.

[9] Lindsay of Birker, review of S. G. Raybould, *The English Universities and Adult Education* (London, 1951), *Universities Quarterly*, 6/1 (Nov. 1951), 82–6.

attending local WEA classes, and their replacement by 'housewives', was taken as evidence that liberal adult education was no longer 'the most obvious vehicle for anyone's social conscience'.[10]

The fallacies here were legion. The Principal of Ruskin College and the then Vice-President of the WEA, H. D. Hughes, argued in reply, and with relevant statistics, that many working-class people were still deprived of the university education they merited.[11] Another don pointed out that the decline in the proportion of manual workers in extramural classes had to be 'set against the declining proportion of manual workers in the population as a whole'. He wondered also if there were really 'no social, economic or political problems which adults urgently need the chance to understand(?)'.[12] And Raymond Williams, also writing in 1961 in his last year as an Oxford extramural tutor, questioned the facile assumptions behind commentaries of this sort:

> Many people will tell you that the WEA's historic mission is over. With the coming of better opportunities in the schools, the exceptional mind in the poor family is spotted young, and is given a real chance. Yes, but this was never at the heart of the WEA's purpose. Of course the exceptional minds must get their chance, but what about everyone else? Are they simply to be treated as rejects? The WEA stands for purposes which some people, including some reformers, cannot even begin to understand. It stands for an educated democracy, not for a newly mobile and more varied élite.[13]

Even if the adult scholar of old, without formal education and qualifications, was a rarity by the 1960s, and even if the best of the young were now able to gain a full education, there remained a responsibility to broaden the understanding of the ordinary citizen, whatever his or her class. The juxtaposition of manual workers and housewives in the argument of *The Oxford Magazine*, meanwhile, suggesting that the education of the latter was somehow less important than that of the former, betrayed an ignorance of the contribution women had always made to the extension and extramural movements, not to mention an unattractive sexism. And reference to 'social conscience' showed a misunderstanding of the nature of the historic engagement of academics with workers' education. Few dons had ever taught classes because they felt guilty about their

[10] *Oxford Magazine*, 25 May 1961, p. 363.
[11] *Oxford Magazine*, 1 June 1961, p. 386.
[12] *Oxford Magazine*, 8 June 1961, p. 402. (The don in question was J. R. Sargent of Worcester College, Honorary Treasurer of the local district of the WEA.)
[13] Raymond Williams, *An Open Letter to WEA Tutors* (London, 1990; first pub. 1961), 4. It seems safe to assume that Williams was answering the editorial in the *Oxford Magazine*, directly.

privilege; few looked upon the enterprise in terms of charity. Most recognized a social obligation to spread learning; most sympathized with the political aspirations of their students, and most saw their relationship with them in terms of a partnership of equals. In effect, this critique and others like it wanted it all ways: the movement was damned for standing still and relying on its 'great tradition', now adjudged inapplicable to a changing society; it was damned also if it tried to adapt and develop new functions by working with different groups, in this case middle-class women.

Some of the criticism may have been ill-informed and superficial. Nevertheless, as the set of related problems became evident in the 1950s the adult education movement fell into 'an uncreative malaise' in Asa Briggs's phrase.[14] Indeed, with a measure of hindsight, it is clear that it was sidetracked into sterile debates on educational standards and the demarcation of effort between the universities and the WEA at a time when it should have been responding imaginatively to the changing context of its work. The arguments, essentially between leading figures in the extramural departments of the civic universities, were focused on the contentions of the Director of Extra-Mural Studies at Leeds University, Sidney Raybould, that the movement should continue to focus on workers' education above all, on the traditional three-year tutorial class, and on the social sciences rather than the liberal arts.[15] There were supplementary disagreements over the precise roles of extramural departments and the WEA: should the WEA attempt work of university standard and should universities be allowed to trespass on traditional WEA functions?[16] After 1945 many extramural departments sought to loosen their ties with the Association and so gain freedom to 'experiment in new methods'.[17] Raybould was a traditionalist and a fundamentalist hoping to turn back the tide, and he set the narrow terms of this debate on the adherence to tradition, when a more realistic course of action beckoned: to accept social and educational diversity, be it in the form of one-year classes on English literature predominantly frequented by the middle classes, and to build on

[14] Asa Briggs, 'Sixty-four years of the WEA', *Workers Education*, 1 (spring/summer 1987), 10.

[15] Blyth, *English University Adult Education*, 197–206. See Sidney Raybould, *University Standards in WEA Work* (London, 1948), *The WEA: The Next Phase* (London, 1949) and *The English Universities and Adult Education* (London, 1951).

[16] Blyth, *Adult Education*, 159–60.

[17] The quotation is taken from the report of a conference held in 1945 by the universities of Oxford, Cambridge, and London which considered the future position of university adult education. See Blyth, *Adult Education*, 160.

the unconventional, but highly successful developments of the war years.

Though extramural departments obviously differed in how they responded to new circumstances, there is a sense in which the traditional adult education movement failed to take its opportunities in the 1950s and 1960s and marked time, caught between an understandable reverence for its past and an uncertainty about the future. It was sidelined also by the establishment of new universities and the expansion of intramural student numbers in the period we associate now with the recommendations and principles of the *Robbins Report* of 1963.[18] The focus of university life was elsewhere; extramural departments began to look very out of date; and several of the finest tutors moved across the divide to take advantage of new opportunities. Richard Hoggart went from the extramural department at Hull to Leicester University and then, in 1962, to the innovative Centre for Contemporary Cultural Studies at Birmingham; Edward Thompson went from the Leeds extramural department to the new Centre for the Study of Social History at Warwick University; and Raymond Williams went from the Oxford Delegacy to a lectureship in English at Cambridge.

There is no more obvious symbol of the self-absorption and prevarication in traditional university adult education than the projection and establishment of the Open University in the mid- and late-1960s. Its rapid and remarkable success after 1969 in offering formal university qualifications to thousands of adults showed just how much latent demand existed which extramural departments and their parent universities had failed to recognize and tap in the years after 1945. It demonstrated also that the traditions of a movement long opposed to qualifications as the reward for study, were outmoded, and, arguably, were depriving students of due recognition for their work and of their abilities. Moreover the Open University had been established deliberately without connection to the extramural movement and without reference to 'the old types of adult education'. Raymond Williams, among many others, regretted this, hoping that the project might have led 'to a reshaping of adult education' in general, and to a connection between distance learning 'and the kind of tutorial class education which had been so well developed by the WEA'. He regretted that the Open University had 'little of our old educational democracy'. Nevertheless the minister responsible, Jennie Lee, rejected such a strategy, making a clean

---

[18] *Higher Education: Report of a Committee appointed by the Prime Minister (The Robbins Report)* (London, 1963).

break with the past, and this may be taken as evidence of the traditional movement's decline in the generation after 1945. It did not seem to be answering the needs of the moment.[19]

In Oxford the break with the past was evident in the cession of territory to a new generation of universities as the map of adult education was rationalized once more. In 1959 Oxford passed over responsibility for provision in Lincoln to Nottingham University. In 1963 the Delegacy gave up responsibility for Swindon to Bristol University, and Heaton Moor in Cheshire was passed to Manchester. Then in 1969 responsibility for East Sussex was passed to the new University of Sussex. In 1972 the boroughs of Bexley and Bromley were transferred to the University of London. And finally in 1975 university adult education in Kent was transferred to the new University of Kent at Canterbury. But the most painful dissociation was in North Staffordshire. In April 1962 the annual rally of the WEA District was a final celebration of the old alliance between Oxford and the Potteries: on 1 August 1962 extramural responsibilities were handed over to Keele University and with it went Oxford's last links with the communities of the industrial working class.[20]

Keele owed its origins, in large measure, to the imagination and enterprise of the Oxford Delegacy. Oxford had helped build up a unique educational tradition in the region. It had also inspired institutional initiatives: first a North Staffordshire Joint Advisory Committee in 1925 which brought together Oxford, the WEA District, and other local educational agencies; then, from 1944, the North Staffordshire Committee for Adult Education, including as well representatives from the various local educational authorities. Over time the individuals involved—notably Lindsay and Cartwright from Oxford—'came to share a common aspiration', the establishment of a University College in the Potteries. And the Oxford Delegacy, and Lindsay, of course, played an important role in stimulating enthusiasm for the project, lobbying on its behalf and bringing all the parties to it together during and immediately after the war.[21]

When Lindsay became Principal of the new foundation he hoped that an extramural department there would be able to accept responsibility for the area within a year of opening. But Keele found

[19] Raymond Williams, *Politics and Letters: Interviews with New Left Review* (London, 1979), 371; W. B. Gallie, *A New University: A. D. Lindsay and the Keele Experiment* (London, 1960); Scrimgeour, *Fifty Years A-Growing*, 93–100.

[20] *Annual Report of the WEA North Staffordshire District 1961–2* (Hanley, 1962), 3.

[21] Sir James Mountford, *Keele: An Historical Critique* (London, 1972), 25.

itself with many other pressing matters to deal with, and in Oxford there were misgivings. The Delegacy had fifteen full-time tutors in North Staffordshire in the late 1940s, a tremendous loyalty to the region, and wished to maintain the relationship with working-class education that responsibility for the region permitted. Its very sense of itself and of the purpose of adult education was bound up with the mythology of Tawney at Longton in 1908 and all the achievements that had flowed from that. On the other side there were many in the Potteries who valued the old and established link with Oxford. Disentangling one set of associations and developing new ones was not smooth and generated some ill will.[22] It may explain why the first Director of the new Department of Extra-Mural Studies at Keele, Roy Shaw, chose to distance himself and his department from the established WEA infrastructure and experiment with new types of adult education.[23] There were similar, if more muted tensions in the transfers to Kent and Sussex universities. The WEA South-Eastern District was also reluctant to cut the link with Oxford, not least because the resources set aside for extramural work by the two new universities were 'meagre' in comparison.[24]

Losing contact with outlying centres in the 1920s had been accompanied by the countervailing establishment of Rewley House and of a more formal extramural presence in Oxford. Similar compensation accompanied the cession of extramural territory after 1960. In the year that North Staffordshire passed to Keele, the Delegacy's constitution was revised and the two committees for extension lectures and tutorial classes were united into a single body. At the same time representatives from each of the main University faculties were attached to the Delegacy to integrate it more closely with the academic life of Oxford.[25] Seven years later the University established a committee under Sir John Habakkuk, Principal of Jesus College 'to review and make recommendations about the University's policy for extramural studies'.[26] The process of integration was taken a stage further in their recommendations, subsequently enacted in 1971, that the Delegacy be reconstituted as a new Department for External Studies under the formal oversight of the General Board of Faculties. Extramural education was now, at least constitutionally, similar to all other activities in the University. As the

[22] Ibid. 192–7; Drusilla Scott, *A. D. Lindsay: A Biography* (Oxford, 1971), 381.

[23] Scrimgeour, *Fifty Years A-Growing*, 99–114.

[24] Jack Woolford, 'The South-Eastern District of the WEA 1945–80', pp. 2–4, unpub. paper, WEA South-Eastern District Archives, Rochester, Kent.

[25] *Oxford Delegacy for Extra-Mural Studies Annual Report 1961–2*, 14–15.

[26] *Report of the Committee on Extra-Mural Studies* (Oxford, 1970), 3.

Director of the new Department put it with a touch of exaggeration, 'at one time we were irregulars skirmishing on the periphery; now we are part of the establishment'.[27] The extramural empire that Michael Sadler had created in the late nineteenth century had been relinquished: compensation took the form of an established place within the University.

Losing contact with North Staffordshire in the early 1960s compounded a more general recognition that the social basis of adult education was rapidly eroding. In 1957, in *The Uses of Literacy*— a sustained lament for the old culture of the working class then beginning to dissolve—Richard Hoggart paid tribute to the 'earnest minority' among the working class who had 'an influence on this group out of all proportion to their numbers' and he enjoined this minority to use that influence to prevent the 'spiritual deterioration' of working people. He feared that the working class was coming 'to accept a mean form of materialism as a social philosophy'.[28] The 'earnest minority' was the group classically attracted to adult education. But for how much longer would this section of the working class exist? Their children, if not they themselves, could be expected to leave the places and culture of their origins: the working-class lad from a respectable home who went up to university or made his way in the world was the stuff of any number of novels and plays in the 1950s and 1960s in Britain. It was also unclear whether this élite could continue to exert their traditional influence in a period of flux when working-class communities were breaking up, their inhabitants rehoused on new estates outside the cities, and when many working-class institutions—clubs, friendly societies, and the like—were disappearing. *Oxford and Working-Class Education* in 1908 had pictured the successful tutorial class spreading its influence and 'leaven[ing] a whole town'.[29] Further back, university extension had enjoyed its greatest success in working-class districts with a strong consciousness of community, and a web of interlocking institutions to sustain lectures and classes. The collapse of 'community', damaging enough to the labour movement as a whole, was peculiarly damaging to the traditional adult education movement which depended so heavily on community solidarity and on coming together for political purposes outside the home. The movement, in other words, had been premised not so much on the individual

[27] *Oxford University Department for External Studies Annual Report 1975–6*, 5.
[28] Richard Hoggart, *The Uses of Literacy: Aspects of Working-Class Life With Special Reference to Publications and Entertainments*, 2nd edn. (1958, Harmondsworth), 318–23.   [29] See p. 104 above.

scholar, as on communities and their organizations, and the development of a corporate desire for education. But what may be termed the overall 'privatization of living' which has refocused daily life on the home, television, and more individual styles of recreation, has undermined the sources of a labour culture. It was not merely that the 'earnest minority' was dissolving in the postwar period, as the working class of intellect were syphoned-off through a more meritocratic educational system; arguably, the more fundamental development was the decline of the civic culture of the working class.

By the mid-1950s it was clear in Oxford that a growing proportion of students were drawn not from the working class, whether earnest or otherwise, but from what was termed in 1948 'the salariat'—'scientists, technicians and social welfare workers' among others.[30] The *Annual Report* of the Oxford Delegacy for 1954–5 attempted to sketch the occupational structure of the average tutorial class: it consisted of 'three housewives; three manual workers, perhaps a fitter, a printer, and a postman; five non-manual workers— a shop assistant, a couple of clerks, a nurse, and a social worker or bank manager; three teachers and one retired person, or a zealous older schoolboy or schoolgirl'.[31] Six years later a survey of Oxford classes was more precise. Housewives made up 27 per cent of all students; technical workers some 24 per cent; teachers 16 per cent; professionals 10 per cent. Ten per cent of students were not in paid work (a considerably smaller proportion than is the case in the 1990s when a substantial section of students are retired) and the social background of 3 per cent of students was unknown. That left only 10 per cent from the manual working class.[32] The rough similarity between a student body of this type and the social composition of extension lecture audiences in the Home Counties at the turn of the century is worth noting. So also is the increasing proportion of women in extramural education after 1945. They had always been well-represented in some areas: 'domestic and home workers' comprised the largest single occupational category among WEA students in the South-Eastern District in the 1930s, for example. And by 1952 over 60 per cent of all students in Kent and East Sussex were women.[33] In 1965 women made up nearly 55 per cent

[30] Thomas Hodgkin, 'Introductory Note', *Rewley House Papers*, 2 (1948–9), 6; *Annual Report of the Oxford Extra-Mural Delegacy 1957–8*, 4.
[31] *Annual Report of the Oxford Extra-Mural Delegacy 1954–5*, 4.
[32] F. W. Jessup, 'A Survey of Oxford Extra-Mural Work 1957–62', *Rewley House Papers*, 4/1 (1962–3), 28.
[33] See the *Annual Report of the WEA South-Eastern District 1951–2*.

of all extramural students in the country.[34] In the early 1990s in Oxford, perhaps as many as two-thirds of students in liberal adult education are women.

One response to changing social imperatives was to break with the liberal tradition, develop vocational education and thus find ways of reaching key groups within the new welfare state and labour movement. Courses for social workers, teachers, probation officers, health professionals, and so forth became standard in the 1950s and 1960s. They fulfilled an obvious social function and could be construed as falling within the ideological parameters of the movement. But vocationalism was controversial because it broke with the fundamental imperative to provide a liberal education on which the development of the movement, dating back to Jowett and Green, had been premised. And the controversy demonstrated the difficulty in the postwar period of simultaneously honouring and departing from inherited assumptions and traditions. These courses tended to be short and intensive, and depended on residence in Oxford or at an outlying centre such as Kingsgate College in Kent or the Wedgwood Memorial College in Staffordshire. The growth in such courses explains why it became not merely desirable but necessary to add a residential centre to Rewley House in Oxford in the early 1960s.

One particular type of vocational education was especially important to the Oxford Delegacy: courses in trade union education which developed in the years immediately following the war and flourished until the 1970s. They seemed to square the circle; they were a response to new expectations that extramural departments should make themselves relevant to economic life and they renewed contact between Oxford and the working class, or at least a specific group within it. The architect of the whole programme, Frank Pickstock, who became Secretary of the Tutorial Classes Committee in 1949 and then Deputy Director of the Delegacy until he retired in 1978, justified the project in three ways: trade union education would obviously meet the educational needs of the unions; it would maintain one of Oxford's traditional aims, 'to educate for political and social responsibility'; and it would counteract 'the post-war trend of declining working class participation in adult education'.[35] Over

---

[34] Thomas Kelly, *A History of Adult Education in Great Britain*, 1st edn. (Liverpool, 1970), 343.

[35] Frank Pickstock, 'The Teaching of Industrial Relations, with Special Reference to Trade Union Education', p. 1, unpub. paper, 29 Jan. 1962, 'Trade Union Education Policy Documents from 1947', file marked 'F. Pickstock', DES/F/4/1/1, Oxford University Archives.

time the University established a pioneering school of trade union studies in which the Delegacy played an important role. In 1947, when the experiment was first suggested, the resources to hand were meagre. With some notable individual exceptions (among them that of G. D. H. Cole) there had been no systematic academic work on trade union structure and function since the Webbs. Though several economists in Oxford were interested 'in aspects of trade union problems . . . there was little relevant research in progress and few up-to-date publications of value for teaching'.[36] With remarkable prescience Pickstock, in 1948, charted the actual course of trade union education in Oxford over the next three decades:

The information on these practical problems is not easily available and a fair amount of research work will be entailed in obtaining it and sorting it out. Successful teaching in this field then, and original research must go hand in hand. It calls for close co-operation between extra-mural tutors and University research institutes like Nuffield and the Institute of Statistics. The advantage of this would not be one-sided. If the University gives adult tutors facilities for and guidance in research, the extra-mural field provides in return a social laboratory which could be of the utmost value to the University.[37]

Teaching in this new field depended on simultaneous research, in other words, and as such, the project brought the Delegacy into active association with different parts of the University. The Delegacy became one base among several in Oxford for academics who helped establish Industrial Relations as an academic discipline in Britain in the 1950s and 1960s. Its courses provided contact with trade unionists and trade unions, and fertile ground for investigation. A large grant from the Leverhulme Trust in the late 1950s, for example, allowed for pioneering research into collective bargaining in three industries—engineering, coal-mining, and road passenger transport—and the development from this of standardized teaching resources. Taken together, the 'New Oxford Group' that developed from these initiatives, consisting of, among others, Hugh Clegg, Alan Flanders, Alan Fox, Arthur Marsh, Derek Robinson, and Bill McCarthy (who had been a Delegacy Scholar as a student at Oxford), were collectively distinguished by their empiricism and pragmatism—by a 'thorough-going concern to get the facts about plant and union organizaton right'. They held to what was described as

[36] Ibid. 2.
[37] F. V. Pickstock, 'Development of Trade Union Education in the Oxford Extra-Mural Area', p. 1, unpub. paper, DES/F/4/1/1, file marked 'F. Pickstock', Oxford University Archives.

an 'institutional bias' and 'their ideology [was] tempered with a thorough knowledge of the possible'.[38] Their influence was largely responsible for the recommendations of the Royal Commission on Trade Unions and Employers' Associations (the Donovan Commission) in regard to trade union reform and the subsequent (and highly controversial) White Paper on industrial relations in 1969, *In Place of Strife*.[39]

The courses they developed, and the very outlook and approach of the 'school' in other ways, were essentially different from the model set out in 1908 in *Oxford and Working-Class Education*. Their emphasis was on the development of skills, rather than a liberal education. Trade unionists were trained for their functions in bargaining with employers and leading other workers: they were not educated as working men as this had been traditionally understood. At the outset, in 1948, Pickstock had justified this approach because 'trade unionists are busy men and sufficient numbers will not attend classes unless they feel they are of direct help with their immediate problems. Teaching has got to start with the practical problems of the Trade Union Secretary, the branch or the Workshop and lead outwards.'[40] Some of the evidence proves him right. By 1953 only a single miner was attending a tutorial class in North Staffordshire, but miners' participation was revived by residential courses on 'Problems of the Mining Industry' as part of the annual Summer School in Oxford in 1954 and 1955.[41]

Assessing the project of trade union education in 1962 Pickstock acknowledged that 'by degrees economic and structural problems' had been subordinated to 'the central issues now grouped under the emerging subject of "industrial relations", i.e. the study of the institutions and relationships involved in collective bargaining between trade unions and employers'.[42] He acknowledged 'misgivings' about the narrowness of the education also. Trade union education on the Oxford model was criticized as 'too much akin to training' and as unlikely to lead the workers involved to take an interest in more general adult education. Its novelty and specialized nature led some to question whether it was an appropriate function for university extramural departments.[43] As early as 1953, indeed, Cole was

[38] Jeremy Bugler, 'The New Oxford Group', *New Society*, 11/281 (15 Feb. 1968), 221.
[39] Brian Harrison, 'Oxford and the Labour Movement', *Twentieth Century British History*, 2/3 (1991), 268–70.
[40] Pickstock, 'Development of Trade Union Education', 1.
[41] Pickstock, 'The Teaching of Industrial Relations', 4–5.
[42] Ibid. 2.   [43] Ibid. 3.

warning against a 'tendency to narrow workers' education down to the immediate tasks of the trade union and co-operative bodies', and was promoting instead 'a wide, constructive conception of the tasks of workers' education'.[44] And the Oxford School has been criticized in similar terms more recently for its focus on the technical issues of trade unionism rather than the economic and political education of workers which might have allowed them to take a broader view of their position in society.[45] At the time, members of the 'school' defended the educational work they were engaged in, variously arguing that traditional approaches had to change to reach a new generation of workers and questioning whether their approach really was as narrow as their critics presumed.[46] There is an irony here, of course: trade union education as developed in Oxford in this period was arguably the Delegacy's most significant academic achievement in the postwar period. But it was an achievement seen to be at odds with the 'Oxford tradition' going back to the earliest tutorial classes in economics and industrial history. The difficulties of responding to present imperatives while respecting the past are evident once more.

It was not only in trade union education that the content and subject-matter were changing. From the 1950s literature, the arts, archaeology, and local history began to attract an increasing number of students; the traditional core of economics, politics, social history, and sociology—the subjects hitherto valued as the keys to political and social emancipation—declined further in popularity. From the early 1960s the traditional three-year tutorial class also began a rapid decline, to be replaced by courses generally lasting a single year—though it was, and still is possible for classes to link together annual courses to make an academically coherent programme lasting several years.

Facile explanations for these related developments affecting all extramural departments—that the traditional adult education movement was no longer capable of serious academic work, for example, or that its students were now of an inferior quality—miss entirely the complex educational and cultural trends making for the change.

[44] G. D. H. Cole, 'Independent Voluntaryism in Workers' Education', unpub. paper delivered to the International Federation of Workers' Educational Associations (1953), 9, in Rewley House Adult Education Reference Library, Box 2(A) (ii).

[45] John McIlroy, 'Trade Union Education for a Change', in Brian Simon (ed.), *The Search for Enlightenment: The Working Class and Adult Education in the Twentieth Century* (London, 1990), 251–4.

[46] e.g. see A. I. Marsh, 'Trade Union and Workers' Education', *Rewley House Papers*, 3/6 (1957–8), 27–36.

First, by the mid-1950s it was evident that university adult education in Oxford as elsewhere was increasingly 'educating the educated', the products of the grammar schools, technical colleges, and universities. Lindsay had worried that such people, if drawn from the working class, would be lost to the movement for good. In fact, it was just as likely that having received a formal education they would make contact with adult education in maturity: possessing an education was no bar to wanting more of it. Long before, the *1919 Report* had recognized that improvements in the education of children and adolescents would not 'supersede the need of education for adults' but 'accentuate' it.[47] But what these new students required was rather different. The initial tutorial classes had offered students their first contact with higher learning and demanded that they develop skills of expression and analysis for the first time. But many of the students coming to classes in the 1950s and 1960s had learnt how to compose essays and express their ideas at college, if not at school. They felt little need to go through the disciplines of a tutorial class; in many cases these had been mastered at an earlier stage. Rather, they required an education to sustain their intellectual and cultural interests outside their working or professional lives.

As Thomas Kelly, the Director of Extra-Mural Studies in the University of Liverpool and author of the standard history of British adult education, pointed out in 1953, the three-year tutorial class was superfluous for many of the better-educated students: 'The grammar school public also requires a wide provision of shorter courses—courses designed to supplement their existing education, to open up new interests, and to provide light and leading on the important questions of the day.'[48] The emphasis was shifting towards continuing education as a form of individual recreation and stimulation rather than as a means to intensive self-education and collective social advancement—though the transition was gradual and for many students then (as now) extramural classes still functioned as a first encounter with serious academic work. Nor is it clear that 'standards' fell. Less was written, certainly, but there is no reason to think that engagement with the subject and the quality of discussion in classes largely composed of students who had already enjoyed a decent education was inferior to what had gone before.

[47] 'Covering Letter from the Chairman to the Prime Minister', *Ministry of Reconstruction: Adult Education Committee, Final Report*, PP 1919, Cmd. 321, xxviii. 6.

[48] Thomas Kelly, 'The Extra-Mural Function of Universities', *The Universities Review*, 25/2 (1953), 102.

In explaining the shift in interest away from the traditional social sciences, meanwhile, it is necessary to consider not only the altered political context in which the Labour Party could now present itself, however mistakenly, as 'the natural party of government'—a context that seemed to render a political education for the assumption of power superfluous—but also the new cultural context of education of all types in the age of television and the mass media. There was no intrinsic conflict between the modern media and adult education; indeed, the movement had enjoyed successful collaboration with radio from the first. As early as 1924 William Temple's address on his retirement as President of the WEA was broadcast by the BBC from the Sheldonian Theatre in Oxford; two years later a WEA tutor gave a course of radio talks on 'One Hundred Years of Working Class Progress'.[49] But in the 1960s and 1970s the quality of television programmes on news, current affairs, and social and international issues during a particularly creative phase in the history of broadcasting in Britain, probably satisfied, if not saturated, the curiosity of many potential students. Gaining knowledge from television may be an essentially passive experience as compared with discussion in a tutorial class, and it brings to mind A. L. Smith's trenchant criticism of the old extension lecture: 'sitting in rows at desks with your mouths open, while a person standing in front squirts jets of information into them—that's not education.'[50] Nevertheless areas of the traditional adult curriculum could not compete with the flow of information and analysis that television began to provide, and students attracted to adult education seem to have felt sufficiently well informed to turn to new subjects. Adult education had to learn to live with a diverse mass media and wherever possible turn it to advantage. As A. H. Halsey has pointed out, giving 'twenty-minute talks on Radio Three' reaches 'more people than Tawney spoke to in the whole of his career as an adult educationist'.[51]

The new media opened new opportunities, in other words; the implication for dons who, in the best traditions of the movement, sought a broad audience, was clear. It is not merely coincidental that the extramural movement in this period was notable for initiating discussion on the role and impact of television and the printed word: Raymond Williams's book on *Communications*, for example,

---

[49] Mary Stocks, *The Workers' Educational Association: The First Fifty Years* (London, 1953), 103.   [50] Scott, *Lindsay*, 65.

[51] 'Transcript of the Seminar at Corpus Christi College, Oxford, on 17 Feb. 1989 on "The Department for External Studies Since 1945"', History of the University of Oxford, p. 16, Oxford University Archives.

developed out of his extramural teaching for Oxford in the 1950s.[52] Adult education tutors who did not have to teach to a prescribed syllabus were especially well placed to assess the effects of television and the popular press on the attitudes, tastes, and preferences of the students they met in their classes—and to reflect on the declining social impact of their work in view of the massive audiences that television could hold and sway. But many have also used the academic interests that television can initiate and maintain in subjects as varied as the arts, natural history, and current affairs, as a basis for successful courses and as a means of reaching new students.

Taking all these contextual, social, and educational changes into account, is the history of university adult education in Oxford since the war to be read as history of decline? It may invite that interpretation at first sight. But an assessment based on the whole history of the movement might also suggest the reverse: that these were the problems of success. In a very real sense the tradition examined in this book has been self-liquidating. It has stood for educational advance, improved social welfare, and the greater participation of the working classes in social and cultural life. And these things seemed to have been secured in the generation after 1945, thus raising questions about the role of university adult education and what may be termed 'the Oxford tradition' in the process. Like many effective movements for reform, university adult education found itself having to justify its continuation in the 1950s and 1960s in a new situation it had striven itself to create: one of expanding educational provision (though by no means adequate to the task of unlocking the full potential of British society). Since the days of Green, Acland, and Sadler, Oxford extension had campaigned for improved secondary education and it had played a part in founding new provincial colleges like Bristol and Reading, not to mention Keele. Its progeny may be said to have usurped the parent: in the words of A. H. Halsey, 'The extension movement so brilliantly led in Rochdale by R. H. Tawney was largely displaced by the provincial university colleges after 1918, by the Open University in the 1960s and by the polytechnics in the 1970s'.[53] The founders, especially Jowett, who had always wanted provincial colleges established with Oxford's assistance, would not have been displeased to see higher education placed on a permanent and established basis and reaching a much larger constituency, even at the expense of their own 'mission'.

[52] Raymond Williams, *Britain in the Sixties: Communications* (Harmondsworth, 1962).

[53] A. H. Halsey, *The Decline of Donnish Dominion: The British Academic Professions in the Twentieth Century* (Oxford, 1992), 68.

We can see the same process at work, though on a smaller scale, in regard to trade union education after the war. In 1962, at the height of the Oxford School's influence, Pickstock argued that the Delegacy should assist unions in building up their own teaching staff and education programmes and hand over to them routine teaching and training.[54] This duly occurred, and by the early 1980s Oxford's role in trade union education was effectively at an end. In assessing the postwar history of Oxford's efforts in adult education, therefore, it is useful to recall Raymond Williams's observation that it is a characteristic of the 'Long Revolution' he described and analysed, and by which British society has been democratized and reformed over the past two centuries, that social aims, 'once achieved, are quite quickly absorbed, and either new expectations are commonly defined, or in their absence there is a mood of stagnation and restlessness'.[55] Both responses to the achievements of the movement are evident in the recent history of adult education. On the one hand stagnation and dispute attended vain efforts to remain faithful to a powerful and revered educational tradition that had achieved much but was losing its relevance. On the other, in many new areas the movement showed itself capable of responding to change, and of attracting and holding increasing numbers of students. When Richard Hoggart published *The Uses of Literacy* in 1957 he estimated that approximately one hundred and fifty thousand people were participating in liberal adult education organized by voluntary bodies and extramural departments.[56] Thirty years later university extramural departments alone had an annual enrolment approximately double this figure.[57]

II

Choosing particular episodes or individuals who were representative of this complex period of change at the end of the tradition this book has examined, is not easy. But one phase in the later history of Oxford's engagement with adult education and one particular

---

[54] Pickstock, 'The Teaching of Industrial Relations', 6–7. It should be added that Pickstock envisaged that the Oxford Delegacy would thereafter concentrate on 'research, providing teaching material and advising on the planning of courses'.

[55] Raymond Williams, *The Long Revolution*, 2nd edn. (1965, Harmondsworth), 13.   [56] Hoggart, *Uses of Literacy*, 320.

[57] *Universities Council for Adult and Continuing Education Annual Report, 1986–7*. The total enrolment in extramural non-residential and part-time courses was 180,172. The enrolment in extramural courses involving consecutive attendance was 122,374, making a total of 302,546.

tutor from this era are worth investigating further for the light they throw on, respectively, the politics of the movement and its intellectual concerns. In the late 1940s the Oxford Extra-Mural Delegacy was caught up in a series of political controversies concerning some of its tutors and its relationships with other co-operating agencies and the state, that have achieved notoriety as, apparently, the most flagrant example of the influence of the Cold War in British universities. In the 1950s Raymond Williams used his experience of adult education and his understanding of its intellectual history, to reinterpret the movement's traditions and present them to a much wider audience. Both have attracted attention, both have been misunderstood, and both tell us something more about the political and intellectual contributions of the Oxford tradition to recent British history.

Political friction between tutors, between tutors and students, and between the Delegacy and local and national educational authorities was common and to be expected: it was an inevitable feature of an educational movement with political intent. Domestic disputes within the movement tended to take the form of disagreements between different positions and strategies on the left of British politics. Occasionally there were external disputes between the movement, or parts of it, and public bodies concerned about the misuse of public funds for partisan purposes, and in these cases they inevitably tended to be of a straightforward left–right variety. George Wigg, when District Secretary of the WEA in North Staffordshire in the late 1930s, apparently claimed 'that there were very few weeks when he did not have some complaint to deal with'—complaints that were both 'domestic' (between people or organizatons within the movement) and from public authorities and Conservative opponents outside it.[58] The WEA South-Eastern District seems to have spent most of the academic year 1933–4 trying to clear itself of the charge of political bias, for example. This followed a day-school at Chatham in April 1933 organized jointly with the local Labour Party at which H. L. Beales of the London School of Economics lectured on 'The Development of Russian Industrialism'. According to the inaccurate information supplied afterwards to the parliamentary secretary to the Board of Education, Beales declared his support for 'the present system in Russia . . . and the advantages of living under a Communist and classless regime' while 'his views on religion were of a negative character'. Political literature 'of a Socialist and Communist character' was said to have been available

---

[58] Roger Fieldhouse, 'Bouts of Suspicion: Political Controversies in Adult Education, 1925–1944', in Simon (ed.), *The Search for Enlightenment*, 165.

and the course ended with a resolution critical of 'the National Government's attitude on Russian questions'. It did not help matters that the prospective Labour candidate for Chatham, Hugh Gaitskell, was also present and that the day-school was immediately followed by a meeting of the local Labour Party in the same place.[59] Most of this account was open to dispute; it was contended by the WEA District that the lectures and the arrangements were not as reported to the Board. But attempts to set the record straight were not immediately successful and the District apparently 'felt repercussions from a number of unexpected quarters throughout the year', whatever that meant.[60]

Most examples of this sort ended in protestations of innocence, messy apologies from tutors and WEA branches, or withdrawals on the part of ill-informed and hasty Conservative councillors and aldermen. Close up they tend to have their comical side, though some incidents were more serious and long-lasting, and there was always the fear that grants would be stopped. But the political problems that affected the whole adult education movement, and Oxford in particular, in the late 1940s, were of a different order. In these affairs, academic reputations and careers were at stake and the controversies could not be contained within departments and WEA Districts but drew in University authorities and became a subject of national political concern. Crucially, many of these disputes were of a 'domestic' type in origin. But whereas controversies within the movement were usually reconciled without attracting public interest, in this case divisions between different wings of the labour movement could not be contained. And whereas most political disputes in the movement hitherto had been essentially local affairs, at this time the disputes were largely caused by, and were understood in the context of, the ideological conflict at the onset of the Cold War in the late 1940s.

But if they were of a different order from the minor, everyday political irritations of the interwar years, the problems in Oxford and elsewhere after 1947 cannot be so easily divorced from political

[59] It may have been as a consequence of this affair that Gaitskell's local Labour Party stopped him appearing in public with Communists and 'fellow travellers'. See Margaret Cole, 'Discovering the Labour Movement', in W. T. Rodgers (ed.), *Hugh Gaitskell 1906–1963* (London, 1964), 46.

[60] See the letter to Mr Firth, probably a member of the Kent Education Committee, from the Board of Education, 29 May 1933; the 'Memorandum on Joint One-Day School held at Chatham, 8 April 1933' written by the South-Eastern District Secretary; and the 'Annual Report of the WEA South-Eastern District 1933–4', in the WEA South-Eastern District Archives, Rochester, Kent.

controversies sparked by army education during the war itself. Some of these concerned singular figures like the Polish emigré, Dr S. F. Osiakovski, whose vigorously pro-Soviet lectures led to many complaints and the termination of his contract by the Oxford and Reading Committee in 1943. But there were several other cases where lecturers were warned, disciplined, or dispensed with after army officers raised questions about their politics.[61] A. J. P. Taylor's highly critical views of Franco apparently met with two complaints, though from left-wing army officers rather than traditional colonel blimps. In characteristic fashion, Taylor 'went straight to Lindsay . . . and asked him to defend my freedom of expression. He did so in letters to the two officers which he showed me.' But Lindsay apparently also left instructions in the office to 'Keep Taylor off Spain' which provoked Taylor's scorn: 'such was the liberal defence of freedom,' he remarked.[62] Lindsay, as Chairman of the Committee, was 'occasionally quite ruthless' in such affairs, though it seems plausible to contend that this arose from his desire to ensure that army education succeeded and was not compromised as a result of such friction, rather than from his hostility to any particular political position.[63] If Lindsay does not quite emerge with honour intact from Taylor's story, at least his *public* defence of free speech deserves credit. As Lindsay probably saw it, the greater good demanded compromises of this sort, and though it is easy to condemn any infringements of free expression, the difficulties of Lindsay's position deserve some sympathy. Nevertheless, as Chairman of the Oxford Delegacy until 1947, he was at the centre of the postwar controversies and it is possible that illiberal habits learned in the extraordinary situation of wartime died hard. Certainly the Oxford Delegacy had experience of dealing with left-wing tutors who had overstepped some political mark or other, well before the events in North Staffordshire between 1946 and 1949 that led to the controversy.

The precise context for the problems in the Oxford Delegacy has already been sketched. The successes of the war years, the optimism that they could be built on in peacetime, the expectations caused by the election of a Labour government, the increase of central funding, the increase in numbers of tutors—all of this contributed to a renewed sense of social relevance in the movement. And it brought into university adult education a new generation of young and politically committed tutors, some of whom were members of the

---

[61] S. P. Mackenzie, *Politics and Military Morale: Current Affairs and Citizenship Education in the British Army 1914–1950* (Oxford, 1992), 105–7, 143–4.
[62] Ibid. 80; A. J. P. Taylor, *A Personal History* (London, 1983), 152.
[63] Mackenzie, *Politics and Military Morale*, 80.

Communist Party and others who were 'fellow-travellers', who had formed their outlook during the later 1930s when attempts to construct a 'Popular Front' brought students into contact with the Party.

The new Secretary of the Delegacy, appointed in June 1945, Thomas Hodgkin, was the son of a Provost of Queen's College and a grandson of A. L. Smith. In 1937 he married the chemist and later Nobel laureate, Dorothy Crowfoot. After a first in Greats at Balliol, he spent a formative few years in the mid-1930s as a British official in the Palestine mandate—an experience that determined his life-long opposition to colonialism. On his return to England in 1936 he drifted into work with the unemployed, organizing classes for them under the auspices of the Friends' Service Council in West Cumberland. This was his introduction to adult education. In 1939 he became a Staff Tutor for the Tutorial Classes Committee in North Staffordshire, and he taught there throughout the war. He was described by one who worked with him at this time as 'a central animating figure among his colleagues and students' in the region, where he 'threw himself with attractive panache into the tradition of teaching out of which the WEA District had been born'.[64] His reports on the work of the Delegacy during the war, co-authored with Lindsay, and his articles on adult education in *Rewley House Papers*, are fluent and exciting testimony to his belief in the potential of the movement: like the pioneers, he had a sense of 'mission'.

Hodgkin had been a member of the Communist Party since 1938.[65] Many of the difficulties that he and the Delegacy ran into were caused by the appointment of other young members or sympathisers during and after the war who were allowed to concentrate in the Potteries. In 1938 there were three full-time tutors in North Staffordshire appointed by the Tutorial Classes Committee; by 1945 there were eleven.[66] Out of a total academic staff of thirty-one in the Delegacy, one estimate of the number of Communist Party members and fellow-travellers runs as high as fourteen or fifteen. Professor Fieldhouse, who has extensively investigated this episode through archival sources and interviews with participants, puts the figure at ten.[67] Whatever the number, it is not unreasonable to

[64] Scrimgeour, *Fifty Years A-Growing*, 58–9; see also *The Times*, 26 Mar. 1982, p. 10.	[65] *The Times*, 26 Mar. 1982, p. 10.

[66] *North Staffordshire Committee for Adult Education. Memorandum on the Future Development of Adult Education in North Staffordshire* (Hanley, 1947), in the A. D. Lindsay Papers, Keele University Archives, File L.174.

[67] Roger Fieldhouse, *Adult Education and the Cold War: Liberal Values Under Siege 1946–51* (Leeds, 1985), 33. Professor Fieldhouse conducted meticulous research on this episode in the Oxford University Archives and took evidence in a very wide range of interviews with participants. Unfortunately, some of the

contend that Hodgkin showed a lack of professional judgement in the nature and deployment of these new appointees. Indeed, an affair that has generally been seen in terms of a political purge inside the Oxford Delegacy is, as will be argued, better seen in terms of professionalism, competence, and good judgement—or their absence.

For some of those involved in the disputes in Oxford that followed, membership of the Party was itself incriminating. In the eyes of many trade unionists and WEA activists on the right of the Labour Party, like the General Secretary of the WEA, Ernest Green, who was instrumental in raising allegations of bias and malpractice against certain Oxford tutors, membership of the Communist Party was incompatible with the traditions of workers' education developed by the WEA and universities. It was widely believed that Communists would obey the party line and would thus be inappropriate as tutors in a movement that believed itself to be liberal, open, and committed to the free exchange of views. And as Professor Fieldhouse shows, though Hodgkin never acted as if a Party functionary, he did come under pressure from the Party's Education Secretary when the the activities of certain tutors were under investigation by the University in 1948–9.[68] In itself, membership of the Party or sympathy for it should not have been at issue: the private views of tutors and teachers of any sort cannot be of relevance to any authority unless they influence the nature of the education given. But this was the point: it was contended by complainants that some tutors had allowed personal commitments to influence what they taught and how they taught it. Even so, for some of those involved in the events in North Staffordshire after 1947, membership of the Communist Party, or sympathy with it, was a central issue, and enough in itself to damn any tutor suspected of such an affiliation. Bridget Hill recalls being summoned to a meeting in 1948 with George Wigg, by then a Labour MP and an advisory member of the Tutorial Classes Committee, at which she 'was cross-questioned for a very long time and most aggressively on which of my colleagues were party members'.[69] Even though the *actions* of the Oxford

documents he saw when conducting his research, notably the Report of the Sub-Committee of the Tutorial Classes Committee, which investigated allegations of malpractice and bias in 1948–9, cannot now be located. The extent of his research and the fact that he has seen relevant documents that cannot be traced have led me to rely on his account of events at a number of places, though I have interpreted the whole episode differently.

[68] Fieldhouse, *Adult Education and the Cold War*, 13–14.
[69] Letter to the author, 17 Aug. 1994.

Delegacy, as we shall see, were relatively mild, the affair was played out in a climate of suspicion in which personal political commitments were no longer treated as private matters. As such, accusations that the affair amounted to a political purge have some force to them.

Proving political bias in cases like this is notoriously difficult. It depends on what was said (and sometimes not said) in a class; it depends on speculating as to why one candidate rather than another was appointed to a particular position. For that reason any account of events like these must be tentative: it is almost impossible at this distance to reconstruct what went on in a seminar, or what was said and heard in a lecture. Oral testimony taken a generation after the event is subject to many obvious defects; the written record is fragmentary and incomplete. But it is clear that there were complaints about some tutors through 1947, and that in 1948 formal allegations were made about a trade union school on 'Problems of Trade Unions Today' held in April in Queen's College, Oxford, and more generally about the administration and education at the Wedgwood Memorial College in North Staffordshire. The complaints came directly from Ernest Green, but emanated from several sources, including the General Council of the TUC, which alleged Communist bias on the trade union course.[70]

The significance of the trade union school, and thus the sensitivity of the affair, has sometimes been overlooked. It had been organized as a conscious 'first step' in the project of trade union education, designed to bring together 'a group of trade union officers, internal and extra-mural tutors and research workers', for initial interchange and the establishment of mutual confidence.[71] A few weeks before it was held, Pickstock had set out a blueprint for the development of trade union education in Oxford and had emphasized the need for the 'official backing of the T.U.C'.[72] Instead, the Delegacy received its official complaints, and the project of working with the unions looked to be in jeopardy from the start. The course had been organized jointly by the Tutorial Classes Committee and the Workers' Educational Trade Union Committee (WETUC). Over the week the participants looked at three themes: wages and economic policy; control of industry; and the future of trade unionism. Most of the students were full-time trade union officials; others were adult tutors drawn from the WEA and extramural departments, including

[70] Fieldhouse, *Adult Education*, 38–40.

[71] Pickstock, 'The Teaching of Industrial Relations', 2.

[72] Pickstock, 'Development of Trade Union Education', 2. The paper is dated 29 Jan. 1948.

the Oxford Delegacy. Some of the lectures were given by national trade union officers, others by university figures: among those listed to speak were Asa Briggs, Hugh Clegg, Maurice Dobb and G. D. H. Cole. After each plenary lecture the participants split into tutorial groups to debate the issues raised and then returned for further plenary discussion.[73] Though it is difficult to be precise, it would seem that the conference divided between its academic participants who were prepared to discuss issues from any perspective in accordance with academic conventions, and trade unionists who were suspicious of anything unorthodox or outside the parameters of traditional Labourism. Apparently Cole was heckled by officials of the Transport and General Workers Union 'when he pointed out some of the shortcomings of the Government's nationalization and wages policy and argued against the tendency towards trade union centralization and for more local autonomy'.[74]

In June 1948 the Tutorial Classes Committee set up a subcommittee to investigate the allegations, comprising John Lowe, the Vice-Chancellor of Oxford; Lucy Sutherland, the historian, who held strong Conservative views; Henry Clay, the Warden of Nuffield; Lindsay and Cole. In its report, presented in March 1949, the committee effectively dismissed the accusations against tutors at the trade union school, discounting many of the complaints as inappropriate and finding no precise evidence to support others. They concluded that 'neither the organization nor teaching gave undue prominence to the communist point of view'. They specifically contested the assumption that Communists, by virtue of their politics, were not fit to serve as tutors, and that presenting a Communist perspective on an issue was illegitimate. In essence the committee defended the right of tutors to express themselves freely.[75] A subsequent 'review of the course' by the Tutorial Classes Committee also suggested that the frictions were as much the result of cultural differences between academics and trade unionists as of straightforward political disagreements.

Some trade unionists were inclined to look only at the immediate practical implications for them of every idea mooted and sometimes inclined to weigh their words as though they were at a trade union conference where it may be dangerous to speculate. An example of this was their treatment of any ideas which might be labelled 'Marxian' (whether in fact this was

[73] See 'Oxford University Tutorial Classes Committee: Course on Problems of Trade Unions To-Day, The Queen's College, 3–10 April 1948', DES/F/4/1/1, Oxford University Archives.
[74] Fieldhouse, *Adult Education and the Cold War*, 41.   [75] Ibid. 42.

a proper label or not); anyone putting forward such ideas for consideration was regarded at first as an opponent in a trade union conference might be regarded.[76]

This is substantiated by some comments made by the Director of Studies at the next trade union school in 1949, J. A. Mack. He was an experienced Oxford tutor who had begun his career teaching tutorial classes in philosophy in the Potteries. According to Mack, 'the exhilaration of last year's school arose out of the clash, not of opinion, but of methods of discussion, in which the method of free discussion won in a fair fight'. He recalled that 'the essential difference between an Oxford school and a policy conference was demonstrated in a series of vigorous midnight and official sessions'; the 1948 conference, whatever the differences between participants, had 'ended with a general feeling that the Oxford method of following the argument wherever it goes had again justified itself'. This would seem to sustain the investigating Committee's conclusions. Nevertheless, if many of the problems had stemmed from some participants' unfamiliarity with academic culture, Mack recalled specifically political problems also: 'Whether implicit or explicit, there was last year a left-wing tendency to try and rig the discussion—as in some trade union meetings—so as to produce a "swing" towards an already approved "line". I found this (on my arrival on the Monday) being openly discussed and resented by the non-left-wingers.' Interestingly, he wrote of 'the high standard' of the 1948 trade union school and compared the 1949 school unfavourably because it 'seemed to be duller, more conformist'.[77]

In regard to the administration of the Wedgwood Memorial College, however, the Committee upheld some of the allegations made. Though they found no evidence that tutors had turned classes into vehicles for their own views, they were more critical about the political balance of the programmes for trade union schools and conferences at the college.

In these courses a very large proportion of the tutors and lecturers have been persons known to be in sympathy with the Communist Party. The evidence before the Committee does not, in their opinion, support a suggestion that

[76] Quoted by Fieldhouse, ibid. 41. The extract is from the Tutorial Classes Committee's 'review' of the school, apparently written afterwards for the students who attended, and in the 'trade union course (Queen's 1948) file' in the Oxford University Archives. This file cannot be located.

[77] J. A. Mack, 'Course on Trade Unions, Planning and Industrial Management, The Queen's College, Oxford, 2–9 July 1949. Report of Director of Studies', unpub. paper in 'Trade Union Education. Policy Documents from 1947', DES/F/4/1/1, Oxford University Archives.

intentional partiality was shown in the teaching provided at these courses—indeed, they have reliable testimony to the contrary—but they believe that when highly controversial contemporary problems are under discussion a body of teachers drawn from a narrow range of political opinion is unlikely to present an adequate and comprehensive picture of the issues involved.[78]

The committee concluded that the Warden of the college, J. O. N. Vickers, a Communist Party member appointed by Hodgkin in 1946 and responsible for the academic programme there, had committed 'an error of judgement . . . in not taking care to balance the disproportionate element among tutors' in trade union courses.[79] Vickers had read History at Cambridge in the late 1930s and had learnt the craft of a tutor—and he was a very gifted teacher—holding classes in prisoner-of-war camps across Europe between 1940 and 1945.[80] In North Staffordshire he had tried to establish around him a like-minded group to undertake the work with trade unions. Tutors with a different politics were effectively excluded, and their complaints at this treatment were also important in prompting the Delegacy's investigation.[81] It would seem that Vickers demurred when asked by the Delegacy to ensure a wider range of opinion on the courses he organized. He thus set down one of the key problems between himself and Oxford: 'My inability to see my way to agree to impose political tests on my full-time colleagues, or to be guided in the choice of tutors by any other considerations than teaching ability, integrity, and knowledge of the subject on the one hand, and student demand on the other.'[82] But this was not the only problem. Hodgkin actually referred to Vickers in a letter from this period as 'uncontrollable' and it would seem that his forceful views on the type of education that should be provided—and who should provide it—led to problems in his relationships with others.[83] Lucy Sutherland wrote that he 'had not shown those qualities of balance,

[78] Quoted by Fieldhouse, *Adult Education and the Cold War*, 48, from the Report of the Sub-committee of the Tutorial Classes Committee, 1949.

[79] Ibid.

[80] Staff Tutor's File, J. O. N. Vickers, DES/F/10/3/2, Oxford University Archives. See Vickers's application to the Oxford Delegacy and supporting testimonials.

[81] Discussion with D. J. Wenden, All Souls College, Oxford, 16 Aug. 1988. Wenden was appointed to North Staffs in 1948. He recalled that the tutors already there confidently expected another candidate, a Communist Party member, to be given the job, and isolated him on his arrival. Wenden took over temporarily as Warden of Wedgwood Memorial College after Vickers left.

[82] J. O. N. Vickers to T. L. Hodgkin, 25 May 1949, Vickers, Staff Tutor's File.

[83] T. L. Hodgkin to H. P. Smith (n.d., but probably written in the spring of 1949 because of the reference to 'J.V. going'), Vickers, Staff Tutor's File.

tact and capacity to work with other bodies and individuals which they believe to be essential in the Warden of a residential College'.[84] Vickers himself accepts that he behaved 'unwisely', and, in his own words, 'deserved to go'.[85] His three-year contract was not renewed in 1949. But his undoubted qualities as a teacher and leader, which the Tutorial Classes Committee certainly recognized, led to letters of protest and concern from several local union branches and trades' councils.[86]

At the same time the contract of another tutor in North Staffordshire, J. W. Campbell, was not renewed as well. Yet this would seem to have been for purely professional reasons: at a time when the standard of extramural education had become a sensitive issue, Campbell was adjudged to be teaching below the level required, and, as Hodgkin wrote to him, 'the decision was taken on academic grounds'.[87] Campbell was a highly unconventional figure—a black American Unitarian minister who had 'been socialist candidate for the Governorship of Massachussets three times' in the 1930s.[88] In one letter to Hodgkin protesting about his treatment, Campbell reminded Hodgkin that his jaw had dropped when Lindsay had appointed him.[89] Campbell spent a year studying at the University of London in 1939–40. He taught classes for the Eastern District of the WEA and for the Cambridge Board of Extra-Mural Studies from 1941, and in 1945 was appointed by the Oxford Delegacy. There is evidence that he was genuinely gifted at stimulating students who lacked an academic background, but it did not save him.[90] It would seem that he was counselled about his teaching at

[84] Lucy Sutherland to 'Dear Master' (A. D. Lindsay?), 7 July 1949, Vickers, Staff Tutor's File.

[85] Discussion with J. O. N. Vickers, Rewley House, Oxford, 4 Nov. 1988. Letter to the Author from J. O. N. Vickers, 5 Aug. 1994.

[86] See letters to the Oxford Delegacy from A. Goodwin, Assistant Secretary of the National Society of Pottery Workers, 13 June 1949; W. E. Myatt, Secretary of the Newcastle and District Trades Council, 16 June 1949; M. C. Dunn, District Secretary of the Amalgamated Engineering Union in North Staffs, 15 June 1949 in Vickers, Staff Tutor's File.

[87] T. L. Hodgkin to J. W. Campbell, 28 Oct. 1949, J. W. Campbell, Staff Tutor's File, DES/F/10/3/1, Oxford University Archives.

[88] See the testimonial from Professor John MacMurray in Campbell, Staff Tutor's File.

[89] J. W. Campbell to T. L. Hodgkin, 4 Nov. 1949, Campbell, Staff Tutor's File.

[90] See Campbell to Hodgkin, 24 May 1945, in which he discusses the reaction of his students on learning that he would be leaving the Delegacy. See also Hodgkin to Campbell, 28 Oct. 1949: 'We know your admirable qualities, and I should have liked to have seen it possible for you to continue to do the kind of work which specially appeals to you and for which you have a special gift.' See also the letter

some stage but 'deliberately chose to follow his own path instead'.[91] It has been suggested that Campbell was a Trotskyist and that he may have been a victim of a political purge also.[92] All that can be said in response is that the file of papers concerning his case makes no reference to politics as a cause for the non-renewal of his contract, though that is hardly conclusive. And in three long letters that Campbell sent to Hodgkin and to H. P. Smith, the Secretary of the Tutorial Classes Committee, about his case, he did not discuss his opinions or affiliations at all but concentrated on the issue of his academic abilities.[93] The only reference to politics is of an oblique kind: in his letter to Smith he compared the high-handed behaviour of the Tutorial Classes Committee to similar behaviour recently on the part of the Labour Party and TUC in regard to the 'rank and file'. It is a significant comparison, of course, because the supposedly dictatorial methods at issue were being applied to the left wing in the Labour Party and unions at this time, but Campbell did not give any hint that such methods were applied to him because of his opinions. He was only making a comparison to explain *the way* he had been treated.[94] The absence of evidence of a political motive in Campbell's case is hardly proof that politics were not at issue: it is in the nature of things that political disputes are often presented in other ways. But the academic reasons given for the non-renewal of his contract are plausible. Both testimonials sent to the Delegacy in support of his application in 1945 suggested a lack of academic distinction. One admitted that 'He is not brilliant intellectually; but he is adequate on American History and on social philosophy in the widest sense'.[95] And according to the other, from H. L. Beales, 'Not

of support for Campbell from G. Penkethman, 1 Apr. 1949, and H. P. Smith's response to a letter from Mrs A. Sylvester of the Baddeley Green WEA branch, 10 June 1949. Campbell, Staff Tutor's File.

[91] H. P. Smith to T. L. Hodgkin, 10 Nov. 1949, Campbell, Staff Tutor's File.

[92] Fieldhouse, *Adult Education and the Cold War*, 50–1.

[93] See Campbell to T. L. Hodgkin, 24 May 1949 and 4 Nov. 1949; Campbell to H. P. Smith, 11 Oct. 1949, Campbell, Staff Tutor's File. In the letter to Smith, Campbell recalled an incident at a 'refresher course' in Balliol when he had publicly contended that he would 'not try to explain Hitler without reference to Kant' and elicited a 'loud guffaw'. It obviously pained him and may have focused concerns about his teaching. To have linked idealism to Nazism in Balliol of all places, where Lindsay had written several books on Kant, could only have been a bad move.

[94] Campbell to Smith, 11 Oct. 1949, Campbell, Staff Tutor's File. As Campbell put it in regard to the National Executive of the Labour Party and the TUC, 'The decisions of these bodies may be wise, but the method by which they are effected is killing any reality of democracy for the majority.'

[95] Testimonial from Professor J. MacMurray, Campbell, Staff Tutor's File.

primarily the scholar, he has all the other gifts for a full-time tutor-ship & he is not deficient in the academic equipment, either. He is sometimes underrated by academic people—they all come to respect him & his intellectual power in the end.'[96] The evidence points to a simple and prosaic conclusion: that a mistake had been made in appointing Campbell in the first place at a time when a large number of staff were engaged in a hurry. Lindsay may be convicted of a failure of personal judgement in 1945 but there are no grounds for contending that this was part of a purge. Campbell's case was a separate matter from that of Vickers, but became entangled with it in the spring and summer of 1949 and hence associated with politi-cal differences between the Oxford Delegacy and some of its tutors.

The affair was complicated further because, in the late 1940s the Delegacy also fell foul of the Colonial Office over the involvement of several Oxford tutors in the attempt to establish extramural education in association with universities in Nigeria and the Gold Coast. There were many ironies in this episode. The idea of work-ing in West Africa had come from George Wigg. He had visited West Africa towards the end of the war to report on army education and had suggested to Lindsay that the University consider planting liberal adult education classes in the region. The 'impressions gained there by countless talks with Africans and Europeans, convinced [Wigg] that an enormous and vigorous field for work on Extension course lines is ready to be developed in the larger centres of popu-lation in West Africa.'[97] But the responsibility for doing this fell on Hodgkin, who was a totally committed supporter of movements for colonial independence. Wigg believed that 'a conception of educa-tion which did not lead to a job, but rather to unpaid service to the community, will be something very new on the coast, but some day it must be started if self-government is not to remain a meaningless slogan'. Hodgkin seemed to agree: 'I believe that even a small nu-cleus of people trained to think out their own answers to the prob-lems which face them, could make a big contribution to the future of their country.'[98] But whether Wigg and Hodgkin really meant the same thing, and would have concurred on the desirable form of self-government in the future, is debatable.

[96] Testimonial from Mr H. L. Beales, 29 July 1945, Campbell, Staff Tutor's File.
[97] 'University Extension Lectures Committee. Proposal Regarding University Extension Courses in West Africa. 9 March 1946', Oxford University Archives, DES/F/16/6/1, fos. 1–2. For an account of the affair, see Michael Omolewa, 'Ox-ford University and the Planting of Adult Education in Nigeria 1945–50', *Journal of Educational Administration and History*, 7 (1975), 28–39.
[98] T. L. Hodgkin, 'Secretary's Visit to Nigeria 1947', DES/F/16/6/1, fo. 11.

Hodgkin visited West Africa in early 1947 to assess the situation, and his subsequent report certainly recognized the likelihood of political difficulties ahead, but ironically again, he saw them as emanating from Nigerians rather than the British government. He noted

a general tendency to suspicion on the side of groups that I met of the motives of Oxford University in putting forward this scheme. A number of those with whom I talked thought that these courses might be intended as a substitute for a degree course . . . Others tended to believe that the initiative must in reality have come from the Colonial Office or from the Nigerian Government rather than from Oxford. Others, that no tutor sent from England could conceivably handle controversial problems objectively, and would inevitably act as an apologist for the Government.[99]

The Colonial Office was aware of these expected difficulties and suggested limiting the involvement of the colonial governments in order not to compromise the project 'in the eyes of certain leaders of African opinion'.[100]

In the event, such suspicions were allayed: 'Students, who, almost without exception, expected to be subjected to propaganda, became co-operative once they were convinced that it was not part of the scheme to change, or to confirm, their existing opinions, but rather to impart information and set certain standards of logic and relevance in discussions on controversial topics.'[101] After a successful pilot project in the summer of 1947,[102] Oxford tutors, including Tony McLean, a veteran of the International Brigade in the Spanish Civil War, who had found his way into ABCA and then into the Oxford Delegacy, and Henry Collins, the distinguished labour historian, went out to the region and began teaching standard courses on 'Problems of Modern Government', 'Political Theory' and 'The Making of Modern Nations'.[103] This was staple, uncontroversial fare back home, but such courses inevitably raised issues connected with colonial independence. Perhaps the tutors concerned were too mindful of their students' preconceptions and prejudices and tried

[99] Ibid., fo. 8.

[100] 'University Extension Lectures in West Africa. Copy of a letter received from the Colonial Office', 29 May 1946, DES/F/16/6/3.

[101] 'Report on Extra-Mural Classes held in the Western Provinces of Nigeria, May–July 1948', DES/F/16/6/1, fo. 2.

[102] T. L. Hodgkin, 'Extension Courses in West Africa', 23 Oct. 1947, DES/F/16/6/1.

[103] For Hodgkin's suggested syllabuses, see 'Report on Secretary's Visit to the Gold Coast, 1947', DES/F/16/6/3. On McLean, see Jack Woolford, 'Tony McLean: A Memoir', Box 2(A) i, 'Personalia, Obituaries and Memoirs', Adult Education Reference Library, Rewley House Library, Oxford.

too hard to conciliate them. More likely, they were sympathetic to their aspirations for self-government and independence. But the real problem was extramural education itself, the kind of subjects it examined, and the open discussion it promoted. The whole ethos of adult education was at odds with the interests of British colonial administration at this time.

There is something essentially comical in the enterprise since nothing could have been more likely to stir up political unrest than a few free exchanges between left-wing tutors and professional, well-educated, English-speaking West Africans, all of whom had benefited from a secondary education, in a WEA-type class.[104] There is no reason to doubt the good faith of the Delegacy: Wigg, Hodgkin, Lindsay and others evidently believed that adult education could be extended to the overseas colonies just as it had been extended to the English provinces half a century before, and believed that it was needed at this stage more than ever. But their conceptions of what political and civic purpose might be achieved by this new form of university extension probably differed very considerably, and, like almost everyone else, they may have miscalculated the speed and strength of the development of indigenous independence movements in the wake of the Second World War. It proved impossible to deliver staid, traditional, and uncontroversial liberal adult education courses in such circumstances. Official unease grew inside the Colonial Office through 1948 and 1949, after which the Delegacy's assistance and influence in the region was formally curtailed: the Colonial Office 'sheered away from us for political reasons' as Thomas Hodgkin explained to his successor, Frank Jessup, in 1952.[105] As Raymond Williams put it, 'the Delegacy was perceived not simply as an internal conspiracy but subversive externally'.[106] It remains to add that several Oxford tutors also fell foul of the armed forces in this period. Service education continued after the war and was largely provided by tutors from extramural departments. But after 1947–8 and the onset of the Cold War, the armed forces became far more suspicious of tutors suspected of Marxist opinions or Communist Party connections. Some Oxford tutors were among those from various extramural departments from whom the services

[104] On the social and educational background of the students, see 'Report on Extra-Mural Classes held in the Western Provinces of Nigeria, May–June 1948', fo. 2.

[105] T. Hodgkin to F. Jessup, 6 May 1952, File 'Appointment of New Secretary', Papers of Frank Jessup, Rewley House, Oxford.

[106] Williams, *Politics and Letters*, 80.

withdrew accreditation: they were no longer acceptable as teachers of service personnel.[107]

The action of the Delegacy in response to its internal problems has been referred to as 'an early form of British McCarthyism'. In an example of 'establishment ruthlessness' the Delegacy 'was ruthlessly purged'.[108] The association of the Oxford Delegacy with some sort of political witch-hunt in the late 1940s is widespread and there are many legends about what happened. Allegations of political bias in education and investigations into it are intrinsically distasteful and automatically evoke laudable and honourable liberal protest in support of freedom of expression. This is as it should be. But an automatic ascription of blame to 'the establishment' in this affair should be resisted. There is a case to be made in defence of the actions of the Tutorial Classes Committee and senior figures in Oxford.

First, was this purge 'ruthless'? Complaints from several quarters were investigated carefully and at length. Many were simply dismissed; indeed, in regard to the 1948 trade union school, the Committee effectively held some of the more narrow-minded trade unionists responsible for the disruptions and disagreements. Some allegations, essentially concerned with the professionalism and judgement of one tutor, were upheld in regard to a specific situation. And as a result, when his contract was up for review, it was not renewed.[109] That is the sum of it, and the tutor concerned and central figure in the affair admits that he behaved 'unwisely'.[110] It is true that from March 1949, when Frank Pickstock became Secretary of the Tutorial Classes Committee, the atmosphere in the Delegacy changed and relationships were tense for several years into the mid-1950s. Over time, other tutors implicated in these events left, though of their own accord. Hodgkin's position became untenable, for example; his judgement had been called in question, he had evidently lost control of members of his staff, and though it would seem that he dissociated himself from Vickers in early 1949, left him to his fate, and placed himself on the side of the Tutorial

[107] Fieldhouse, *Adult Education and the Cold War*, ch. 5, esp. pp. 85–7.

[108] R. W. Johnson, 'Moooovement', *London Review of Books*, 12/3 (1990), 5–6. (A review of books about Raymond Williams.)

[109] It is important to note that until the recommendations of the Habakkuk Committee were enacted in the early 1970s, Staff Tutors did not have tenure. It was standard practice to renew contracts every three or five years.

[110] I have discounted Campbell's case because it is not clear that politics were involved in it.

Classes Committee, he lacked the confidence of all parties.[111] He resigned in 1952 and left to travel through Africa, making contact and friendships with some of the most influential African leaders of the period, including Kwameh Nkruma, Tom Mboya, Julius Nyrere and Franz Fanon. He became a distinguished historian of that continent, held a post in the University of Ghana, and eventually returned to an Oxford lectureship in the Government of New States in 1965.[112] But several tutors who were known to be members of the Communist Party continued to work for the Delegacy in the 1950s, including Michael Carritt, Tony McLean, and Henry Collins, who had collaborated with Vickers in North Staffordshire and who was apparently given to wondering through the 1950s why he had not been forced out as well.[113] The case of Vic Allen, who specialized in trade union education and history is also instructive. As a WEA tutor in South Lancashire he came under pressure for his public support of the Chinese Revolution and his opposition to the Korean War, and was threatened with dismissal. Yet he was appointed to a position in the Oxford Delegacy in 1951.[114] Another tutor, A. T. D'Eye, who was based in Kent and who was a very public supporter of all things Soviet, was a constant embarrassment to Oxford over three decades but nothing was done to dislodge him. D'Eye had antagonized the WEA District and, because of his forthright pro-Soviet views, could not be found classes; groups did not want him as a tutor. He strained relations between the WEA and Oxford in the south-east and between the WEA and local organizations in the District. But he was tolerated throughout. The Delegacy merely monitored the situation from time to time, and tried, where possible, to smooth over the problems he caused.[115] In other words, there is relatively little evidence of ruthlessness. Party members, fellow-travellers and academic Marxists continued to work for the Delegacy after 1949, though it had been made clear that there was now a firm prohibition on mixing together personal politics and teaching. 'New limits had been drawn and a minority of Marxists would be

---

[111] For evidence that all amity had broken down between them, see Vickers to Hodgkin, 14 June 1949, Vickers, Staff Tutor's File. The evidence in the personal files of Vickers and Campbell suggests that Hodgkin went along with the decisions, and that he was influenced and guided in his conduct towards both men by Smith. Note Smith's comment to Hodgkin in a letter dated 10 Nov. 1949: 'How they would rejoice to drive a wedge between you and the Committee', Campbell, Staff Tutor's File.   [112] *The Times*, 26 Mar. 1982, 10.
[113] I owe this point to Douglas Hewitt who was a colleague and friend of Collins.   [114] Fieldhouse, *Adult Education and the Cold War*, 24–5.
[115] Ibid. 26–7.

tolerated so long as they did not come to exercise more than a minority influence.'[116]

Secondly, was this McCarthyism? Aspects of the affair undoubtedly bear a resemblance to the contemporary political purges in the United Sates, where membership of the Communist Party, or suspicion of socialist or pro-Soviet sympathies, often was the issue, and was enough, in itself, to justify dismissal and public opprobrium. But in the United States there was no tolerance whatsoever for Marxist academics, Party members and sympathizers; nor for more moderate socialists or innocents of no particular politics whatsoever, who nevertheless fell foul of authorities, often acting arbitrarily, in all walks of American life, and who were to be numbered in their thousands. While it is easy enough to pigeon-hole the affair as a local form of McCarthyism, and while in some respects that is understandable and also justifiable, in other respects the affair was not a clear-cut example of a political purge, and the authorities did not behave in an obviously illiberal, arbitrary, and dictatorial manner.

Thirdly, who or what was 'the Establishment' in this affair? The committee that inquired into the allegations included, in Lindsay, Clay, and Cole, three of the most senior figures in the adult education movement who hardly fit the conventional image that the term evokes. The enquiry might have been undertaken by true conservatives; in fact it was left to people who in many respects had established the very traditions and conventions of the adult education movement at issue. Cole would probably have found his ascription to the 'establishment' a great joke. And it is important to note that it was not the Delegacy and University which prosecuted the purge; rather, they reacted to the complaints of senior figures in the WEA and trade union movement. If an 'establishment' of any type was involved, it was of a right-wing Labourist variety. The Delegacy found itself caught up in a wider Cold War conflict within the labour movement between right and left. To its credit, the committee's comments on the allegations raised against tutors at the Queen's College trade union school showed a degree of contempt for the crude anti-Communism of the more dedicated Labour cold warriors.

Sympathy for the group of tutors at the centre of the affair is certainly not misplaced. Many of them were exhilarated by Labour's victory in 1945 and believed that the movement's time had come once again: that adult education could assist in the building of a new society and a new popular consciousness. The entire tutorial

[116] John McIlroy, 'Border Country: Raymond Williams in Adult Education', pt. 1, *Studies in the Education of Adults*, 22/2 (Oct. 1990), 139.

team in North Staffordshire apparently went canvassing for George Wigg in Dudley at the 1945 election to prove the point, though they may have come to regret their enthusiasm for the candidate in time.[117] They can more easily be convicted of misplaced idealism than political conspiracy. Indeed, their youth may be a key to understanding the episode; they lacked the restraints of experience and came into conflict with an older generation who had as little sympathy with their methods as with their politics. This is captured in Smith's comment to Hodgkin that 'these boys have shown that they are prepared to break the work to which many others have given a lifetime of devotion, just to get their own way'.[118] They evidently saw adult education as an important arena in which to develop a socialist politics and build a socialist culture, not least because of its contacts with the trade unions. It was this that drew them to North Staffordshire. They also grew critical of what they saw as the timorousness of Attlee's administration. Domestic reforms seemed half-hearted, as in the case of a nationalization programme that stopped short of workers' control of industry, and they opposed the government's anti-Sovietism. In 1945 they may have believed they spoke with and for their students. By mid-1947 the public mood had changed, the Cold War was an accepted reality, and as a group, these tutors were no longer in step with majority opinion within the Labour movement.[119] There was a parallel to this in the fortunes of the army's renamed Bureau of Current Affairs, which by 1947, was 'consciously attempting to preserve an attitude to foreign affairs now accepted only by an increasingly isolated minority', and which, in consequence, lost influence in, and control over, postwar army education.[120]

As public attitudes altered, so the sensitivity and professionalism of the traditional tutor should have supervened. If we think back to the first tutorial classes, what is so striking is the sympathy of the tutors for the opinions and experience of their students. Tawney and his colleagues worked with the grain, respecting the attitudes they came across. If these were to change it was to be as a product of the education itself rather than as the consequence of any propagandizing by the tutor. In a letter Tawney wrote to Mansbridge in 1923 he explained that 'what is wanted in Tutorial Classes is . . . teaching which takes account of, and is related to, the dominant

---

[117] Letter from Bridget Hill to the author, 17 Aug. 1994.
[118] H. P. Smith to T. L. Hodgkin, 10 Nov. 1949, Campbell, Staff Tutor's File.
[119] For evidence of the change in public mood, see Mass Observation, *Peace and the Public* (London, 1947), 23.
[120] Mackenzie, *Politics and Military Morale*, 205.

interests of the students'. It was easy enough for the tutor to teach undergraduates and lead 'them through the conventional course'. But 'in extra-mural work the students' interests determine the direction of the study & he must follow them'. Extramural students 'are not worse educated but differently educated from himself and his academic friends'. Contact with them should lead him 'to revise his own conclusions . . . and to supplement his ignorance by their experience'.[121] As Cole had written in 1912, 'We must always keep in mind the general principle that it is our business, not to force our own whimsies on an ungrateful people, but ourselves to be grateful for the privilege of giving intelligent men and women what they want'.[122]

What was lacking at Wedgwood Memorial College in the late 1940s was this quality of sympathy. In pursuing a political project without respect for the views of some of their students, tutors antagonized them, which was hardly likely to assist them in the enterprise (if this it was) of infiltrating and influencing the trade union movement. Adult education was supposed to be about winning the confidence of the community. Instead, local people in Barlaston knew the college as 'the Kremlin'.[123] As one tutor who was then teaching in Kent and East Sussex put it, such partisanship and stridency was 'a weapon in the hands of critics and an alienator of potential students'.[124] And in antagonizing the WEA and trade unions, they compromised the Tutorial Classes Committee in Oxford and undermined confidence in it—and mutual confidence was a crucial element in the relationship between dons and workers. It is for this reason that those involved were guilty of a lack of professionalism, and it was professionalism rather than politics that was at the heart of the affair. In an important part of the *1919 Report* concerning 'the state and adult education' it was argued that 'the basis of discrimination between education and propaganda is not the particular opinions held by the teacher or the students, but the intellectual competence and quality of the former and the seriousness and continuity of study of the latter'.[125] Though it is commonly believed that this episode was about 'the particular opinions held by the

---

[121] R. H. Tawney to A. Mansbridge, 12 June 1923, Mansbridge papers, lxiiiA, British Library, Add. MS 65257, fos. 97–9.

[122] G. D. H. Cole, 'Socialism and Education 12/8/12', G. D. H. Cole Papers, Nuffield College, Oxford, B2/16, fos. 10–11.

[123] Fieldhouse, *Adult Education and the Cold War*, 45.

[124] Woolford, 'The South-Eastern District of the WEA', 8. Woolford was actually referring to Kent and East Sussex.

[125] *Adult Education Committee, Final Report*, 118.

teacher(s)' and though this certainly was an issue, it would be more accurate to see it as a question of 'intellectual competence and quality'.

Professor Fieldhouse would seem to hold the first of these two positions. He has contended that in the late 1940s 'the liberal tradition of adult education was besieged by cold war anticommunism'. This anticommunism threatened 'to eliminate the liberal approach ... which aimed to give students access to a whole range of arguments and to develop their critical faculties so that they could question all assumptions, formulate alternative interpretations, and come to their own conclusions about the important issues of the day'.[126] This argument could be turned on its head if applied specifically to events in Oxford. In the eyes of Lindsay and Cole, who had helped to create and sustain that very liberal tradition, it was threatened also by naïve tutors abusing the privilege of their position and the trust invested in them by their students. Pushing the Party line and lining up a series of like-minded tutors seemed to them equal threats to the breadth and tolerance of traditional liberal adult education. A generation and more before these events, the Plebs had sought to mix education and political commitment and had chosen the honest course of trying to establish their own institutions and educational independence. As a method of action it commands the respect Cole gave it. But Cole, as we have seen, believed implicitly in the liberal tradition, and apparently reacted with some determination when he learnt of attempts to undermine it from within in 1948.[127] In other words, if the issue is taken to be the tradition of liberal open-mindedness and tolerance in the adult education movement there is another and obverse way of understanding it, in which the threats to the liberal tradition came not from crude anticommunism but from a form of clumsy and incompetent propagandism. Whether the affair is seen in these political terms or, as I think more appropriate, in terms of competence and professionalism, the limited action taken by the Tutorial Classes Committee in Oxford seems justifiable, if hardly to be welcomed or applauded.

III

Raymond Williams had joined the Delegacy in 1946 and was to spend sixteen years teaching for it. His role in the events of the late

---

[126] Fieldhouse, *Adult Education and the Cold War*, 92.

[127] D. J. Wenden apparently told Cole about the situation he had discovered in North Staffs after his appointment there in 1948. Cole began moves inside the

1940s, or rather the lack of a role, has recently been questioned.[128] Williams was not involved in any direct way because the political problems of the late-1940s did not affect Kent and East Sussex where he was based. He was never implicated in any allegations of malpractice, and there is no evidence of his views on the conduct of colleagues or on the affair as a whole at the time. Yet he gave at least two versions of his later responses, and they are strikingly different. Reflecting on these events in the interviews in 1979 conducted by the *New Left Review* that comprised the book *Politics and Letters*, he spoke of 'a violent assault' on the organization of the Delegacy which 'was seen as a Communist cell' and which amounted to 'a sharp local form of the Cold War'.[129] Yet in 1983 in a memorial lecture for his friend and extramural colleague, the much-loved Tony McLean, that was given before a WEA audience, he was critical of 'crude versions which would have converted this educational practice [of adult education] into ideological training and propaganda'. He spoke of the generation who came into adult education in the 1930s and who wished to build a 'social consciousness' adequate to deal with 'the crises of modern capitalist society'. He noted 'the resulting complications—the emotional, intellectual, and social complications of that generation, which entered with that kind of intention'. As he explained further,

The whole problem was that people arriving with a message, their kind of message in the bottle, had to learn, if they were to enter in any sustained way the experience of Adult Education, that even people who agreed that the point of Adult Education was the building of an adequate social consciousness, didn't, in that sense, want messages. I mean they didn't want the conclusions of arguments: they wanted to reach their own conclusions.[130]

It is difficult to reconcile these two accounts. Williams himself certainly wanted to 'reach [his] own conclusions'. Though he had been a member of the Communist Party while first at Cambridge, his formal membership lapsed in 1941, and he distanced himself from the party over time.[131] By 1958 he could express his opposition to 'the Marxist interpretation of culture' for its 'insistence that if you honestly want socialism you must write, think, learn in prescribed ways', though he returned to Marxism and it informed his academic work in the 1970s and 1980s.[132] Perhaps his greatest

Delegacy to find out what was happening at the Wedgwood Memorial College. Discussion with D. J. Wenden, 16 Aug. 1988.

[128] Johnson, 'Moooovement', 5.   [129] Williams, *Politics and Letters*, 80.
[130] Williams, 'Adult Education and Social Change', 12, 21.
[131] Williams, *Politics and Letters*, 52–3, 92–3.
[132] Raymond Williams, *Culture is Ordinary* (London, 1990; first pub. 1958), 11.

quality as a teacher and critic was this very independence in his outlook and judgement: it was certainly noted by many people who came into contact with him. But the prevalent conception of Williams as an isolated intellectual who singlehandedly redrew the historical map of British culture in books written 'on the margins' whilst he was an Oxford extramural tutor needs substantial revision. It misconceives the adult tradition itself and shows a fundamental misapprehension of what Williams was doing in books like *Culture and Society* and *The Long Revolution*.

Williams came into adult education through the archetypal postwar route of army education. From a Welsh working-class and grammar school background he had spent the years 1939–41 at Trinity in Cambridge studying for Part I of the English Tripos. He went into the army and became an officer in an antitank regiment of the Guards Armoured Division, participating in the Normandy landings and the advance on Germany. For two years he was also an Army Education Officer.[133] He returned to Cambridge in the autumn of 1945 for his final year at the university. During this he taught a class for the Eastern District of the WEA. As the District Secretary wrote in a reference that helped him get his job with the Oxford Delegacy,

Williams, upon returning here from the B[ritish] A[rmy] O[f] [the] R[hine], fired by his experience of educational work with 'the chaps' in Germany and by what he heard of the W.E.A. came to see me to offer his services. Though he was reading English, he was prepared to offer Current International Affairs on the basis of his background of reading, plus his varied wartime experiences. I tried him out with a Terminal Course on International Affairs with a group in the Fenland, largely composed of agricultural workers, and he was a great success. Subsequently, single talks by him in other places earnt great praise from our branch members.[134]

Williams sat his finals, took a first, and then began work for the Oxford Delegacy. On his application he had offered to teach literature and drama, politics, and international relations: his first three classes in East Sussex during the winter of 1946–7 were in the last of these disciplines.[135] He spent the years between 1946–60 in the district, living in Seaford and Hastings. He then spent a single year in Oxford as a Senior Staff Tutor for the Berkshire, Buckinghamshire, and Oxfordshire District in 1960–1, before he was appointed to a lectureship in English at Cambridge.

[133] See Williams's application for a Staff Tutorship in the Oxford Delegacy, July 1946, Williams, Staff Tutor's File, DES/F/10/3/4, Oxford University Archives.
[134] Frank Jacques to H. P. Smith, 18 July 1946, Williams, Staff Tutor's File.
[135] F. Pickstock to W. E. Styler, 8 Jan. 1962, Williams, Staff Tutor's File.

As Frank Pickstock wrote soon after his departure, 'to say that he was successful as tutor is understating the case'. He was always in demand as a teacher and 'in later years he was almost too successful, and one or two of his classes became more like Extension Lecture Courses'. In 1946–7 the Delegacy organized five classes in East Sussex: in his last year there were twenty-two and Pickstock saw this as a measure of Williams's influence. He noted also Williams's great effect on his colleagues, and he concluded that he 'had something else; this something else was not just an academic brain, but the personality and purpose of an inspired educator'.[136] The judgement accords with Frank Kermode's recollection of Williams at his first Oxford Summer School in 1947 as 'the centre of academic attention. Though himself not long out of the Army, he struck me as a young man of enviable assurance and authority, exactly aware of what he was doing.'[137]

When Williams reflected on his years in adult education in *Politics and Letters* his remarks were notable for their criticism of the Oxford Delegacy and their extreme detachment from the whole experience of teaching adults. This may explain why another tutor of English in the Delegacy who knew Williams and who had worked with him, spoke of a sense that he had 'rather fouled his own nest' after moving to Cambridge.[138] Williams recalled problems over his syllabuses, which were unconventional because interdisciplinary. This was at the time, in the early 1950s, when the debate on standards in extramural classes, led by Raybould, was at its most intense. He was also critical of the turn towards management education in the Oxford Delegacy after 1960: 'it was at this point that I knew I wanted to move on.' His reservations were widely shared at the time, and latent tensions between liberal and vocational adult education are still a feature of extramural education today.

But there is something rather obtuse and self-righteous about Williams's impatience with 'these dreadful refresher courses for managers'.[139] As he would have known, extramural education was coming under increasing pressure to make itself 'relevant' to economic

---

[136] Ibid. (The letter was written to provide Styler, Professor of Adult Education at Hull University, with information on adult tutors who had also made a major contribution to scholarship for an article he was writing. See W. E. Styler, 'Recent Adult Education in Great Britain', *International Review of Education*, 8 (1962–3), 166–74.

[137] Frank Kermode, 'Professor Raymond Williams', *The Independent*, 28 Jan. 1988, p. 25.

[138] The remark was made by Douglas Hewitt, a Staff Tutor in English in the Oxford Delegacy from 1956–1988 in a discussion on the history of adult education in Oxford on 5 Jan. 1989. [139] Williams, *Politics and Letters*, 78–83.

life; the income generated by such courses could be used to subsidize traditional functions in liberal adult education like his own literature classes; and courses for managers had political utility for a department already so closely associated with the trade unions.[140] Management education was also a logical development of the empirical and pragmatic approach to industrial relations of the Oxford school of trade union studies. It had a rationale in purely institutional terms, in other words. More generally, it is not immediately clear why even a socialist should find the education of managers inappropriate for an extramural department. As one policy document put it some time later, 'Though the Delegacy's experience has been primarily with workers, it has developed an expertise which seems to render it specially well-qualified to enlarge the horizons and deepen the understanding of management in handling social relationships'.[141] Educating, and in the process, humanizing, the bosses may have a very obvious function and worthwhile outcome when seen in terms of working-class interests. There is a hint of unreality in Williams's remarks, therefore, even ingratitude, which is difficult to accept from a scholar who had the support and admiration of his colleagues, who gained so much from adult education that he used in his own work, and who wrote on hearing of his appointment in Cambridge 'that in many ways I am very sorry to be leaving'.[142]

Like the great tutors in the tradition, Williams learnt from his students and used their insights and his experience of teaching them, to inform his own thinking and writing. His pioneering study of *Communications* was based on 'classes for members of the Workers' Educational Association and for trade unionists'.[143] In his evening classes in East Sussex he set some of the texts and tried out some of the ideas later to be incorporated in *Culture and Society*.[144] And in a final statement before leaving Oxford and WEA teaching, he

---

[140] In 1983 Williams referred to 'the pressure, backed by funding, to train people for roles and jobs as preferable to the general education of human beings and citizens' (Williams, 'Adult Education and Social Change', 23). Though he is not specific about where the pressure was coming from, it suggests some awareness of the broader context in which university adult education was turned towards vocational education.

[141] 'Trade Union and Related Studies Committee. Future Policy' (n.d., probably 1969 or 1970), an anon. unpub. paper in 'Trade Union Education. Policy Documents from 1947', DES/F/4/1/1, Oxford University Archives.

[142] Williams to Pickstock, 26 Ap. 1961, Williams, Staff Tutor's File.

[143] Williams, *Communications*, 13.

[144] Tony McLean, 'Working with the South-Eastern District of the WEA: Some Reminiscences 1945–56', in *Adult Education and Social Change* (WEA South-Eastern

wrote of having 'discussed D. H. Lawrence with working miners' and 'television with apprentices in training'. These were 'formative experiences' in which 'I have learnt as much as I have taught'.[145] He was conscious, also, of the debt owed to the pioneers of adult education before him: indeed, it has been suggested that Williams himself came to hold 'a position similar to that occupied by Tawney and G. D. H. Cole in earlier years in Britain'.[146] And he used the tradition that linked him to them as a way of understanding the present. When he wrote about student unrest in the late summer of 1968, for instance, he related it to the struggle of working men to win not just an education but one in which they participated as equals. And he used the example to critique the notion of 'student power' and replace it with the more honourable conception, as he saw it, of an educational democracy.[147] He had earlier defined his 'own social purpose as the creation of an educated and participating democracy'.[148]

Williams gained from the adult tradition as much as he contributed to it, in other words. It gave him political anchorage, a model of educational practice, and, for a scholar deeply interested in lineages and historical development, whether of writers, concepts, or 'keywords', a deep personal attachment to a social and intellectual tradition. For these reasons we should be sceptical of portraits of Williams in the 1950s as isolated and unassociated with mainstream academic life. Perhaps he was, from some vantage points, at a sort of 'academic periphery'[149] and he did describe himself and his fellow-tutors taking classes through each winter 'as independent intellectuals'.[150] Indeed, at a particularly difficult moment in late 1950, when he felt overwhelmed with work, he tentatively asked for a transfer, 'as I should like to be nearer Oxford for many reasons, and in particular so as to be able to see more of, and work closer with two or three members of the English Faculty I have come to know'.[151] But it is simply wrong to contend that his most enduring work, *Culture and Society*, was 'written in isolation in the 1950s'

District, 1983), 38. See also Raymond Williams, 'Literature in Relation to History: 1850–1875', *Rewley House Papers*, 3/1 (1949–50), 36–44.

[145] Williams, *Open Letter to WEA Tutors*, 5.

[146] Derek Tatton, 'Raymond Williams, the WEA and "Towards 2003"', *Workers Education*, 3 (spring/summer 1988), 27.

[147] Raymond Williams, 'Different Sides of the Wall', *Guardian*, 26 Sept. 1968, 14.

[148] Williams, *Open Letter to WEA Tutors*, 3.

[149] Kermode, 'Raymond Williams', 25.

[150] Williams, 'Adult Education and Social Change', 10.

[151] Williams to Pickstock, 17 Nov. 1950, Williams, Staff Tutor's File.

and 'outside of any university discipline'.[152] Put simply, Williams's work in this period drew on the adult tradition, especially as it had been developed in Oxford since the late nineteenth century, and may be said to have presented this intellectual lineage and way of under-standing society to a large and receptive audience, many of them from a new generation of students, and part of a new socialist culture, who were unfamiliar with the themes it was rehearsing and reinterpreting.

Williams actually said this himself: *Culture and Society*, he wrote, 'gathered and tried to restate an existing tradition'.[153] For its subject was the same as that developed in Toynbee's lectures and Tawney's first classes on the history of economic transformation: the experi-ence of, and responses to, industrial capitalism in Britain. The dif-ference came only in the medium of analysis: Williams used literary and cultural evidence rather than the data of economic and social history to explain his theme. He united the traditional subject matter of the Oxford adult tradition—the attempt to explain to students where they, their jobs, and their communities came from—with the study of his own discipline, English literature. According to Williams, 'There was a time as an adult tutor when you felt a second class citizen if you were not teaching Economics or Politics, because that had been the first interpretation of what the business of creating social consciousness was'.[154] He helped change that himself. In effect, for a later generation of adult students more given to reading novels than accounts of eighteenth-century enclosures or of devel-opments in industrial technology, Williams attempted to create this social consciousness using the tools of a literary scholar—the analy-sis of texts and cultural traditions. As he explained in the book, his analysis of culture was attempting to subsume other ways of approaching these issues, and other discourses:

It might be said, indeed, that the questions now concentrated in the mean-ings of the word *culture* are questions directly raised by the great historical changes which the changes in *industry*, *democracy*, and *class*, in their own way, represent, and to which the changes in *art* are a closely related response. The development of the word *culture* is a record of a number of important and continuing reactions to these changes in our social, eco-nomic and political life, and may be seen, in itself, as a special kind of map by means of which the nature of the changes can be explored.[155]

---

[152] Alan O'Connor, *Raymond Williams: Writing, Culture, Politics* (Oxford, 1989), 55, 60.

[153] Williams, *The Long Revolution*, 8, 'Foreword to the Pelican edn.'.

[154] Williams, 'Adult Education and Social Change', 22.

[155] Raymond Williams, *Culture and Society 1780–1950*, 3rd edn. (Harmonds-worth, 1963), 16.

The subject of the book would have made sense to the students at Longton and Rochdale in 1908, certainly: it was 'an account and an interpretation of our responses in thought and feeling to the changes in English society since the late eighteenth century'.[156] They also had wanted to understand these changes, the better to control social developments in the future. Perhaps the conservative voices in the tradition—Burke positing a traditional, hierarchic, and reciprocal community in opposition to laissez-faire liberalism, or Southey's romantic organicism—were unfamiliar to the students of early tutorial classes. But a tradition including Cobbett's incantations against the destruction of an older, rural England; Owen's pioneering communitarianism; the early political and social rebellion of the Romantic poets; and the attempts to explore and understand industrial life in the novels of Dickens, Gaskell, Disraeli, Kingsley, and George Eliot, was known to many of the students of the late-Victorian and Edwardian eras. As Robert Roberts noted, the pre-1914 working class élite were dedicated readers of Ruskin, Dickens, Kingsley, and Carlyle.[157] And when Williams himself turned to Carlyle and Ruskin, he was going over the themes set before the many extension audiences in the industrial north lucky enough to have attended Hudson Shaw's great lectures on these figures, not to mention the young pioneers of extension in Oxford in the 1880s like Sadler and the 'Inner Ring', who actually heard Ruskin lecture for themselves.

William Morris, meanwhile, is the pivotal figure in Williams's tradition, for he transmuted a critique of materialism, industrialism, and capitalism into a positive political commitment to socialism, and wrote extensively about the true definition and meaning of culture in his essays on politics and aesthetics in the 1880s and 1890s. And Morris was the inspiration for very many extramural courses, students, and tutors, from G. D. H. Cole down. Indeed, he is still, as I know myself, having taught many courses on him to extramural classes in the late 1980s. It is no coincidence that in 1930 the Stoke Tutorial Class gave an original likeness of Morris, drawn in 1882 by H. Hopwood, to be hung in the Common Room at Rewley House, for Morris was in the bloodstream of the movement.[158] Williams also signalled his intellectual affiliations very clearly when he included a perceptive analysis of Tawney in *Culture and Society*. Williams noted Tawney's debt to Ruskin and Arnold: adult

[156] Ibid. 11.

[157] Robert Roberts, *The Classic Slum: Salford Life in the First Quarter of the Century*, 2nd edn. (Harmondsworth, 1973), 177.

[158] 'Notes and News', *Rewley House Papers*, 1 (1931), 175.

education, which had grown up on the critical tradition these two had established in the mid-Victorian period, was now fused with that tradition in the person of a professional historian who was also, like Ruskin and Arnold, 'a social critic and moralist'.[159] Adult education was now a part of the 'Culture and Society tradition' itself; that tradition had always been a part of adult education as developed through the alliance of dons and workers.

Similar points may be made about other books Williams wrote, notably *The Country and the City*. As he explained in the introduction to this study, the exploration of the relationship between these two environments, territories, concepts, and states of mind, owed a great deal to his own upbringing and experience. But the book was premised on the idea that images 'of country and city have been ways of responding to a whole social development'[160]—that writers in the past and 'many millions of people' living today have understood social and economic transformation in terms of the way it has altered landscapes, townscapes, their sense of space, and their relationship to the natural and built environment.[161] Thus an analysis of literary depictions of country and city became, in Williams's hands, an analysis of capitalism itself: 'the division and opposition of city and country, industry and agriculture, in their modern forms, are the critical culmination of the division and specialization of labour which, though it did not begin with capitalism, was developed under it to an extraordinary and transforming degree.'[162] Tawney wrote about enclosures; Williams about Goldsmith's 'Deserted Village'. Again, the central themes of economic and social history were approached by him through literary and cultural analysis.

The adult tradition was not identical to the lineage Williams constructed, of course: several of the twentieth-century authors he examined either lived and wrote too late to have been subsumed into it, like Orwell, or were, like Eliot, critics of a democratic culture. But it was close to it, overlapping constantly. Williams had taken his inheritance as an Oxford tutor, and used it to explore the same themes as his predecessors. But the exploration was in a different discourse, and was now presented for a conventional academic audience. There were other influences in Williams's work, of course: the practical criticism of I. A. Richards, the high moralism of Leavis, and Marxism. But it was as an adult tutor that Williams

---

[159] Williams, *Culture and Society*, 214.
[160] Raymond Williams, *The Country and the City*, 2nd edn. (London, 1975), 356. My understanding of this book has been assisted by discussion with my colleague at St Peter's College, Dr Eric Swyngedouw.
[161] Ibid. 11.   [162] Ibid. 366.

was especially well placed for such a reinterpretation of English cultural history: he was already part of an oppositional tradition which had grown out of the desire of tutors and students to comprehend and to assess what Toynbee had called, before working-class audiences, 'the Industrial Revolution'. And in so far as he was part of that tradition, *Culture and Society*, his most important work while he was in adult education, was not a definitively new account of its subject. It was a reinterpretation and 're-presentation'. It synthesized, but it did not truly innovate. It brought together the intellectual elements of the adult tradition, and fused them with the academic mainstream. Indeed, in a very real sense it made the adult tradition *into* the mainstream.

Williams's work has attracted a great deal of critical attention since his death. But rather little of it has examined his years in adult education and his debts to it.[163] We are now in a better position to appreciate what is wrong with some of the accounts of Williams's writing which are not grounded in an appreciation of his fidelity to the adult tradition. According to Stuart Hall, in *Culture and Society* Williams 'not so much engaged the map of English culture as redrew it' revealing 'a new configuration in the architecture of English critical thought, which we hardly glimpsed before'.[164] The configuration was not new, but axiomatic to an older socialist tradition with which young postwar intellectuals had lost contact. According to Terry Eagleton, Williams 'almost singlehandedly . . . transformed socialist cultural studies in Britain from the relative crudity of 1930s Marxism to an impressively rich, subtle and powerful body of theory'. Again Williams is pictured as an isolated pioneer, when he had behind him a whole tradition of learning and scholarship which he was linking to the academic mainstream.[165] In an otherwise helpful and insightful study of Williams as an adult tutor John McIlroy has argued that 'his distinctive contribution was largely an independent and individual one rather than made as part of a wider movement'.[166] In so far as Williams always demonstrated great self-possession and independence of institutional ties and constraints, this may be right. But his publications while an Oxford tutor owed

---

[163] John McIlroy and Sallie Westwood (eds.), *Border Country: Raymond Williams in Adult Education* (Leicester, 1993) is the honourable and most interesting exception.

[164] Stuart Hall, 'Only Connect: The Life of Raymond Williams', *New Statesman*, 115/2,967 (5 Feb. 1988), 20–1.

[165] Terry Eagleton, 'Professor Raymond Williams', *Independent*, 28 Jan. 1988.

[166] McIlroy, 'Border Country', pt. 2, *Studies in the Education of Adults*, 23/1 (Apr. 1991), 19.

a tremendous amount to the 'wider movement', in this case the specifically intellectual inheritance of adult education which formed the basis of his teaching and writing. Hence it is difficult to accept the argument that *Culture and Society* 'remains a major achievement in its reconstitution of a lost or suppressed tradition of opposition to the organization of society since the industrial revolution'.[167] The tradition was never lost, nor suppressed, but provided the intellectual and ideological basis for the university extension movement and the original alliance between dons and workers through the WEA in the early years of the century. And if in *The Long Revolution* Williams developed 'the central idea of a learning community, the cultural empowerment of the majority of the population, the excluded and disinherited', was he not at one with the central propositions of *Oxford and Working-Class Education* and the *1919 Report*?[168] Was not this what Green and Tawney and Temple and Smith had wanted also? It is in the nature of things that such ideas must be restated in each generation. But their restatement in this form by Williams, in a book about the historical development of education, literacy, and the institutions of culture more generally, was at one with the adult tradition he was part of himself.

Williams was fully conscious of the ways in which the adult tradition was fusing with conventional academic life at this time. Looking back in 1983 he noted how the interdisciplinary study of art, culture, history, and literature which had been going on for decades in the WEA was suddenly discovered by intramural higher education and proclaimed as the new subject of 'Cultural Studies' when taken across the divide by extramural tutors like Richard Hoggart and himself in the early 1960s.[169] And Edward Thompson as a tutor in the Leeds Extra-Mural Department was also drawing on the traditions and themes of adult education in ways consonant with Williams for his great books on William Morris and on *The Making of the English Working Class* at the moment of most profound social and economic transformation after 1780—the latter growing out of his classes to WEA groups in West Yorkshire in the 1950s and early 1960s.[170] Expressing sentiments that would have been axiomatic to the founders of the extension movement, Thompson explained that he 'went into adult education because it

---

[167] Ibid. 9.   [168] Ibid. 10.

[169] Williams, 'Adult Education and Social Change', 17.

[170] E. P. Thompson, *William Morris: Romantic to Revolutionary* (London, 1955); id., *The Making of the English Working Class* (London, 1963).

seemed to me to be an area in which I would learn something about industrial England, and teach people who would teach me. Which they did.'[171] In the late 1950s and early 1960s the study of literature, history, and modern culture more generally was invigorated, not to say transformed, by contact with the adult tradition. It is another example of innovations on 'the academic periphery' of adult education that have changed conventional university education in the past century.

Williams's themes were not new; it was the audience that had altered. By the early 1960s he was speaking to growing numbers of students in new university departments who eagerly accepted his ideas but had no sense of their provenance, and, therefore, of what they themselves owed to a former and rather different political and educational tradition. They were encountering his ideas on culture and its development at a time when the tradition that had helped form these ideas was itself in something of a decline. *Culture and Society* has won many plaudits over the years. If the present analysis is correct, it may be taken as the end point and apotheosis of the intellectual tradition established through the alliance of dons and workers. As Toynbee had seen in the early 1880s, the dons were rejecting orthodox economic theory and the workers were rejecting economic practice simultaneously. Together they developed a critical tradition, based on certain canonized writers, texts, and ideas, that informed their understanding of society and politics. Williams knew this tradition, and some of his early books were based on teaching it to adult classes. He encapsulated it, and he brought it into the mainstream at a singular moment when a new audience was open and ready to receive it in the early years of the 1960s. Like Hoggart, Thompson, and others, he transferred the adult tradition at a moment when it was itself under threat as extramural education was forced to find new functions and appeal to new audiences.

The tradition continues to have relevance in adult education as recent personal experience confirms. No book evoked as much interest, controversy, and personal identification in the extramural courses I taught in the 1980s as Martin Wiener's study of *English Culture and The Decline of the Industrial Spirit*, concentrating as it

[171] Henry Abelove, Betsy Blackmar, Peter Dimock, and Jonathan Schneer, 'E. P. Thompson', in id. (eds.), *Visions of History* (New York, 1983), 13. Thompson discussed the relationship of his teaching to his writing in the television programme, *A Life of Dissent: Remembering E. P. Thompson*, 'Rear Window', Channel 4, 18 Sept. 1993.

does on literary and cultural responses to industry and the national ambivalence to the values associated with business and enterprise.[172] And William Morris is still a protean figure. Courses on his life and work open up several different ways of connecting students with the traditional themes of adult education. To many students when they first enter a classroom, Morris may now be a pioneer of environmental politics rather than a pioneer socialist, but that in itself is a measure of his continuing relevance and a good point of departure. Morris's laments at the destruction of the countryside, the ugliness of towns and cities, the decline of taste in an 'age of shoddy', and the decay of community; his ideas on work and art; and the utopianism of *News from Nowhere*, still have the capacity to stimulate and move students as they did in the 1890s and early 1900s.

[172] Martin J. Wiener, *English Culture and the Decline of the Industrial Spirit 1850–1980* (Cambridge, 1981).

8

OXFORD AND WORKING-CLASS EDUCATION: AN ASSESSMENT

I

When Raymond Williams came to assess the contribution of adult education to general educational advance, he picked out three features of special note: 'the student's choice of subject, the relation of disciplines to actual contemporary living, and the parity of general discussion with expert instruction'.[1] He contrasted the 'rigid selection and distribution of specialized minority roles' in the modern university with the essence of adult education 'in which the whole society is seen as a learning process, and in which, consequently, access is open, not only for all people but for all their questions, across the arbitrary division of quotas and subjects. This is what adult education embodied, as a demand, at once educational and social; in fact political'.[2]

It was not merely a matter of celebrating those features of the tradition that made for democracy, flexibility, and relevance. To Williams, the tradition also embodied a vision of how society might be, 'a society in which it is assumed that society itself is an educative process, that society is a method of association and co-operation'.[3] Adult education was more than 'a matter of remedying deficit' or of 'meeting new needs': 'the deepest impulse was the desire to make learning part of the process of social change itself.'[4] In assessing the adult tradition, in other words, we must go beyond merely educational success to consider also its wider social aims and aspirations. It is proposed to do this by breaking down the tradition into its component parts and considering in turn the educational achievements

---

[1] Raymond Williams, *The Long Revolution*, 2nd edn. (Harmondsworth, 1965 edn.), 165.
[2] Raymond Williams, 'Different Sides of the Wall', *Guardian*, 26 Sept. 1968, 14.
[3] Raymond Williams, 'The Common Good', *Adult Education*, 34/4 (Nov. 1961), 192.
[4] Raymond Williams, 'Adult Education and Social Change', *Adult Education and Social Change. Lectures and Reminiscences in Honour of Tony McLean* (WEA South Eastern District, 1983), 12.

of the movement, the gains and losses to the workers, the contribution of the dons, and the specific relationship between Oxford and the labour movement as mediated through adult education.

Williams pointed to the method of adult education as one of its most distinctive contributions to the wider culture. Its traditions of voluntarism, self-governance, and dialogue between tutor and students over what is to be studied, look all the more distinctive, and all the more attractive, in an age when the state has begun to dictate what should be learnt and how. Internal democracy was highly prized: it gave students the opportunity to study what they believed answered their intellectual needs, and tutors the sense that what they were teaching was of unambiguous advantage to the groups before them. It was also, as Tawney and Cole recognized, a microcosm of 'the good society' to which the movement aspired. Adult education organized itself as a functioning model of the social aims it desired to achieve. But the educational contributions go further than this, for on the periphery of the modern university, adult education has had the freedom to experiment and innovate. In Oxford in particular, the ideals and the experience of adult education influenced the conceptualization of the PPE course, and, more recently, have shaped trade union education. Generally, the university disciplines of Geography, Economic History, English and more recently, Industrial Relations and Cultural Studies, owe a debt to adult education and the space it has given to teachers and students to follow unconventional ideas to their conclusions. And that very space, combined with the idealism of students and tutors alike, has helped preserve the idea of a liberal education at the heart of the adult tradition even to this day, in the face of political pressure to teach skills and to train rather than educate. It may seem paradoxical that on the periphery Jowett's ideas flourished and still flourish. It arises from the flexibility and the democracy that Williams admired: if a class wishes to spend a year studying *Paradise Lost* there is nothing to stop it. If groups decide that contemporary events dictate a knowedge of Russian history the only constraint is the availability of a qualified tutor. In 1875 *The Times* may be said to have set a challenge to the ancient universities:

The spirit of learning for learning's sake which Oxford and Cambridge have always kept alive must be planted in the new centres if the Universities are to extend their influence as well as their teaching . . . to bring the means of culture and intellectual advancement within the reach of all who are fitted by nature to profit by it is a task not unworthy of our great Universities.[5]

[5] *The Times*, 23 Sept. 1875, 7.

To have attempted this with some success for more than a century and to be doing it still is not an inconsiderable achievement. It is certainly an achievement to have protected liberal adult education (indeed, actually expanded it in terms of student numbers in Oxford in the past two decades) when extramural departments have found the financing of their traditional classes increasingly difficult.

The movement also has an honourable record in reaching the educationally underprivileged. The literature on the history of adult education is littered with laments for the failure to attract sufficient numbers of working-class men into lecture halls and classes. And the revelation that many audiences were socially mixed, if not lower-middle-class, in composition, is the message of many learned articles. This book merely echoes the message: at most times working-class males comprised a minority of students, and those who were drawn in from working-class communities were from Hoggart's 'earnest minority' or what one local extension enthusiast had called 'the cream of the working class'. Reaching further down to the unskilled and unassociated was much more difficult. But I do not see the need to lament this. For much of the period covered by this book the educational opportunities open to most of the people of Britain were meagre; in this sense, the majority, from many different classes, were educationally underprivileged, and the movement surely served a useful function if it attracted and held the middle and lower-middle classes as well as the workers. As John Carey has shown, the self-improving, intellectually aspiring clerk was the subject of the literary intelligentsia's contempt in the late-Victorian and Edwardian periods.[6] So much the worse for the littérateurs. But the type was a mainstay of extension and of tutorial classes, and in providing opportunities for such people the movement may be said to have made an honourable social contribution. Indeed, we may go further and question the assumptions about social attitudes and political behaviour that most historians bring to the study of this group. As the history of adult education suggests, many lower-middle-class students shared the consciousness as well as the income of working-class students and many contributed their skills to organizing the movement. The clerks were an important component of early Labour organizations and were especially notable for the idealism and desire for transcendence that characterize the adult tradition. It is when historians of the labour movement

---

[6] John Carey, *The Intellectuals and the Masses: Pride and Prejudice among the Literary Intelligentsia 1880–1939* (London, 1992), ch. 3, 'The Suburbs and the Clerks'.

forget the spirit and zeal of the pioneers that they also overlook the clerks. Their earnest desire for self-improvement should never be satirized; nor should they be left out of any history of labour's consciousness.

But the most important group of the underprivileged in this story are women. When Stuart began extension lecturing in the late 1860s, it was to groups of women. When Percival called for an initiative to tie together 'the Universities and the Great Towns' he could see that it would bring 'the essentials of a university education within reach of an indefinite number of young women'.[7] When Green introduced the first Oxford extension lecture in 1878 he included women among the groups likely to benefit from the scheme. And yet, as Maude Royden suspected when she suggested the creation of 'a Ruskin College for working-women . . . to a prominent member of the WEA' and he seemed close to fainting, the movement always thought and spoke in terms of working-class men, and may be said to have achieved its greatest social and educational success in a fit of absent-mindedness.[8] Indeed, if this book has been relatively silent about women in adult education it is because the sources themselves are unyielding on this subject; a movement run by men with men in mind, which nevertheless has been most successful in attracting women, has left rather little about its most faithful students. Part of the reason for this may be the existence of other organizations designed for the self-improvement of women—Women's Institutes which claimed the attention of at least one Oxford woman don, Grace Hadow;[9] the National Union of Townswomen's Guilds, the Women's Co-operative Guild, the Women's Voluntary Service, and so forth. Even if the ostensible aim of organizations like these was service to the community, they were important foci for educational activity, and probably reached a section of women that university adult education always neglected. But even those who *were* students in the movement were neglected. Many Oxford lecturers thought the less of the matinée 'sealskins': they forgot that provision for the higher education of the daughters of the middle classes has been inadequate in Britain until the present generation. Of whatever class, women take their place as the underprivileged group who have gained most from the adult tradition, as they do still.

---

[7] John Percival, *The Connection of the Universities and the Great Towns* (London, 1873), 14.

[8] Maude Royden, 'Equality of Opportunity', *The Highway*, 1/4 (Jan. 1909), 62.

[9] Helena Deneke, *Grace Hadow* (London, 1946), ch. 12, esp. pp. 172–3.

II

The Oxford tradition was premised on the belief that the future belonged to the workers; that mass democracy must give them power. For some tutors it was therefore necessary to educate them for their new responsibilities, and we can see this expressed in *Oxford and Working-Class Education*. To others, working-class communities and consciousness embodied the same collective values that they stood for themselves. Toynbee had spoken of the professor and workman agreeing, from different perspectives, that the old doctrine of *laissez-faire* was inhumane and inefficient. Tawney's generation took this further, building the movement on an identity of political aspirations shared by dons and workers. The dons discovered also that their reverence for education was shared by many who came to their classes. Again there was an identity, this time of the spirit. For many working-class scholars, the adult education movement also brought them into contact with the national culture. Whatever the complex emotions and ambivalence they felt about Oxford, they could believe they had achieved a measure of social acceptance and recognition in association with the University. As the state and the political parties had come to recognize the reality and power of working-class institutions and communities from the mid-nineteenth century onwards, and had accommodated them, so in adult education the centres of culture offered another sort of recognition a generation or so later. And for each student individually, the movement offered personal gains of an intangible nature, as their testimony suggests, irrespective of the collective advances promised by adult education and the construction of a 'learning community'. Indeed, a survey of 410 tutorial class students and 128 former students from Ruskin College undertaken in the mid-1930s discovered that 'personal enrichment' stood 'half a pace ahead of social service' as a motive for study.[10]

Yet collective achievements and the collective ethos itself are probably the most distinctive features of working-class adult education. Williams defined 'working-class culture' as 'the basic collective idea, and the institutions, manners, habits of thought, and intentions which proceed from this'. The authentic products of this culture included 'the collective democratic institution, whether in the trade unions, the co-operative movement, or a political party' or,

---

[10] W. E. Williams and A. E. Heath, *Learn and Live: The Consumers' View of Adult Education* (London, 1936), 8.

we might add, in adult education.[11] The belief in a highway for the many, rather than a ladder for the few; the rejection of examinations and qualifications by the tutorial classes movement; the rejection also of scholarships to the University for the outstanding students in the pioneer classes at Longton and Rochdale—these things characterize the movement, and were designed to subvert traditional conceptions of education as a race to be won by the chosen few, leaving the majority to contemplate failure and experience intense personal frustration. Workers' education as pioneered by Oxford and the WEA was authentically 'collectivist' and this is what made it special.

But, at the end of the tradition, and looking backwards, it is legitimate to ask how much was gained by the working class from this authentic collectivism? To ask whether alternative educational strategies might not have resulted in greater empowerment and social emancipation? To ask whether workers' education on this model really assisted the working class? One comparison to make is with the Open University, the success of which has shown how strong is the demand for qualifications and individual advancement among the many who missed or were denied opportunities in the past, and earlier in their lives. The 'great tradition', whatever its merits, could not satisfy them. Another comparison, and one worth examining at some length, is with a different educational tradition altogether, that of the United States. For in the United States the values and aims of adult education have been at variance with those in England. Indeed, in the 1890s an attempt was made to replicate the university extension movement in America, but it did not succeed and university adult education developed there on a different model. And this difference, combined with an understanding of the reasons for the failure of extension on the English model in America, may be employed in a critique of the adult tradition in Britain.

Until the later nineteenth century, the provision of education for adults in the United States was not unlike that in Britain. It was a patchwork of voluntary agencies, including Mechanics' Institutes for artisans, the Free Public Library movement that developed in New England in the 1820s and 1830s, and the Lyceum movement, a national network of lecture audiences and local study groups found in most towns across the north and mid-west by the 1830s and 1840s.[12] This was one feature of the associational culture that

[11] Raymond Williams, *Culture and Society 1780–1950*, 3rd edn. (Harmondsworth, 1963 edn.), 313.

[12] Malcolm S. Knowles, 'Historical Development of the Adult Education Movement', in id. (ed.), *Handbook of Adult Education in the United States* (Chicago, 1960), 7–12.

many, most famously de Tocqueville, noted in the new republic.[13] But if Britain and the United States were comparable in terms of voluntary educational activity, there were also sharp distinctions. In America, universal white manhood suffrage and the early development of the public school, diminished the interest of the emergent labour movement in education for purely working-class purposes— in education for social and political emancipation. And the passage in 1862 of the Morrill Land Grant Act, which provided public lands for the support of state universities, exemplified a popular interest in providing accessible facilities for higher education, and a responsive political will to match it. The Land Grant colleges were designed to teach scientific agriculture and home economics to farmers and their families; subsequently, their curricula broadened to allow for liberal studies also.

The extension movement in England adapted one authentic feature of American voluntarism for its own purposes, the Chautauqua. Described by one gentle critic in 1892 as a 'mixture of science, fresh-air, flirtation, Greek reminiscence, and devoutness', the Chautauqua, as we have seen, was a model for the Oxford and Cambridge Summer Meetings from the late 1880s.[14] But a more powerful influence flowed in the opposite direction. The classic example is the university settlement. Jane Addams had first visited London in 1883, knew of the settlement movement before returning to the East End in June 1888, visited Toynbee Hall on that occasion, and went back to replicate it in Hull House in Chicago, the model for dozens of 'settlements' in late-nineteenth and early-twentieth-century urban America that brought charity and civic leadership to the slums.[15] Indeed, Addams's account of her visit to Oxford, of her discussions there with Sidney Ball and another Master of Balliol, Edward Caird, of her sense of intellectual fellowship with Oxford scholars in the vanguard of philosophical idealism, complete with appreciative references to the examples of Ruskin, Green, and Toynbee, is very suggestive evidence of the impact of this distinctive British social creed on contemporary American social reformers.[16] And English

[13] Alexis de Tocqueville, *Democracy in America*, ed. Phillips Bradley (New York, 1954; first pub. 1835), ii. 114.
[14] George Herbert Palmer, 'Doubts About University Extension', *Atlantic Monthly*, 69/413 (March 1892), 370.
[15] Allen F. Davis, *American Heroine: The Life and Legend of Jane Addams* (New York, 1973), 48–51; Christopher Lasch, *The New Radicalism in America 1889–1963: The Intellectual as a Social Type* (New York, 1965), 25; Jane Addams, *Twenty Years at Hull House* (New York, 1981; first pub. 1910), 60–3, 70–4.
[16] Addams, *Twenty Years at Hull House*, 42–5.

university extension, in many eyes an analogue to the university settlement movement, also had influence in the United States.

In 1887, Herbert Baxter Adams, Professor of History at Johns Hopkins University, advocated the development of university extension in America. Adams was a key figure in the development of American academic culture during this formative period for the modern American university. On the basis of a doctorate taken at Heidelberg, he was one of the initial appointments at Johns Hopkins when the new university opened its doors to provide specialist postgraduate training in 1876. He went on to teach and prepare many of the new faculty members in history and the social sciences in America's burgeoning colleges. He was also the founder and first secretary of the American Historical Association.[17] Every inch the model of the new professional scholar, as opposed to the traditional don, he nevertheless saw great virtues in English university extension, though it has been suggested that Adams's model of extension was also influenced by the German seminar method of instruction he had experienced for himself.[18] In an address to the American Library Association in September 1887, he urged that America's public libraries should serve as centres for extension education. As he later explained,

There is a most extraordinary movement in England called university extension. It means the extension of university instruction in popular form by lectures from the great university centres at Oxford and Cambridge, throughout the great towns and manufacturing districts of England ... Antagonism between the classes and the masses has broken down. Capital and labour have joined hands for the elevation of society. The attention of entire communities has been directed to the burning questions of our time. Now my notion is that the same results can be accomplished in America, through the agency of our great public libraries, by utilizing the highest educational forces within their reach.[19]

[17] Daniel T. Rodgers, 'Professorial Socialists: The Economics Profession in the United States and Germany in the Late Nineteenth Century', unpub. paper delivered to the Organization of American Historians (Chicago, 1992); *Dictionary of American Biography*.

[18] Edward A. Gallagher, 'The American Society for the Extension of University Teaching: A Productive Pioneer of University Extension', unpub. paper, pp. 2–3. I am grateful to Dr Gallagher of Oakland Community College, Auburn Hills, Mich., for use of this paper and other assistance.

[19] Quoted in J. M. R. Owens, '"Fifteen Lean Years"—The Experiment of "English" University Extension in the United States', *Rewley House Papers*, 3/5 (1956–7), 13. The quotation is from an article Adams wrote in the *Springfield Daily Republican* in Sept. 1887.

Three years later, under the wing of the University of Pennsylvania, the Philadelphia Society for the Extension of University Teaching was founded, changing its name within six months to the American Society for the Extension of University Teaching (ASEUT).[20] Its secretary came immediately to Britain to prepare a report on English university extension.[21] Following the English model, the American Society organized voluntary branches at a local level; it also sought the co-operation of local colleges and universities in supplying qualified lecturers.[22] Among others, Woodrow Wilson, then a Professor at Princeton, gave three lecture series under its auspices.[23] Indeed, the Society did not lack the support and patronage of leading academic figures, and with their assistance extension was tried in a number of universities in the early 1890s: at a conference at the end of 1891 it was reported that lectures were under way in twenty-eight states and territories.[24] There were some modest initial achievements. An annual average of eighteen thousand students attended lectures under the auspices of the American Society in the 1890s. In ten years it put on 954 courses, mainly in Philadelphia, New York, and surrounding areas. When in 1895 the Society reviewed its first five years it noted that its main success had been with people who were already educated, especially women. It had also touched 'teachers, clerks, businessmen, mechanics and factory operatives' though it admitted that attracting the participation of workers was difficult.[25] Several lecturers from Oxford and Cambridge were invited to give classes for the ASEUT, including Sadler, Mackinder, Hudson Shaw, C. R. Ashbee, Graham Wallas, and R. G. Moulton.

Yet English university extension, transplanted to the United States, was ultimately a failure. Audiences fell away and the movement never succeeded in attracting the diversity of social classes and groups that it sought. Those universities that had tried to develop extension on the English model generally gave up within a few years. According to the report of United States Commissioner of Education for 1894, 'the institutions seemed more ready to provide lecturers than

---

[20] George F. James (ed.), *Handbook of University Extension* (Philadelphia, 1893), 17–18.

[21] Owens, ' "Fifteen Lean Years" ', 14.

[22] Gallagher, 'The American Society', 4.

[23] *Ten Years' Report of the American Society for the Extension of University Teaching 1890–1900* (Philadephia, 1901).

[24] Malcolm S. Knowles, *A History of the Adult Education Movement in the United States*, 2nd edn. (New York, 1972), 48.

[25] Owens, ' "Fifteen Lean Years" ', 16–17.

the people were to take advantage of them'.[26] Adams himself explained this failure in organizational terms: 'First, lack of suitable extension lecturers; second, lack of financial support; third, inability of university men to carry the extra burden of travel and teaching; fourth, the greater claims of academic service on college campuses where enrollments were just then increasing; fifth, the development of less expensive ways of popular education.'[27] Add to this the impact of the Panic of 1893 and the subsequent economic depression, and more recent historians of American higher education would be in agreement.[28] But there were other reasons for its failure as well. The American free public high school, with no counterpart in England, filled the gap at the secondary level which English university extension was in part trying to cover. An editorial in the *Educational Review* also dismissed extension as insufficiently rigorous: 'as a substitute for a college or even an academic training, it is utterly useless and misleading.'[29] But the most searching critique came from a Harvard Professor of Philosophy, George Herbert Palmer. He made the point that extension was necessary in Britain in a situation of relative stasis in higher education. In comparison, the American system of higher education was expanding rapidly: 'A Western state is no sooner settled than it establishes a state university, and each of the sects start from one to three colleges beside.'[30] In a situation of relatively cheap, expanding, full-time educational provision, university extension on this model was superfluous.[31] But his emphasis was on the differences between the respective societies and cultures. In England

the movement is as much social as scholarly, and accompanies a general democratic upheaval of an aristocratic nation; it springs up in the neighborhood of universities to which the common people do not resort, and in which those subjects which most concern the minds of modern man are little taught; in its country other facilities for enabling the average man to capture knowledge—public libraries, reading clubs, illustrated magazines, free high schools—are not yet general.

The American context was different:

[26] Ibid. 15.

[27] Quoted in James Creese, *The Extension of University Teaching* (New York, 1941), 49.

[28] See Baldwin M. Woods and Helen V. Hammarberg, 'University Extension Education in the United States of America', *Universities in Adult Education* (UNESCO, Paris, 1952), 131. F. H. Harrington, *The Future of Adult Education* (San Francisco, 1977), 16. Gallagher, 'The American Society', 9.

[29] *Educational Review* (New York), 3 (March 1892), 297.

[30] Palmer, 'Doubts About University Extension', 372.   [31] Ibid. 369.

From the first the American college has been organized by the people and for the people. It has been about as much resorted to by the poor as by the rich. Through a widely developed system of free public schools it has kept itself closely in touch with popular ideals. Its graduates go into commercial life as often as into medicine, the ministry or the law.[32]

Palmer idealized the accessibility of the American college, and he painted an excessively bleak picture of the sources for public instruction in England. Nevertheless, his comparison was valid, explaining why an educational movement with roots in the nature of English society would be inapplicable in the United States. One other point is also worth making: extension of a liberal education on the English model also failed because it did not meet the more utilitarian needs of potential American students. While the American Society was struggling to find, let alone build an audience, many metropolitan institutions in the 1890s began to organize evening courses as a preparation for full-time study or as a part-time alternative to it. 'Typically, their students were fully-employed adults, enrolled part-time and determined to fight their way up the social and economic ladder . . . both then and now, adult education has served to broaden opportunity for American citizens . . . [who] found that success in modern America depended increasingly on learning or at least on the ability to produce a diploma.'[33] Indeed, the failure of English university extension in America 'shows what has so often happened since to brave attempts to promote the liberal education of mature citizens, in view of adult preference for more useful fare'.[34] As university extension on the English model floundered, so a new and durable type of university adult education, designed to develop and reward individual achievement, in which students could study in their own time for the same qualifications as conventional undergraduates, was being established in many different universities and colleges. As the *1919 Report* noted, 'the extension system in the United States . . . aims more at providing preparatory work in University subjects for qualifications for degrees than at general instruction'.[35]

The new pattern could be divined in the foundation of the University of Chicago in 1892. Under the influence of its first President, William Rainey Harper, a former director of the Chautauqua, the university comprised five colleges, one of which was the Division of

---

[32] Ibid. 368.   [33] Harrington, *Future of Adult Education*, 15, 21.
[34] Ibid. 16.
[35] *Ministry of Reconstruction: Adult Education Committee, Final Report*, PP 1919, Cmd. 321, xxviii. 360.

University Extension. And this Division was able to include stand-ard university and college courses, lifted from the internal curriculum, credits and all. At the new University of Chicago, in other words, extension was integral to the university's structure and mission, and degree work could be undertaken by part-time students.[36]

But it was at the University of Wisconsin that the most influential experiments in extension were pioneered. From 1891 the university had tried to provide extension lectures on the English model. One of the most famous figures in American academic life in this period, the historian Frederick Jackson Turner, gave seven extension lecture courses on American History in the winter of 1891–2. As he wrote to Herbert Baxter Adams in January 1892, 'In one little community of 600 inhabitants—farmers etc.—I have an audience of over 200 people'.[37] A high point was reached in 1895–6 when the University of Wisconsin offered fifty-seven courses in forty-three communities in Wisconsin and northern Illinois.[38] But in the late 1890s the pro-gramme declined as the best lecturers, Turner among them, with-drew to concentrate on their academic research and the novelty wore off. By the first years of the century the extension programme was effectively moribund. It was revived after 1906 through the combination of University President Charles R. Van Hise and a new director of extension education, Louis E. Reber. But in place of a liberal academic education, the new emphasis was on the university serving all the people of the state by providing a range of facilities adapted to their diverse educational needs.

The new curriculum was more vocational and utilitarian: as Reber explained,

Right or wrong, you find here a type of university extension that does not disdain the simplest form of service. Literally carrying the University to the homes of the people, it attempts to give them what they need—be it the last word in expert advice; courses of study carrying University credit; or easy lessons in cooking or sewing. University Extension in Wisconsin endeavors to interpret the phraseology of the expert and offers the benefits of research to the household and the workshop, as well as to municipalities and state.[39]

[36] Knowles, *History of the Adult Education Movement,* 48; Owens, ' "Fifteen Lean Years" ', 14.

[37] Merle Curti and Vernon Carstensen, *The University of Wisconsin 1848–1925: A History,* 2 vols. (Madison, 1949), i. 724.   [38] Ibid. 727.

[39] Louis E. Reber, 'The Scope of University Extension and Its Organisation and Subdivision', in *Proceedings of the First National University Extension Conference, March 10–12, 1915* (Madison, 1915), 25.

Expert advice was thus offered by the university to the state administration as well as to the people; what became known as 'the Wisconsin idea' saw the entry of the university-based expert into government to assist in technical and social planning. This is clear in the titles of the many journal and magazine articles about Wisconsin's extension work published after 1906: 'A University in Public Life', 'A University that Runs a State', 'Tutoring Lawmakers', and most famously of all, Lincoln Steffens's article in 1909, 'Sending a State to College'.[40] Steffens was the most celebrated 'muckraking' journalist of the age, given to exposés of corruption and urban destitution, and author in 1904 of the most famous muckraking text of all, *The Shame of the Cities*. But he enthused over the university at Madison which offered 'to teach anybody—anything—anywhere' and he listed machine shops, model dairy farms, a housekeepers' conference, and other examples of grass roots utility he had discovered when he visited the campus. He pictured the University of Wisconsin as a sort of living reference library for the state, a resource for the community.

The University of Wisconsin is as close to the intelligent farmer as his pig pen or his tool house. The university laboratories are a part of the alert manufacturer's plant. To the worker the university is drawing nearer than the school around the corner, and is as much his as his union is his. Creeping into the minds of his children with pure seeds, into the opinion of voters with impersonal knowledge, the State University is part of the citizen's own mind.[41]

This was the reverse of the usual Steffens style, the antithesis of muckraking. If he usually demonstrated what was wrong with American life, in Madison, Wisconsin he had found a model of civic virtue. To quote a later phrase of his that has now entered the language, he 'had seen the future and it worked'.

The Wisconsin idea cannot be divorced from its political context. It depended on the support of the state governor and quintessential American Progressive, Robert M. La Follete. La Follette believed in spreading knowledge; he believed also in the value of expertise in running the state, and encouraged the participation of university faculty members on official enquiries, commissions and so forth.[42] The state legislature was also persuaded: appropriations earmarked

---

[40] Curti and Carstensen, *University of Wisconsin*, ii. 588–90.
[41] Lincoln Steffens, 'Sending a State to College', *American Magazine*, 67/4 (Feb. 1909), 364; see also Laurence R. Veysey, *The Emergence of the American University* (Chicago, 1965), 107.
[42] Robert M. La Follette, *La Follette's Autobiography* (Madison, 1913), 30–1.

for university extension in the state rose from $20,000 in 1907 to
$225,000 in 1914.[43] The University of Wisconsin had become the
darling of the Progressives in America. Progressivism, that broad
movement for political and social reform that swept America in the
first years of the century, favoured knowledge, enlightenment, popular
education, and revelation. For knowledge allowed citizens to judge
the motives of corrupt politicians and all-powerful business trusts;
and the way to end evils was to expose them to a receptive, dis-
criminating mass audience. Knowledge and its accessibility also
prompted innovation and reform: one magazine speculated that so
many political initiatives originated in Wisconsin because the university had organized the state as a vast forum for public ideas.[44]
This was the Progressives' dream—a nation of informed, responsive, and responsible citizens, and delegations of educationalists,
politicians, and social reformers came to Madison to see it at first
hand.[45] There was some awareness of the educational experiment at
Wisconsin in Britain during this period, and the *1919 Report* noted
the specific work of the university's bureau on municipal government and the general social functions of the American university as
a centre of social expertise: 'The University in the United States has
other activities besides Extension work which, although not strictly
Adult Education in our sense of the term, have immense influence
in the non-academic world. Many Universities have set up bureaus
of information, advice and instruction on all social problems for the
use of any workers.'[46]

By 1914 thirty state universities had organized extension divisions and they were joined by several private universities including
Chicago, Brown, Tulane, Pittsburg, Northwestern and, the most
ambitious of all, Columbia in New York.[47] The Wisconsin model
was admired and imitated, though most institutions stopped short
of the whole 'Wisconsin idea', not least because the political context
in which they functioned was frequently less encouraging than in
Wisconsin itself, with obvious consequences for funding. Some chose
not to offer instruction below undergraduate standard; others re-
frained from offering the more vocational services; many were not

[43] Curti and Carstensen, *University of Wisconsin*, ii. 571.
[44] Ibid. 590.   [45] Ibid. 562 n, 591.
[46] *Adult Education Committee, Final Report*, 360. See also L. E. Reber to
A. Mansbridge, 8 Jan. 1914, Mansbridge Papers, lxiiiA, British Library Add. MS
65257, fos. 38–9.
[47] Charles R. Van Hise, 'The University Extension Function in the Modern
University', *Proceedings of the First National University Extension Conference*,
12–13.

invited to participate in the administration of state government.[48] But the model of an adaptive, flexible educational servant of the people, and of the university as responsible to the whole adult community, had been established. And it was a model that was premised on allowing the citizen to gain the skills and qualifications he or she needed for individual advance.

At roughly the same time in both England and the United States, therefore, an initial model of university extension was being thrown over for new types of adult and community education. But the differences between the model developed in America and that pioneered in Longton and Rochdale and set down in *Oxford and Working-Class Education* are plain. Tutorial classes were embodiments of the liberal ideal and brought élite styles of education—the tutorial, the academic essay, and so forth—to an élite of the working-class. University extension on the Wisconsin model was more utilitarian and far more responsive to the demands of a diverse range of students. In Britain the pattern pioneered by Oxford and replicated in other universities was for the university to decant certain new functions into peripheral administrative units (extramural delegacies, local lecture syndicates, and the like), leaving the heart of the university untouched and unencumbered. In contrast, the model pioneered at Wisconsin and Chicago involved turning the university inside out and making the various extension functions central to the administration and ethos of the institution. Above all, the alliance of Oxford and the WEA was designed to provide education for a specific class, and, indeed, a specifically élite group within that class. At Wisconsin, extension was viewed as a resource for all the citizens.

This difference between the education of the individual and the education of a socio-economic class is illustrated in the most interesting study by Margaret Hodgen of *Workers' Education in England and the United States* published in 1925. In 1922 she had sent requests for information on provision for specifically working-class students to 125 extension departments in the United States. She received 68 replies but only fourteen institutions were able to provide her with any information on student occupations, and 'only two, judging by the character of courses offered or the care with which occupational data was compiled, appeared to have the education of the working-class, as a class, in mind'.[49] This was confirmed by the

---

[48] Harrington, *Future of Adult Education*, 18–19.
[49] M. T. Hodgen, *Workers' Education in England and the United States* (London, 1925), 250 n.

early experience of the Workers' Educational Bureau in the United States. Modelled on the WEA in England, the Bureau had been established in April 1921 at a meeting of workers and educationalists in New York. But in its first years it had great difficulty interesting university extension departments in co-operating in the provision of higher education for trade unions and workers' groups. At least until the Depression in America, the workers' educational movement operated in relative isolation from the universities.[50] Hodgen had discovered that the idea of 'workers' education' had little resonance in an educational system designed to maximize individual opportunities and satisfy specific individual needs. American society has always been premised on socio-economic mobility upwards, even if the degree to which this has been achieved has often been exaggerated. It has seen education as a crucial means for the achievement of this aim, and universities and colleges have consequently developed qualities and educational programmes which reflect this spirit. In American universities, and following to a greater or lesser extent the Wisconsin idea, extension has sought to expand individual access to university resources rather than provide an élite education for a small social group at many removes from the university itself.

In many ways this comparison and brief, compressed history of American adult education merely confirms a familiar distinction between the individualism and class-consciousness of, respectively, American and British society. For most of the past two centuries educational debate in Britain has generally taken as its unit the socio-economic class and its educational needs—generally defined by people who are not of the class concerned—rather than the individual. Conversely, in the United States, the forms of educational provision, extension among them, have reflected an intensely individualistic culture. When extension emerged in England in the 1870s it was essentially an initiative in the relationship between classes. And the tutorial classes movement continued to conceive of its role in terms of equalizing opportunities as between classes, and training an emergent class for the exercise of power. George Herbert Palmer was correct in seeing university extension in Britain as essentially a social rather than an educational movement, and for this reason, correct in arguing that it must fail in a very different social context in the United States.

This comparison may merely confirm archetypal views of both

<hr>

[50] See Spencer Miller, Jr. (Secretary of the Workers' Educational Bureau of America), 'Workers' Education and University Extension', in *Proceedings of the Eighth Annual Conference of the National University Continuing Education Association at St Louis, Missouri, April 19 1923* (St Louis, 1923), 13–20.

societies, therefore. But it also raises another question: whether the British concentration on the education of a class as an exercise in social and political emancipation, has been, in the long run, either durable or effective? The 'Wisconsin idea', as developed and adapted in dozens of extension departments across the United States since the early years of the century, has enabled millions of Americans to obtain qualifications by part-time study and has been far more effective in drawing in the disadvantaged and in pushing up participation rates in higher education towards the 40 per cent mark. Conversely, the association of British universities and the WEA, the dominant theme in university adult education until at least the 1970s, may have actually narrowed the base of adult education. It literally foisted an Oxford curriculum onto the working class, which suited the few, but which, it may surely be argued, was unsuitable for the needs of the many. And it was an Oxford curriculum without degrees at the end: three years of university-standard work in a tutorial class was wonderful for the soul, but it gave no equivalent qualifications. It also allowed British universities to pay scant regard to adult students because structurally, extramural education in association with the WEA, and aimed at a specific group of male workers, did not necessitate any changes in the organization of the university. 'Working-class education' sustained the alliance of dons and workers that late-Victorian Oxford sought, and this alliance played its part in assisting the political emergence of Labour. But it may be argued that eighty and ninety years later there is little left to show for this conception of adult education. Indeed, in the past ten or fifteen years university extramural departments in Britain have belatedly recognized the strengths of the 'Wisconsin idea' and have been turning themselves into expressions of it. It is worth noting that it was an American model—university extension at Chicago University—that influenced Harold Wilson's idea of an Open University in the 1960s.[51]

This is not to dismiss any of the achievements discussed in this book: the social project that inspired Tawney and his generation was self-evidently relevant to the context of Edwardian Britain, and the successes of the educational alliance then fashioned were obvious and important. But that project is arguably less relevant today, or at least, cannot be approached in the same way, using the same methods, in a society in which the political context has changed and in which the traditional rhetoric of an education for social emancipation seems,

[51] Harold Wilson, *Memoirs: The Making of a Prime Minister 1916–64* (London, 1986), 189–90.

at best, inappropriate. For a society belatedly beginning to embrace and understand the meaning of mass higher education, the American model is proving to be a better guide to fulfilling new functions and meeting new demands than the old adult tradition.

III

The 'earnest minority' gained immeasurably; the majority of workers were untouched by the movement and may even have been deterred by it. That may be a realistic assessment of the adult tradition over the past century in Britain as it has influenced the working class. What, then, of the dons? It has been an argument of this book that they gained quite as much as they have given to this relationship. Adult education gave many dons the satisfaction of helping to integrate the working class into national life—a process that began in political terms in the 1850s and 1860s and to which they added a cultural dimension from the 1880s. Educational service also provided a new civic project for generations losing their religious belief; it met the need to be of assistance to fellow men and women, but without the obligation to take orders and to have faith. It was also an almost automatic social function for Oxford students and tutors touched by philosophic idealism, who believed in community and common values and hoped to create these things through education. And it was especially rewarding to find that values they held dear were also prized in the working-class communities they visited. Many students were also searching for something to fill the void once taken up by Christianity; many believed in the virtues of study for its own sake in a mirror-image of Jowett's liberal ideal. And the collective ethic was at the heart of working-class culture: as Williams argued, it actually defined it. It was therefore very easy to feel a common bond with students who believed that education would assist social advance and who sought in it a means for their own personal spiritual transcendence. The dons went down to meet their students as their students came up to meet them. The forces and themes in this intellectual enterprise were cherished and experienced in common. Values, aims, approaches were not passed down only, but passed up also. The virtues of the higher life that attracted dons to their calling were virtues also in the eyes of their new students.

The history of adult education thus provides an almost classic example of the 'organicist' position that John Goldthorpe has distinguished as one of three distinct responses on the part of intellectuals to the working class during the past century in Britain—the other two he styles the 'liberal' and 'left' positions. Intellectuals of the 'left' convinced themselves, without reason or evidence, of the revolutionary potential of the workers, only to be rudely disabused. Those who adopted the liberal position looked forward to the incorporation and decomposition of the working class as living standards rose, educational opportunities broadened, technology changed the nature of work, and old neighbourhoods were rehoused. The 'organicists', on the other hand, found regenerative virtues in working-class institutions and outlooks, and prized existing working-class culture rather than its dissolution. To organicists—and Raymond Williams is one of Goldthorpe's exemplars of the position—the collective ethos of working-class life offered alternatives to individualism and the potential 'for an entirely new moral order'. The working classes were seen as 'the bearers of "oppositional" values'. It is Goldthorpe's contention that all three positions have misunderstood the workers and misinterpreted the evidence before them: in the case of 'organicists', they mistook working-class communitarianism and solidarity for a positive moral commitment to anticapitalist values when they were, in fact, merely strategic and instrumental responses to adversity. The communal life of the working class was a practical reaction to the problems of existence; with affluence it has perished because no longer needed. Goldthorpe may be right; it is certainly a helpful typology of intellectual attitudes.[52] Nevertheless, through adult education dissenting intellectuals were put in touch with communities that had developed similar critiques of existing economic and social relationships, and the essential identity of attitudes on both sides was a source of mutual confidence and strength.

Workers' education was also an appropriate project for an intellectual élite whose function was to teach. Oxford may have produced minds of great distinction but they were teachers also, indeed foremost. It is not difficult to explain why other European university traditions have not developed comparable movements and why European intellectuals have always found it difficult to reconcile academic distinction with adult education: their traditions of instruction are generally very different. Professors are at one or more removes from their students; research has generally been accorded more respect than teaching. In such circumstances, the idea of the professor going out of the university to teach groups without any

---

[52] John H. Goldthorpe, 'Intellectuals and the Working Class in Modern Britain', in David Rose (ed.), *Social Stratification and Economic Change* (London, 1988), 39–56.

formal position in it, and in intimate social contact with them, may have seemed an example of English eccentricity. Indeed, we might go further: it was not just that dons found a useful function in adult education because they had been trained to value teaching and to see themselves as teachers. The very success of Hudson Shaw, Tawney, and their fellows owed something to the nature of the academic culture inside Oxford. For it is one of the great virtues of the tutorial system that it promotes equality and open dialogue between tutor and student; that it is informal; that it depends not just on the student's respect for the tutor but on the tutor taking the ideas of the tutee seriously; and that it promotes personal friendship and close interest in the student's welfare and progress.

These features and qualities had immediate and obvious relevance for the education of communities and groups lacking any previous contact with higher learning. Tutors naturally treated their students as equals, treated their ideas and, above all, their experience, with respect; sympathized with them, built no barriers between themselves and their classes, made themselves available, and sought to become members of the communities they visited. As the inspectorate's report on Oxford's tutorial classes in 1924 observed, 'Without exception the relations between tutors and classes reproduce what is best in the college life of the older Universities to a degree which is remarkable when the actual circumstances are borne in mind'.[53]

Arguably, the relationship between dons and workers grew out of the academic culture of the ancient universities. This was, and is still, an essentially democratic culture, predicated on self-governance, service to students, and a type of equality linking junior and senior members in the college community. It is a culture that is frequently caricatured, misunderstood, and underestimated, and it is one that is under threat, because such educational intensity is expensive and time-consuming. But the remarkable success of many young dons in otherwise alien communities of the working class from the 1880s owed a great deal to it.

But the 'don as teacher' has given way in the past generation to the 'don as researcher'. The professionalization of academic life and the primacy given to the uncovering of new knowledge have altered the function and self-image of the don with consequences for the adult tradition. For this had depended on the tutor able to teach what was required by the group and innovate if need be; it required

[53] Board of Education: Report by H. M. Inspectors upon University Tutorial Classes under the Supervision of the Joint Committee of the University of Oxford, for the period ending 31st July, 1924 (n.d.). Oxford University Archives, 'Copies of Special Reports, Memoranda etc . . .', DES/F/2/1/8, folder 3, p. 4.

adaptability and flexibility of a sort common enough to the college tutor used to turning his hand to any number of subjects in an amateurish way. But in more recent decades these qualities have become less common: the don has been replaced by the subject specialist, learned in a narrow range of issues and more given to spend spare hours in research than in further teaching beyond the walls. In turn, the function and image of the modern university has changed; the teaching of an educational élite may still be one view of Oxford, but it is just as likely to be seen as a centre of primary research, whether in the humanities or natural sciences. In addition, the very expansion of knowledge as more resources and time have been devoted to research has built a new division between the public and the specialists. These related developments have all had their effects on the nature and function of university adult education. The university is seen as a centre of new knowledge rather than a keeper of the ancient, classical wisdom. The university lecturer (rather than don) is now a dedicated specialist who may be called on to elucidate new developments in his or her field. And extramural education has turned to the explanation of this new knowledge to broad audiences as one of its key functions.

Lindsay had anticipated this as early as 1951: 'there is some case' he wrote 'for the revival of university extension of the old kind. We do very badly need some machinery through which the ever-increasing scientific discoveries of the universities may permeate the population as a whole.'[54] In Oxford and in other universities, the extramural day-school now provides for this, bringing scholars and researchers before lay audiences to explain the results and import of their research and keep the public aware of what is being said and written in remote areas of the academic world. But the change has been rather more profound than this: to some degree, as the social and political functions of university adult education have declined in relevance, these explanatory academic functions have grown to take their place. Rewley House in Oxford is now a place to come to learn about current understanding in any number of subjects, a window in the wall allowing contact between the research within and the curious and concerned public without. This may always have been an aspect of the adult tradition, but it is now a central function in Oxford and elsewhere. That it meets real educational need and fulfils an important social function is evident in the size of weekly audiences for such events.

---

[54] Lindsay of Birker, review of S. G. Raybould, *The English Universities and Adult Education* (London, 1951), in *Universities Quarterly*, 6/1 (Nov. 1951), 86.

In explaining why university adult education is no longer so concerned with the social aims of its forbears it is necessary, therefore, to consider the changing conception and role of the don. The early extension lecturers were self-consciously attempting to build a common culture linking the social classes together in the shared appreciation of texts, authors, and ideas. John Ruskin had influenced Oxford in the 1880s and that influence, in turn, was spread more widely through the population by the early extension lecturers. There was an evangelical belief in the adult education movement, which endures still, that culture was not exclusive but integrative, and that it could and should be shared more widely. As a consequence, the adult tradition has encouraged popularization in the best sense of that term—making accessible, not cheapening or diluting. Johnson, the first Oxford lecturer, Hudson Shaw, Marriott, Smith, Lindsay, and many others, were accomplished popularizers, though they contributed little in print that is read now or which is thought to have been important. It was not simply that they wanted to widen the audience for intellectual culture; they also wanted to break down the barriers between the intellectual and the wider world. Their energies went into this function—a function that was taken more seriously and accorded more respect than now—rather than the uncovering of new knowledge or the taking of a new view.

But it cannot be denied that in recent years the popularizing impulse, and with it, the social vision of the dons, has declined. In part this is because the modern academic profession lacks the confidence, we might almost say the audacity, of the late-Victorian and Edwardian dons. The early extension lecturers and tutors had the temerity to believe they had something to offer educationally disadvantaged communities. No doubt it was easier in a more strictly class-conscious society to have confidence that a 'university man' would get an attentive audience merely by virtue of being a 'university man'. But academic position and distinction no longer induce the same awe. In the past decade or so there even may have been a conscious attempt to marginalize and ignore academic wisdom because it holds to values and beliefs at odds with prevailing political and social opinion. In such circumstances it is far harder for the university lecturer to command attention. And the combination of declining public esteem, deteriorating conditions of work, declining institutional and personal autonomy, and increasing pressures from bureaucracy, have contributed to a growing academic insularity in which professional and, above all, internal financial concerns take precedence at the expense of the social engagements that moved

Tawney's generation. It is difficult to imagine a meeting such as took place on 10 August 1907 in the Examination Schools in Oxford taking place now, and this is not just because it would be surprising if two hundred working-class organizations felt that Oxford had something tangible to offer that could not be found elsewhere. Rather, the sort of ambition and breadth that inspired such occasions is lacking. This is not a criticism of Oxford or any other university; it is merely an observation on the changing nature of academic life. Lecturers come before audiences as specialists; the vocation of the don as a public educator with that sense of social 'mission' that inspired the founders is rare indeed.

But the contraction in ambition and aspiration may also follow from the way in which adult education has been structured in Oxford and other universities. It is not only the dons who have specialized but also the university itself. The growth of knowledge and the diversification of functions in a modern university have encouraged a proliferation of independent institutions with separate remits. Where once the 'missionaries' of university extension conceived their purpose as the permeation of the whole university with their ethos, adult and continuing education has more recently been defined in terms of a designated institution and building, constitutional independence, and separate and adequate funding. While no one would wish to return to a situation in which adult education in Oxford is once more dependent on the goodwill and the generosity of the wealthier colleges, the very facts of dependency and poverty in the past encouraged collaboration across the University, and made university extension and the early experiment with tutorial classes a matter of academic and personal interest to a spectrum of people and institutions in Oxford. Self-governance, separate and adequate facilities, and self-sufficiency are all obvious advantages, but the very fact of institutional independence delimits adult education physically, institutionally, and thus psychologically. Adult education, organized and taught by specialists in the field, goes on in one corner; other functions are found elsewhere. Obligations to the wider community are discharged successfully, but the conception of adult education as an integral component of all aspects of university life, expressed so eloquently in the *1919 Report*, is much more difficult to realize. This, too, is not a criticism, but merely a reflection on the complexity and differentiation of university life now, as compared with the simpler structures Sadler, Marriott, and Temple had to manipulate in a university in which there were fewer institutional boundaries to cross and fewer barriers to break down.

IV

Something else has changed also; it is not just that the old working class has disappeared, that an older conception of the don is passing, and that higher education has become more complex, bureaucratic, and specialized. There have been fundamental political changes which have undermined the basis of Oxford's relationship with the labour movement. It is necessary first to establish the identity and nature of this political association. And one way of doing so is by reference to the social democratic tradition that Peter Clarke has sketched.[55] For Clarke there is a fundamental distinction to be made in the history of the left in Britain between those versions of socialism premised on class conflict and the eventual victory of the working class, and those 'social democratic' versions which have striven for social justice and equality as the means by which to end class conflict and class distinctions. On one side are those theorists who have seen class conflict as the solution to injustice; on the other, those who have seen such conflict as intrinsically part of the problem and who have preferred to take the reformist and parliamentary road to socialism as a means of eradicating class distinctions altogether and enhancing the opportunities of the majority of the people.

Clearly, the greater portion of Labour's strategists have fallen into the second camp; indeed, one of the problems with Clarke's differentiation is the difficulty of finding a senior and influential figure in the history of socialist thinking and Labour politics in Britain who has ever stood for the former position. Clarke's social democratic tradition explicitly comprises the New Liberals, J. A. Hobson and L. T. Hobhouse; the early Fabians; Tawney, Durbin, Crosland, and the Gaitskellites.[56] Each of these in turn developed a version of social democracy appealing 'to the interests of the community as a whole, to a model of economic co-operation and social harmony, immanent if not fulfilled'.[57] The fundamental similarity to the political programme that inspired Oxford's engagement with adult and workers' education is clear: the adult tradition sits squarely within this social democratic consensus about the means and aims of social transformation.

But we may go further, for the figures who comprise Clarke's social democratic tradition overlap with the Oxford tradition described in this book. Arthur Acland may have left politics before the

---

[55] Peter Clarke, 'The Social Democratic Theory of the Class Struggle', in Jay Winter (ed.), *The Working Class in Modern British History* (Cambridge, 1983), 3–18.

[56] Ibid. 5.   [57] Ibid. 8.

advent of New Liberalism in the Edwardian period, but his credentials as a founder of the movement seem secure. Hobhouse, as an undergraduate at Corpus Christi in the early 1880s, was a member of Acland's 'Inner Ring', his name appears on the list of the Oxford committee which organized the first Summer Meeting in 1888, and he assisted the new tutorial classes with his favourable report on them for the Board of Education in 1910. As Kadish has pointed out, he was prevented from greater involvement in the work of Oxford Extension by the conditions of his fellowship.[58] Hobson taught for the Oxford Delegacy through the 1890s when his heterodox views closed off extension lecturing elsewhere. Of Tawney's engagement with adult education and its role in the development of his mature political thought little more need be said. Meanwhile Durbin and Gaitskell himself may be said to have made contact with Labour through the port of entry that was adult education. Even Crosland was not untouched; as a young don in the late 1940s he taught on trade union courses for the Oxford Delegacy. And as Secretary of State for Education and Science in 1965 he was on hand to open the new residential centre at Rewley House and emphasize not only the then Labour government's strong commitment to adult education, but the links that many members of that administration had with it 'either as teachers ourselves or by being taught'.[59] Only the Fabians are out of place; their élitism and instrumentalism were rejected by Tawney and Cole because such strategies, though they might gain something in the short term, did not depend on the strength and democracy of the working-class movement itself; they merely sought to use the existing structures of the state in new and advantageous ways. That said, individual Fabians, like Sidney Ball, still made a contribution to adult education.

No doubt this stretches things too far; some of these connections are tangential and coincidental, and the Oxford tradition this book has examined includes several key figures who have no place in Clarke's lineage—though it would not be difficult to find a place in it for T. H. Green and Arnold Toynbee (who both clearly anticipated New Liberalism) as well as William Temple and even G. D. H. Cole. But Clarke's social democratic tradition is composed of several figures who came out of Oxford, and several for whom the experience of adult education was formative and lasting. It would be foolish to claim that adult education has ever played a central

---

[58] Alon Kadish, *The Oxford Economists in the Late Nineteenth Century* (Oxford, 1982), 97. The same restrictions applied to Sidney Ball at St John's and may explain why he was a propagandist for the movement but did not teach for it.
[59] *Oxford Mail*, 20 Mar. 1965.

role in the *institutions* of the labour movement. But it did have considerably greater influence on the general consciousness of Labour, and because it was one obvious route into the movement for intellectual figures, it had a particular impact on several of those who have defined Labour's ideological position in the past century. In Tawney's case the impact was profound; in other cases it was merely one of several influences. But it is incontestable that adult and workers' education, particularly as developed in Oxford, has played an important and intrinsically interesting role in the education and socialization of the intellectual leaders of Labour since the late-Victorian period. Through the history of the Oxford tradition in adult education may be traced the continuous project to reach out to, and assist, the working class in modern Britain on the part of intellectuals, from Green at one extreme to Williams at the other.

Yet one Oxford historian has recently suggested that the relationship between Oxford and the labour movement may be 'destined for permanent decline' and 'may eventually come to be seen as a completed historical episode'.[60] In the 1950s and 1960s the Labour front bench was dominated by the products of Oxford, many of them graduates of the PPE school (which would surely have pleased Lindsay), and several of them former dons. In the 1980s no new Oxford generation came to take their place. In the past, the very presence of such figures gave the party an appeal beyond its natural constituency. But the labour movement now is less given to intellectual deference than once it was, though in this it merely reflects wider social attitudes.[61] Bearing in mind the reverence of Mansbridge and his movement for the universities and higher learning, Halsey has noted the 'tacit and diluted feeling of hostility to the elitist and allegedly unresponsive universities' on the part of 'the modern parliamentary left'.[62] Yet the election to the leadership of the Labour Party in July 1994 of Tony Blair, educated at St John's College, Oxford, and John Prescott, educated at Ruskin College, suggests that the relationship may not be quite finished. The balance of St John's, Sidney Ball's college, and the wealthiest in the university, and Ruskin, Noah Ablett's college, is an intriguing reminder of the rival traditions of adult and workers' education, and of the traditions

[60] Brian Harrison, 'Oxford and the Labour Movement', *Twentieth Century British History*, 2/3 (1991), 270–1.

[61] R. W. Johnson, 'Going for Gould', *London Review of Books*, 9/14 (23 July 1987), 7. Brian Harrison, 'Politics', in id. (ed.) *The History of the University of Oxford*, viii, *The Twentieth Century* (Oxford, 1994), 411.

[62] A. H. Halsey, *The Decline of Donnish Dominion: The British Academic Professions in the Twentieth Century* (Oxford, 1992), 36.

of left and right in the Labour Party. Both traditions owe something to Oxford, as does the leadership and thought of the Labour Party over several generations.

Yet the relationship between Oxford and the labour movement may have broken down not merely because the Party is no longer as open as it once was to intellectual leadership. It has also forgotten the importance of education in its own history and as a force for social change. By this I do not mean the system of general public education, but the education of its members, supporters, and the rest of the community in order that they might better understand the case Labour is making. It was as contributors to this project that the dons had a special role and service to offer: as this aspect of the labour movement has withered, so the universities have had less to contribute to the movement, and no obvious means through which to make contact with the organizations of the working class.

To Tawney and his generation, the education of the movement was obligatory: in 1924 he welcomed 'the recognition by ever wider sections of the working-class movement that if it is to solve its own problems, mobilise its own forces, and create a social order more in conformity with its own ideals, it must attend to the education of its members with the same deliberation and persistence which it has brought to the improvement of their economic position'.[63] A few years earlier 'a Manchester Socialist' had told Harold Begbie that 'when Labour comes it must be to stay. And Labour cannot hope to stay unless it is trained for its work. That's why I say that nothing is so important as education.'[64] But since 1945 the movement has had the problem of finding ways of reactivating the educational project that had been a part of its advance towards power. In the late 1940s Cole was critical of Labour 'for its neglect of socialist education and hence of popular participation in the business of social reform and social ownership'.[65] At a Fabian Society dinner in 1954 Tawney asked that socialism make its appeal not only to men's 'interests' but 'to men's imaginations'.[66] And at his eightieth birthday celebrations in 1960 he returned to the theme, asking for 'a much more real effort on the part of the Labour Party to give

[63] R. H. Tawney, 'Introduction', in T. W. Price, *The Story of the Workers' Educational Association from 1903 to 1924* (London, 1924), 7.

[64] H. Begbie, *Living Water: Being Chapters from the Romance of the Poor Student* (London, 1918), 111–12.

[65] A. W. Wright, *G. D. H. Cole and Socialist Democracy* (Oxford, 1979), 234.

[66] Ross Terrill, *R. H. Tawney and His Times: Socialism as Fellowship* (London, 1974), 261.

more instruction'.[67] The party has developed competence in elec-
tioneering; but it is doubtful if supporters can be made and opponents confuted in the crude propagandism of campaigns. As the
very earliest British socialists recognized, a machine for winning
votes is not enough. If Labour is to construct the civic culture it
needs to sustain its political challenge it should remember its traditions and the part that education once played in the movement.

Oxford's involvement in adult education and the relationship that
grew from it between dons and workers was premised on an educational crusade: the use of such a term is deliberate, for the movement had a 'mission'. In the days of Green and Acland the mission
was to make responsible, democratic citizens and smooth the passage of the working class into the nation. In the days of Tawney
and Temple it sought to give the working majority the understanding and the skills for government. That sense of mission, that very
reverence for education in the labour movement, has declined in
recent decades, and the political fortunes of the movement have
declined with it. If the argument of this book is correct, this is not
merely coincidental. Heed the words of Charles Gore, then Bishop
of Birmingham, who had been a mentor to Albert Mansbridge, and
who had assisted in constructing the alliance of dons and workers
in 1907. He gave a short address at the end of a WEA conference
in Reading in 1910 that Mansbridge declared to have been the
greatest speech in the history of the Association. In language redolent of the bible, and of a biblical crusade of right against might
that tells us something important about the way the movement
perceived itself, he expressed the faith of many of the pioneers when
he linked together social advance and education:

You may become strong and clamorous, you may win a victory, you may
effect a revolution, but you will be trodden down again under the feet of
knowledge unless you get it for yourselves; even if you win victory you will
be trodden down again under the feet of knowledge if you leave knowledge in the hands of privilege; because knowledge will always win over
ignorance.[68]

---

[67] 'Dr Tawney's Call To Socialists—More Effort Needed to Inform Public', *The
Times*, 12 Dec. 1960, 14.
[68] G. L. Prentice, *The Life of Charles Gore: A Great Englishman* (London,
1935), 283–4. Mary Stocks gave the 1909 Annual Meeting of the WEA as the time
and place of this speech, but Prentice is probably more reliable; see Mary Stocks,
The Workers' Educational Association: The First Fifty Years (London, 1953), 36.
See also A. Mansbridge, *Edward Stuart Talbot and Charles Gore* (London, 1935),
61.

APPENDIX RECORDS OF EXTRAMURAL EDUCATION IN THE UNIVERSITY OF OXFORD

The records of the present Department for Continuing Education in Oxford, dating back to the beginnings of the extension movement in Oxford, were transferred from Rewley House to the Oxford University Archives in 1983. They comprise the largest and most frequently consulted section of the Archives. The papers deposited there contain minutes, meeting papers, and the financial accounts of all the varied organizations that have overseen extramural education in the university, including a file of 'Early Papers' (EP/1/1–8) from which it is possible to piece together aspects of the early history of extension lecturing. The collection also contains detailed printed syllabuses for extension lectures, dating back to 1886, and syllabuses for tutorial classes from 1907. These make it possible to recreate the extramural curriculum as it has developed across the history of the movement. To give an example, DES/SB/2/4–8 includes syllabuses of tutorial classes given by R. H. Tawney (1907–14), Henry Clay (1909–15), F. W. Kolthammer (Cuthbertson) (1911 and 1915–17) and T. W. Price (1925–9). There are also programmes and syllabuses for the Summer Meetings dating back to 1889. There are volumes of examination papers, set for the students of university extension in the late-Victorian and Edwardian period. As well as the annual reports of the Extension Lectures Committee and the Tutorial Classes Committee, there are well-preserved reports, written by lecturers, tutors, and local and/or class secretaries, on individual courses. There are some class registers. The collection contains letter books for the period 1889–1934, including copies of all letters sent out by the Delegacy and the Tutorial Classes Committee.

The collection also contains a range of specialist files containing material on particular aspects of the University's extramural work, or on particular projects. These include correspondence between the Secretary of the Delegacy and Ruskin College and the WEA (DES/F/1/4/1); files on trade union education between 1944 and 1977 (DES/F/4); and files on services' education 1939–72 (DES/F/6). There are files on the adult students' scholarship scheme which brought mature students to study in the university (DES/F/2/6); on the WEA summer school at Balliol, with material in it dating back to 1911 (DES/F/5/3); and on that marvellous tribute to the strength of the movement in the Potteries, the North Staffordshire Miners' Higher Education Movement (DES/F/2/3). There are also files on 'Inquiries into University Extension Work' including material on the 1908 *Report*, the Royal Commission of 1919–22, and the Habbakuk Committee of 1970 (DES/F/14). The collection contains personal files on tutors for the period 1890–1981, though the majority of these concern full-time tutors employed since the Second World War. There are also files of press cuttings for the period 1878–1939. And the collection includes the papers of one of the great servants of the adult education movement, E. S. Cartwright, Organizing Secretary of the Tutorial Classes Committee between 1912 and 1945.

The items in the collection have not been catalogued, but a handlist gives some general guidance to the contents of files and to the extent of the collection.

BIBLIOGRAPHY

MANUSCRIPT SOURCES

A. H. D. Acland MSS, 'College', Broadclyst, Devon.
Balliol College Minutes and uncatalogued MSS, Balliol College, Oxford.
Papers of Edward Stuart Cartwright, Oxford University Archives.
G. D. H. Cole Papers, Nuffield College, Oxford.
Papers of the Department for Continuing Education, University of Oxford, Oxford University Archives.
Papers, memorabilia and ephemera on Reuben George, Central Library, Swindon.
T. H. Green Papers, Balliol College, Oxford.
Hebdomadal Council Papers, Oxford University Archives.
F. W. Jessup Papers, Rewley House, Oxford.
Benjamin Jowett Papers, Balliol College, Oxford.
A. D. Lindsay Papers, University Archives, University of Keele.
J. Ramsay MacDonald Papers, Public Record Office, London.
Albert Mansbridge Papers, British Library, London.
Ministry of Reconstruction Adult Education Committee Papers, Public Record Office, London.
Miscellaneous papers on adult education, Adult Education Reference Library, Rewley House, Oxford.
Royal Commission on Oxford and Cambridge Universities 1919–1922 MSS, Bodleian Library, Oxford.
A. Maude Royden MSS, Fawcett Library, Guildhall University, London.
Ruskin College Strike Papers, Ruskin College, Oxford.
M. E. Sadler Papers, Bodleian Library, Oxford.
A. L. Smith Papers, Balliol College, Oxford.
Workers' Educational Association Papers, Temple House, Bethnal Green, London.
Workers' Educational Association South-Eastern District MSS, Rochester, Kent.
Workers' Educational Association North Staffordshire District MSS, Cartwright House, Hanley, Staffordshire.
A. E. Zimmern Papers, Bodleian Library, Oxford.

NEWSPAPERS AND JOURNALS

The American Magazine
Atlantic Monthly
Barnsley Chronicle
Birmingham Daily Gazette

The Blue Book
Bournemouth Visitors' Directory
Brighton Herald
Co-operative News
Educational Review (New York)
Fortnightly Review
The (Manchester) Guardian
Hereford Times
The Highway
The Independent
International Woman Suffrage News
Justice
The Labour Leader
London Review of Books
The New Age
New Society
New Statesman
Oldham Industrial Co-operative Record
Oxford Magazine
Oxford Mail
Oxford Times
Oxford University Extension Gazette
Plebs
Review of Reviews
Rewley House Papers
The Round Table
Staffordshire Sentinel
Swindon Advertiser
The Times
Times Educational Supplement
Transactions of the National Association for the Promotion of Social Science
University Extension Journal
Universities Quarterly
The Universities Review
The Welsh Outlook
The Westminster Gazette
Workers Education

OFFICIAL PUBLICATIONS

Report of Her Majesty's Commissioners Appointed to Inquire into the State, Discipline, Studies and Revenues of the University and Colleges of Oxford, PP (Parliamentary Papers) 1852, no. 1482, vol. xxii.
Report of the Commissioners Appointed to Inquire into the Property and Income of the Universities of Oxford and Cambridge, PP 1873, C. 856, xxxvii, Pt. 1.

University of Oxford Commission 1877: Part 1: Minutes of Evidence taken by the Commissioners, PP 1881, C. 2868, lvi.

Ministry of Reconstruction: *Interim Report of the Adult Education Committee of the Ministry of Reconstruction on Industrial and Social Conditions in Relation to Adult Education*, PP 1918, Cd. 9107, ix.

Second Interim Report on Education in the Army, PP 1918, Cd. 9225, ix.

Third Interim Report on Libraries and Museums, PP 1918, Cd. 9237, ix.

Ministry of Reconstruction: Adult Education Committee, Final Report, PP 1919, Cmd. 321, xxviii.

Hansard['s Parliamentary Debates], 4th series.

Royal Commission on Oxford and Cambridge Universities, Report, PP 1922, Cmd. 1588, x.

Royal Commission on Oxford and Cambridge Universities: Appendices to the Report of the Commissioners (London, HMSO, 1922).

MAIN PRINTED PRIMARY SOURCES

Annual Reports of the Committee of the Delegates for Local Examinations Appointed to Carry into Operation the University Statute for the Establishment of Lectures and Teaching in the Large Towns of England and Wales (Oxford, 1886–92).

University of Oxford: Delegacy for the Extension of Teaching Beyond the Limits of the University: Annual Reports (Oxford, 1892–1924).

Delegacy for Extra-Mural Studies: Annual Reports (Oxford, 1925–71).

Department for External Studies: Annual Reports (1971/2–).

Oxford University Extension Delegacy: Tutorial Classes Committee: Annual Reports (Oxford, 1909–62).

Annual Reports of the Workers' Educational Association.

OTHER PRINTED PRIMARY SOURCES (IN CHRONOLOGICAL ORDER)

Oxford University Extension (London, 1866).

Report of a Public Meeting held at Bristol to Promote the Establishment of a College of Science and Literature for the West of England and South Wales (Bristol, 1874).

The Fourteenth Annual Co-operative Congress of 1882 (Manchester, 1882).

Report of a Conference in the Examination Schools, Oxford, of Representatives of the Local Committees Acting in Concert with the Committee of Delegates of Local Examinations Appointed to Establish Lectures and Teaching in Large Towns and of others Interested in the Extension of University Teaching on April 20 and 21 1887 (Oxford, 1887).

Report on the Peripatetic Teaching in Scientific and Technical Subjects Carried on in Various County Districts Under the Supervision of the Oxford Delegates for University Extension Acting in Concert with the Technical Instruction Committee of County Councils During the Winter 1891–92 (Oxford, 1892).

The English Universities and the English People. Report of a Conference

*on the Extension of University Teaching Among Workmen, Oxford,
3 August 1892* (Oxford, 1892).

*Ten Years' Report of the American Society for the Extension of University
Teaching 1890–1900* (Philadelphia, 1901).

*The Higher Education of Working Men, Being the Official Report of the
Joint Conference between Co-operators, Trade Unionists, and University Extension Authorities, Held at Oxford, on Saturday August 22nd
1903* (London, 1903).

*Papers Submitted to the National Conference of Working Class and Edu-
cational Organisations, Held in the Examination Schools, High Street,
Oxford, on Saturday, August 10th, 1907* (London, 1907).

*Oxford and Working-Class Education: Being the Report of a Joint Com-
mittee of University and Working-Class Representatives on the Relation
of the University to the Higher Education of Workpeople,* 2nd edn.
(Oxford, 1909).

The Democratic Control of Ruskin College, Oxford (Leicester, 1909).

*Ruskin College and Working-Class Education: Its Trials: A History of the
Dispute: Future Development of the College* (n.d. [1909]).

*Special Report on Certain Tutorial Classes in Connection with the Work-
ers' Educational Association* (J. W. Headlam HMI and Prof. L. T.
Hobhouse), Board of Education, Special Reports, No. 2 (n.d. [1910]).

*Report on the Working of the Summer Classes held during the Long
Vacation at Oxford in Balliol College and New College* (Oxford, 1912).

*Proceedings of the First National University Extension Conference at
Madison, Wisconsin, March 10–12, 1915* (Madison, Wisc., 1915).

*Annual Reports of the Workers' Educational Association North Stafford-
shire District* (1921/2–89).

*Board of Education: H. M. Inspector's Report on University Tutorial
Classes 16 May 1922* (1922).

*Board of Education: Report by H. M. Inspectors upon University Tutorial
Classes under the Supervision of the Joint Committee of the University
of Oxford, for the Period Ending 31st July 1924* (n.d.).

*Annual Reports of the Workers' Educational Association South-Eastern
District* (1926/7–).

Adult Education in Kent and East Sussex (WEA South-Eastern District,
1945).

*The Further Education of Men and Women: A Task of the 1944 Educa-
tion Act* (Nuffield College) (London, 1946).

Wedgwood Memorial College: Barlaston Hall: Annual Reports (Hanley,
1946–).

*North Staffordshire Committee for Adult Education: Memorandum on the
Future Development of Adult Education in North Staffordshire* (Hanley,
1947).

*Higher Education: Report of a Committee appointed by the Prime Min-
ister (The Robbins Report)* (London, 1963).

Report of the Committee on Extra-Mural Studies (The Habakkuk Report)
(Oxford, 1970).

Universities Council for Adult and Continuing Education Annual Report 1986–7 (n.d.).

WORKS OF REFERENCE

Dictionary of American Biography, ed. Dumas Malone (London, 1928–37).
Dictionary of Labour Biography, ed. Joyce M. Bellamy and John Saville, 7 vols. (London, 1972–84).
Dictionary of National Biography.
International Biography of Adult Education, ed. J. E. Thomas and Barry Elsey (Nottingham, 1985).
Who's Who of British Members of Parliament 1832–1979, ed. M. Stenton and S. Lees, 4 vols. (Brighton, 1976–81).

INTERVIEWS AND OTHER ORAL SOURCES

D. J. Wenden, All Souls College, Oxford, 16 August 1988.
Mr J. O. N. Vickers, Rewley House, Oxford, 4 November 1988.
Karen and Douglas Hewitt, Oxford, 5 January 1989.
Bridget Hill, Rewley House, Oxford, 2 May 1989.
Harold Marks, London, 30 September 1992.
Transcript of a seminar at Corpus Christi College, Oxford, 17 February 1989, on 'The Department for External Studies Since 1945', History of the University of Oxford, Oxford University Archives.

BOOKS AND ARTICLES

ABBOTT, EVELYN, and CAMPBELL, LEWIS, *The Life and Letters of Benjamin Jowett*, 2 vols. (London, 1897).
ABELOVE, HENRY, BLACKMAR, BETSY, DIMOCK, PETER, and SCHNEER, JONATHAN, 'E. P. Thompson', in id. (eds.), *Visions of History* (New York, 1983), 3–25.
ABRAMS, PHILIP, 'The Failure of Social Reform 1918–20', *Past and Present*, 24 (1963), 43–64.
ACLAND, A. H. D., 'The Education of Co-operators and Citizens', in *The Co-operative Wholesale Society Ltd. Annual Diary 1885* (Manchester, 1885).
—— and JONES, BENJAMIN, *Working Men Co-operators: What they have done and what they are doing* (London, 1884).
ACLAND, ANNE, *A Devon Family: The Story of the Aclands* (London, 1981).
ACLAND, T. D., *Some Account of the Origin and Objects of the New Oxford Examinations* (London, 1858).
ADDAMS, JANE, *Twenty Years at Hull House* (New York, 1981; first pub. 1910).
ADDISON, PAUL, *The Road to 1945* (London, 1975).

ALLAWAY, A. J., 'David James Vaughan: Liberal Churchman and Educationalist', *Transactions of the Leicestershire Archaeological and Historical Society*, 33 (1957), 45–58.

ANDREWS, LAWRENCE, *The Education Act 1918* (London, 1976).

ANONYMOUS, 'The Labour Party and the Books that Helped to Make It', *Review of Reviews*, 33/198 (June 1906), 568–82.

ARNOLD, MATTHEW, *Culture and Anarchy* (London, 1869).

ASHLEY, MAURICE, and SAUNDERS, C. T., *Red Oxford* (Oxford, 1930).

ATKINS, HENRY, 'Oxford and Working-Class Education', *Justice*, 25/1,301 (19 December 1908), 6–7.

BALL, OONA HOWARD (ed.), *Sidney Ball: Memories and Impressions of 'An Ideal Don'* (Oxford, 1923).

BALL, SIDNEY, 'What Oxford Can Do for Workpeople', in *Papers Submitted to the National Conference of Working Class and Educational Organisations, held in the Examination Schools, High Street, Oxford, on Saturday, August 10th, 1907* (London, 1907), 9–16.

BARKER, ERNEST, 'Politics and Political Philosophy', in Oona Howard Ball (ed.), *Sidney Ball: Memories and Impressions of 'An Ideal Don'* (Oxford, 1923), 219–27.

BARKER, T. C., 'The Beginnings of the Economic History Society', *Economic History Review*, 2nd ser., 30/1 (February 1977), 1–19.

BARNETT, HENRIETTA, *Canon Barnett: His Life, Work and Friends*, 2 vols. (London, 1918).

BEATON, WINIFRED, 'The Tutorial Class Movement', in G. D. H. Cole *et al.* (eds.), *The WEA Education Year Book 1918* (London, 1918), 253–61.

BEGBIE, HAROLD, *Living Water: Being Chapters from the Romance of the Poor Student* (London, 1918).

BELLAMY, JOYCE, and BING, H. F., 'Acland, Sir A. H. D.', in Bellamy and Saville (eds.), *Dictionary of Labour Biography*, i. 6–7.

BERNBAUM, GERALD, *Social Change and the Schools 1918–1944* (London, 1967).

BETJEMAN, JOHN, 'School Days and After', in W. T. Rodgers (ed.), *Hugh Gaitskell 1906–63* (London, 1964), 15–18.

BLOUET, BRIAN, *Sir Halford Mackinder 1861–1947: Some New Perspectives*, Research Paper No. 13, University of Oxford, School of Geography (1975).

BLYTH, JOHN A., *English University Adult Education 1908–1958: The Unique Tradition* (Manchester, 1983).

BOWRA, MAURICE, 'Oxford in the Nineteen Twenties', in W. T. Rodgers (ed.), *Hugh Gaitskell 1906–63* (London, 1964), 19–30.

BRIGGS, ASA, 'Sixty-Four Years of the WEA', *Workers Education*, 1 (spring–summer 1987), 8–11.

BRITTAIN, VERA, *Testament of Youth* (London, 1933).

—— *Chronicle of Youth: Vera Brittain's War Diary 1913–1917*, ed. A. Bishop (London, 1981).

BROWN, GEOFFREY F., 'Independence and Incorporation: The Labour

College Movement and the Workers' Educational Association before the Second World War', in Jane L. Thompson (ed.), *Adult Education for a Change* (London, 1980), 109–25.

—— 'The Workers' Educational Association and Educational Reform', in G. D. H. Cole *et al.* (eds.), *The WEA Education Year Book 1918* (Nottingham, 1981 repr.; first pub. 1918), 15–26.

BROWN, GEORGE, *In My Way* (London, 1971).

BRYCE, JAMES, 'The Future of the English Universities', *The Fortnightly Review*, NS 33 (March 1883), 382–403.

BUGLER, JEREMY, 'The New Oxford Group', *New Society*, 11/281 (15 February 1968), 221.

BULLOCK, ALAN, 'The Universities and Adult Education', *The Highway* (May–September 1952), 1–7.

BURROWS, JOHN, *University Adult Education in London: A Century of Achievement* (London, 1976).

—— 'The Teaching of Economics in the Early Days of the University Extension Movement in London 1876–1902', *History of Economic Thought Newsletter* 20 (spring 1978), 8–14.

CAMPBELL, LEWIS, *On the Nationalisation of the Old English Universities* (London, 1901).

CANTOR, L. M., 'Halford John Mackinder', in J. E. Thomas and Barry Elsey (eds.), *International Biography of Adult Education* (Nottingham, 1985), 375–8.

CAREY, JOHN, *The Intellectuals and the Masses: Pride and Prejudice among the Literary Intelligentsia 1880–1939* (London, 1992).

CARTWRIGHT, E. S., 'The Extra-Mural Student at the University', *Journal of Adult Education*, 3/1 (October 1928), 60–70.

[——] 'Looking Backwards: A Tutorial Class Anniversary. By an Old Student', *Rewley House Papers*, 2 (February 1929), 66–73.

CHESTER, NORMAN, *Economics, Politics and Social Studies in Oxford 1900–85* (London, 1986).

CHILDS, DAVID, *Britain Since 1945*, 2nd edn. (London, 1986).

CHILDS, WILLIAM H., *Making a University: An Account of the University Movement at Reading* (London, 1933).

CLARKE, PETER, *Liberals and Social Democrats* (Cambridge, 1978).

—— 'The Social Democratic Theory of the Class Struggle', in Jay Winter (ed.), *The Working Class in Modern British History* (Cambridge, 1983), 3–18.

CLAY, HENRY, *Economics: An Introduction for the General Reader* (London, 1916).

COLE, G. D. H., 'An Oxford Summer School', *The Blue Book*, 1/5 (March 1913), 389–96.

—— *The World of Labour: A Discussion of the Present and Future of Trade Unionism* (London, 1913).

—— 'Trade Unionism and Education', in id. *et al.* (eds.), *The WEA Education Year Book 1918* (London, 1918), 370–3.

—— 'The Tutor', *The Highway*, 44 (April 1953), 280–5.

COLE, G. D. H., 'Independent Voluntaryism in Workers' Education', unpublished paper, Adult Education Reference Library, Rewley House (1953).

—— FREEMAN, ARNOLD, MACTAVISH, J. M., TAWNEY, R. H., TEMPLE, WILLIAM, and ZIMMERN, A. E. (eds.), *The WEA Education Year Book 1918* (London, 1918).

COLE, MARGARET, *Growing Up Into Revolution* (London, 1949).

—— 'Discovering the Labour Movement', in W. T. Rodgers (ed.), *Hugh Gaitskell 1906–63* (London, 1964), 31–47.

—— *The Life of G. D. H. Cole* (London, 1971).

COLLINGWOOD, R. G., *An Autobiography* (Oxford, 1939).

COLLINS, H. P., *John Cowper Powys: Old Earth-Man* (London, 1965).

CORDER, PERCY, *The Life of Robert Spence Watson* (London, 1914).

COTTLE, BASIL, and SHERBOURNE, J. W., *The Life of a University* (Bristol, 1951).

CRAIK, W. W., *The Central Labour College 1909–29* (London, 1964).

CRAWFORD, ALAN, *C. R. Ashbee: Architect, Designer and Romantic Socialist* (New Haven, 1985).

CREESE, JAMES, *The Extension of University Teaching* (New York, 1941).

CROSSMAN, RICHARD, *The Diaries of a Cabinet Minister*, ii (London, 1976).

—— *The Crossman Diaries: Selections from the Diaries of a Cabinet Minister 1964–70*, ed. Anthony Howard (London, 1979).

CURTI, MERLE, and CARSTENSEN, VERNON, *The University of Wisconsin 1848–1925: A History*, 2 vols. (Madison, 1949).

CURZON OF KEDLESTON, LORD, *Principles and Methods of University Reform: Being a Letter Addressed to the University of Oxford* (Oxford, 1909).

DALYELL, TAM, *Dick Crossman: A Portrait* (London, 1989).

DAVIDSON, WILLIAM, *Reuben and I* (Swindon, 1922).

DAVIES, MRS HUWS, 'Women and Adult Education', in R. St John Parry (ed.), *Cambridge Essays on Adult Education* (Cambridge, 1920), 133–54.

DAVIS, ALLEN F., *American Heroine: The Life and Legend of Jane Addams* (New York, 1973).

DE LEON, DANIEL, *Two Pages from Roman History. I. Plebs leaders and labor leaders. II. The Warning of the Gracchi* (New York, 1903).

DENEKE, HELENA, *Grace Hadow* (London, 1946).

DENNIS, NORMAN, and HALSEY, A. H., *English Ethical Socialism: Thomas More to R. H. Tawney* (Oxford, 1988).

DE TOCQUEVILLE, ALEXIS, *Democracy in America*, ed. Phillips Bradley (New York, 1954; first pub. 1835).

DRAPER, W. H., *Sir Nathan Bodington: First Vice-Chancellor of the University of Leeds: A Memoir* (London, 1912).

—— *University Extension: A Survey of Fifty Years 1873–1923* (Cambridge, 1923).

DURBIN, ELIZABETH, *New Jerusalems: The Labour Party and the Economics of Democratic Socialism* (London, 1985).

DURBIN, E. F. M., *The Politics of Democratic Socialism: An Essay in Social Policy* (London, 1940).

—— *What Have We to Defend? A Brief Critical Examination of the British Social Tradition* (London, 1942).

EAGLETON, TERRY, 'Professor Raymond Williams', *The Independent*, 28 January 1988.

ELIOT, VALERIE (ed.), *The Letters of T. S. Eliot*, i, *1898–1922* (London, 1988).

EMERY, ALBERT, 'In the Early Tutorial Classes, (1) Longton', *The Highway*, 44 (April 1953), 253–6.

[EMES, JOSEPH], 'Impressions of a Summer Meeting VIII, By a Gloucestershire Miner', *Oxford University Extension Gazette*, 3/25 (October 1892), 4–5.

ENGEL, ARTHUR, *From Clergyman to Don: The Rise of the Academic Profession in Nineteenth Century Oxford* (Oxford, 1983).

FASNACHT, G. E., 'Education in H. M. Forces: A Lecturer's Impressions', *Rewley House Papers*, 2/4 (March 1941), 146–7.

FIELDHOUSE, ROGER, *The Workers' Educational Association: Aims and Achievements 1903–1977* (Syracuse, NY, 1977).

—— 'The Ideology of English Adult Education Teaching 1925–1950', *Studies in Adult Education*, 15 (September 1983), 11–35.

—— 'Conformity and Contradiction in English Responsible Body Adult Education 1925–1950', *Studies in the Education of Adults*, 17/2 (October 1985), 121–134.

—— *Adult Education and the Cold War: Liberal Values Under Siege 1946–51* (Leeds, 1985).

—— 'The 1908 Report: Antidote to Class Struggle?', in Sylvia Harrop (ed.), *Oxford and Working-Class Education* (Nottingham, 1987), 30–47.

—— 'Bouts of Suspicion: Political Controversies in Adult Education 1925–1944', in Brian Simon (ed.), *The Search for Enlightenment: The Working Class and Adult Education in the Twentieth Century* (London, 1990), 153–72.

FLETCHER, SHEILA, *Maude Royden* (Oxford, 1989).

FOWLER, W. S., 'The Influence of Idealism upon State Provision of Education', *Victorian Studies*, 4/4 (June 1961), 337–44.

FURNISS, HENRY SANDERSON, *Memories of Sixty Years* (London, 1931).

GAITSKELL, HUGH, 'At Oxford in the Twenties', in Asa Briggs and John Saville (eds.), *Essays in Labour History: In Memory of G. D. H. Cole* (London, 1960), 6–19.

GALLAGHER, EDWARD A., 'The American Society for the Extension of University Teaching: A Productive Pioneer of University Extension', unpublished paper.

GALLIE, W. B., *A New University: A. D. Lindsay and the Keele Experiment* (London, 1960).

GEORGE, REUBEN, 'To the Comrades of the WEA', in William Davidson, *Reuben and I* (Swindon, 1922).

GEORGE, REUBEN, '*The Path We Trod*': *Twenty-five Years' Comradeship with the WEA*, Wiltshire Pamphlet No. 103 (Swindon, 1933).

GILBERT, E. W., *Sir Halford Mackinder 1861–1947: An Appreciation of his Life and Work* (London, 1961).

GILL, L. V., 'What Can we Learn from History?', *The Highway*, 40 (October 1949), 255–9.

GOLDMAN, LAWRENCE, 'The Social Science Association 1857–1886: A Context for Mid-Victorian Liberalism', *English Historical Review*, 100/1 (1986), 95–134.

GOLDTHORPE, JOHN H., 'Intellectuals and the Working Class in Modern Britain', in David Rose (ed.), *Social Stratification and Economic Change* (London, 1988), 39–56.

GORDON, PETER, and WHITE, JOHN, *Philosophers as Educational Reformers: The Influence of Idealism on British Educational Thought and Practice* (London, 1979).

GOVER, REV. CANON, 'Report of the Edinburgh Ladies' Educational Association', *Transactions of the National Association for the Promotion of Social Science 1868* (London, 1869), 451–2.

GRATTON, NIGEL J., 'Reuben George and the WEA in Swindon', unpublished paper, Swindon Reference Library, L911 (92) GRA (1973).

GRAVES, RICHARD PERCEVAL, *The Brothers Powys* (Oxford, 1984).

GREEN, T. H. *Prolegomena to Ethics* (London, 1883).

—— *The Witness of God and Faith. Two Lay Sermons* (ed. A. Toynbee) (London, 1883).

—— 'Lecture on the Grading of Secondary Schools', in R. L. Nettleship (ed.), *Works of T. H. Green*, 3 vols. (London, 1888), iii. 387–412.

GREENWOOD, ARTHUR, *The Education of the Citizen: Being a Summary of the Proposals of the Adult Education Committee* (London, 1920).

—— 'Labour and Adult Education', in R. St John Parry (ed.), *Cambridge Essays on Adult Education* (Cambridge, 1920), 111–32.

GRIER, LINDA, *Achievement in Education: The Work of Michael Ernest Sadler 1885–1935* (London, 1952).

GRIGGS, CLIVE, *The Trade Union Congress and the Struggle for Education 1868–1925* (Lewes, 1983).

HAIG, A. G. L., 'The Church, the Universities and Learning in Later Victorian England', *The Historical Journal*, 29/1 (1986), 187–201.

HALL, STUART, 'Only Connect: The Life of Raymond Williams', *New Statesman*, 115/2,967 (5 February 1988), 20–1.

HALSEY, A. H., *The Decline of Donnish Dominion: The British Academic Professions in the Twentieth Century* (Oxford, 1992).

HALSTEAD, ROBERT, 'Working Men and University Extension', *Oxford University Extension Gazette*, 3/32 (May 1893), 108–10.

—— 'Impressions of a Summer Meeting', *University Extension Journal*, 5/49 (October 1894), 5–6.

HARRINGTON, F. H., *The Future of Adult Education* (San Francisco, 1977).

HARRIS, JOSE, 'Political Thought and the Welfare State 1870–1940: An

Intellectual Framework for British Social Policy', *Past and Present*, 135 (1992), 116–41.

HARRISON, BRIAN, 'Oxford and the Labour Movement', *Twentieth Century British History*, 2/3 (1991), 226–71.

—— 'Politics', in id. (ed.), *The History of the University of Oxford*, viii, *The Twentieth Century* (Oxford, 1994), 377–412.

HARRISON, J. F. C., *Learning and Living 1790–1960: A Study in the History of the English Adult Education Movement* (London, 1961).

HARROP, SYLVIA (ed.), *Oxford and Working-Class Education*, rev. 2nd edn. (Nottingham, 1987; 2nd edn. pub. 1909).

HARVIE, CHRISTOPHER, *The Lights of Liberalism: University Liberals and the Challenge of Democracy 1860–1886* (London, 1976).

HEYCK, T. W., *The Transformation of Intellectual Life in Victorian England* (London, 1982).

HOBSBAWM, ERIC, 'The Forward March of Labour Halted?', in Martin Jacques and Francis Mulhern (eds.), *The Forward March of Labour Halted?* (London, 1981), 1–19.

HOBSON, J. A., 'The Influence of Henry George in England', *Fortnightly Review*, NS 372 (December 1897), 835–44.

—— *Confessions of an Economic Heretic* (London, 1938).

HODGEN, MARGARET T., *Workers' Education in England and the United States* (London, 1925).

HODGKIN, T. L., 'Some War-Time Developments in Adult Education', *Rewley House Papers*, 2/4 (March 1941), 141–5.

HOGGART, RICHARD, *The Uses of Literacy: Aspects of Working-Class Life with Special Reference to Publications and Entertainments*, 2nd edn. (Harmondsworth, 1958).

—— 'The All-Important Minority', *Guardian*, 26 September 1968, p. 12.

HOWARD, ANTHONY, *Crossman: The Pursuit of Power* (London, 1990).

HOWARTH, JANET, 'The Edwardian Reform Movement', in M. G. Brock and M. C. Curthoys (eds.), *History of the University of Oxford*, vii, *The Nineteenth Century*, pt. 2 (Oxford, forthcoming).

HUGHES, H. D., 'A General Introduction to the Year Book', in G. D. H. Cole *et al.* (eds.), *The WEA Education Year Book 1918* (Nottingham 1981 repr.; first pub. 1918), 7–11.

IREMONGER, F. A., *William Temple, Archbishop of Canterbury: His Life and Letters* (Oxford, 1948).

JACOBS, NICHOLAS, 'The German Social Democratic Party School in Berlin 1906–14', *History Workshop Journal*, 5 (spring 1978), 179–87.

JAMES, GEORGE F. (ed.), *Handbook of University Extension* (Philadelphia, 1893).

JENKINS, ROY, *A Life at the Centre* (1991, London; repr. 1992).

JENNINGS, BERNARD, *Albert Mansbridge* (Leeds, 1973).

—— 'The Oxford Report Reconsidered', *Studies in Adult Education*, 7 (1975), 53–65.

—— *Albert Mansbridge and English Adult Education* (Hull, 1976).

JENNINGS, BERNARD, *New Lamps for Old? University Adult Education in Retrospect and Prospect* (Hull, 1976).

—— 'Revolting Students: The Ruskin College Dispute 1908–9', *Studies in Adult Education*, 9/1 (April 1977), 1–16.

—— *Knowledge is Power: A Short History of the Workers' Educational Association 1903–1978* (Hull, 1979).

—— 'The Reception of the Report', in *The 1919 Report: The Final and Interim Reports of the Adult Education Committee of the Ministry of Reconstruction 1918–1919* (Nottingham, 1980), 39–44.

—— 'The Making of the Oxford Report', in Sylvia Harrop (ed.), *Oxford and Working-Class Education* (Nottingham, 1987), 11–29.

JEPSON, N. A., 'Staffing Problems During the Early Years of the Oxford University Extension Movement', *Rewley House Papers*, 3/3 (1954–5), 20–33.

JESSUP, F. W., 'A Survey of Oxford Extra-Mural Work 1957–62', *Rewley House Papers*, 4/1 (1962–3), 17–42.

JOHNSON, R. W., 'Going for Gould', *London Review of Books*, 9/14 (23 July 1987), 7.

—— 'Moooovement', *London Review of Books*, 12/3 (8 February 1990), 5–6.

JONES, JOHN, *Balliol College: A History 1263–1939* (Oxford, 1988).

JONES, RUSSELL L., 'The Invasion of a University', *The Highway*, 3/35 (August 1911), 173–4.

JONES, THOMAS, *Whitehall Diaries*, i, 1916–1925, ed. R. K. Middlemas (London, 1969).

JOWETT, BENJAMIN, 'Suggestions for University Reform' (1874), in Lewis Campbell, *On the Nationalisation of the Old English Universities* (London, 1901).

—— 'Memoir', in Arnold Toynbee, *Lectures on the Industrial Revolution in England* (London, 1884), pp. v–xxvii.

KADISH, ALON, *The Oxford Economists in the Late Nineteenth Century* (Oxford, 1982).

—— *Apostle Arnold: The Life and Death of Arnold Toynbee 1852–1883* (Durham, NC, 1986).

—— 'University Extension and the Working Classes: The Case of the Northumberland Miners', *Historical Research*, 60/142 (June 1987), 188–207.

—— 'Rewriting the *Confessions*: Hobson and the Extension Movement', in Michael Freeden (ed.), *Reappraising J. A. Hobson: Humanism and Welfare* (London, 1990), 137–66.

—— 'Oxford Economics in the Later Nineteenth Century' and 'The Teaching of Political Economy in the Extension Movement: Cambridge, London and Oxford', in Alon Kadish and Keith Tribe (eds.), *The Market for Political Economy: The Advent of Economics in British University Culture 1850–1905* (London, 1993), 42–77; 78–110.

KEARNEY, ANTHONY, *John Churton Collins: The Louse on the Locks of Literature* (Edinburgh, 1986).

KELLY, THOMAS, 'The Extra-Mural Function of Universities', *The Universities Review*, 25/2 (Feb. 1953), 99–103.

—— *A History of Adult Education in Great Britain*, 3rd edn. (Liverpool, 1992; first pub. 1970).

KENT, JOHN, *William Temple: Church, State and Society in Britain* (Cambridge, 1992).

KERMODE, FRANK, 'Professor Raymond Williams', *The Independent*, 28 January 1988, p. 25.

KNOWLES, MALCOLM, 'Historical Development of the Adult Education Movement', in id. (ed.), *Handbook of Adult Education in the United States* (Chicago, 1960), 7–28.

—— *A History of the Adult Education Movement in the United States*, 2nd edn. (New York, 1972).

KRAMNICK, ISAAC, and SHEERMAN, BARRY, *Harold Laski: A Life on the Left* (London, 1993).

LA FOLLETTE, ROBERT M., *La Follette's Autobiography* (Madison, 1913).

LANGLEY, J. N., 'The South Staffordshire Association for the Promotion of Adult Education', *Transactions of the National Association for the Promotion of Social Science 1868* (London, 1869), 447–8.

LASCH, CHRISTOPHER, *The New Radicalism in America 1889–1963: The Intellectual as a Social Type* (New York, 1965).

LAWSON, JOHN, and SILVER, HAROLD, *A Social History of Education in England* (London, 1973).

LECLERC, MAX, *Le Role Social des universités* (Paris, 1892).

LEVY, CARL, 'Introduction: Historical and Theoretical Themes' and 'Education and Self-Education: Staffing the Early ILP', in id. (ed.), *Socialism and the Intelligentsia 1880–1914* (London, 1987), 1–34; 135–210.

LEWIS, RICHARD, *Leaders and Teachers: Adult Education and the Challenge of Labour in South Wales 1906–1940* (Cardiff, 1993).

LINDSAY, A. D., *The Essentials of Democracy* (London, 1929).

—— 'Foreword', in A. S. P. Woodhouse (ed.), *Puritanism and Liberty* (London, 1935).

—— 'The Education of a Citizen Army', *Rewley House Papers*, 2/5 (March 1942), 198–9.

LIVINGSTONE, RICHARD, *The Future in Education* (London, 1941).

LOCKHART, C. G., *Cosmo Gordon Lang* (London, 1949).

LONGFORD, ELIZABETH, *The Pebbled Shore* (London, 1986).

LOWE, R. A., 'The North Staffordshire Miners' Higher Education Movement', *Educational Review*, 22/3 (June 1970), 263–75.

—— 'Some Forerunners of R. H. Tawney's Longton Tutorial Class', *History of Education*, 1/1 (January 1972), 43–57.

—— 'Early University Extension Work in North Staffordshire', unpublished paper, Adult Education Reference Library, Rewley House, Oxford (n.d.).

LUNN, W. J., 'Adult Scholars at Oxford Since the War', *Rewley House Papers*, 3/2 (1953), 66–9.

MacDonald, J. Ramsay, 'Oxford and the Democracy', *The Labour Leader* (27 November 1908), 757.

McIlroy, John, 'The Triumph of Technical Training?' and 'Trade Union Education for a Change', in Brian Simon (ed.), *The Search for Enlightenment: The Working Class and Adult Education in the Twentieth Century* (London, 1990), 208–43; 244–75.

—— 'Border Country: Raymond Williams in Adult Education' (2 pts), *Studies in the Education of Adults*, 22/2 (October 1990), 129–66; 23/1 (April 1991), 1–23.

—— and Westwood, Sallie (eds.), *Border Country: Raymond Williams in Adult Education* (Leicester, 1993).

Macintyre, Stuart, *A Proletarian Science: Marxism in Britain 1917–33* (Cambridge, 1980).

Mack, John A., *The History of Tunstall II Tutorial Class 1913–34* (Stoke-on-Trent, 1935).

Mackenzie, S. P., *Politics and Military Morale: Current Affairs and Citizenship Education in the British Army 1914–1950* (Oxford, 1992).

McKibbin, Ross, 'Why was there no Marxism in Great Britain?' in id., *The Ideologies of Class: Social Relations in Britain 1880–1950* (Oxford, 1990), 1–41.

—— 'The "Social Psychology" of Unemployment in Inter-War Britain', in id., *The Ideologies of Class* (Oxford, 1990), 228–58.

Mackinder, H. J., and Sadler, M. E., *University Extension: Past, Present and Future*, 3rd edn. (London, 1891).

McLean, Tony, 'Working with the South-Eastern District of the WEA: Some Reminiscences 1945–56', in *Adult Education and Social Change: Lectures and Reminiscences in Honour of Tony McLean* (WEA South-Eastern District, 1983).

Mactavish, J. M., 'The WEA: Its Propaganda, Organisation and Method', in G. D. H. Cole *et al.* (eds.), *The WEA Year Book 1918* (London, 1918), 328–34.

Mann, Tom, 'Mr Tom Mann on University Teaching Among Workmen', *Oxford University Extension Gazette*, 2/1 (October 1892), 5–7.

Mansbridge, Albert, 'Co-operation, Trade Unionism and University Extension', *University Extension Journal*, 8 (January; March; April, 1903), 53; 85; 118.

—— *University Tutorial Classes* (London, 1913).

—— *An Adventure in Working-Class Education* (London, 1920).

—— *The Older Universities of England* (London, 1923).

—— 'The Beginning of the WEA', *The Highway*, 16/3, (summer 1924), 132–5.

—— *Arnold Toynbee* (n.d.).

—— *Edward Stuart Talbot and Charles Gore* (London, 1935).

—— *Fellow Men: A Gallery of England 1876–1946* (London, 1948).

Marriott, J. A. R., 'Hudson Shaw', *Rewley House Papers*, 2/8 (March 1945), 308–10.

—— *Memories of Four Score Years* (London, 1946).

MARRIOTT, STUART, 'Extensionalia: The Fugitive Literature of Early University Adult Education', *Studies in Adult Education*, 10/1 (April 1978), 50–72.

—— 'Dr Welch on "Oxford and University Extension": A Critical Note', *Studies in Adult Education*, 11/1 (April 1979), 12–27.

—— 'The Whisky Money and the University Extension Movement: "Golden Opportunity" or "Artificial Stimulus"?', *Journal of Educational Administration and History*, 15 (1983), 7–15.

—— 'Oxford and Working-Class Adult Education: A Foundation Myth Re-examined', *History of Education*, 12/4 (1983), 285–99.

—— *Extramural Empires: Service and Self-Interest in English University Adult Education* (Nottingham, 1984).

—— 'Collins, John Churton'; 'Marriott, John Arthur Ransome'; 'Shaw, George William Hudson' in J. E. Thomas and Barry Elsey (eds.), *International Biography of Adult Education* (Nottingham, 1985), 104–10; 399–408; 533–40.

MARSH, ARTHUR, 'Trade Union and Workers' Education', *Rewley House Papers*, 3/6 (1957–8), 27–36.

MARWICK, ARTHUR, *The Deluge: British Society and the First World War* (London, 1965).

MASS OBSERVATION, *Peace and the Public* (London, 1947).

MILLAR, J. P. M., *The Labour College Movement* (London, 1979).

MILLER, SPENCER, JR., 'Workers' Education and University Extension', in *Proceedings of the Eighth Annual Conference of the National University Continuing Education Association at St Louis, Missouri, April 19, 1923* (St Louis, 1923), 13–20.

MILNER, LORD ALFRED, 'Reminiscence', in Arnold Toynbee, *Lectures on the Industrial Revolution in England*, 3rd edn. (London, 1908), pp. ix–xxx.

MOONEY, TED, *J. M. Mactavish: General Secretary of the WEA 1916–27: The Man and His Ideas* (Liverpool, 1979).

MOORE, W. E., 'E. H. Birchall', *Rewley House Papers*, 4/1 (1962–3), 43–4.

MORLEY, JOHN, *Recollections*, 2 vols. (London, 1917).

MORRIS, CHARLES, 'Lindsay of Balliol', *Rewley House Papers*, 3/2 (1953), 9–12.

MOUNTFORD, SIR JAMES, *Keele: An Historical Critique* (London, 1972).

MUMMERY A. F., and HOBSON, J. A., *The Physiology of Industry: Being an Exposure of Certain Fallacies in Existing Theories of Economics* (London, 1889).

MYERS, F. W. H., 'On Local Lectures for Women', *Transactions of the National Association for the Promotion of Social Science 1868* (London, 1869), 450–1.

NETTLESHIP, R. L., 'Memoir', in id. (ed.), *Works of Thomas Hill Green*, 3 vols. (London, 1888), vol. iii, pp. xi–clxi.

NIELD, WALTER, 'What Workpeople Want Oxford To Do', in *Papers Submitted to the National Conference of Working Class and Educational Organisations, Held in the Examination Schools, High Street, Oxford, on Saturday, August 10th, 1907* (London, 1907), 3–7.

O'CONNOR, ALAN, *Raymond Williams: Writing, Culture, Politics* (Oxford, 1989).

OMOLEWA, M., 'Oxford University and the Planting of Adult Education in Nigeria 1945–50', *Journal of Educational Administration and History*, 7 (1975), 28–39.

OWENS, J. M. R., ' "Fifteen Lean Years": The Experiment of "English" University Extension in the United States', *Rewley House Papers*, 3/5 (1956–7), 10–24.

'AN OXFORD TUTOR', 'The Place of Oxford in a Democracy', *New Stateman*, 1/22 (6 Sept. 1913), 682–4.

PAKENHAM, LORD FRANK, *Born to Believe: An Autobiography* (London, 1953).

PALMER, GEORGE HERBERT, 'Doubts About University Extension', *Atlantic Monthly*, 69/413 (March 1892), 367–74.

PARKER, C. S., *Academical Endowments* (London, 1875).

PARKER, JOHN, 'Oxford Politics in the Late Twenties', *The Political Quarterly*, 45/2 (April–June 1974), 216–31.

PARKER, W. H., *Mackinder: Geography as an Aid to Statecraft* (Oxford, 1982).

PATTISON, MARK, *Suggestions on Academical Organisation with Especial Reference to Oxford* (London, 1868).

—— 'What Measures are Required for the Further Improvement of the Universities of Oxford and Cambridge?', *Transactions of the National Association for the Promotion of Social Science 1868* (London, 1869), 385–90.

PERCIVAL, JOHN, 'By What Means can a Direct Connection be Established between the Elementary and Secondary Schools and the Universities?', *Transactions of the National Association for the Promotion of Social Science 1870* (London, 1871), 310–16.

—— *The Connection of the Universities and the Great Towns* (London, 1873).

PETERSON, WILLIAM S., *Victorian Heretic: Mrs. Humphry Ward's* Robert Elsmere (Leicester, 1976).

PHILLIPS, ANNE, and PUTNAM, TIM, 'Education for Emancipation: The Movement for Independent Working-Class Education 1908–1928', *Capital and Class*, 10 (spring 1980), 18–42.

PICHT, WERNER, *Toynbee Hall and the English Settlement Movement*, trans. by Lilian A. Cowell (London, 1914).

PIPES, RICHARD, *Social Democracy and the St. Petersburg Labor Movement 1885–1897* (Cambridge, Mass., 1963).

POLLINS, HAROLD, *The History of Ruskin College* (Oxford, 1984).

POSTAN, MICHAEL, 'Politics and Intellectual Progress', in W. T. Rodgers (ed.), *Hugh Gaitskell 1906–63* (London, 1964), 49–66.

POWYS, JOHN COWPER, *Autobiography* (London, 1934).

PRENTICE, G. L., *The Life of Charles Gore: A Great Englishman* (London, 1935).

PREST, JOHN, 'The Asquith Commission, 1919–1922', in Brian Harrison (ed.), *The History of the University of Oxford*, viii, *The Twentieth Century* (Oxford, 1994), 27–43.

PRICE, T. W., *The Story of the Workers' Educational Association from 1903 to 1924* (London, 1924).

RAYBOULD, SIDNEY, *University Standards in WEA Work* (London, 1948).

—— *The WEA: The Next Phase* (London, 1949).

—— *The English Universities and Adult Education* (London, 1951).

REBER, LOUIS E, 'The Scope of University Extension and its Organisation and Subdivision', in *Proceedings of the First National University Extension Conference, March 10–12, 1915* (Madison, 1915), 25–39.

RÉE, JONATHAN, 'Idealism and Education', *History of Education*, 9/3 (1980), 259–63.

—— *Proletarian Philosophers: Problems in Socialist Culture in Britain, 1900–1940* (Oxford, 1984).

—— 'Socialism and the Educated Working Class', in Carl Levy (ed.), *Socialism and the Intelligentsia 1880–1914* (London, 1987), 211–18.

RICHTER, MELVIN, *The Politics of Conscience: T. H. Green and His Age* (London, 1983 repr.; first pub. 1964).

ROACH, J. P. C., *Public Examinations in England 1850–1900* (Cambridge, 1971).

ROBERTS, ROBERT, *The Classic Slum: Salford Life in the First Quarter of the Century*, 2nd edn. (Harmondsworth, 1973).

RODGERS, DANIEL T., 'Professorial Socialists: The Economics Profession in the United States and Germany in the Late Nineteenth Century', unpublished paper, delivered to the Organization of American Historians (Chicago, 1992).

ROSE, JONATHAN, 'The Workers in the Workers' Educational Association 1903–1950', *Albion*, 21/4 (winter 1989), 591–608.

ROWBOTHAM, SHEILA, ' "Travellers in a Strange Country": Responses of Working Class Students to the University Extension Movement 1873–1910', *History Workshop Journal*, 12 (autumn 1981), 62–95.

ROWLEY, CHARLES, *Fifty Years Work Without Wages* (London, 1912).

ROWLEY, EVE, *A History of the WEA in Longton* (Stoke-on-Trent, 1988).

ROYDEN, A. MAUDE, 'Women's Work in Education', *The Highway*, 1/1 (October 1908), 4–5.

—— 'A Chance for Women', *The Highway*, 1/3 (December 1908), 46–7.

—— 'Equality of Opportunity', *The Highway*, 1/4 (January 1909), 61–2.

—— 'A. Maude Royden C.H., D.D.', in Margot Asquith (ed.), *Myself When Young: By Famous Women of To-Day* (London, 1938), 361–82.

—— *A Threefold Cord* (London, 1947).

RUMSEY, REV. JAMES, 'Oxford Extension', *Transactions of the National Association for the Promotion of Social Science 1866* (London, 1867), 379–85.

SADLER, M. E., *The Development of University Extension* (Philadelphia, 1892).

—— 'Sir Arthur Acland', *Oxford Magazine*, 21 October 1926, pp. 13–14.

—— *Selections from Michael Sadler: Studies in World Citizenship*, ed. J. H. Higginson (1979).

SADLEIR, MICHAEL, *Sir Michael Sadler: A Memoir by his Son* (London, 1949).

SCHUCHARD, ROBERT, 'T. S. Eliot as an Extension Lecturer' (2 pts.), *Review of English Studies*, NS 25 (1974), 163–73; 292–304.

SCOTT, DRUSILLA, *A. D. Lindsay: A Biography* (Oxford, 1971).

SCRIMGEOUR, C. A., *Personalities and Partners in the North Staffordshire WEA District 1921–1971* (Stoke-on-Trent, 1972).

—— *Fifty Years A-Growing: A History of the North Staffordshire District, the Workers' Educational Association 1921–1971* (Stoke-on-Trent, 1973).

SEED, W. H. (ed.), *The Burning Question of Education: Being an Account of the Ruskin College Dispute, its Causes and Consequences* (Oxford, 1909).

SEWELL, WILLIAM, *Suggestions for the Extension of the University: Submitted to the Rev. The Vice-Chancellor* (Oxford, 1850).

SETH, ANDREW, and HALDANE, R. B. (eds.), *Essays in Philosophical Criticism* (London, 1883).

SHAW, W. HUDSON, 'A. Maude Royden 1901–1920', *International Woman Suffrage News*, 14/8 (May–June 1920).

SIMON, BRIAN, *Education and the Labour Movement 1870–1920* (London, 1974).

—— 'The Struggle for Hegemony, 1920–1926', in id. (ed.), *The Search for Enlightenment: The Working Class and Adult Education in the Twentieth Century* (London, 1990), 15–70.

SKED, ALAN, and COOK, CHRIS, *Post-War Britain: A Political History*, 2nd edn. (Harmondsworth, 1984).

SLEE, PETER, *Learning and a Liberal Education: The Study of Modern History in the Universities of Oxford, Cambridge and Manchester 1800–1914* (Manchester, 1986).

SMITH, A. L., *The Christian Attitude to War* (Oxford, 1915).

—— *Arthur Lionel Smith: Master of Balliol (1916–1924): A Biography and Some Reminiscences by his Wife* (London, 1928).

SMITH, BARBARA (ed.), 'Truth, Liberty, Religion': *Essays Celebrating Two Hundred Years of Manchester College* (Oxford, 1986).

SMITH, EDWIN, 'The Educational Work of the Birmingham and Midland Institute', *Transactions of the National Association for the Promotion of Social Science 1868* (London, 1869), 447–8.

SMITH, H. P., 'Adult Students at the University', *Rewley House Papers*, 2/8 (March 1945), 313–20.

—— 'Edward Stuart Cartwright: A Note on his Work for Adult Education', *Rewley House Papers*, 3/1 (1949–50), 8–24.

—— *Labour and Learning: Albert Mansbridge, Oxford and the WEA* (Oxford, 1956).

—— 'A Tutorial Class Makes History', *Adult Education*, 31/4, (spring 1959), 271–80.

SOMMER, DUDLEY, *Haldane of Cloan* (London, 1960).

SPENDER, J. A., *Sir Robert Hudson: A Memoir* (London, 1930).

STANFORD, PETER, *Lord Longford: A Life* (London, 1994).

STEDMAN JONES, GARETH, 'Class Expression versus Social Control? A Critique of Recent Trends in the Social History of Leisure', *History Workshop Journal*, 4 (autumn 1977), 163–70.

STEFFENS, LINCOLN, 'Sending a State to College: What the University of Wisconsin is Doing for its People', *The American Magazine*, 67/4 (February 1909), 349–64.

STOCKS, MARY, *The Workers' Educational Association: The First Fifty Years* (London, 1953).

STUART, JAMES, *Letter on University Extension Addressed to the Resident Members of the University of Cambridge* (Cambridge, 1871).

—— *University Extension* (Leeds, 1871)

—— 'On the Work of the Universities in Higher Education', *Transactions of the National Association for the Promotion of Social Science 1871* (London, 1872), 372–6.

—— 'Inaugural Address', *Report of the Second Summer Meeting Held in Oxford, August 1889* (Oxford, 1889), 17–36.

—— *Reminiscences* (London, 1911).

STYLER, W. E., 'Recent Adult Education in Great Britain', *International Review of Education*, 8 (1962), 166–74.

—— 'The Report in Retrospect', in Sylvia Harrop (ed.), *Oxford and Working-Class Education* (Nottingham, 1987), 48–64.

SUTHERLAND, JOHN, *Mrs Humphry Ward: Eminent Victorian, Pre-Eminent Edwardian* (Oxford, 1990).

SYMONDS, RICHARD, *Oxford and Empire: The Last Lost Cause?* (London, 1986).

TATTON, DEREK, 'Raymond Williams, the WEA and "Towards 2003"', *Workers Education*, 3 (spring/summer 1988), 27–31.

R. H. TAWNEY ['LAMBDA'], 'The University and the Nation', *The Westminster Gazette*, 15, 16, 17, 23, 24 February; 2, 3, 10 March 1906.

—— *The Agrarian Problem in the Sixteenth Century* (London, 1912).

—— 'An Experiment in Democratic Education', *The Political Quarterly*, 2 (May 1914), 62–84.

[R. H. TAWNEY], 'Democracy or Defeat: By a Soldier', *The Welsh Outlook*, 4/37 (January 1917), 8–13.

—— 'Introduction', in T. W. Price, *The Story of the Workers' Educational Association from 1903 to 1924* (London, 1924), 5–9.

—— 'In Memoriam: The Master of Balliol', *The Highway*, 16/3 (summer 1924), 146–7.

—— 'The Future of the Workers' Educational Association', *The Highway*, 21 (October 1928), 3–5.

—— 'Preface', in *The Adult Student as Citizen: A Record of Service by WEA Students Past and Present* (London, 1934).

[R. H. TAWNEY], 'The Workers' Educational Association in Wartime', *The Highway*, 32 (November 1939), 4–6.

—— 'William Temple: An Appreciation', *The Highway*, 36 (January 1945), 44–5.

—— 'Programme for Action: A Speech Delivered to the Annual Conference 1947', *The Highway*, 39 (November 1947), 3–4.

—— 'Mr. E. S. Cartwright: A Leader in the Adult Education Movement', *Manchester Guardian*, 16 August 1950, p. 3.

—— 'Mansbridge', *The Highway*, 44 (November 1952), 42–5.

—— 'A Fifty Years' Memory', *Manchester Guardian*, 5 November 1956, p. 4.

—— 'Tawney on A. P. Wadsworth', *The Highway*, 48 (January 1957), 82–4.

—— 'The WEA and Adult Education', in id., *The Radical Tradition: Twelve Essays on Politics, Education and Literature* (London, 1964), 82–93.

—— *R. H. Tawney's Commonplace Book*, ed. J. M. Winter and D. M. Joslin (Cambridge, 1972).

TAYLOR, A. J. P., *A Personal History* (London, 1983).

TAYLOR, JOHN A., 'The Making of the 1919 Report', in *The 1919 Report: The Final and Interim Reports of the Adult Education Committee of the Ministry of Reconstruction 1918–1919* (Nottingham, 1980 edn.), 27–36.

TEMPLE, WILLIAM, *The Life of Bishop Percival* (London, 1921).

—— 'Leading Facts in the History of the Workers' Educational Association', in G. D. H. Cole *et al.* (eds.), *The WEA Education Year Book 1918* (London, 1918), 324–7.

TERRILL, ROSS, *R. H. Tawney and His Times: Socialism as Fellowship* (London, 1974).

THOMPSON, E. P., *William Morris: Romantic to Revolutionary* (London, 1955).

—— *The Making of the English Working Class* (London, 1963).

TILLYARD, A. I., *A History of University Reform from 1800, with Suggestions Towards a Scheme for the University of Cambridge* (Cambridge, 1913).

TOYNBEE, ARNOLD, *Lectures on the Industrial Revolution in England* (London, 1884).

—— *Progress and Poverty: A Criticism of Mr. Henry George* (London, 1883).

TOYNBEE, C. M., 'Prefatory Note', in Arnold Toynbee, *Lectures on the Industrial Revolution in England* (London, 1884), pp. xxix–xxxi.

TOYNBEE, GERTRUDE, *Reminiscences and Letters of Joseph and Arnold Toynbee* (London, n.d.).

TREVELYAN, JANET PENROSE, *The Life of Mrs. Humphry Ward* (London, 1923).

TSUZUKI, CHUSHICHI, 'Anglo-Marxism and Working-Class Education', in Jay Winter (ed.), *The Working Class in Modern British History* (Cambridge, 1983), 187–99.

TURNER, FRANK M., *The Greek Heritage in Victorian Britain* (New Haven, 1981).

VAN HISE, CHARLES R., 'The University Extension Function in the Modern University', *Proceedings of the First National University Extension Conference, March 10–12 1915* (Madison, 1915), 7–24.

VEYSEY, LAWRENCE R., *The Emergence of the American University* (Chicago, 1965).

WALLACE, STUART, *War and the Image of Germany: British Academics 1914–18* (Edinburgh, 1988).

WARD, W. R., *Victorian Oxford* (London, 1965).

WARD, MRS HUMPHRY, *Robert Elsmere* (London, 1888).

—— *Marcella* (London, 1984; first pub. 1894).

WATSON, R. SPENCE, 'On the Best Method of Providing Higher Education in Boroughs', *Transactions of the National Association for the Promotion of Social Science 1870* (London, 1871), 363–6.

WEBB, BEATRICE, *My Apprenticeship* (London, 1926).

—— *Diaries of Beatrice Webb*, ed. N. and J. Mackenzie, 4 vols. (London, 1982–5).

WELCH, EDWIN, *The Peripatetic University: Cambridge Local Lectures 1873–1973* (Cambridge, 1973).

—— 'The London Society for the Extension of University Teaching, 1875–1902', *Guildhall Studies in London History*, 3/1 (October 1977), 55–65.

WEST, LINDEN, 'The Tawney Legend Re-examined', *Studies in Adult Education*, 4/2 (October 1972), 105–19.

WIENER, MARTIN J., *English Culture and the Decline of the Industrial Spirit 1850–1980* (Cambridge, 1981).

WIGG, GEORGE, *George Wigg* (London, 1972).

WILLIAMS, PHILIP M., *Hugh Gaitskell: A Political Biography* (London, 1979).

WILLIAMS, RAYMOND, 'Literature in relation to History 1850–1875', *Rewley House Papers*, 3/1 (1949–50), 36–44.

—— 'The Common Good', *Adult Education*, 34/4 (November 1961), 192–9.

—— *Britain in the Sixties: Communications* (Harmondsworth, 1962).

—— *Culture and Society 1780–1950*, 3rd edn. (Harmondsworth, 1963).

—— *The Long Revolution*, 2nd edn. (Harmondsworth, 1965).

—— 'Different Sides of the Wall', *Guardian*, 26 September 1968, p. 14.

—— *The Country and the City*, 2nd edn. (London, 1975).

—— *Politics and Letters: Interviews with New Left Review* (London, 1979).

—— 'Adult Education and Social Change', in *Adult Education and Social Change: Lectures and Reminiscences in Honour of Tony McLean* (WEA South-Eastern District, 1983).

—— *An Open Letter to WEA Tutors (1961) and Culture is Ordinary (1958)* (London, 1990).

WILLIAMS, W. E., and HEATH, A. E., *Learn and Live: The Consumers' View of Adult Education* (London, 1936).

WILSON, HAROLD, *Memoirs: The Making of a Prime Minister 1916–64* (London, 1986).

WILSON, J. DOVER, 'Adult Education in Yorkshire', *The Journal of Adult Education*, 3/1 (October 1928), 47–59.

WILTSHIRE, HAROLD, 'A General Introduction to the Report' in *The 1919 Report: The Final and Interim Reports of the Adult Education Committee of the Ministry of Reconstruction 1918–1919* (Nottingham, 1980 edn.), 7–23.

WINTER, J. M., 'R. H. Tawney's Early Political Thought', *Past and Present*, 47 (May 1970), 71–96.

—— *Socialism and the Challenge of War: Ideals and Politics in Britain 1912–18* (London, 1974).

WOODS, BALDWIN M., and HAMMARBERG, HELEN V., 'University Extension Education in the United States of America', *Universities in Adult Education* (UNESCO, Paris, 1952), 128–68.

WOOLFORD, JACK, 'Tony McLean: A Memoir', unpublished paper, Adult Education Reference Library, Rewley House, Oxford (1983).

—— 'The South-Eastern District of the WEA 1945–80', unpublished paper delivered at the Wedgwood Memorial College, 28 February 1981, WEA South-Eastern District, Rochester, Kent.

WRIGHT, A. W. 'From Fabianism to Guild Socialism: The Early Political Thought of G. D. H. Cole', *Bulletin of the Society for the Study of Labour History*, 32 (spring 1976).

—— *G. D. H. Cole and Socialist Democracy* (Oxford, 1979).

—— *R. H. Tawney* (Manchester, 1987).

YEO, STEPHEN, 'A New Life: The Religion of Socialism in Britain, 1883–1896', *History Workshop Journal*, 4 (autumn 1977), 5–56.

YORKE, PAUL, *Ruskin College 1899–1909*, Ruskin Students' Labour History Pamphlets, no. 1 (Oxford, 1977).

ZIMMERN, A. E., 'The Workers at the Summer Meeting', *Oxford Magazine*, 24 October 1907, pp. 23–4.

—— *The Greek Commonwealth: Politics and Economics in Fifth Century Athens* (Oxford, 1911).

—— 'Education and the Working Class', *The Round Table: A Quarterly Review of the Politics of the British Empire*, 14 (March 1914), 255–79.

INDEX